Power and Peril

MICHAEL W. HIGGINS
DOUGLAS R. LETSON

Power and Peril

The Catholic Church at the Crossroads

HarperCollins*Publishers*Ltd · Toronto · 2002

Power and Peril:
The Catholic Church at the Crossroads
Copyright © 2002 by Michael W. Higgins
and Douglas R. Letson.
For information address
HarperCollins Publishers Ltd,
55 Avenue Road, Suite 2900,
Toronto, Ontario, Canada M5R 3L2

www.harpercanada.com

HarperCollins books may be purchased for educational,
business, or sales promotional use.
For information please write:
Special Markets Department,
HarperCollins Canada,
55 Avenue Road, Suite 2900,
Toronto, Ontario, Canada M5R 3L2

First edition

Canadian Cataloguing in Publication Data

Higgins, Michael W.
Power and peril : the Catholic Church at the crossroads

Includes bibliographical references and index.
ISBN 0-00-255745-2

1. Catholic Church – History – 1965– .
2. John Paul II, Pope, 1920–
I. Letson, Douglas Richard, 1939–
II. Title

BX1390.H53 2002   282'.09'045   C2001-902525-4

HC 9 8 7 6 5 4 3 2 1

Printed and bound in the United States
Set in Bulmer

Timothy Radcliffe, former Master General of the Dominicans, has written that what most afflicts us in the church today is a "fear of debate." We wish to dedicate our book to the memory of one Catholic— father, husband, educator, cabinet minister, and university chancellor—who understood the high value of debate in both his professional and in his faith life:

John Sweeney (1931–2001)

Contents

INTRODUCTION   1

1   *Peter's Unsteady Barque*   7

2   *Health Care and Education: The Perils of Secular Society*   93

3   *And the Greatest of These Is Virginity: Sex and Marriage*   184

4   *The Curse of Clericalism*   254

5   *Spiritual in Essence and Form*   329

ENDNOTES   383

BIBLIOGRAPHY   413

PERMISSIONS   431

INDEX   433

Introduction

Power and Peril is the product of years of experience, both lived and literary. Our lived experience is partly rooted in our respective personal and professional engagement with the Roman Catholic Church. That engagement springs from a belief in the Church's essential role in the human pilgrimage, and it also includes the conviction that we belong to a pilgrim Church—a Church that, like the rest of us, is actively engaged in the perennial quest for perfection.

Our lived experience includes several years of philosophical study for the priesthood—the Scarboro Fathers in the case of Michael Higgins and the Congregation of the Resurrection in the case of Douglas Letson. Both of us are happily married, and our lived experience also includes a sum total of more than sixty years of teaching and administrative experience in a Roman Catholic milieu at the university level, over which time we have both taught and learned from thousands of students and scores of fellow faculty.

Our literary experience includes more than 300 interviews with prominent Roman Catholics worldwide as part of our research for the five books we have jointly written to date, as well as attending several Episcopal Synods in Rome as accredited writers. In addition, we have studied literally thousands of books in preparation for those interviews as well as for our years of lectures within the university and the wider communities. We also served as the chief editors of *Grail: An Ecumenical Journal* during its fourteen-year run. All of which is to say that the conclusions and suggested directions contained in this book are not scientific in any sociological sense, nor are they merely anecdotal or narrowly personal. There is no pretense here of a carefully controlled subject group as a basis for numerical analysis, nor is this a formal theological study—we are academics, but we are not theologians. There is, rather, the results of many years of research, reflection, debate, day-to-day encounters with the theoretical nuances of the academic world, as well as with the more tangible implications of the *realpolitik* both within the Church and within the extended society. *Power and Peril* is the product of trial, reflection, intellectual engagement, and personal growth. The suggestions and conclusions in this book, therefore, are hardly the rantings of dissident Catholics. They are the honest conclusions of two scholars who can claim from first-hand and far-reaching experience that the views expressed are widely held and deserve our collective attention.

Like the pilgrims in Geoffrey Chaucer's fourteenth-century *Canterbury Tales*, the Church, and society itself, is by human necessity an aggregate of saints and sinners; as with Chaucer's pilgrims, there is in all of us—as individuals and as Church—a perennial need for contrition and reformation. In the Church and in society one will find cause for both hope and joy, but one will also find cause for both pain and sorrow. *Power and Peril*, as a consequence, contains both celebration and suggestion. Centuries of experience teach, however, that suggestions for change are not always welcome within the Church: too often the Church, both the institutional Church and vocal groups within the Church universal, have reacted to calls for reformation by attacking the messengers and ignoring the message. This is, in a sense, the easy way out since it does not address the issues.

Despite its long intellectual history, the Catholic Church also has an unenviable tradition of banning books and harassing authors. It is ironic that Stephen Dedalus, in James Joyce's *A Portrait of the Artist as a Young Man*, is accused of reading too much and, as a result, of developing doubts about his Catholicism; this same suspicion of the written word is directed against a penitent university student in Morley Callaghan's *Such Is My Beloved*; similarly Nora, in Henrik Ibsen's *A Doll's House*, recognizes that opinions that subjugate women are to be found in books, books sanctioned by the Christian Churches in general. The imaginative artist has the mimetic capacity to fuse textual insight with vicarious experience and so to image the human struggle. It is precisely the kind of study that the Second Vatican Council's germinal document on joy and hope, *Gaudium et spes* (the *Pastoral Constitution on the Church in the Modern World*), urges upon the university since the Council Fathers reason that the arts and social sciences capture the longing of humankind to perfect both ourselves and our world. It is precisely this cross-fertilization that Donald Cozzens has in mind when he suggests in *The Changing Face of the Priesthood* that an engagement with poetry, novels, film, and the theatre will revitalize not only the clerical imagination but the heart, the soul, the homily, and general pastoral care as well.

Ironically, the Catholic Church's penchant for the *argumentum ad auctoritatem*, a deference to past authority, is rooted in a manuscript tradition; yet, the Church has all too often shown a censorious suspicion of the written word. Such censorship is doubly ironic, given the emphasis that *Gaudium et spes* places on the need for research and freedom of expression, and given that *Dignitatis humanae* (the *Declaration on Religious Freedom*) emphasizes the essential requirement for freedom of inquiry as a necessary means to freedom of conscience and one's ability to make an appropriately informed decision—a theme repeated in *Gravissimum educationis* (the *Declaration on Christian Education*), the Council's document on education. It is a peculiarity of Roman Catholicism that it often views as sacrosanct the scholarly reflection of ages long gone, but has difficulty in dealing with research in the immediate present. It ought to be possible to examine the Church in the modern world without suspicion, rancour, or recrimination. The Second Vatican Council said no less of the Roman Catholic Church in *Lumen gentium* (*Dogmatic Constitution on the Church*) when, for example, the Council Fathers observed that "the Church, embracing sinners in her bosom, is at the same time holy and always in need of being purified, and incessantly pursues the path of penance and renewal."

Monsignor Ronald Knox, translator, essayist, homilist of distinction, and Catholic chaplain to Oxford University, is reputed by biographer Penelope Fitzgerald to have once observed with a right mixture of whimsy and seriousness: "He who travels in the barque of Peter had better not look too close into the engine-room."

This may be good pastoral advice, but not appropriate if you wish to bring a scholarly perspective to bear on such issues as the making and unmaking of a tradition, the crises of an institution in the throes of transition, and the acute spiritual challenges facing a vital community of faith. Peter's barque is not unaccustomed to turbulent seas. After all, it has successfully charted its way for two millennia, remains one of the world's oldest institutions and perduring forms of government, and has defied those who would seek its extinction with a spiritual elasticity and nose for survival equal to none.

The need for Catholics and others to try and understand what goes on in the Church is inexhaustible. The history of the Roman Catholic Church is a history replete with examples of heroic vision and villainous behaviour, reformist zeal and oppressive edicts, holiness and perfidy. It is an institution like any other: human, flawed, lumbering, resistant to change, and intolerant. It is also, for believers, *the mystical body of Christ* and *the Pilgrim People of God.*

Catholic writers must keep both notions in mind while they labour to make sense of the past, account for the present, and dream for the future.

To go near the engine room is to get close, perhaps for most Catholics too close, to the operating apparatus of the barque. We often prefer to trust in the expertise of the captain, finding a mite of security in the knowledge that those in command must know what they are doing. But the Church is more than its captain, crew, or passengers and all have a stake in the effective running of the engine room. Catholics have an obligation, by virtue of their baptism, to participate fully in the life of the Church, and Catholic leaders, scholars, and teachers have an obligation to help Catholics engage with their Church and its traditions and practices by knowing the history, charisms, and experiences of their Church. In short, being an informed Catholic or being informed about the Catholic Church takes work.

We undertook to write this book as a public sign of our conviction that knowledge liberates. And we have done so in a manner that reflects our belief that a critical fidelity to the tradition demands an honest investigatory approach to the reality of the Church. We concur with Jesuit theologian Cardinal Avery Dulles when he says in his study *The Craft of Theology: From Symbol to System:* "commitment to the Church is a normal prerequisite for competently criticizing the Church."

At the very beginning of the third millennium of Christianity, we believe that the doctrines, ecclesiastical structures, political and social agendas, ecumenical and interfaith strategies, internal reforms, and plenitude of spiritual movements and personalities of the Roman Catholic Church demand vigorous attention, intelligent debate, and an openness to change.

For these reasons, we believe it important, nay imperative, not to contribute to what playwright Tom Stoppard calls in *The Invention of Love* "the fudge and flim-flam, the hocus-pocus and plain dishonesty that parade as scholarship in the journals," as well as memoirs, polemics, and tendentious tomes that seek to demolish the Church without heed to the deeper truths at stake.

This study is not an exercise in deconstruction; it is a summons to hope.

It is a primer for a new time.

Many of the people with whom we met as we prepared for writing this book spoke to us with passion, with conviction—they spoke bluntly. Too often conviction is interpreted as naysaying in the Catholic club. Passion, conviction, bluntness ought rather to be seen as commitment, commitment to what has been and what can be. We are grateful indeed for the many people who spent some time with us and who have spoken their minds. Through the exchange of ideas we can all become meaningfully engaged in the essential act of unending reformation. As Father Stephen Dowling, the Christ-like protagonist of Morley Callaghan's *Such Is My Beloved*, confesses when the usual platitudes fail him in his efforts to console a sick and impoverished mother pregnant with her twelfth child: "There may be much that we don't understand."

There may, indeed, be much that we do not understand. It is a sentiment not often heard from a Vatican that seems more intent on pontificating, on providing the last word, than entering into a respectful dialogue; it is, however, a sentiment often articulated by priests and even by some bishops and cardinals as well. This book is a call for positive dialogue so that through honest and open discussion, we who are Church might all come to understand just a little bit better how to make the Church a more credible witness in a world increasingly in need of evangelization.

As *Lumen gentium* points out on several occasions—and as both *Apostolicam actuositatem* (the *Decree on the Apostolate of the Laity*) and *Gaudium et spes* confirm—by virtue of their baptism and hence of their sharing in the priesthood of Christ the High Priest, the laity not only have a role to play, but have a responsibility to assume that role in the service of Church and society in a manner commensurate with their training and ability. Nor is that role limited to the minutiae of practical administration, maintenance of plant, or the raising of funds. The Council Fathers also invited the laity to engage in a process of positive criticism, noting in *Lumen gentium* that "An individual layman, by reason of the knowledge, competence, or outstanding ability which he may enjoy, is permitted and sometimes even obliged to express his opinion on things which concern the good of the Church." For her part, the Church "is not set up to seek earthly glory, but to proclaim humility and self-sacrifice, even by her own example." Hence the Council's persistent reference to the Church's pilgrim state and hence its repeated call for the collaborative involvement of the People of God as it is anticipated in 1 Peter 2:9–10.

Cardinal Gerald Emmett Carter, the archbishop emeritus of Toronto, is fond of quoting an inscription etched into a medieval church and accorded to Augustine of Hippo: *In necesariis unitas, in dubiis libertas, in omnibus caritas*—With respect to those things that are essential, there needs to be single-mindedness; concerning those things that are doubtful, there must be a freedom to investigate; in all things, charity must reign. It is a noble starting point. And it too is where we would like to stake our claim. Implicit in this threefold approach to faith and understanding is the assumption that there is a bedrock on which one builds—it is what Cardinal Joseph Bernardin called the Common Ground. At the same time, there are subjects that need to be explored if they are to be better understood, if we, both as individuals and as Church, are to grow, to become more perfect, to be fit beacons on the human pilgrimage in troubled times.

St. Jerome's University
WATERLOO, ONTARIO

1

Peter's Unsteady Barque

The challenges facing the contemporary Roman Catholic Church are myriad. Issues of doctrine, ecclesiastical discipline and governance, morality, spirituality, and institutional reform are immediate and pressing. And although the best Catholic theology teaches that the Church is not to be exclusively identified with its hierarchical incarnation, it is an essentially Catholic "thing" to begin at the top.

Before we examine in discrete chapters the *particular* features of the Catholic Church at the crossroads, we will look at the foundation of the modern papacy and the current pontificate. And an historical overview of the last century will be helpful in isolating for special attention those defining features of the papacy that have contributed to the current deluge of institutional and intellectual challenges.

There can be few institutions more fascinating—or more perplexing—than the papacy. In recent years, the papacy has been the subject of countless studies, documentaries, film specials, and general-interest books in spectacular full colour. The papacy sells. It always has, in a way. Eamon Duffy, reader in Church History at the University of Cambridge, reminds us:

> . . . that the papacy is a fact, as the institutional Church is a fact, the end-product of the unimaginably complex journey through time in which the word of God announces itself to humankind. As Catholic Christians

we can neither undo the past nor start with a blank page, for we know that the dwelling of God is among us, and all of us creatures of time, constituted and given identity as much by what has happened to us, by our own past, as by anything we ourselves choose to do. The papacy is one of the concrete forms in which order, unity and fidelity to the truth have been preserved within the Church; we might not have designed it had we been given an entirely free hand, but free hands, like free lunches, are not a feature of life as we know it. The papacy is the way things have worked out. . . . It is because Catholics place so high a value on the papacy that we need constantly to remind ourselves that it is, like everything else in this sublunary world, a creature of time and circumstance. It has not always been so, it will change beyond our imaginings, and one day it will pass away. At papal coronations, as the pope was carried into St. Peter's, it was once the task of a barefoot Franciscan to step into the route of the procession and to light a torch of flax, which flared and went out. The Franciscan cried out, "*Sancte Pater, sic transit gloria mundi*" ("Holy Father, thus passes away the glory of the world"). The ritual has long since been abolished, but I like to think that in the work of the historian its spirit lives on.[1]

Historian Duffy nicely encapsulates the *reality* of the papacy for contemporary Roman Catholics and avoids the easy attractions offered by revisionists, reformers, and advocates of the status quo. Quite simply, the papacy is a *given*. But how the papacy functions in postmodern times, how it achieves its intricately interlaced goals—political, spiritual, social—calls for serious scrutiny. For all its citadel-like firmness, its formidable history, and its impressive property in central Rome, the papacy is neither hostile nor resistant to change in spite of appearances to the contrary. But it wasn't always thus, as Sir Peter Ustinov makes clear in his introduction to "The Third Millennium," the concluding part of his six-hour series, *Sir Peter Ustinov's Inside the Vatican*:

In the nineteenth century the Church was suspicious of everything that made up what we would come to see as the modern world: democracy, socialism, science. It found itself engaged in a century-long struggle within which it had to opt for spiritual values against secularism and materialism, community values against individualism, and international order against various forms of nationalism.[2]

The papacy's multivalent struggles in the 1800s provided a solid foundation for the kind of engagements with the secular world that came to dominate in the 1900s. Although after the establishment of the Italian state in 1870—the culmination of the Resurgence, the great eruption of Italian nationalism directed by Mazzini, Cavour, and Garibaldi—the papacy was forced to relinquish the Papal City States, and indeed Rome itself, to the newly created Italy, it never really retreated from the world. It simply withdrew. The redoubtable Pius IX, or Pio Nono, the Pope at the time of the annexation of the papal territories, was ever the astute player. He knew he had lost this hand, but there would be other games to play. In the meantime, he would withdraw; he would become the Prisoner of the Vatican. As a result of the victory of the Italian unificationists, the pope withdrew into the sealed womb of the Basilica of St. Peter's and the Apostolic Palace, denouncing as he did so the spiritual perils of liberalism and the spirit of revolution. He would pout, pray, and ponder. The papacy became self-entombed.

By the time Cardinal Pietro Gasparri, secretary of state under Pius XI, had successfully negotiated the Lateran Treaties with Benito Mussolini in 1929, thereby securing the creation of the sovereign state we call Vatican City, the papacy was already in the process of emerging from its 1870-imposed cocoon. It had survived the devastation of the Great War that pitted one Catholic country against another, and although leery of modernity, it was making occasional gestures at rapprochement. But the spectre of totalitarianism had to be confronted.

As early as 1926 Pope Pius deplored the emergence of "a theory of the State which is directly repugnant to Catholic doctrine, namely that the State is its own final end, that the citizen only exists for the State." At the beginning of the Pope's controversy with Mussolini in 1929—the very year in which the Lateran Treaties were signed—Pius declared: "The State does not exist to absorb, swallow or annihilate the individual and the family: that would be absurd and unnatural." The papal encyclical protesting against Italian Fascism, *Non abbiamo bisogno*, was published in 1931. The attack on Nazism, *Mit brennender sorge* and the condemnation of atheistic Communism, *Divini redemptoris*, appeared within days of each other in March 1937.[3]

The history of the papacy's complex relationship with the despotic regimes in Europe from the 1920s up to the end of the Second World War in 1945 is fraught with controversy, cheap accusation, misdirected loyalty, and precipitous and incautious judgments. Benito Mussolini—Il Duce—and his Fascisti; Adolf Hitler—Der Führer—and his National Socialists; Ante Pavelich—Poglavnic—and his Ustashe; Francisco Franco—La Caudillo—and his Falangists: all these dictators sought in various ways to negotiate concordats or treaties with the Vatican that would ensure them some measure of moral legitimacy as governing powers. It was essential for them—especially given that they were all cradle Catholics and all but one from predominantly Catholic countries— to have, if not the Vatican's benediction, at least some sign of validation. The papacy negotiated with a clear-headedness about these regimes and their immediate ambitions—a stark sense of *realpolitik*—and yet at the same time with an appalling naïveté concerning the deeper villainy of their motives. The papacy was to pay a heavy cost both then and—in the eyes of many contemporary commentators and historians—now.

Still, one should not forget that when these regimes unravelled, some with the fury of the Thousand-Year Reich and some with the peaceful gradualism of post-Franco Spain, the Vatican remained—unthreatened, secure, and a mite triumphant. As recorded in a German Foreign Office report of 1925:

"We Communists," said Chicherin, the Soviet Foreign Minister, in 1925 to Msgr. D'Herbigny, "feel pretty sure we can triumph over London capitalism [*sic*]. But Rome will prove a harder nut to crack. If Rome did not exist, we would be able to deal with all the various brands of Christianity. They would all capitulate before us. Without Rome, religion would die. But Rome sends out for the service of her religion propagandists of every nationality. They are more effective than guns or armies. . . . The result of the struggle, my friend, is uncertain. What *is* certain is that it will be long."[4]

And long it was—not for Nazism, or Fascism, or even for the more long-lasting Falangism, but for Marxist Communism. For Chicherin, the struggle's conclusion was clear: the annihilation of the Church, of religion itself, and the victory of dialectical materialism. The reality was to prove otherwise. Although Communism would mushroom into an empire of considerable proportions, and although there would be various iterations of the Marxist creed, the Church of Rome never established a meaningful and enduring modus vivendi with its archenemy. Not that it didn't try. Particularly during the pontificate of Pope Paul VI, substantial efforts were made to find some ground for agreement with the Communist powers. The principal architect for what became known as Ostpolitik was Paul VI's urbane secretary of state, Cardinal Agostino Casaroli, who undertook to preserve what little leverage the Church had in Communist countries like Poland, Hungary, East Germany, and Czechoslovakia by negotiating various agreements with the political authorities, sometimes over the objections of the local bishops. Paul VI and Casaroli had both concluded that Communism was going to be around for some time and that the institutional Church would lose far too much—its right to appoint bishops, run its own schools, publish Church newspapers and magazines—if it did not find some way of accommodating at least a few of the pressing demands of these basically hostile and atheistic regimes. The Church had shown many times before in the twentieth century its remarkable versatility in coping with persecution by dictatorial governments. It could do so again. After all, Paul VI and his secretary of state knew implicitly that the Holy Roman Apostolic and Catholic Church was in for the long haul. They could afford to wait out the passing of these antipathetic governments. But not at all costs.

After all, the Church of Rome is not just a supernatural construct, an object of faith; it is also an institution with specific requirements for survival like schools and centres of learning to pass on the faith, means of communication that are unfettered, clergy and religious personnel unhampered in their pastoral labours, and bishops who are sanctioned by Rome. In his efforts to guarantee at least some signs of religious freedom—although much circumscribed by a fearful ideology—Casaroli was prepared to bargain with the devil. Better to protect a few liberties than to suffer the eradication of all. To that end, the Vatican was prepared to recall tenacious and patriotic prelates like Josef Beran of Prague, József Mindszenty of Budapest, and Josyf Slipyi of Kiev in order to accommodate the Communist powers, to save them the continuing embarrassment of having in their conquered capitals cardinal archbishops of unbending resistance.

This was a heavy price to pay—the Vatican would be severely criticized by local Catholics for selling out their brave leadership in order to get some paltry concessions from cynical and corrupt powers—and the politically suave and seasoned approach of master diplomats like Pope Paul VI and Cardinal Casaroli would be largely abandoned by Paul's successor, John Paul II. Interestingly, although the Polish Pope would be far less accommodating when dealing with Communism, he retained Casaroli as his secretary of state for many years as he was more keen on shifting the emphasis than exploding the strategy.

Questions of Vatican polity are in the end not sufficiently explainable in terms of the civil service—the Roman Curia with its many dicasteries or congregations—but by the personality, interests, skills, history, and spirituality of the Holy See's CEO: the Pope. In short, the papacy is shaped by the popes and not the other way round. As we enter the third millennium of the Christian faith, the current occupant of the Chair of Peter is a formidable leader whose will, fidelity, intellect, and energy have defined Catholicism for his time, and very possibly for some time to come.

Elected after the very short pontificate of Albino Luciani, patriarch of Venice, who became John Paul I and who reigned for only thirty-three days—August 26 to September 28, 1978—Karol Wojtyla, cardinal archbishop of Krakow, became Pope on October 16 and, choosing the name of his immediate predecessor, became John Paul II. It is reasonable to conclude that in the matter of papal style and priorities, this was pretty well all that these men shared in common.

To understand the direction of the Roman Catholic Church in this new century, to understand the initiatives, censures, negotiations, and political and social alliances that characterize current Vatican policy, we need to understand the makeup of John Paul II—the intellectual and spiritual forces that have shaped him personally and the political and moral crises that have marked his pontificate.

First, we must appreciate that the turmoil and divisions that mark much

of contemporary Catholicism are the result of an array of complex historical processes, including secularization, that John Paul II has attempted to
stem or at least ameliorate. Such a task is gargantuan, even for one as
gifted as Wojtyla and, arguably, he has contributed as much to the
tensions as to the harmonies that exist in his Church. This "state of the
Church" is neatly summarized by the Canadian theologian and spiritual
writer Ronald Rolheiser:

> Recently I attended a meeting of the major superiors of the Oblates of
> Mary Immaculate (my order) in Europe. More than a dozen countries,
> from both western and eastern Europe, were represented. My job was
> only to listen and there was a lot to hear. . . . Several of the presenters
> used the term "post" to prefix more than just the words "modern" and
> "ecclesial." They spoke too of being "post-communal," in that the
> Church, and indeed society as a whole, struggles to create community
> as it once did. . . . For every one of them, there was the memory of a
> time when the Church in their country "worked" better than it does
> now. . . . We are not, it seems, so much post-Christian as we are post-
> ecclesial (not that this is good). Things are very mixed. We are experi-
> encing some real religious and moral gains, along with some losses.
> Christianity is more like a detached retina (through which we used to
> see and through which we originally formed our vision of things) than
> something that is past its time.[5]

Certainly, John Paul II is not unaware of the decline of institutional
religion in Europe or in the affluent countries of the Americas, and he has
set his face like flint against the soulless progressivism of the age, the anti-
transcendent bias of a rationalistic humanism, the supreme folly of
comprehensive political systems that diminish the human in search of
the collective dream, and the moral relativism that undermines the
genuinely communal in the interests of the individual.

Prior to John Paul II, very few modern religious philosophers have
understood better the cult of the leader—and the consequences to society
of this perverse deference to the force that is power—than Simone Weil.
She knew first-hand the terror and perfidy of the cult of the leader in the
Hitlerism she saw spreading over Europe. While she fought Hitler and his

legions in her way and Wojtyla did so in his, they both knew intimately the spiritual threat that is totalitarianism.

During Weil's life (she died at the age of thirty-four in 1943 while in exile in England, having fled the Nazis in France), the bureaucratic state gave rise in turn to the cult of the leader. She accounts for this cult as follows: "The state is a cold concern which cannot inspire love, but itself kills, suppresses everything that might be loved; so one is forced to love it, because there is nothing else. That is the moral torment to which all of us today are exposed. . . . Here lies perhaps the cause of that phenomenon of the leader, which has sprung up everywhere nowadays and surprises so many people. Just now, there is in all countries, in all movements, a man who is the personal magnet for all loyalties. . . . Being compelled to embrace the cold metallic surface of the state has made people by contrast hunger for something to love which is made of flesh and blood. This phenomenon shows no sign of disappearing, and however disastrous the consequences have been so far, it may still have some very unpleasant surprises in store for us."[6]

Weil was to be spared the more unpleasant surprises by her death, but Wojtyla would be given no such reprieve. We need to appreciate the political climate in which Wojtyla grew to maturity in order to assess fairly his policies and pastoral strategies, for the totalitarian state left an indelible stamp on his soul and his sensibility.

So, too, did the ecclesial world that existed prior to the Second Vatican Council, the world that formed the young Pope-to-be, a world distinguished by the appearance of homogeneity, an intimidating bulwark against the assaults of secularism, an international body indifferent to the modern "plagues" of pluralism, religious freedom, and theological and philosophical diversity. That world began to change abruptly, drastically, and irreversibly. And Wojtyla was there for it all, even as a Council bishop.

But the Second Vatican Council did not happen as the consequence of human whim or caprice. In an important way, it was prepared for. In the nineteenth century, the First Vatican Council had been convened amid the great political and intellectual turmoil that marked the new Italy. The Council, under Pius IX, reacted strenuously to the threats of a hostile and largely anticlerical Europe by affirming the integrity of the Catholic Church and the rights and prerogatives of its supreme pastor, the Pope. It was at this Church council that the teaching of papal infallibility was formally declared as Catholic dogma. There were those at the time who felt that the moment was not propitious for such a solemn promulgation, and although they did not deny the doctrine, they found its proclamation inopportune. In fact, this faction or group in the Church became known historically as the Inopportunists, and among their number was none other than John Henry Newman.

THE NEWMAN LEGACY

Throughout his long life Newman fought for an ecclesiastical recognition of the plurality of gifts in the Church. For instance, he understood the role of the laity as indispensable to Catholic life, Catholic doctrine, and Catholic liturgy. He entertained the wrath of some key papal critics and the general suspicion of many a high-placed cleric when he dared to argue, as he did in *On Consulting the Faithful in Matters of Doctrine*, that the faithful ensured the Church's orthodoxy when the pastors of the Church succumbed to heresy. For Newman, the faithful, the laity, who for centuries remained unschooled or at least uninitiated into the mysteries of the sacred sciences, are not marginal to the Church's life. The laity are not passive recipients of the Church's wisdom, a *tabula rasa* upon which can be written the mandates of the hierarchy. They *are* the Church and it is necessary to consult them in matters of doctrine because they have their own charism or gift, their own sense of the Church. By boldly defending the "theological" competence of the laity in a way that had not been done before, Newman had no intention of confounding the rightful ministries of lay and ordained persons. Rather, he sought to guarantee a proper regard for the role of the laity, a role that his contemporary and enemy, the redoubtable Monsignor George Talbot, reduced to not much more than "to hunt, to shoot, to entertain. These matters they understand, but to meddle with ecclesiastical matters they have no right at all." In addition, the historian and prelate Cardinal Aidan Gasquet listed only three positions for the layperson: kneeling before the altar, sitting below the pulpit, and putting hand in purse. Newman aimed higher.

Many a theologian and Council Father has argued that Newman was *the* theologian who best adumbrated the insights of the Second Vatican Council, its *éminence grise* as it were. There is no doubt that his theory of the development of Christian doctrine and his encyclopedic knowledge of and love for the apostolic tradition made him a central influence on the Council's deliberations. His championing of the laity by means of a carefully reasoned argument reverberated throughout the largest assembly of Catholic churchmen in history, an assembly convened nearly seventy years after his death. When his own contemporary, Bishop W.B. Ullathorne of Birmingham, once asked him "Who are the laity?" he, reluctant to debate matters self-evident, answered curtly, "The Church would look foolish without them." Indeed.

Newman's tolerance for novel or conflicting ideas, his sturdy faith in the evolutionary capacity of ideas, and his conviction that truth need fear nothing were comforting notions for those theologians depressed by various Roman edicts designed to centralize and render uniform all theological inquiry. Newman's own personal distaste for those who delate others to Rome (he himself suffered under such an affliction throughout most of the pontificate of Pius IX) and his distaste for Rome's penchant for premature involvement in ecclesial-theological debates prompted his observation that the reason why the scholars and clerics of the Middle Ages were so vigorous in their debates and inquiries was simply that they were allowed "free and fair play . . . [and] not made to feel the bit in their mouths at every other word they spoke." Newman was not one to despise authority or its rightful exercise. He had, after all, defended the authority of Rome against its numerous detractors by examining its apostolic record, its critical role during the doctrinal crises of the patristic period, and its claim of continuity with the primitive Church. His credentials as pro-Roman could not be denied, save by his enemies and the ignorant.

Newman argued for the vital and free interplay of intellect and authority, of freedom and discipline, in a way that assured the necessity of both—poised in tension but ever struggling—to apprehend the deepest truth. James M. Cameron, the eminent Newman scholar, made these observations:

One of his most famous writings was called *On Consulting the Faithful in Matters of Doctrine*, and this was the document that got him into terrible trouble in Rome. And indeed, it was the cause of his living under the shadow of Rome's displeasure for most of his Catholic life. What Newman brings out in this work, and indeed in many of his other writings, is the extent to which the gifts that belong to the Church are in fact diffused throughout the community. They're not exclusively localized in particular centres of authority who, as it were, stand at the centre of a bureaucratic or quasi-military network and tell us what we are to do and what we are to believe. The great providential gift of the Pope, the Bishop of Rome, and of the other bishops, is the gift of being able to articulate the faith that we all share.[7]

There were others besides Newman, of course, who wrote and preached before the Second Vatican Council, who sought the revitalization of theology, and who saw the need for reform and for continuing renewal. There were various theologians and philosophers around the beginning of the twentieth century in France, Germany, and to some extent England as well, who took up the challenges posed by contemporary biblical and historical scholarship, asking unsettling questions about the historical Jesus, the place of dogmatic teaching, and the role of the Church in modernity. They were condemned and every effort was made to wipe out their influence in the seminaries and theological faculties, with often disastrous consequences. But theologically innovative and prophetic thinking continued in the work of such luminaries as Marie-Dominique Chenu, Yves Congar, and Henri de Lubac, who struggled to bring the world back into theology. The value of the secular, the role of the laity, the importance of tradition, and the very drama of atheistic humanism were all matters that occupied their attention and energy.

PAPA RONCALLI

Besides the ideas and the labours of the theologians and philosophers, there was a need for leadership at the very pinnacle of the Catholic world: the papacy. In 1958, the princely Eugenio Pacelli, Pius XII, died and the Chair of Peter was vacant for the first time in nearly twenty years. The august Pius XII was a remote and imperious presence in the Church; he was the shepherd as monarch. His successor was the shepherd as peasant, an unlikely candidate by the name of Angelo Roncalli, and he would take the name of John. He would be known to history as Pope John XXIII.

Papal biographer and Vaticanologist Peter Hebblethwaite wrote a magisterial biography of Roncalli, which he followed with an equally thorough biography of the next pope, Paul VI. An historian, journalist, and former Jesuit editor, Hebblethwaite was known and respected for his wit, learning, occasional acidity, and matchless familiarity with the machinery of the Vatican. He could be tart and cynical in his judgments but he remained throughout his life Roncalli-friendly. In the following extract, he describes at some length the man and his formation:

Roncalli was educated at the Roman College, or the Roman Seminary as it was then known, and which later developed into the Lateran University. In fact, it was Pope John himself who turned it into a university. Immediately after his ordination in 1904, or almost immediately afterwards, he became secretary to the Bishop of Bergamo, his diocese, and a city at the foothills of the Alps. It was an ardent diocese, and indeed some people have called it the Brittany of Italy. Bergamo never had a university or a court, so the church was the patron of the arts and so on. It is a very proud city, full of local achievements—artistic, musical, and otherwise. Roncalli was very much a Bergamist. Known as the bishop's shadow he remained secretary for ten years at the same time that he was a professor of church history. He made no great claims to be a scholar, but he was more than serviceable as an historian, his life's work being an edition in five volumes of the Acts of the Visitations of St. Charles Borromeo, the great reformer and Bishop of Milan. In fact, Borromeo was canonized as a bishop according to the mind of the Council of Trent. It was the saint's reforming zeal that very much appealed to Roncalli and that is why, when Pope John thought of the Council of Trent in the sixteenth century, he thought of it not as an anti-Protestant council but as a reforming one. There is this very curious thing that when, on December 2, 1962, Pope John said we are going to end this council in 1963, he remarked on how wonderful it was to think that the Council he convened—the Second Vatican Council—would end on the

400th anniversary of the end of the Council of Trent. It is sadly ironic to note that this speech, which he gave at the end of the First Session of the Second Vatican Council, would be his last. Everybody knew that he was dying and that he would not see the end of the Council, no matter what the date of its conclusion. He was the historian to the end. He would not have delighted in the knowledge that many Catholics saw Trent as a byword for obscurantism and reaction. He was always the historian, from Bergamo to Rome. After his stint as secretary, Roncalli received many diplomatic postings—Bulgaria for ten years, Turkey for nearly ten years, and France for nine years. And then, finally, he came to rest, sailing home graciously into port at the age of seventy-two, as the Patriarch of Venice, and everybody thought how nice for the old boy, for he's now come to the end of his days. Little did they know.[8]

The patriarch of Venice would soon be the first among equals, the *primus inter pares*. The cardinals gathered in Rome to elect, as they had done for centuries, a new supreme pontiff. The one they would choose to succeed Pius XII would be more than anyone could have bargained for, a surprise for all, insiders and otherwise. In fact, the conclave itself proved to be rather difficult in some respects.

One of the problems of this conclave—and one must say this fairly brutally—involves the simple fact that Pius XII left the Church, and the College of Cardinals in particular, in a sorry state. There were only fifty-three of them when he died, and two more died before the conclave began. So, simply put, there were only fifty-one out of a possible seventy at that date and, believe it or not, half of them were older than Roncalli himself at seventy-seven. Consequently, the choice was not very extensive and to those older cardinal-electors who voted for him, he was a sprightly youngster. They thought they were appointing a younger man. The great rival in that papal election was Cardinal Gregory Peter Agagianian XV, patriarch of the Armenians. He was born in Russia and had a beard to prove it, but he was really more Roman than Rome. There is a wonderful remark of Roncalli's on the eve of the Council—a very indiscreet remark—when he observed that people said they wanted to elect Agagianian because he was a foreigner, but he had no idea how to relate to people from the East because he had been entirely romanized. Still, Agagianian was always very friendly to his archrival and there appears to have been no animosity between them, even though, as Roncalli noted, throughout the conclave the votes went up and down like two beans in a pot cooking. It was by no means a clear-cut conclave.

Contrary to the conventional wisdom, I don't believe that Roncalli was elected as a stop-gap pope. Sure, in a sense he was precisely that, for after all his age worked against longevity in office, but the real choice made by the conclavists had to do with the issue of continuity. Did they want a change? After the long pontificate of Pius XII (1939-1958), a glittering pontificate marked by tremendous oratory, great anti-Communist rallies, and firm leadership, the cardinal-electors were nonetheless resentful that the bishops of the world could not get to see the Pope, for he was often isolated. They wanted someone who would be accessible. And accessible Roncalli would prove to be. After his election on October 28, 1958, Roncalli saw all the cardinals, all his electors, one by one—especially the foreigners and the ones who were scheduled to leave Rome—and he asked each of them what they thought he should do. Now, clearly, they didn't say call a Council of the Church, but they did tell him the difficulties they faced in their respective jurisdictions. One example that his secretary, Loris Capovilla, recalls is illustrative of the Roncalli touch. It involves the case of a cardinal who was also a knight, Cardinal Sir Norman Gilroy of Sydney, Australia. Evidently, Gilroy informed the new Pope that Australia, which was still technically mission territory and therefore fell under the jurisdiction of Propaganda Fide, had just suffered the indignity of having two of its dioceses divided up in such a way that made sense on the map but absolutely no sense if you knew the geography of the place. This happened, argued Gilroy, because nobody thought to appoint an Australian to Propaganda Fide. This silly little instance of the cleavage between what was happening on the periphery of the Church and the centre highlighted one of the serious problems in Church governance.

Examples multiplied throughout all the interviews. There were things going on in the local churches that were good things—the biblical movement, patristic renewal, liturgical renascence—yet somehow they received no encouragement from Rome. Within three days of his election, Roncalli made a note about investigating the idea of calling a Council as the only way to deal with a situation that had gotten out of hand. The reason such an idea was surprising, if not alarming, was simply that the First Vatican Council of 1869–1870 defined papal infallibility as a dogma of the Church and some theologians concluded that as a consequence they no longer needed Councils. Although theoretically the idea of a Council remained in Canon Law, it was not really necessary, they reasoned, because the Pope could do it all. Now John, an obedient man throughout his life, could not *not* obey the Holy Spirit, could not but be faithful to the Church. When he called the Council—and the tepidity and resistance of the curial cardinals to the idea was palpable—he argued that it was not so much a divine inspiration as an insight tested in prayer.[9]

Within a year of his death in 1963 Roncalli wrote that "when on the 28th of October, 1958, the cardinals of the Holy Roman Church designated me for the supreme responsibility of governing the universal flock of Jesus Christ, there was a widespread belief that I would be a provisional, a transitional pope. But, instead, here I am on the eve of the pontificate's fourth year with an immense program of work in front of me to be carried out before the whole watching, waiting world. As for me, I am like St. Martin: he neither feared to die nor spurned to live."[10]

Indeed, his immense undertaking of work, the Second Vatican Council, would continue under his successor, Pope Paul VI, thereby ensuring John XXIII a very special place in Catholic history. The Council, John's "insight tested in prayer," accomplished many things that have virtually reshaped the structure of the Church beyond the point of mild adaptation but falling short of a radical facelift: decentralization of some decision making; strong support for the principle of collegiality; deep recognition of the importance of meaningful dialogue both within the Church and between the Church and other religions; and internationalization of the Roman Curia. The Council, by the time it had concluded on December 8, 1965, had produced sixteen documents of varying weight, quality, and authority: *Lumen gentium* (*Dogmatic Constitution on the Church*); *Dei verbum* (*Dogmatic Constitution on Divine Revelation*); *Sacrosanctum concilium* (*Constitution on the Sacred Liturgy*); *Gaudium et spes* (*Pastoral*

Constitution on the Church in the Modern World); *Inter mirifica* (*Decree on the Instruments of Social Communication*); *Unitatis redintegratio* (*Decree on Ecumenism*); *Orientalium ecclesiarum* (*Decree on the Eastern Catholic Churches*); *Christus dominus* (*Decree on the Bishops' Pastoral Office in the Church*); *Optatam totius* (*Decree on Priestly Formation*); *Perfectae caritatis* (*Decree on the Appropriate Renewal of Religious Life*); *Apostolicam actuositatem* (*Decree on the Apostolate of the Laity*); *Presbyterorum ordinis* (*Decree on the Ministry and Life of Priests*); *Ad gentes divinitus* (*Decree on the Church's Missionary Activity*); *Gravissimum educationis* (*Declaration on Christian Education*); *Nostra aetate* (*Declaration on the Relationship of the Church to Non-Christian Religions*); and *Dignitatis humanae* (*Declaration on Religious Freedom*). These documents have been received and implemented with varying degrees of success since the Council. Some of them served as a springboard for serious change, others provided foundational shifts in ecclesiological thinking that have had an impact on Catholic self-understanding that will endure for generations, and still others proved insufficiently relevant in content and focus.

The composition of these documents, the politics of lobbying for their promulgation, the Curial manoeuvrings to either stymie or significantly retard those documents that the conservative faction perceived as limiting Curial power and that of the pontiff, the endless jostlings behind the scene as reformers and conservatives struggled to prioritize and direct the workings of the Council—all these factors contributed in the end to the design and structure of the documents, as Hebblethwaite carefully points out:

The Council documents have a certain structure and basically answer three questions. The first question is: What is the Church? It is a curious thing in a way that the church had not reflected on what it was. You don't find a theory about what the church is until the nineteenth century with people like Johann Adam Mohler and then later in the twentieth century with Karl Adam and Yves Congar. It was necessary, then, for the Council Fathers to arrive at a self-understanding of the church which was faithful to tradition, of course, but which unveiled aspects of tradition that had been forgotten. The main thing was to see the church as the people of God on a march through history, a history in which everybody is endowed with charismatic graces. From the start there is a radical equality among the people of God, a point that is underscored in the opening paragraphs of *Lumen gentium* and then and only then do you move on to talk about the priesthood, the episcopate, the papacy. The ordering is right and revolutionary in its way.

The second question flows from the first: What are the different roles in the church and how are they to be understood? On this point you will note that the Council documents go through the role of the bishop, the role of the priest, the role of the religious, and the role of the laity quite systematically, and then they move on to the various, if you like, activities of the church. For instance, the liturgy. The life of prayer in the church undergoes some serious re-evaluation: we now have the introduction of the vernacular and the slow elimination of Latin. You can't have, argue the Council Fathers, a strange barrier coming between the people and the expression of prayer.

And, finally, the third question: With this new understanding of the church and the altered roles exercised by its members, how are the church's complex and multivariegated relationships with society and other faith groups defined? On this point, what you see evolving is a discovery or rediscovery of the church's fundamental Christian humanism and a recognition of the supreme importance of relating to other Christians through a shared baptism, of acknowledging the special question of the Jews, the value of religious liberty, and the pastoral demands to respond to the joys and hope, anxieties and pain, of the modern world. This structure or plan can actually be found in a private letter written by Giovanni Battista Cardinal Montini, Archbishop of Milan, to Pope John on October 18, 1962, just one week after the Council had started. Montini noticed that during the First Session of the Council the bishops and their *periti* (learned advisers) or theological experts were confused, frustrated, angry, with no direction or focus, and so by the end of this Session on December 5, he got up and announced that we needed a plan and then proceeded to provide the one he had outlined two months earlier in his correspondence with the pope. Everybody applauded. But he was not alone in his planning: there were the likes of Suenens of Belgium, Lercaro of Italy, and Léger of Canada.[11]

There were many who opposed the unfolding intentions of the progressive wing of the Council, however, and traditionalists or conservatives found themselves pitted against the reformers or liberals, although these labels were to prove inadequate in defining the genuine shades of difference that often existed among the bishops as well as among the bishops and some of their theological experts.

THE POLISH BISHOP

Karol Wojtyla was a Council bishop and his debut in the *aula*—his intervention in the great aisle of St. Peter's Basilica—if not a grand epiphany nor earth-shattering in its implications nonetheless confirmed him as a man of the Council.

It is interesting to look at his very first intervention at the Council on November 21, 1962, when he was forty-two years old. The circumstances were not propitious. By that date it was obvious that Cardinal Alfredo Ottaviani's draft text on *De Fontibus revelationis* (*On the Two Sources of Revelation*) would be rejected as inadequate; indeed, it had been rejected the previous day, but had not had the necessary two-thirds majority against it to be thrown out. Pope John XXIII waived this point and the text went back to the drawing board. But before that wise decision had been announced, there were still some Council Fathers who wanted to speak, among them Bishop Wojtyla. What did he do in his first appearance on the international scene and in his first address to the universal Church?

Wojtyla gave the Council Fathers a semantic mini-lecture on the meaning of the word *fons*. The term *fons* or "source," he observed, was applied in the strict sense only to the origin or wellspring of the water supply; it was applied only analogously to the well or cistern that contained the original spring water. He concluded that if the draft text were to be retained, its title would have to be changed, for there were not two "sources" of revelation but only one, God speaking. It followed that "scripture and tradition" were not sources at all, except by analogy. It is unlikely that anyone found this particularly helpful. The draft was doomed anyway, so its pedantic dissection was neither here nor there. It cannot be candidly said, as the hagiographers would have us believe, that on November 21, 1962, those present nudged each other and said: "One day Karol Wojtyla will be Pope." They did not. But at least they were able to distinguish him from the other Polish bishop who wanted to change the creed to read: "I believe in the Holy, Catholic and *Petrine* Church."

Despite Karol Wojtyla's not-very-auspicious debut, the Vatican Council was a great event in his life. It brought him out of intellectual isolation to some extent, he soon found that his dialectical skills allowed him to compete with Western theologians with apparent equality, and he won the confidence of Pope Paul VI. Without the Council and the Synods that derived from it, there was no way in which Karol Wojtyla could have become Pope.[12]

Clearly, the future John Paul II was a product of the Council, shaped by its dynamic, intellectual debates, strategic alliances, and (of supreme importance for the Church universal under the Johannine aspect of its updating), its *aggiornamento*. Wojtyla could see first-hand the papal commitment to the Council; there were no compromises or regrets on the part of either John XXIII or of Paul VI. Quite simply, the Council was the work of the Spirit. Although Wojtyla was not unfamiliar with Rome—he had been a graduate student there—the exposure he experienced at the various sessions of the Council gave him access to a world outside the secure boundaries of Catholic Poland. He learned something of the dignity of the Petrine Office, of the rich history of this essential ministry in the Church, and of the nature of papal leadership in the context of the college of bishops. By simply being present at the Council, Wojtyla could see in action the consultation, deliberation, collegiality, and co-responsibility that define effective episcopal stewardship. He learned how to listen:

The Council was a unique occasion for listening to others, but also for creative thinking. Naturally, the older and more expert bishops contributed the most to the development of the Council's thought. At first, since I was young, I learned more than I contributed. Gradually, however, I came to participate in the Council in a more mature and creative manner. . . . The Council was a *great experience of the Church*; it was—as we said at the time—*the "seminary of the Holy Spirit."* At the Council the Holy Spirit spoke to the Church in all its universality, which was reflected in the presence of bishops from the whole world and by the presence of representatives of many non-Catholic Churches and communities.[13]

Wojtyla was changed by the Council. He was also changed by the pontificate of Paul VI, the Pope as Hamlet, the Pope as indecisive leader, the Pope as pawn of Church factions and conflicting political ideologies. Paul was an intellectual, a Vatican bureaucrat of exceptional skill, a trusted confidante of John XXIII, and a bishop committed to seeing the Council decrees implemented in the life of the universal Church. But for all his learning and diplomacy, Paul underestimated the assaults of modernity, the ecclesiastical squabbles that arose in the Council's wake, and the challenges to a papal authority that seemed both unremitting and unforgiving.

It was Paul who issued the encyclical *Sacerdotalis coelibatus* (*Priestly Celibacy*) reaffirming the practice of celibacy for Latin rite clerics, who painstakingly negotiated with Communist powers rather than resorting to denunciation, who argued strenuously for the poor in his encyclical *Populorum progressio* (*Progress of Peoples*), who began the tradition of papal travels outside of Italy, and who advanced ecumenical relations with his quantum leap of official visitations with Michael Ramsey, the primate of the Anglican Commonwealth and archbishop of Canterbury, and with Athenagoras II, the ecumenical patriarch. It was a pontificate of small gains, gentle surprises, oscillating between the demands of progressives and traditionalists, a papacy marked by a tone of pastoral gradualism. It was also a pontificate scarred by intense controversy and acrimonious division. Paul was the Pope who issued the encyclical *Humanae vitae* (*Of Human Life*), which reaffirmed the Church's comprehensive ban on all forms of artificial birth regulation and as a consequence unleashed a torrent of private anguish and public rebellion not hitherto experienced by the Church. In addition, he struggled unsuccessfully to reconcile Marcel Lefebvre and his schismatic band of ultratraditionalists who questioned the authority of the Council and defied the pontiff. And in the end he failed even to save the life of his old friend, the distinguished Italian Christian Democrat Aldo Moro, who had been captured by the terrorist group, the Red Brigades. Moro's bodyguard was gunned down and he was held prisoner for fifty-five days, the Brigade callously repudiating the entreaties of the pontiff. Paul was determined to do whatever he could for Moro and found little help in the way of co-operation with the ruling government of Giulio Andreotti, so he acted alone.

Paul vi resolved to appeal personally to Moro's captors. In a public letter he lauded Moro's virtues, recalling their student friendship, describing Moro as a son of the Church and a decent and honourable man. "I beseech you to free Aldo Moro, simply and unconditionally," wrote the Pope, "not because of my humble and well-meaning intercession, but because he shares with you the common dignity of a human brother and because I dare hope that in all conscience you do not wish the cause of true human progress either to be stained with innocent blood or to be tortured by unnecessary suffering." The Pope even offered to ransom his old friend.[14]

Nothing worked. Moro was murdered and Paul publicly expressed his grief and anger at a memorial service in his own basilica, St. John Lateran. His deep disappointment was palpable and his reproach of Moro's assassins brave and categorical. But he gave every evidence of being a broken man. And he was. Within three months of Moro's obsequies, Paul himself was dead. It was time for a conclave and a new pope.

The election of Paul's successor was swiftly achieved. One hundred and eleven cardinals met in conclave on August 25, 1978. The following day Albino Luciani was chosen with 101 votes on the fourth ballot. He was God's candidate, said Cardinal Basil Hume. Luciani's choice of title was to combine those of John and Paul—no other pope had ever had two names. He had risen through the ranks, both as an academic and as a pastor. His family had been socialist and, though he had moved to the right, especially while patriarch of Venice, he was able to establish good relations with members of the Communist Party when need

be. He was a humble man, rejecting the ceremonial of a papal corona-
tion. At a press conference—itself a novelty—he admitted that had he
not entered the priesthood, he might well have become a journalist. On
the morning of September 28, 1978 he was found dead in his bed.
Rumours immediately suggested he had been murdered, perhaps to
stop him investigating the Vatican Bank affair or because officials had
discovered he was about to reverse the teaching on birth control. More
confusion was created by concealing the fact that he had been found by
a nun, who was bringing him an early-morning cup of coffee.[15]

Luciani's death is the stuff of drama. Indeed, it has proven to be the stuff
of fantasy as well. British investigative journalist David Yallop published
his exposé of the manner of the Luciani death with its accompanying
horror of conspiracy, prelatical intrigue, venal Vatican bureaucrats, and
underworld links in 1984, a book he tantalizingly titled *In God's Name*,
thereby unleashing a torrent of charges and countercharges that shocked
and titillated the Catholic and non-Catholic world alike. Yallop argued
that the Pope had been murdered and went so far as to identify any one of
six possible candidates as either the assassin or the mastermind behind a
plot of Borgian proportions. He also reasoned that it was possible there
was collusion among some or all of the candidates. And these candidates
constituted an impressive list: Cardinal Jean Villot, Pope Paul's indefati-
gably loyal secretary of state; Cardinal John Cody, archbishop of
Chicago; Archbishop Paul Marcinkus, head of the Vatican Bank or IOR
(Istituto per le Opere di Religione); bankers and financiers Michele
Sindona and Roberto Calvi; and Licio Gelli, master of Masonic Lodge P2.

The collapse of the Banco Ambrosiano in Milan in 1982 and the mysterious murder of Calvi shortly after—found hanging on Blackfriars Bridge
in London—along with the disappearance of Gelli, the complicated extra-
dition hearings concerning Sindona, and the Vatican's reluctance to allow
Marcinkus to appear before an Italian judicial inquiry all compounded the
intrigue associated with the charge levelled by Yallop against his six
suspects.

Yallop cleverly chose to ground his allegation that something was radically amiss with the death of Pope John Paul I on the knowledge that there
have been wide discrepancies in the various reports concerning the

discovery of the Pope's death. At first it was Sister Vincenza, who discovered him dead at 4:45 A.M., but then a later official bulletin established that it was Father John Magee (later named a bishop) who discovered the Pope at 5:30 in the morning. In addition, wild and sundry claims concerning the reading matter that he held in his hands at the time of death ranged from a hit list of imminent Vatican firings to a copy of the classical devotional work *The Imitation of Christ*. Various contradictions and confusions contributed to the widening credibility gap. Yallop was correct in taking to task a central Church administration with little sense of accountability and an exaggerated taste for baroque secrecy. Yallop also made good sense when he decried the Victorian prudery and far from candid manner with which Vatican officials, senior and junior, dealt with the secular world. In truth, the Vatican does itself little good by often insisting on a code of behaviour that is more fitting for a Jacobean court than a sanctuary consecrated to God's service. But it was one large leap, and Yallop was clearly fond of such leaps in his investigative work, from voicing strong misgivings regarding the Vatican's resistance to openness to passionate denunciations of grave malfeasance.

Armed with moral rectitude—or at least the appearance of it—and with the necessary information his "sources" had given him, Yallop was determined not only to chronicle Vatican blunders but to establish beyond them a conspiracy of alarming magnitude. In Yallop's view, Cardinal Villot was vigorously committed to upholding the policies of Paul VI, particularly on the issue of birth control as articulated in *Humanae vitae*, and had sufficient cause to believe that John Paul I was about to reverse the papal position on artificial birth regulation with devastating consequences for papal authority. Quite simply, John Paul I had to be prevented from changing the teaching on contraception. And now to Cardinal Cody.

Yallop was convinced that Cody feared that the influential bishop-maker, Cardinal Sebastiano Baggio, had prevailed upon the Pope to seek his removal from Chicago because of scandals associated with his episcopal leadership in the "windy city." This was not to be. Yallop further argued that Marcinkus lived in dread that Luciani, respected for his fiscal honesty in all his previous posts including Venice, would not tolerate the kind of skullduggery rumoured to be rife in the corridors of the Vatican Bank. This housecleaning must not happen.

So much for our scheming prelates. The other candidates—Sindona, Calvi, and Gelli—had every reason, purports Yallop, to preserve the status quo because Vatican monies were inextricably linked with their international dealings. They were not unaccustomed to acting decisively and ruthlessly when they saw their interests threatened.

There is no question that Vatican initiatives in the area of finance have often proven ill-advised. There have been some shady negotiations and a plethora of bad judgments. Paul VI himself was aware of many of them, but seemed largely powerless to effect any substantial changes. John Paul II convened a special gathering of cardinals to address the increasingly troublesome question of Vatican culpability in the event, as with the Banco Ambrosiano, of the collapse of a financial institution with Vatican investments or support. Among the experts John Paul turned to was Cardinal-Archbishop Gerald Emmett Carter of Toronto:

When it came to practical and administrative advice, John Paul himself did not hesitate to draw on Carter's financial expertise, and Carter was only too willing to offer it. On the matter of annual financial statements, fiscal accountability and the sorry state of Vatican investments, Carter was vigorously blunt. Appointed to the powerful Council of Cardinals for Study of Organizational and Economic Problems of the Holy See, and following the disastrous collapse of the Banco Ambrosiano in 1982 and the loss of millions, coupled with the incalculable loss of face for the Vatican, Carter urged immediate and drastic reforms. He deplored the Roman obsession with secrecy and insisted that unless they broke out of that centuries-old style of thinking they could not raise the necessary funds from those prosperous countries accustomed to open books and open budgets. Along with like-minded cardinals, including Philadelphia's Krol and New York's O'Connor, he eventually succeeded. In a news item published in *The Tablet* following a fall 1989 meeting of the Council of Cardinals, Carter announced "that for the first time the figures were being independently audited and a certified financial report would be sent to every diocese in the Church. His council, he said, had fought 'quite a battle' with the Vatican officials over that: 'Every year we were pounding on at the same thing, and finally we got it done.'"[16]

Yallop was correct when he launched his broadside against fiscal mismanagement by various Vatican officials, but his allegations of grand conspiracy by a cabal of Mafiosi, Masonic leaders, disgruntled clerics, and fearful papal advisers is fantastically wide of the mark. Yallop's book is more fiction than investigation and the truth behind the death of the amiable and short-lived John Paul I is more pathetic than tragic.

John Cornwell, the British journalist, researcher, and scholar, wrote a masterful study of the death of Albino Luciani called, with due biblical resonance, *A Thief in the Night: The Death of Pope John Paul I*, and in his work, exhaustively thorough and scrupulously fair, he concluded that "the whisperings, the rumours, the theories—far-fetched, sensational, fantastic—all serve a purpose: they detract from the most obvious and shameful fact of all: that John Paul I died scorned and neglected by the institution that existed to sustain him."[17]

There are some delicious ironies in the Cornwell investigation: in the process of securing Vatican assistance and disproving the wild assertions of Yallop, Cornwell established a reputation in Vatican circles—or at least among some in certain Vatican circles—of trustworthiness and judiciousness. And then came Cornwell's own Yallopesque *Hitler's Pope: The Secret History of Pius XII* exactly a decade later. And a new controversy, or better yet new/old, commenced. But that's in the future. On the fateful day when Luciani died, the Catholic world was stunned. Once again all eyes—Catholic or otherwise—were on Rome. The papacy, not for the first time, became the centre of universal attention—rapt, curious, and worried.

Although many of the grand claims made for the papal office during the darkest days of the nineteenth century were no longer advanced, at least in public, by the defenders of the institution, Catholics of varying degrees of theological sophistication recognized the enduring attraction of the institution and its unquestionable capacity to survive. Paul Johnson, the Catholic journalist, editor, and historian, makes the case rather well:

We may dispute the truths of Christianity. We may deny the primacy of Roman Catholicism within the Christian communion. We may reject the dogma of Papal Infallibility. But we cannot dispute that the papacy itself, purely as a human institution, is unique. The historian bows his head in humble respect at its antiquity, continuity and durability, and observes in awe its endless splendours and shadows as they flicker across the centuries. It has now survived two entire millennia with its essential functions intact. It is granitic in its capacity to endure. "Thou art Peter, and upon this rock I will build my Church." The Church is still there. The pope is still the rock on which it leans for guidance and leadership. The papacy is the last of the ancient autocracies, the only one where the autocrat himself has preserved his essential powers intact. Caesars and tsars, kaisers and Holy Roman Emperors, mikados and sultans and Moguls have vanished or shrunk into mere constitutional functionaries, no more significant today than the high priests of the Israelites or the pharaohs of ancient Egypt. But the pope is still there, and a larger congregation than ever before—over one billion people of all races—acknowledges his spiritual sovereignty.[18]

Johnson's rhapsodic celebration of the papacy's powers of survival is not without its appeal for both the partisan and the detached. After all, what he says has the historian's ring of truth about it: the papacy is still around while other institutions of like structure and universal scope have either declined in importance or simply disappeared. But there is much that Johnson's panegyric leaves out, and at the time of the death of John Paul I, the papacy had about it the air of a dispirited and directionless institution. Paul VI's dying months were a depressing chronicle of powerlessness—the Moro crisis being just the most dramatic of them all—and the short-lived reign of John Paul I, which had promised so much, seemed now a harbinger of grim days to come. But this was all to change with the election of the cardinal-archbishop of the venerable royal and university city of Krakow, Poland: Karol Wojtyla.

The papacy had reached a low point at the time of Paul's death, only to be compounded shortly after with John Paul's early demise. The election of the theologian-philosopher-poet-bishop from Poland offered a new energy and focus for a languishing leadership. The papacy itself had been changed by many of the new theological insights, or better yet emphases, emerging from the Second Vatican Council. The Pope was increasingly seen as the true *first among equals*, a bishop like other bishops, but by virtue of the Petrine Office called to exercise a special ministry of unity and not of overlordship. The Pope, the Bishop of Rome, is more a symbol of genuine communion and far less a potentate. From now on, the Council Fathers supposed, the primatial authority of the Pope would be fraternal and not monarchical in intention and in function. Ecclesiologist and ecumenist J.M.R. Tillard—Dominican friar, *peritus*, and a friend of John Paul II—outlined the postconciliar view of the papacy in a major address to the North American Academy of Ecumenists in 1997:

> It is his task to make possible and to maintain a kind of ping-pong game, a back and forth movement, a to-and-fro dynamism, between local groups of bishops (in dialogue with their local churches) and himself. Through this process, opinions may be clarified, the hidden truth of some positions be discovered, the complexity of the matter be unveiled, the legitimacy of a variety of expressions be acknowledged, the necessity of counterbalances in the *praxis* of the Church be recognized. Since the Bishop of Rome has the capacity to distance himself from national, ethnic, or racial fervor or interests, he has in the whole process the mission to prevent his brothers to be in their research of the common good the slaves of their local and immediate agendas. He has also the task to help them resolve the difficult conflicts around rights, customs, traditions of diverse groups. Yet he does this more by persuading than by ordering. . . . The Bishop of Rome is called by God to be a leader, opening new ways, guiding the local churches in evangelical endeavors their own bishop may be unable to discern in isolation, insisting on moral issues dangerously jeopardized in some philosophical circles, tracing the limits of Christian submission to the ideals of political societies. In the life of the Catholic Church the voice of the Bishop of Rome plays an essential role. But this voice has always to be pronounced in the episcopal brotherhood, never outside of it. The Catholic Church would not really be the Catholic Church without the Bishop of Rome, the Bishop of Rome would not really be the Primate of the Catholic Church without the brotherhood of what has been called since Cyprian the episcopal college.[19]

Tillard identified Paul VI's reintroduction of the Episcopal Synod as an occasional body called to exercise a consultative role in assisting the Petrine Office in the exercise of its ministry as a bold undertaking that was sadly doomed to failure. The Synod's structure and limitations were such as to prevent it from being anything more than a powerless listening post. "The synod only exists in order to let the Roman pontiff know its opinion. It is not able to address the Church directly so as to express, in communion with the pope but not simply preparing the pope's own decision, the judgement of the universal episcopate on the matters at issue."[20] Synods were to fare no better under John Paul II's pontificate. Indeed, they appear to have fared worse.

The 1985 Extraordinary Synod of Catholic Bishops that convened at the Vatican to "review" the twenty years that elapsed since the conclusion of the Second Vatican Council is a perfect template for the politicking, frustrations, and aborted hopes that have come to define the failure of synodical governance as practised by the papacy. Not that important issues were not raised and healthy debate engaged. For instance, Bishop James Malone, a delegate of the United States, spoke of the Synod as a great success characterized by fraternal candour and noted that the Synod provided the opportunity to further strengthen the ties that link the national episcopal conferences with the Successor of St. Peter, "from whom we receive inspiration, direction, and confirmation in the apostolic faith." By contrast, the germane observations of Cardinal Aloisio Lorscheider of Brazil lack the convoluted tone of so much of the discussion that occurred around the topic of national conferences of bishops and synods as institutional expressions of collegiality. His contributions were pointed, orthodox, and yet devoid of that simpering and deferential tone that frequently infects episcopal prose: "this form of communion and participation—synods; regional conferences; etc.—does not at all damage the primacy of the Roman Pontiff, but rather realizes what the ministry of the Pope is already meant to be: the service of unity. The juridical forms can vary over the course of the centuries, but the fundamental reality of communion and participation belongs to the very essence of the Church, and finds its theological and biblical foundation in the very essence of the Church."[21]

Delegates struggled to articulate a view of collegiality that was less theoretical in tone and more practical in expression and did so under the constant constraints of not appearing in any way to be less than respectful of the Pope and his intentions—hardly a forum or context for vigorous debate. And yet, periodically, invitations to honest dialogue arose at press conferences, at the religious equivalents of parliamentary scrums, in the formal *interventions* of the Synod delegates, during the small group discussions or *circuli minores* that occurred after the formal presentations had concluded, and even in the summations provided by the formidable Sala Stampa della Sante Sede or Press Office of the Holy See—perhaps the most poignant being the gentle and yet profound counsel of Bishop Georges Singha of the Congo, who observed that "unity is not a synonym for uniformity, nor standardization, nor levelling, but must go hand-in-hand with diversity, differences, variety and perhaps multiplicity." This counsel, deeply rooted in the traditional ecclesiology of the Roman Church, has yet to find meaningful incarnation in the structures of governance, and whatever hope may have been invested in the revival of the Episcopal Synod has been scotched by the heavy reality of Curial control and papal prerogative.

Throughout the 1980s and 1990s, calls from several sources for reform of the papacy—or more precisely still, reform of the ways in which the papal office is exercised—have mounted with increasing intensity. Bernard Cooke, a U.S. theologian and former Jesuit priest, calls for a radical shift in the very model of papal leadership from a monarchical model to that of the Grand Facilitator:

> . . . even as we rejoice in papal moral leadership, we cannot avoid questioning other exercises of papal power, exercises of power that involve domination, control, threat and claim to eminence beyond any judgement short of God. God's Spirit does not work in this way. As an alternative, we can envisage a papal role as liaison among communities around the world with their diverse cultural insights into the gospel, with their differing cultural forms of sacramental liturgies, with their diverse patterns of Christian community.[22]

It is the kind of model one might expect from a progressive U.S. theologian, in part built on his experience of democratic governance and his innate belief in its natural superiority over other modes of power and authority. Still, it is not without sensitivity to the historically conditioned reality of papal politics and the exercise of the Petrine ministry. More realistic and influential a contribution to the still largely *sotto voce* discussion around a revitalized and reconfigured papal office can be found emanating from Cooke's contemporary John Quinn, the retired archbishop of San Francisco, who in delivering his Campion Address at Oxford University in 1996 called for an understanding of the papacy that embraced the principles of collegiality and subsidiarity and went further still: Quinn reminded his audience that Pope Eugene III had been a monk under the great abbot–theologian, the "Last Father of the Church," St. Bernard of Clairvaux, and that in a letter written to the newspaper on the occasion of his election Bernard admonished him, in light of the pontifical preference to be more the successor of the Emperor Constantine than of the fisherman Peter, to abjure the pomp and ceremony of papal public appearances. The Second Vatican Council, Quinn argues, has ushered in a new and welcome simplicity to the modern papacy, but there continue to be deep ecclesial concerns. For instance, the political model of leadership with its emphasis on order and control should not, in Quinn's episcopal opinion, exclude the ecclesial model with *its* emphasis on communion and the discernment of gifts. These models must co-exist in tension.

Quinn's argument that the ecclesial model be given equal time with the political model is especially interesting given the decidedly political occupations of John Paul II, his adroit handling of complex and competing political interests—Poland, Haiti, Philippines, Rwanda—and his passionate commitment to basic human rights and their protection worldwide. In addition, although he has been hard on clergy in political life, Ernesto Cardenal in Nicaragua and Robert Drinan in the United States being particularly outstanding cases, he has not hesitated to enter the political arena himself when he saw the outcome serving the Catholic and common good. The Constantinian legacy is never far from Rome; in fact, it imbues Rome, and the counterinfluence of the Gospel then becomes yet more imperative. The catacombs reside in the shadow of the *imperium* still.

Quinn's Campion lecture and his subsequent book, *The Reform of the Papacy: The Costly Call to Christian Unity* (1999), actually arise out of a challenge posed by John Paul II himself in his 1995 encyclical *Ut unum sint* (*That They May Be One*), when he called for a constructive dialogue whose object would be "to find a way of exercising the primacy, which while in no way renouncing what is essential to its mission, is nonetheless open to a new situation." John Paul II is genuinely open to ecumenical dialogue and is earnest in his efforts to heal the scandalous rifts that divide Christianity, for they are many and they run deep. He knows that the Successor of St. Peter is often perceived as the major obstacle to eventual unity and the crushing irony of this not invalid perception weighs on him heavily. After all, the Pope is supposed to be the symbol of unity. Again and again on his numerous peregrinations, he has encountered reminders that his office and the way it is historically exercised have prevented serious efforts at full union. This pains him. But John Paul is not a compromising kind of person; he prefers the gradualist approach, rejects syncretism, understands the frustrations and impatience attendant on true dialogue, remains committed to unalterable philosophical and theological propositions, and although appreciative of the value of the dramatic gesture, he always prefers substance to theatre. Any change to the way the papacy is understood, its central administration or Curial arm reformed, and the presence of the Vatican on the world stage recalibrated, will depend on who is Pope. As the Benedictine theologian Patrick Granfield remarks: "In the last analysis, the papacy—exalted institution that it may be—is the man. . . . a man, limited by his natural gifts, education, and experience, and by his geographical, social, and cultural milieu."[23] We need to know that man, what shapes him, and what defines him.

In the case of Karol Wojtyla, we begin with Poland. It is critical to understand what Poland means to the Pope—its culture, its spirituality, its mission—in order to appreciate his own rootedness in this land and the unique way in which his own history and destiny are tied inextricably to it. Biographer and theologian George Weigel attaches considerable significance to Wojtyla's deep reading of the soul of Poland:

As Karol Wojtyla's biographer, I am persuaded that he came to a "culture-first" view of history very early in his life, certainly by the end of the 1940s. This conviction was fed from many sources: his immersion as a student in Polish Romantic literature; his experience in the Rhapsodic Theatre and the cultural resistance movement during the Nazi Occupation; his wrestling with the question of revolutionary violence in his drama, *Our God's Brother*; and, above all, his profound Christian conviction that the Word through whom the world was created remains the centre of the world and its history. Because the

Word has overcome the world (Jn 16:33), those conformed to the Word
can speak words of truth to the world of power. A people in possession
of its authentic cultural heritage, Wojtyla came to believe, possessed a
freedom that no tyrant could abrogate entirely. The tools of material
force were, ultimately, incapable of resisting the weapons of spiritual—
cultural—resistance. That was the strategy of resistance that Wojtyla
applied during his years as priest and bishop in Kracow, and that is the
strategy of change he has applied on the world stage in his 22 years as
John Paul II. That, pre-eminently, was what he did in June 1979 in
Poland: by restoring to his people their authentic history and culture,
by giving them permission to say publicly who they were and what had
made them that way, he not only provoked a mass psychological catharsis with long-term political consequences; he created a revolution of
conscience that struck the Communist culture of the lie at its most
vulnerable point.[24]

The spiritual and the cultural are intimately connected in Wojtyla's
mind and they come together in a special synthesis in Poland, a synthesis
that provides him with a template for the world. A people disconnected
from their culture is a people adrift, easy prey to the master weavers of
deceit and enslavement be they Fascist, National Socialist, or Communist. And in the end only the Word truly liberates because the Word is
incarnated in time, history, and culture.

But Wojtyla was not only shaped by the great religious and literary
figures of Poland; they provided him either through their writing or
directly through their own personal intervention with an introduction to
the saints and thinkers that were to prove foundational for the future
Pope's own thought. For instance, as John Paul II notes:

Before entering the seminary, I met a man named Jan Tyranowski, who
was a true mystic: this man, whom I consider a saint, introduced me to
the great Spanish mystics and in particular to Saint John of the Cross.
Even before entering the underground seminary [during the Nazi occupation of Poland], I read the works of that mystic, especially his poetry.
In order to read it in the original, I studied Spanish. That was a very
important stage in my life.[25]

John of the Cross would come to haunt Wojtyla as an intellectual, spiritual, and literary influence, and it took him some time to abandon his idea to join the Discalced Carmelites, the order associated with John of the Cross. As a young man he had had many conversations with Jozef Prus, a Carmelite who frequently visited the palace of the cardinal-archbishop of Krakow, Prince Adam Sapieha. The prince-bishop was not inclined to allow his promising young seminarian, known to all by his nickname Lolek, to move to a Carmelite convent in order to continue his advanced or theological studies disengaged from the mundane world. Sapieha was not willing to lose Lolek to the contemplative life.

Still, the young Wojtyla continued his Carmelite contacts, published his first volume of poems, *Song of the Hidden God*, with a Carmelite publishing house, wrote an honours thesis on John of the Cross, and maintained his contacts with the saintly Tyranowski. The perduring influence of Carmelite thought and spirituality on the Pope can be discovered, perhaps not surprisingly, given that John of the Cross was one of the great poets of the Spanish Golden Age, in Wojtyla's own verse. The Sanjuanist emphases on the apophatic or dark way, the role of emptiness in contemplation, and the genuine passion for God are captured in Wojtyla's "Man of Emotion":

You don't really suffer when love is flooding you:
it's a patch of enthusiasm, pleasant and shallow;
if it dries up—do you think of the void?
Between heart and heart there is always a gap.
You must enter it slowly—
till the eye absorbs color,
the ear tunes to rhythm.

Love and move inwards, discover your will,
shed heart's evasions and the mind's harsh control.[26]

If Wojtyla's episcopal motto were not "*Totus tuus*," a phrase that comes from the writings of the French priest St. Louis-Marie Grignion de Montfort, thereby underscoring the deeply Marian roots of the Pope's spirituality, then it just as appropriately could have been "Love and move inwards," a perfect distillation of the Carmelite vocation. But *Totus tuus* it is and that is as it should be given the centrality of Mary in the devotional and theological life of Karol Wojtyla.

As bishop, Wojtyla chose as his official motto the Latin words *Totus tuus*—"All Yours"—taken from Louis-Marie Grignion de Montfort, the Breton saint, in whose *Treatise* he had found divine inspiration, reading it on the floor of the Solvay factory during the war. Henceforth he placed the motto at the top of the page, in the right-hand corner, on every document and letter he penned the rest of his life.[27]

John Paul II is quite clear about the "Marian thread," as he calls it, running through his life. It was while working during the war in the Solvay chemical works in Krakow that he read the work that would change his life, Louis-Marie Grignion de Montfort's *Traité de la vraie dévotion à la Sainte Vierge* (*Treatise on the Most Excellent Devotion to the Most Holy Virgin*):

The reading of this book was a decisive turning-point in my life. I say "turning-point" but in fact it was a long inner journey which coincided with my clandestine preparation for the priesthood. It was at that time that this curious treatise came into my hands. The *Traité* is one of those books that it is not enough to "have read." I remember carrying it on me for a long time, even at the sodium factory, with the result that its handsome binding became spotted with lime. I continually went back to certain passages. I soon saw that in spite of the book's baroque style it dealt with something fundamental. As a result, my devotion to the Mother of Christ in my childhood and adolescence yielded to a new attitude springing from the depths of my faith, as though from the very heart of the Trinity and Jesus Christ. . . . "Perfect devotion to Mary"— that is how the author of the treatise puts it—that is, the true knowledge of her, and confident surrender to her, grows with our knowledge of Christ and our confident surrender to his person. What is more, this "perfect devotion" is indispensable to anyone who means to give himself without reserve to Christ and to the work of redemption. . . . My devotion to Mary . . . is an integral part of my inner life and of my spiritual theology. . . . I should add that my extremely personal and inward spiritual relation to the Mother of Christ had merged since my youth with the great stream of Marian devotion which has a long history in Poland and also many tributaries. . . . I should like to mention in particular the Marian sanctuary of Kalwaria Zebrzydowska, near Cracow and Wadowice, where I was born, a sanctuary which is so dear to me and which I have visited so often in my youth, and later as priest and bishop. I can tell you that, in the manner of devotion shown by the people to whom I belong, I found there what I had discovered in the treatise.[28]

Mary is critical to all that Wojtyla does and is. He acknowledges her importance in his life and in that of the Church in countless ways: his reflections on the Marian aspect of his priestly life in *Gift and Mystery: On the Fiftieth Anniversary of My Priestly Ordination*; his encyclical dedicated specifically to Mary, *Redemptoris mater*; his numerous invocations of Mary in his apostolic exhortations, papal addresses, Wednesday afternoon sermons, and encyclicals of both broad and narrow focus; his public recognition in a talk to the Roman Curia that the Church, including the Petrine Office that he exercises, takes its fundamental form from Mary in her self-surrender to God with her *fiat*; and in the special significance that he attaches to Marian apparitions, shrines, and titles. Although there is a theological sophistication to the Pope's Mariological reflections, including some interesting (if not unconventional) exegetical interpretations, the appeal of Marian devotion is at a level of deep personal meaning. For instance, although Wojtyla professes a strong attachment to such Polish shrines as Czestochowa, home of the Black Madonna and the last point of the Polish resistance to the Swedish invaders in the seventeenth century, thereby underscoring the *cultural* significance of Marian devotion, he has a personal familiarity with and attraction to many of the great and some more recent Marian moments in Catholic history: Our Lady of Guadalupe, the patron saint of all the Americas, a devotion that originated in the sixteenth century in Mexico; Our Lady of La Salette, named the Reconciler of Sinners, a nineteenth-century French devotion; Our Lady of Lourdes, also a nineteenth-century French devotion, with the most famous and popular of shrines;

and Our Lady of Fatima, a twentieth-century devotion originating in Portugal, which holds special importance in the life of John Paul II.

It was on May 13, 1917 that it all began. Three young Portuguese shepherd children—Lucia de Jesus (ten), Francisco (nine), and Jacinta Marto (seven)—witnessed an apparition of a "Lady brighter than the sun," from whose hands there hung a rosary. The Lady instructed them to pray frequently and invited them to return to the spot of the apparition on several occasions where they could find her. During the last apparition, October 13, 1917, the Lady appeared in the presence of some 70,000 people and informed the children that hereafter she was to be known as Our Lady of the Rosary. In an earlier apparition—July 13—the Lady had requested that Russia (then in the throes of the Communist Revolution) be consecrated to her Immaculate Heart. This request was known as the "secret of Fatima." In time, a commanding shrine would be built on the site of the apparitions, Francisco would die on April 4, 1919 and his sister Jacinta on February 20, 1920, and Lucia would become a Dorothean sister and witness several subsequent apparitions in convents in Pontevedra and Tuy. The "secret" consists of three parts, two of which were disclosed, and the third of which was rumoured to be known to popes alone. This "secret" became the subject of great speculation—wild, apocalyptic, millennarian, doomsday—and stories of popes overcome by the power of the message were rampant. On May 13, 2000 the Vatican revealed the third part at a Mass for the beatification of the two Marto children celebrated at the Shrine of Our Lady of Fatima by John Paul II himself. Cardinal Angelo Sodano, Vatican secretary of state, read an address at the Mass that both revealed the content of the third part and provided a context for interpreting its meaning. The text includes a prophetic vision that graphically describes a scene in which "a bishop clothed in white" makes his way with great effort toward a cross. His path is strewn with the corpses of the martyred—bishops, priests, women and men religious, and laypeople as well—and then he too falls on the same cluttered ground, apparently dead, felled by a fusillade of bullets.

On May 13, 1981 John Paul II was wounded in an assassination attempt in St. Peter's Square by Turkish dissident and terrorist Mehmet Ali Agca. The Pope concluded that, as he said in a meditation with the Italian bishops at the Gemelli Polyclinic in 1994, it was "a motherly hand which guided the bullet's path, enabling the dying pope to halt at the threshold of death." On one occasion when the bishop of the diocese in which the Shrine of Our Lady of Fatima is located visited the Pope, John Paul provided the bishop with the bullet that had pierced him and which had been lodged in the popemobile in order that it may be kept in the shrine. It was later set in the crown of the statue of Our Lady of Fatima.

In addition to the special intervention by the Blessed Virgin Mary to spare the life of the Pope—a conviction that John Paul holds unwaveringly—the Pope also assigns special significance to her intercessory role in the collapse of the Soviet system commencing in 1989. As late as 1997 he continued to invoke Our Lady of Fatima to heal our troubled times in his "Message for the World Day of the Sick" in which he commented that "the Lady of the message seems to read the signs of the times—the signs of our time—with special insight. . . . The insistent invitation of Mary most holy to penance is nothing but the manifestation of her maternal concern for the fate of the human family, in need of conversion and forgiveness."

John Paul's devotion to Mary is a source of inspiration to countless Catholics throughout the world, but it is also the occasion for deep misgivings and distrust on the part of various intellectuals and scholars who see in Wojtyla's proclivity to bestow dubious honours on her a sign of his indebtedness to that most papal of recent popes, Pius IX. This criticism is expressed most directly, if not acidly, by U.S. biographer, classicist, and historian Garry Wills:

The political use of Mary to fight communism, which began with [Count Emiliano Avogardro] della Motta's 1851 book [*An Essay Considering Socialism and the Socialist Teaching and Tendencies*] and continued through Pius IX's reign, was renewed in this century through the call of Our Lady of Fatima to pray for the conversion of Russia, which led to the formation of a worldwide "Blue Army" in her service. Pius XII reported in 1951 that he had a vision replicating that at Fatima in 1917. Pope John Paul's devotion to Our Lady of Fatima is connected with his resistance to communism in his native Poland. But he has larger and grander visions of his service to her, comparable to that of his hero, Pius IX. In 1997 he established a special commission of twenty-three scholars to consider defining Mary as Co-Redemptrix of the human race. This goes beyond the usurpation of the Spirit's activity represented in calling her the Mediatrix of All Graces. Now she is to be made the joint agent of a divine work. Once more the Spirit's intimate action in the body of Christ is removed off to a distance only she can traverse for our sake. Nothing could be more alien from the treatment of Mary in the gospels.[29]

Wills's attack on the current papacy and its "structures of deceit" bears the marks of an urgent broadside and he is less than fair—in fact, he is reductionist—in his treatment of John Paul II and his Marian tendencies. In his effort to excoriate Pio Nono, Wills paints the canvas of his argument with grand liberality and broad strokes and with little regard for the necessary historical distinctions and personal colourations. But he is correct when he identifies the present debate about Mary's presumed co-redemptive role as a further instance of the Pope's "high mariology." The popular pressure on the Pope to name Mary as Co-redemptrix, Mediatrix of all Graces and Universal Advocate, has been mounting for many years. There are international symposia held on the topic in addition to a letter-writing campaign urging the Pope to grant Mary the new honours that has garnered millions of petitioners in nearly 150 countries. Hundreds of bishops and scores of cardinals are well disposed to a theological and pastoral initiative that seems to hold little appeal for the Church's leading thinkers. In fact, French theologian and priest René Laurentin, considered the foremost scholar on Mary in the world, is adamantly opposed to granting these new titles to the Blessed Virgin Mary. His reasons are sound and supported by the overwhelming majority of the Church's theologians and ecumenists, but the pressure on the Pope continues unabated.

The argument for Mary's co-redemptive role is grounded on a distinction made between the "objective redemption" that only Christ can effect and a "subjective redemption" by which Mary's co-operation in distributing the fruits of Jesus's redemptive act is essentially different in kind and degree from that of all the faithful. Historical sources and biblical passages that are recruited to support this special role of Mary are specious, tendentious, and eccentric. But the drafters of the campaign cleverly draw on John Paul's own writings to substantiate the validity and appropriateness of their Marian undertaking. For instance, they find validation in the Pope's general audience address of April 9, 1997: "The collaboration of Christians in salvation takes place after the Calvary event, whose fruits they endeavour to spread by prayer and sacrifice. Mary instead co-operated during the event itself and in the role of mother; thus her co-operation embraces the whole of Christ's saving work. She alone was associated in this way with the redemptive sacrifice that merited the salvation of all mankind."

Whether the Pope will act on the campaign to define Mary's role as Co-redemptrix, Mediatrix of All Graces and Universal Advocate, is conditional upon assuring non-Catholic Christians that this is not a ruse to rank Mary with Jesus and in responding persuasively to the counterarguments advanced by the Church's premier thinkers and leaders who consider the new titles of dubious biblical justification and of questionable theological significance. After all, they reason, Mary has already been the subject of dogmatic definition in terms of her immaculate conception, divine motherhood, perpetual virginity, and assumption. There is no pastoral necessity, ecumenical imperative, or theological urgency that requires a new dogma. John Paul II may well require further persuading, not because he is indifferent to the role of Mary in salvation history, but precisely because his personal devotion to the Virgin is central to his self-definition as a priest, he will move cautiously, protectively, and in consort with his chief theological advisers, including Vatican cardinals Joseph Ratzinger, prefect of the Congregation of the Faith, and Walter Kasper, president of the Pontifical Council for Promoting Christian Unity.

The Pope's spirituality is deeply Polish, connected with culture, engaged with the arts, in dialogue with the best currents of thought, and steeped in history. Poles like St. Stanislaw, patron saint of Poland, are not abstract footnotes in an historical record. They are symbols of the eternal. In fact, as Polish Nobel Laureate Czeslaw Milosz reminds us, one of the salient characteristics of the Polish person is "an extremely strong sense of the communion of saints, namely of the link between the living and the dead. . . . If you go to a cemetery on All Saints Day . . . you will realize that it is the greatest feast in Poland."[30]

The importance that John Paul II attaches to a living history can be seen in his penchant for creating saints—he holds the unassailable record for beatification and canonization in the history of the papacy—and in the value that he places on holding sacred the memory of those who have helped to Christianize culture through their witness. One such inspiring figure was Adam Chmielowski, a painter, religious brother, and a mendicant who identified completely with the underprivileged and stood in solidarity with them and in so doing embodied the radical Christian witness of a St. Francis of Assisi and St. John of the Cross.

Brother Albert has a special place in the history of Polish spirituality. . . . One of my greatest joys as Pope was to raise this poor man of Cracow, who went about in his gray habit, to the honors of the altar, first with his beatification in Blonie Krakowskie during my visit to Poland in 1983, and then with his canonization in Rome, in November of the memorable year 1989. Many writers have immortalized the figure of Brother Albert in Polish literature. . . . I too, as a young priest, when I was curate at Saint Florian's Church in Cracow, wrote a dramatic work in his honor, entitled *The Brother of Our God*. This was my way of repaying a debt of gratitude to him.[31]

Perhaps the example most illustrative of the various strains of Wojtyla's spiritual makeup—contemplative, Marian, Polish—can be found in his canonization of the first saint of the new millennium: Maria Faustina Kowalska of the Most Blessed Sacrament. She was a religious of the Congregation of the Sisters of Our Lady of Mercy. About twenty years old when she entered her religious congregation, she spent her entire life— she died at age thirty-three—given over to the imitation of Christ through sacrifice, humility, and compassion. On February 22, 1931 she had a vision of Christ in her cell with rays of mercy streaming from his heart. He instructed her to have an image painted to represent this vision and that she was to identify as "Jesus, I trust in you." Christ also commanded her to write a diary so that others could come to know and trust him—a work that was eventually published as *Divine Mercy in My Soul*—and she continued to have revelations between 1931 and 1938. Christ continually emphasized the unlimited and non-discriminating nature of his mercy and it was this aspect of Jesus that most appealed to her. She died of tuberculosis on October 5, 1938 on the eve of a war she is said to have predicted. Throughout the years of Nazi rule in Poland, her cult spread and she was, as John Paul II has remarked, "a particular support and an inexhaustible source of hope." Faustina's emphasis on the divine mercy greatly appealed to John Paul and he made a special visit to the Shrine of Divine Mercy in Lagiewniki in June 1997 to pray at her tomb. He provided a personal reflection on the occasion that underlined the attraction to him of the message of the Divine Mercy, "a message that has always been near and dear to me . . . and in a sense forms the image of this pontificate." Even as a young man he had been drawn to her mysticism and her holy witness, visiting her sanctuary on his way to work in the chemical factory, and later as archbishop of Cracow becoming the promoter of her cause for sainthood. As Pope he would acknowledge her influence on his life and thought, especially on his 1980 encyclical *Dives in misericordia* (*Rich in Mercy*).

When he canonized her—number 297 of his pontificate and the first of the new era—he underlined the significance he has consistently attached to the contemplative life, to the self-emptying quality of Mary's total love, and to the unique mosaic that is Polish culture and spirituality.

THE POPE AS WRITER

The Pope's deeply personal spirituality suffuses all his work—pastoral, administrative, intellectual—and is never cut off from its philosophical moorings in Thomism and phenomenology. The Pope, at heart, understands himself to be a philosopher, and some of his own considerable publications are explicitly identifiable as philosophical in root and substance, for instance with *The Acting Person*, his experiment with combining the insights of Thomas Aquinas with those of Max Scheler. It should come as no surprise, then, that some of his papal writings have a philosophical focus or underpinning. As he did with his three pivotal social encyclicals—*Laborem exercens* (*On Human Work*, 1981), *Sollicitudo rei socialis* (*On Social Concern*, 1987), and *Centesimus annus* (*On the Hundredth Anniversary of Rerum Novarum*, 1991)—John Paul has penned three thematically connected "philosophical" encyclicals that highlight his role as teacher, ethicist, and metaphysician.

On August 6, 1993, the Feast of the Transfiguration of the Lord, John Paul issued the first of the trilogy, *Veritatis splendor* (*The Splendour of*

Truth), an encyclical addressed pointedly to all the bishops of the Roman Catholic Church "regarding certain fundamental questions of the Church's moral teaching." Very clearly the alarm bells are sounded in the introduction wherein the Pope intones:

> . . . a new situation has come about *within the Christian community itself*, which has experienced the spread of numerous doubts and objections of a human and psychological, social and cultural, religious and even properly theological nature, with regard to the Church's moral teachings. It is no longer a matter of limited and occasional dissent, but of an overall and systematic calling into question of traditional moral doctrine, on the basis of certain anthropological and ethical presuppositions. At the root of these presuppositions is the more or less obvious influence of currents of thought which end by detaching human freedom from its essential and constitutive relationship to truth. Thus the traditional doctrine regarding the natural law, and the universality and the permanent validity of its precepts, is rejected; certain of the Church's moral teachings are found simply unacceptable; and the Magisterium itself is considered capable of intervening in matters of morality only in order to "exhort consciences" and to "propose values," in the light of which each individual will independently make his or her decisions and life choices.

The remaining 170 pages address this "crisis." The language is often abstract and speaks of first principles, categories of thought, modes of discourse and inquiry that are largely foreign to contemporary readers unfamiliar with Neo-Scholastic and Thomistic thinking. British writer Quentin de la Bedoyere calls it "a strong contender for the most prolix document ever written; only popes and dictators can get away with logorrhea."

The first of the three sections that comprise the encyclical consists of a biblical meditation, one of John Paul II's favourites, the dialogue of Jesus with the rich young man in the Gospel of St. Matthew. The young man asks Jesus: "Teacher, what good must I do to have eternal life?" Jesus's answer to this question, the question itself, and its spiritual significance for all followers of Jesus are examined by the Pope with rudimentary exegetical tools that yield their own rich harvest: "Jesus's way of acting and his words, his deeds and his precepts constitute the moral rule of Christian life. Indeed, his actions, and in particular his Passion and Death on the Cross, are the living revelation of his love for the Father and for others."

The Pope then moves on to the second question of the encyclical. In this section the Pope examines various tendencies in present-day moral theology, reaffirms the validity of universal moral absolutes, deplores the dangerous post-Enlightenment drift into subjectivism, reminds Christians of the true nature of freedom and of the relationship of morality to faith, restates the classic teaching of God's eternal law and of the natural law as the human expression of this eternal law, denounces the liberality of interpretation regarding the role and judgments of conscience, repudiates the arguments of proportionalists, consequentialists, and those ethicists who espouse a "fundamental option" approach rather than a traditional acts-directed ethical methodology, and repeats with vigorous clarity the existence of intrinsically evil acts.

In the third and final section John Paul explores the pastoral dimensions of his argument and reminds the bishops that "before the demands of morality we are all absolutely equal." He especially laments the dechristianization process that has succeeded in severing the interwoven relationship of faith with morality: "Today's widespread tendencies toward subjectivism, utilitarianism and relativism appear as not merely pragmatic attitudes or patterns of behaviour, but rather as approaches having a basis in theory and claiming full cultural and social legitimacy."

The Pope then proceeds to speak of the role and the value of the Magisterium and lobs the following ecclesiological grenade: "Dissent, in the form of carefully orchestrated protests and polemics carried on the media, is opposed to ecclesial communion and to a correct understanding of the hierarchical constitution of the People of God." He concludes with a meditation on Mary.

Not unsurprisingly, the reception of the encyclical varied. *The Globe and Mail*, *Le Monde*, and *The New York Times*, among a legion of others, applauded its publication and the courage of its author. The universal episcopate responded with deference of mind and spirit. Conservative Catholics exploded with pleasure; moderates felt cowed; progressives regrouped; radicals went ballistic. But it was only the first round. There was more to come.

On March 25, 1995, the Feast of the Solemnity of the Annunciation of the Lord, *Evangelium vitae* (*The Gospel of Life*) appeared. This encyclical letter was addressed to bishops, priests, deacons, men and women religious, lay faithful, and all people of goodwill. The Roman Church is nothing if not hierarchical.

Evangelium vitae stands on the foundations set by *Veritatis splendor*. In chapter one of *Evangelium vitae*, John Paul makes clear his case: euthanasia, abortion, contraception, sterilization, doctor-assisted suicide, in-vitro fertilization, surrogacy, and the death penalty are all symptoms and manifestations of a world held captive by an ideology and ethic deeply hostile to the Christian world view:

> While the climate of widespread moral uncertainty can in some way be explained by the multiplicity and gravity of today's social problems, and these can sometimes mitigate the subjective responsibility of individuals, it is no less sure that we are confronted by an even greater reality, which can be described as a veritable structure of sin. This reality is characterized by the emergence of a culture which denies solidarity and in many cases takes the form of a veritable "culture of death." This culture is actively fostered by powerful cultural, economic and political currents which encourage an idea of society excessively concerned with efficiency. Looking at the situation from this point of view, it is possible to speak in a certain sense of a war of the powerful against the weak: a life which would require greater acceptance, love and care is considered useless, or held to be an intolerable burden, and is therefore rejected in one way or another. A person who, because of illness, handicap or, more simply, just by existing, compromises the well-being or life-style of those who are more favoured tends to be looked upon as an enemy to be resisted or eliminated. In this way a kind of "conspiracy against life" is unleashed. This conspiracy involves not only individuals in their personal, family or group relationships, but goes far beyond, to the point of damaging and distorting, at the international level, relations between peoples and States.

The Pope proceeds—this time lacing his argument with an extended meditation on the Cain and Abel story to be found in the Book of Genesis— to outline the consequences of a notion of freedom that is unidimensional, defined in terms of individual rights only, disengaged from truth, grounded on "the shifting sands of complete relativism"—a notion of freedom that has no place for the transcendent.

Freedom for the pontiff is inherently relational. It is tied to the Other. It draws its meaning from the dialectic "between the experience of the uncertainty of human life and the affirmation of its value that so completely defines the life of Jesus":

> He is certainly accepted by the righteous, who echo Mary's immediate and joyful "yes." But there is also from the start, rejection on the part of the world which grows hostile and looks for the child in order to "destroy him". . . . In this contrast between threats and insecurity on the one hand and the power of God's gift on the other, there shines forth all the more clearly the glory which radiates from the house at Nazareth and from the manger at Bethlehem: this life which is born is salvation for all humanity.

The only adequate antidote to the poison of the culture of death is the culture of life embodied in the gospel of life—a life distinguished by its self-donation, self-emptying, *kenosis*. "Jesus proclaims that life finds its centre, its meaning and fulfilment when it is given up."

But the Pope does not restrict himself to biblical reflection and theology. He reviews the Roman Catholic position on many highly controversial areas of sexual morality and restates the Church's uncompromising opposition to any technological undertaking that further sunders the integral relationship of the procreative with the unitive in every single act of sexual intercourse. His forays into biology and history earn him correction by such distinguished thinkers as the Catholic scientist John-Erik Stig Hansen, head of research at the Hvidore Hospital in Denmark, and the late Jesuit ethicist Richard McCormick, professor of Christian Ethics at the University of Notre Dame in the United States. Both make the point that inaccuracies or misunderstandings seriously weaken the credibility of an encyclical that they largely and soundly applaud.

The Pope doesn't hesitate to scold nations that enact legislation that diminishes human life in all its forms. He wrestles with the complex issue of civil and moral law and has little time for a morality governed by poll, personal whim, social licence, or majority opinion.

The Pope is categorical in his defence of life at all its stages and he expects Catholics in political leadership to be unwavering in their support of those measures to be taken to ensure that life is protected at all stages, but especially at the most vulnerable: the beginning and the end. John Paul is neither timid when urging Catholic politicians to take their faith and conscience seriously when performing the duties of elected office, nor in reminding the public at large to value the high office of political leadership itself, something he has frequently noticed and with alarm that has not been the case in many democracies. As he observed in an apostolic exhortation on February 19, 1998: "Members of governments, parliaments, the ruling class, and political parties are often accused of being overly ambitious, obsessed with power, selfish, and corrupt. However, neither those accusations nor the rather widespread opinion according to which politics is an occupation fraught with moral danger, in the least justifies the abstention of Christians from public life."

POLITICS AND FAITH

There isn't a Catholic politician in the world who has not been at some point caught in the vexatious arena of conflict between the dictates of an informed conscience and party loyalty, government policy and moral obligations, riding representation and personal opinion. And on no issue is this more acutely the case than that of abortion, its legality and availability. Quebec luminary Claude Ryan understands the demands of faith and political responsibility and has spent a lifetime shirking neither. A former national secretary of the French section of Catholic Action, editor and publisher of the influential Quebec newspaper *Le Devoir*, leader of the Quebec Liberal Party, leader of the Official Opposition, and variously minister of Education, Higher Education and Science, Public Security, Municipal Affairs and Housing, Ryan retired from politics in 1994. He has written and lectured widely on matters political and religious and knows intimately the perils that accompany ethical leadership:

There is very little room for absolutes in the actual making of political decisions. Politics is the art of the possible. So many interests and opinions must be taken into account before a decision is reached that the end-result is most often a compromise solution which leaves even one's friends more or less satisfied. Society needs above all politicians who are not dogmatic but professionally capable and morally strong. If I had to choose between a candidate who likes to display his religious faith in public but is insensitive to the need of his constituents and rather ineffectual, and a candidate who is not explicitly religious while not being anti-religious, but whose competence is well-established and whose commitment to the public interest is genuine, I would in ordinary circumstances give my vote to the latter. A corollary of this is that the Christian who serves in politics must be the ultimate judge of his decisions as long as he enjoys the trust of his fellow citizens. In line with St. Augustine's principles, he must be prepared at all times to oppose any law or decision which is not in his judgement conducive to peace, forbids the adoration of one God alone, or is objectionable from the standpoint of honest morality. He must be prepared to sacrifice not only his career but also his freedom, and perhaps even his life, in order to remain true to his principles.

In order to arrive at just decisions in such situations, he must have solid notions about what laws can achieve. He must also realize that in practical matters the best is often the enemy of the good. The object of laws, according to St. Thomas Aquinas, is neither to make citizens instantly virtuous nor to eradicate all forms of evil from society. Laws must aim at facilitating the practice of virtue, says Saint Thomas, but they must do so gradually and by taking into account established customs and habits. They must also be tolerant of certain imperfections rather than trying to impose unattainable norms of conduct upon the population. Laws which are too severe risk not being obeyed, and laws which are disobeyed breed contempt, warns St. Thomas with his usual wisdom. *That is why*, he concludes, *human-made laws cannot prohibit all that is prohibited by the natural law* (which is of God). That is also why, as opposed to the natural law which is immutable, human laws must remain subject to change. Let me take the example of abortion. In conformity with his Church's teachings on the inviolable sacredness of life, a Christian politician will in principle be opposed to abortion. But confronted with a piece of legislation dealing with abortion, he will have to study it in collaborating with colleagues sincerely holding other views on this matter. From conversations between parliamentarians, compromise solutions which nobody had originally imagined and which might considerably reduce the incidence of abortion while not totally banning it, may emerge. Hence the dilemma which the Christian politician must resolve. Should he stick to his position to the point of opposing any solution which falls short of a total ban? Or should he support a solution which is not ideal but which appears to a sincere lawmaker as the best possible one in the circumstances?

I do not advocate any particular course of action, since each case must be judged in light of concrete circumstances. I only wish to stress that, in such a situation, a politician should ultimately be guided by his conscience, not by outside pressures. I also wish to think that the Christian politician who sincerely follows his conscience may serve more effectively the principles which he has at heart than the one who makes his decisions on the sole basis of opinion polls or the number of petitions which reach his desk. It also seems to me that Christian voters, when invited to choose their representatives, should in all fairness judge the merits of the candidates on the basis of their whole record and not on the basis of one sole issue to the exclusion of all others.[32]

Ryan's clear and nuanced approach to a Catholic politician's public and private struggle with moral issues might not appeal to every prelate or to those self-styled guardians of Catholic orthodoxy who prefer the categorical judgment to the multitextured one, but it does highlight the prudential approach characteristic of those Catholic political leaders who treasure rather than fear the value of compromise. John Paul II, for all his inclination to the apodictic, understands the need to work with the political order and realizes the supreme futility of simply denouncing policy and direction at odds with Catholic teaching. It is important to effect change from within. In fact, he has called on the laity to engage in, rather than absent themselves from, the political arena.

But abortion, sterilization, euthanasia, and other similar moral challenges must be seen in the light of an authentic, biblically grounded

Christian anthropology, and to that end the Pope has laboured for years to establish a framework as well as a body of knowledge that affirms the uniqueness of Catholic moral teaching. Aware that the teaching of Paul VI's *Humanae vitae* has not been received by the Church, in spite of the repeated iterations of the encyclical's authority by the Magisterium, John Paul began his own strategy of correcting what George Weigel calls the "pastoral and catechetical failure" of *Humanae vitae*. In a sequence of 130 fifteen-minute *ferverini* delivered at weekly papal audiences that began on September 5, 1979 and concluded five years later on November 28, 1984, John Paul produced a body of work that was subsequently compiled and issued under the title *Theology of the Body: Human Love in the Divine Plan*. In this detailed treatment of a Catholic theology of the body that asserts the intersection of the spiritual and the material in such a way as to underscore the sacrality of the erotic and the bodily-ness of the divine, one should expect an intuitive understanding of the essentially sensual nature of an embodied spirituality. But as scripture scholar Luke Timothy Johnson observes in his critique of the Pope's Wednesday noon conferences:

> The pope's subtitle is "Human Love in the Divine Plan," but no real sense of human love as actually experienced emerges in these reflections. . . . John Paul thinks of himself as doing "phenomenology," but seems to never look at actual human experience. Instead, he dwells on the nuances of words in biblical narratives and declarations, while fantasizing an ethereal and all-encompassing mode of mutual self-donation between man and woman that lacks any of the messy, clumsy, awkward, charming, casual, and, yes, silly aspects of love in the flesh. Carnality, it is good to remember, is at least as much a matter of humour as of solemnity. In the pope's formulations, human sexuality is observed by telescope from a distant planet. Solemn pronouncements are made on the basis of textual exegesis rather than lived experience. The effect is something like that of a sunset painted by the unsighted.[33]

The Pope's preference for the philosophical abstraction over the concrete experience—in spite of his phenomenological perspective—should come as no surprise, nor should his yearning for the idealized, his

inclination to the ascetical, and his taste for arduous witness. The Pope
has the personality of a romantic, but it is nicely encased in the head of a
medievalist. In all his musings about love—*agape* and *eros*—the Pope
speaks of the transporting power of love, self-donation, mutuality, reci-
procity, and integration, but he does not speak of the senses and the body
as the senses and the body. Like most churchmen schooled in a tradition
of fear, if not loathing, of the body *qua* body, the Pope is much happier
celebrating the joys of a disembodied intimacy and of simply avoiding any
mention of pleasure at all. As a consequence, his teaching reads as so
much etherealized and disconnected cogitation, laced with countless allu-
sions to the scriptures and suffused with affection for the Virgin Mary.

But if John Paul's persistent and inventive labours to make real and
attractive the Church's teaching on sexuality and morality as crystallized
in *Humanae vitae* and in his own writings have yet to credibly penetrate
the consciousness of the Catholic masses, his efforts to more firmly root
the Catholic communion in its own neglected philosophical tradition may
well be paying off. The third work of his philosophical/ethical trilogy,
Fides et ratio (*Faith and Reason*), was issued on the Feast of the Triumph
of the Cross, September 14, 1998, and was addressed specifically to the
bishops of the Catholic Church on the relationship that exists between
faith and reason, "the two wings on which the human spirit rises to the
contemplation of truth."

Determined to bring philosophy back to its rightful position in the
Church—an autonomous science in search of the truth but conjoined
with theology at some level of shared enquiry—John Paul declares war on
all forms of intellectual and moral nihilism and seeks in *Fides et ratio* to
establish a mutual strategy of constructive response to forces that threaten
both the integrity of philosophy and the integrity of theology, the role of
reason and the role of faith. First and foremost in the Pope's mind is the
struggle to reclaim the validity, the very possibility, of universal and
absolute statements, the bogeyman of all deconstructionists and most
modern philosophical orthodoxies:

> . . . there are signs of a widespread distrust of universal and absolute
> statements, especially among those who think that truth is born of
> consensus and not of consonance between intellect and objective

reality. . . . The lesson of history in this millennium now drawing to a close shows that this is the path to follow: it is necessary not to abandon the passion for ultimate truth, the eagerness to search for it or the audacity to forge new paths in the search. It is faith which stirs reason to move beyond all isolation and willingly to run risks so that it may attain whatever is beautiful, good and true. Faith thus becomes the convinced and convincing advocate of reason.

Trained as a philosopher, the Pope laments the sundering of philosophy's vital connection with theology, the decline of serious philosophical studies in the seminaries, the predominance of philosophical schools that are ensnared by epistemological questions to the exclusion of all others, the persistent post-Enlightenment denigration of metaphysics, and the marginalization of those dimensions that should be at the very heart of philosophical enquiry, particularly that dimension the pope calls *sapiential*, the search

. . . for the ultimate and overarching meaning of life. . . . This *sapiential dimension* [is] all the more necessary today, because the immense expansion of humanity's technical capability demands a renewed and sharpened sense of ultimate values. If this technology is not ordered to something greater than a merely utilitarian end, then it could soon prove inhuman and even become a potential destroyer of the human race.

The recovery of this *sapiental dimension* can only be truly effected once the errors of contemporary philosophy are identified and eliminated. These include eclecticism ("the approach of those who, in research, teaching and argumentation, even in theology, tend to use individual ideas drawn from different philosophies, without concern for their internal coherence, their place within a system or their historical context"), historicism ("the claim that the truth of a philosophy is determined on the basis of its appropriateness to a certain period and a certain historical purpose"), scientism ("the philosophical notion which refuses to admit the validity of forms of knowledge other than those of the positive sciences; and it relegates religious, theological, ethical and aesthetic knowledge to the realm of mere fantasy"), pragmatism ("an attitude of mind which, in making its choices, precludes theoretical considerations or judgements based on ethical principles"), and nihilism ("the denial of the humanity and of the very identity of the human being").

The philosophical merits of the Pope's encyclical are heatedly debated. There are those who derive considerable satisfaction from the pontiff's syllabus of errors, his willingness to engage philosophical method in the service of truth, and his forthright commitment to the system of thought associated with the Angelic Doctor, St. Thomas Aquinas. There are others, however, and Anthony Kenny, former master of Balliol College, Oxford, is one of them, who find the approach of the Pope in *Fides et ratio* in the end unfulfilling:

> Philosophers will be grateful for the compliment which *Fides et ratio* pays to their profession; but they will find it difficult to reciprocate wholeheartedly the papal embrace. An encyclical is, after all, not an ideal medium for the communication of a philosophical message. Poised half-way between the anathemas of old and the *Analecta Husserliana* of today, it lacks the sharp clarity of the first and the scholarly sophistication of the second. Perhaps it is unsurprising that there have hitherto been no philosopher popes: the two professions must be very difficult to combine.[34]

It is certainly true that the encyclical is more concerned about philosophical issues than it is about being an exercise in pure philosophical method. Still, at its very core, the reader will discover both the Pope's passion for philosophy and for a certain kind of philosopher, most especially that philosopher who apprehends the truth of the person Jesus Christ and who pays a terrible price for this knowledge: the price of martyrdom.

> The martyrs know that they have found the truth about life in the encounter with Jesus Christ, and nothing and no one could ever take this certainty from them. Neither suffering nor violent death could ever lead them to abandon the truth which they have discovered in the encounter with Christ. This is why to this day the witness of the martyrs continues to arouse such interest, to draw agreement, to win such a hearing and to invite emulation. This is why their word inspires such

confidence: from the moment they speak to us of what we perceive deep down as the truth we have sought for so long, the martyrs provide evidence of a love that has no need of lengthy arguments in order to convince. The martyrs stir in us a profound trust because they give voice to what we already feel and they declare what we would like to have the strength to express.

THE TROUBLESOME CANONIZATION OF EDITH STEIN

And no one in our time, argues John Paul, better combines the heroic witness of the martyr with the rigorous pursuit of the truth than the philosopher nun Edith Stein. Born in Breslau, Silesia, in 1891 to Auguste and Siegfried, she was one of eleven children of whom only seven survived until adulthood. Her father died when she was quite young and her mother, a devout Jew and able business woman, succeeded in providing a home that was financially secure and loving. Edith did not share her mother's commitment to faith, nor does she appear to have shared her aptitude for commerce, but she did early on betray an intellectual predilection for philosophical speculation, a predilection that she partially satisfied in her studies at Breslau University, but which she would more comprehensively pursue at Göttingen University where she joined the Philosophical Society, a gathering of students of the great philosopher Edmund Husserl. This circle included such thinkers as Max Scheler and Adolf Reinach, the latter a convert to Catholicism who perished at the front in 1917 and who, with his wife Anne, had a deep impact on Stein both intellectually and spiritually.

Stein left Göttingen and studied in Freiburg under Husserl, writing her doctoral dissertation, "On the Problem of Empathy," under his supervision. She also worked as his research assistant for two years, and although they eventually had a parting of the ways, at Stein's insistence in fact, Husserl spoke highly of her work and recommended her for a university post should a position come open for a woman. No such opportunity materialized, however, and Stein continued her private research with no chance of qualifying as a university lecturer, but remained ever hopeful. It was in 1921 that, while staying at the home of fellow philosophers Theodor Conrad and Hedwig Martinus, she came across a copy of the autobiography of St. Teresa of Avila, devoured it, and concluded that "the *Life* of our Holy Mother Teresa happened to fall into my hands [and the] long search for the true faith came to an end." She was baptized on January 1, 1922 in the parish church of St. Martin in Bergzabern and was confirmed one month later in the private chapel of the bishop of Speyer, Ludwig Sebastian. Her life as a Roman Catholic began, like most conversions, in a spirit of intense ardour, but unlike most converts Stein already possessed a profound interior disposition to the contemplative life with a taste for deep private meditation that impressed many with its maturity.

From 1923 to 1931 Stein was occupied with considerable academic activity—she taught at St. Magdalene's in Speyer (a Dominican girls' school), translated many works and composed others, undertook several domestic and foreign lecture tours, and then became an instructor for a short time at the German Institute for Scientific Pedagogy in Münster. In fall 1933 she entered the Carmel in Cologne, following in the steps of her great model, St. Teresa, was clothed as Sister Teresia Benedicta a Cruce six months later, took first vows in 1935 and perpetual vows in 1938. During this period she wrote several of her most important works, including *Finite and Eternal Being*, and then at the end of 1938 she emigrated to the Carmel in Echt, Netherlands, in what turned out to be a vain hope of escaping the expanding Nazi onslaught.

In 1942, following a pastoral by the Dutch bishops denouncing the deportation of Jews, Edith and her sister Rosa, who earlier had found a haven at Echt with Edith, were arrested by the Gestapo, along with all the Jewish converts to Catholicism, deported to the assembly camps at Amersfoort and Westerbork, and from there transported to Auschwitz and Birkenau where they were killed.

As a Carmelite, Edith Stein found her true self in St. John of the Cross. If St. Teresa brought her into the Church, St. John provided the inspiration for her last great and fragmentary work, *The Science of the Cross*. It is not difficult to see the several convergences with the life and thought of Karol Wojtyla—the attraction to the contemplative vocation, the shared passion for phenomenology, the influence of Carmelite thought, the synthesis of philosophy and prayer. In addition, Wojtyla's high regard for the supreme sacrifice demanded of faith finds special expression in his homily at the beatification of Edith Stein at Cologne in 1987:

The church now presents Sister Benedicta a Cruce to us as a blessed martyr, as an example of a heroic follower of Christ, for us to honour and to emulate. Let us open ourselves up for her message to us as a woman of the spirit and of the mind, who saw in the science of the cross the acme of all wisdom, as a great daughter of the Jewish people and as a believing Christian in the midst of millions of innocent fellow men made martyrs. She saw the inexorable approach of the cross. She did not flee in fear. Instead, she embraced it in Christian hope with final love and sacrifice, and in the mystery of Easter even welcomed it with the salutation *ave crus, spes unica*.

Although the beatification of Edith Stein and her subsequent canonization in 1998 made sense to John Paul, these very same acts outraged the Jews and triggered a controversy that threatened to seriously undermine the work the Pope had handsomely accomplished in his efforts to seek healing with the Jewish people. What went wrong? As early as the 1980s, when it was clear that Rome was moving toward Stein's beatification, opposition from Jewish groups continued to mount. The opposition grew around two specific concerns: the fear that a Jewish convert to Catholicism might occasion the development of organized initiatives in the Church focussed on the conversion of other Jews to the Catholic faith, and the appropriation of the Shoah by the Church through the symbolic representation of a martyr like Stein. By the time she was canonized, apprehension over her designation as a martyr—the misunderstandings that can arise over the true nature of her witness and the ugly competition of two religious traditions fighting over the meaning of her death—had reached crisis proportions. Rabbi Dow Marmur of Holy Blossom Temple in Toronto highlights the difficulties most Jews have over the identification of Stein as a martyr:

The problem of Edith Stein as far as Jews [are] concerned is first of all connected with the issue of the Church having a need to declare someone a martyr who was a Jew originally. The Church has a long history of really getting very excited each time a Jew is converted. We know why—after all, the poor pagans don't know any better. But the Jews, from whose midst Jesus came, they should really know and if they should still persist in being Jewish, then there is something radically wrong with them and if someone breaks away and embraces Christianity, that has to be celebrated. To me, this whole business of Edith Stein the martyr is a throwback to that particular tradition. In addition, those who died in the Holocaust did not die as martyrs. Martyrdom means choice, but nobody had a choice. It was premeditated murder; there was no question of martyrdom. As well, Edith Stein died because she had Jewish genes, according to the Nazis, and not because she was a Christian and testified to her faith. Christians have to understand this: she was not killed because of her Christianity but because, as far as the Nazis were concerned, she was as Jewish as the rest of us, and when I say "no" she was not Jewish, it is because I refuse to allow the Nazis to define who is a Jew. The whole question of canonization is so very strange and very peculiar and says so very little about Edith Stein as far as I am concerned, but a lot about Church politics.[35]

But for John Paul, Edith Stein *is* a martyr; of that fact he has no doubt. Although he understood the apprehensions expressed by so many in the worldwide Jewish community over the perceived theological insensitivity and political inopportuneness associated with both the beatification and canonization of Stein, the Pope had already moved beyond any narrow or literal meaning of martyr. Repeatedly, as he did on the occasion of the beatification of 233 martyrs of the Spanish Civil War in 2001, the Pope has reminded Catholics that martyrs are "the most eloquent proof of the truth of the faith [which] is able to give a human face even to the most violent death, and shows faith's beauty even in the midst of atrocious sufferings." The Pope is prepared, however, to nuance what he means by martyrdom. True, it is necessary that one suffer for the faith in order to be recognized as a martyr, that one pay the ultimate sacrifice in the face of *odium fidei* or hatred of the faith, but that does not always mean that one will immediately perish because of one's heroic witness. For instance, when John Paul beatified Cardinal Alojzije Stepinac at the Croatian National Shrine of Our Lady of Marija Bistrica in October 1999, he recognized in his homily that the controversial Croatian prelate was a martyr because for many years he had been the object of hatred and lies by the Communist Party:

Blessed Alojzije Stepinac did not shed his blood in the strict sense of the word. His death was caused by the long suffering he endured: the last fifteen years of his life were a continual succession of trials, amid which he courageously endangered his own life in order to bear witness to the Gospel and the unity of the church. In the words of the psalm, he put his very life in God's hands (Psalms 16:5).

In his homily at the canonization of Edith Stein—both the one following the Gospel and the one delivered after the recitation of the Angelus—the Pope identified the Carmelite as both "an eminent daughter of Israel and faithful daughter of the Church," as "a young woman in search of truth," and along with the Polish Franciscan friar Maximillian Mary Kolbe whom the Pope had canonized in 1982, she was declared a martyr of Auschwitz. In fact, the Pope made clear his own perspective that he was "always convinced that these two martyrs of Auschwitz together would lead us into the future." Understandably, Jewish leaders like Rabbi Marmur were puzzled, disappointed, and, for some, outraged by the Pope's apparent indifference to their protestations. But he wasn't indifferent. He has never been indifferent to Jewish sensitivities. His record of good faith gestures, substantive agreements, and genuine efforts at reconciliation cannot be denied.

In various memoirs and biographies you find the close relationship of the Pope with the Jewish community, and indeed with individual Jews, the object of special scrutiny and wonder. His childhood friend, Jerzy Kluger, continues to play an important though distant role in his life, and the influence of the great French thinker Emmanuel Levinas merits special recognition in the Pope's mind as a "philosopher of dialogue" with that other seminal Jewish savant Martin Buber. The Pope's deep sense of connection with the Jews is not, however, limited to personal companionship rooted in a Polish upbringing, nor with acknowledging the influence of a Jewish philosopher. He has, precisely as Bishop of Rome and Supreme Pontiff, formalized the spirit of dialogue and healing that he sees as an imperative for the Roman Catholic communion.

In 1978 he granted his first papal audience to a Jew, and the very next year he followed up on this precedent with another one. On the first papal tour to Poland, he made a visit to Auschwitz, thereby becoming the first pope to visit this Nazi concentration camp. The symbolism in both cases was arresting. In 1986 he became the first pope in history to actually enter a Jewish house of worship when he made a visit to the chief rabbi in Rome. He chose this occasion to reiterate the Second Vatican Council's condemnation of discrimination against the Jews, and when feelings were running high between Polish Jews and Polish Catholics in the 1980s over the disputed presence of Carmelite nuns in Auschwitz eager to establish a convent on the killing grounds, the Pope intervened when he realized that a made-in-Poland solution was not imminent. This bold gesture was followed in 1993 on the fiftieth anniversary of the uprising of the Warsaw Ghetto with his exhortation to his fellow Catholics and the Jews "to be first a blessing to one another" before we then proceed as sons and daughters of Abraham "to be a blessing for the world."

But for many Jews the first major breakthrough came in 1993 with the formal recognition by the Vatican City State of the state of Israel, with full diplomatic ties guaranteed. Not long after this momentous event, the Pope met with Israel's chief rabbi in the papal summer residence, Castel Gandolfo. The Jewish people responded to these various initiatives with signs of their own heartfelt approval—the Anti-Defamation League of B'Nai Brith published a Hebrew edition of *A Letter to a Jewish Friend* by Jerzy Kluger; the National Jewish Book Award was bestowed on John Paul's collection of writings, *Spiritual Pilgrimage: Texts on Jews and Judaism*; and continued lobbying by many Jewish bodies for a statement or document from the Pope on the Shoah finally came to fruition in 1998 with *We Remember: A Reflection on the Shoah*, prepared by the Vatican's Commission for Religious Relations with the Jews under the presidency of the Australian cardinal, Edward Idris Cassidy. In a letter accompanying the text, the Pope "encourages [the Church's] sons and daughters to purify their hearts through repentance of past errors and infidelities." But many—Jews and Catholics alike—were left dissatisfied with a text that is timid, inclined to blame members of the Church rather than the Church itself for many of the "errors and infidelities" of the past, and which lacks the forthright approach of the French bishops' statement on the Shoah that faced directly the complicities and failures of French Catholics during the Nazi occupation of France. It will be the triumph of his personal visit in 2000 to Yad Vashem, the Jerusalem memorial to the victims of the

Holocaust, that will impress members of both Abrahamic faiths that he is in earnest when he calls the Catholic Church to conversion:

> As bishop of Rome and successor of the apostle Peter, I assure the Jewish people that the Catholic Church, motivated by the Gospel law of truth and by no political considerations, is deeply saddened by the hatred, acts of persecution and displays of anti-Semitism directed against the Jews by Christians at any time and in any place. The church rejects racism in any form as a denial of the image of the Creator inherent in every human being (cf. Gn. 1:26). In this place of solemn remembrance, I fervently pray that our sorrow for the tragedy which the Jewish people suffered in the 20th century will lead to a new relationship between Christians and Jews. Let us build a new future in which there will be no more anti-Jewish feeling among Christians and anti-Christian feeling among Jews, but rather the mutual respect required of those who adore the one Creator and Lord, and look to Abraham as our common father in faith.

These words—delivered in Jerusalem on March 23, 2000—are brave and persuasive. With his actor's natural gift for theatre, Karol Wojtyla chose the right stage at the right time. But there was a darkening shadow on the horizon, one not of his own making but one he could not ignore—the beatification of Pius XII. By proceeding with Pacelli's beatification, especially in light of the *Hitler's Pope* controversy and all that Cornwell's book has generated, he could undo a master accomplishment with wretched timing. Columbia University historian Istvan Deak, in his review of the Cornwell book, fairly and insightfully identifies the papal quandary:

> Pius XII died in 1958, at the age of eighty-two, plagued by many illnesses, of which incessant hiccuping must have been the most excruciating. He was not an evil man. In fact, his behaviour must be judged to have been a little better than that of millions upon millions of other Europeans who were even more indifferent toward their Jewish fellow citizens and other victims of the German and Soviet tyrannies. But then Eugenio Pacelli was the Pope, and while little was expected of the others, much was expected of him. . . . But could not this Pope have

made a single, historic public gesture? If he had, he would likely have saved more Jews, Poles, Serbs, and others than he did through his diplomatic skills. Unfortunately, he proved weak and fallible. He demonstrated no personal courage; he gave no example of the *Imitatio Christi*, which is what the world expects from the head of a church that traces its authority back to the apostles. Pope John Paul II's current attempt to make Pacelli a saint must be judged a very strange undertaking indeed.[36]

Still, without saying so, the Pope appears to have shelved the Pacelli file—at least for the moment. Not because he sees it now as "a very strange undertaking," but because the politics of saint-making demands it. When Jews, First Nations peoples, Muslims, and Catholic critics campaigned against the canonization of Isabella the Catholic—Ferdinand's wife and one of the unifying monarchs of the new Spain in 1492—the cause was dropped. Isabella, symbol of imperial Spain and scourge of Jews and Moors alike, would not be a saint.

PAPAL SILENCE

Pius XII and his silence over the Jewish Question and the Nazis has been fiercely debated by historians, partisans, survivors of the Holocaust, Vatican clerics attached to the Holy See during the Second World War, political and religious leaders implicated by the presumed silence, and investigative journalists with a taste for blood if not truth. Much of the energy for the attack on Pacelli originated with the publication in 1963 of *The Deputy* by German playwright Rolf Hochhuth. Up until that time there was very little in the way of criticism of the Vatican and the Pope during the Nazi era, with some prominent rabbis and Jewish historians actually going out of their way to praise Pacelli for his personal bravery and acts of charity toward Jews. But with Hochhuth's play—translated and performed widely around the world—the floodgates were opened. Numerous books have continued to fuel the debate ever since.

With the publication of the Cornwell book, a new level of intensity in the debate was achieved. Many critics and historians—Catholic and non-Catholic alike—have raised serious objections to the scholarship, methodology, and objectivity of *Hitler's Pope* without dismissing all of the argumentation. As U.S. priest-professor John F. Morley, author of the important *Vatican Diplomacy and the Jews During the Holocaust, 1939–43*, observed:

> . . . despite its serious flaws, *Hitler's Pope* is a book that cannot, and should not, be ignored. Every point that Cornwell raises—whether it is Pacelli's early career, his concordat negotiations, his spirituality and approach to the world, his refusal ever to explicitly criticize Nazi Germany, and his reaction to the Holocaust—is a matter of crucial concern to Catholics. For Catholics to gloss over Pius's actions as if there were no problems, no evidence of short-sightedness, no sacrificing of one principle for another, no infatuation with the notion of the church triumphant, denies the moral purpose of historical study. Pius XII cannot be seen to be above criticism.[37]

Morley is, of course, right. And it would appear that John Paul II agrees with him. In October 1999 an international commission of three Catholic and three Jewish historians was established with the clear mandate to examine critically the eleven volumes of archival material published by the Vatican on the pontificate of Pius XII and the role of the Church during the Holocaust and the Second World War. The Catholic members of the Commission include, in addition to Morley, who is a religious studies professor at the Catholic Seton Hall University, Jesuit historian Gerald Fogarty of the University of Virginia and Eva Fleischner of Montclair State University in New Jersey. The Jewish members of the International Catholic-Jewish Historical Commission, as it is formally called, consist of Bernard Suchecky of the Free University of Brussels, Robert Wistrich of Hebrew University in Jerusalem, and Michael Marrus of the University of Toronto. Their first report was issued in October 2000 and in it they state that in

> . . . discharging our mandate, we hope to establish a more secure documentary basis for analyzing the actions and policies of Pius XII and the Vatican. Our task is not to sit in judgement of the pope and his advisers. Rather, through analysis and study of their actions, statements and

letters, we hope to contribute to a more nuanced understanding of the role of the papacy during the Holocaust.[38]

The report raises numerous questions as it probes for more details, requests additional access to data that is still classified, and asks for "the records of day-to-day administration of the church and the Holy See." One particularly germane question involves Edith Stein. The Commission notes:

In 1933, Edith Stein wrote to Pius XI asking him to issue an encyclical condemning anti-Semitism. [The report then quotes Stein describing her letter itself: "I know that my letter was sealed when it was delivered to the Holy Father; some time later, I even received his blessing for myself and my loved ones. But nothing else came of it. Is it not possible that he recalled this letter on various occasions later on? My fears concerning the future of German Catholics have been gradually realized in the course of the years that followed."] This may have been the first of many appeals made to the Vatican for intervention on behalf of the Jews. . . . How was this letter received? Is the letter itself in the archives, and if so may we see it?[39]

John Paul has little choice, given both his public commitment to truth seeking and his deeply felt attachment to Jewish faith and culture, but to pursue at some personal and institutional cost a policy of openness on the matter of historical accuracy. The context of a universal Jubilee provided him with opportunities for *rapprochement* that he took ample advantage of in his ministry of healing. As of the summer of 2001, however, the Commission ceased to function and John Paul's efforts to build trust between Jews and Catholics were seriously derailed. Persuaded that Vatican authorities were unwilling to give the kind of comprehensive access to information needed to conduct its work, the Commission was scuttled by distrust among its members and anger over perceived Vatican intransigence.

THE WOJTYLA PASTORAL STRATEGY

A Church Jubilee is a "year of the Lord's favour," a time dedicated in a special way to God. The notion of a Jubilee has its origins in the Hebrew Scriptures and was seen as a time, held every seventh or sabbatical year, when according to the Law of Moses the earth was to be left fallow, slaves set free, and debts cancelled. Every fifty years there was to be a specifically designated Jubilee year at which time the customs and traditions of the sabbatical year were to be expanded and celebrated with deeper solemnity. The Jubilee year was seen as an occasion to restore equality among all the children of Israel and was marked by a communal commitment to justice. The Jubilee year was first celebrated in the Catholic Church under Boniface VIII in 1300 and was seen as "a year of pardon and grace," marked by penitential pilgrimages, the granting of exceptional indulgences, and sacramental pardon. In 1343 Clement VI instituted the fifty-year Jubilee, but various popes since have celebrated Jubilees or Holy Years at the twenty-five-year mark. Conceived as a time of rejoicing and forgiveness, the tradition of the Jubilee was formative in the evolution of an organic body of Catholic social teaching, a teaching that increasingly emphasizes the importance of justice as "constitutive of the Gospel," as Paul VI noted in 1974.

John Paul has a fondness for the dramatic value of anniversaries and this has been no more consistently and eloquently expressed than in his attachment to the Great Jubilee of 2000. In his Apostolic Letter, *Tertio millennio adveniente* (*As the Third Millennium Draws Near*), issued on November 10, 1994, John Paul made clear the high personal and ecclesial importance he associated with the Great Jubilee of the Second Christian Millennium: "Since the publication of the very first document of my Pontificate [*Redemptor hominis* (*The Redeemer of Man*, 1979)] I have spoken explicitly of the Great Jubilee, suggesting that the time leading up to it be lived as 'a new Advent'. . . . In fact, preparing for the Year 2000 has become as it were a hermeneutical key of my Pontificate."

The Pope has made forgiveness critical to every act leading up to and including the Great Jubilee and in this he has moved markedly beyond the traditional celebration of these events by addressing not only the sins of individuals and the sins of society, but the sins of the Church itself. In the light of the Second Vatican Council, with its demonstrated openness to the world, and with the terrible memory of our scarred century—concentration camps, total war, horrendous massacres—John Paul concluded that the world needs purification, that it needs conversion. He then orchestrated a series of special religious "moments" designed to highlight our collective need for forgiveness and reconciliation. One of the most effective and controversial of these "moments" was the Pope's public call in his 1998 Bull of Indiction of the Great Jubilee of the Year 2000, *Incarnationis mysterium* (*The Mystery of the Incarnation*), for the "purification of memory" as one of the signs that "may help people to live the exceptional grace of the Jubilee with greater fervour."

Cardinal Joseph Ratzinger, president of the International Theological Commission as well as prefect of the Sacred Congregation for the Doctrine of the Faith, proposed that the Commission respond to the Pope's appeal and prepare a study on the Church and its past faults, specifically in the light of the Pope's Jubilee motif of memory's purification. The result is "Memory and Reconciliation: The Church and the Faults of the Past," in which one of the most delicate issues addressed is the Holocaust.

The Shoah was certainly the result of the pagan ideology that was Nazism, a pagan ideology animated by a merciless anti-Semitism that not only despised the faith of the Jewish people, but also denied their very human dignity. Nevertheless, "it may be asked whether the Nazi persecution of the Jews was not made easier by the anti-Jewish prejudices imbedded in some Christian minds and hearts. . . . Did Christians give every possible assistance to those being persecuted, and in particular to the persecuted Jews?" There is no doubt that there were many Christians who risked their lives to save and to help their Jewish neighbours. It seems, however, also true that "alongside such courageous men and women, the spiritual resistance and concrete action of other Christians was not that which might have been expected from Christ's followers." This fact constitutes a call to the consciences of all Christians today, so as to require "an act of repentance (teshuva)," and to be a stimulus to increase efforts to be "transformed by renewal of your mind" (Rom. 12:2), as well as to keep a "moral and religious memory" of the injury inflicted on the Jews. In this area, much has already been done, but this should be confirmed and deepened.

"Memory and Reconciliation" provoked a torrent of criticism, however, because both within and outside the Church many found the document timidly penitential, fearful of publicly acknowledging institutional culpability, and of rationalizing Church failure as a failure of individuals to live by the standards of the Gospel and thereby minimizing (if not erasing) organizational responsibility for leadership. Church historian Eamon Duffy has warned that the Pope's laudable "purification of memory" must not become a "laundering of memory."

A warmer reception greeted the Pope's Service Requesting Pardon held three months after the publication of "Memory and Reconciliation." The service was held in St. Peter's Basilica on the first Sunday of Lent and was a theatrical tour de force, a classic example of Wojtyla's deep love for a dramatic or symbolic gesture suffused with genuine feeling and conviction. Following the Pope's homily at the Mass, an appropriately designated Vatican or dicastery official led a prayer in one of the following seven categories: confession of sins in general; confession of sins committed in the service of truth; confession of sins that have harmed the unity of the Body of Christ; confession of sins against the People of Israel; confession of sins committed in actions against love, peace, the rights of peoples, and respect for cultures and religions; confession of sins against the dignity of women and the unity of the human race; confession of sins in relation to the fundamental rights of the person. Immediately after each of these prayers, the Pope offered his own invocation. The penitential ceremony—a cantor chanting amen, an assembly intoning *Kyrie eleison*, silent prayer, a lamp lit before the crucifix following each petition for forgiveness, all culminating with the Pope embracing and kissing the crucifix—provided a special dramatic focus at the beginning of the first Lent of the Third Millennium.

The Great Jubilee has figured prominently in the Pope's ecclesial and pastoral strategies. As said earlier, "preparing for the Year 2000 has become as it were a hermeneutical key to my Pontificate." Themes like forgiveness and repentance, celebration and communion, have dominated

much of the Pope's theology in the past decade. But running through this
majestic score as the principal leitmotif is John Paul's fervid attachment to
that exemplarity of Christian life most dramatically evidenced in the
witness of the saints. In his Apostolic Letter, *Novo millennio ineunte* (*At the
Beginning of the New Millennium*), released just after the Jubilee year
ended, the Pope underscores his commitment to the "lived theology of the
saints," and in so doing he reminds us that the saints

> . . . offer us precious insights which enable us to understand more
> easily the intuition of faith, thanks to the special enlightenment which
> some of them have received from the Holy Spirit or even through their
> personal experience of those terrible states of trial which the mystical
> tradition describes as the "dark night." . . . I thank the Lord that in
> these years he has enabled me to beatify and canonize a large number of
> Christians, and among them many lay people who attained holiness in
> the most ordinary circumstances of life. The time has come to re-
> propose wholeheartedly to everyone this high standard of ordinary
> Christian living: the whole life of the Christian community and of
> Christian families must lead in this direction.

Although the Pope is calling for all the baptized to take seriously the
injunction to be holy and to recognize that the personal path to holiness
must be supported by the solidarity provided by all believers, whether by
means of the "traditional forms of individual and group assistance" or by
means of support provided by more recent "associations and movements
recognized by the church" (Communion and Liberation, Opus Dei, etc.),
he continues to assign special meaning to the martyrs, the blood of whom
is the seed of Christian life:

> *Sanguis martrum semen Christianorum.* This famous "law" formu-
> lated by Tertullian has proved true in all the trials of history. Will this
> not also be the case of the century and millennium now beginning?
> Perhaps we were too used to thinking of the martyrs in rather distant
> terms, as though they were a category of the past, associated with the
> first centuries of the Christian era. The jubilee remembrance has
> presented us with a surprising vista, showing us that our own time is

particularly prolific in witnesses, who in different ways were able to live the Gospel in the midst of hostility and persecution, often to the point of the supreme test of shedding their blood.

John Paul, schooled as he has been in the horror of the camps and gulags, is devoted to the memory of those who have paid the highest price in their opposition to lies and butchery, who have stood loyal to the cross in the shadow of the swastika and of the hammer and sickle. He has regularly and vigorously praised the heroic fidelity of the "church of silence," the Church of Communist Europe, and he has stood by the struggling churches of Latin America, Asia, and Africa as they battle hostile powers, totalitarian regimes, and corrupt military leaders, but not at the cost of ecclesiastical orthodoxy, as the disciples of the theology of liberation have discovered to their dismay. On matters of doctrine and Church law, John Paul has proven to be a formidable warrior-pope giving little ground, taking few hostages, and not inclined to negotiate weak treaties.

As the many bishops, theologians, and women and men religious who have run afoul of the Vatican line can attest, with John Paul there is no quarter. The list of those who have been interrogated, investigated, censured, suspended, cautioned, rehabilitated, and reconciled is not short. John Paul and his primary enforcer of doctrinal orthodoxy, the redoubtable Cardinal Ratzinger, have been nothing less than thorough in their determination to see to it that the faith is taught in its integrity, that dissent is contained if not minimized, and that the organic teaching of the Church is enunciated with clarity and indivisibly by a Magisterium unhampered by a fractious theological academy. Among the many who have been invited "to correct their errors" during the pontificate of John Paul II are Hans Küng, Edward Schillebeeckx, Jacques Pohier, Charles Curran, Leonardo and Clodovis Boff, John J. McNeill, Tissa Balasuriya, Jacques Dupuis, and Roger Haight. The discipline meted out has ranged from dismissal to silencing to excommunication, and those who have experienced the methods of the Congregation for the Doctrine of the Faith have been disappointed or outraged by the secrecy and tardiness that attend much of the investigation.

At the same time, the process has been improved during the Wojtyla pontificate with efforts made to streamline the investigation and assure fairness. Especially identified for scrutiny are those theologians who have engaged in serious dialogue with Marxism—no longer a credible threat to Catholicism—and those involved in interfaith explorations in the area of theology and spirituality—the most threatening and challenging of theological encounters in an increasingly pluralistic world. On matters of sexual morality as well, Rome is ever vigilant in the Wojtyla years for any hint of a softening of official Church teaching on contraception.

John Paul has little stomach for dissent and dissenters. As he remarked in his first encyclical *Redemptor hominis* (1979), "it is the right of the faithful not to be troubled by theories and hypotheses." To further strengthen the Pope's resolve to limit (if not eliminate) dissent in the Church, the Congregation for the Doctrine of the Faith issued *Donum veritatis* (*The Gift of Truth*) in 1990, an instruction on the ecclesial vocation of the theologian, which boldly declares that dissent frequently "appeals to a kind of sociological argumentation which holds that the opinion of a large number of Christians would be a direct and adequate expression of the 'supernatural sense of the faith.' Actually, the opinions of the faithful cannot be purely and simply identified with the *sensus fidei*." This is a firm warning to the faithful and theologians alike that not all the ideas that arise among the People of God are in any way reconcilable with the faith. What is especially disturbing to the Vatican officials and the Pope is the disproportionately determinative influence of the media, the power of mass communications to disseminate ideas that are incompatible with official teachings and that fail to weigh the comparative authority of the Magisterium with those of bone fide theologians, renegade theologians, investigative journalists, educated laity, the religiously uninformed, the devoutly ignorant, and craven opinion-shapers. The rampant egalitarianism of the media, coupled with its insatiable taste for controversy, make life for the Magisterium one sustained siege experience. But John Paul II prefers to take the offensive.

Not everyone, however, in authority in the Church shares the Pope's hardline tactics. Several leading churchmen have opted for a more irenic approach when dealing with dissent, seeing the issue more in terms of pastoral strategy than canonical enforcement. The Catholic Church in England and Wales provides a good and dramatic illustration of the difference in approach that exists between the shepherd as listener and the shepherd as hammer. The late Cardinal Basil Hume, archbishop of West-minster and primate of the Catholic Church in England and Wales, was a deeply loved pastor, respected national figure (more than any other Catholic churchman since Cardinal Henry Edward Manning in the nine-teenth century), admired contemplative and writer, who managed to achieve a delicate balance of conflicting ecclesial interests and still hold the Church together. In an address videotaped shortly before his death and played at a conference of U.S. Catholic bishops, Hume reminded his fellow members of the episcopacy how complex the issues are that face a modern bishop, not the least of which is

> . . . how to deal with dissent, when authority tends not to be respected and moral judgments, being so subjective, are unashamedly relativist. It seems to me that it is important that a bishop should aim to keep the whole of his flock within the one fold. There will be in the flock consid-erable differences of opinion, mutual antagonisms, and the exchange of unkind comments. This is a recipe for disaster for the Gospel. This kind of situation demands of us exceptional gifts of charity, patience and understanding. I am constantly being urged to suppress this group of people or that group, or drive out of the church this lot or that lot. I do not believe that this is right. I believe that as a bishop I have to try to lead people from where they are to where they never dreamt they might go. If you drive a person out of the Church you have taken a very grave responsibility on yourself.[40]

Although Hume could be firm with those who publicly flout the teach-ings of the Church, and although he could be protective of his jurisdic-tional obligations and prerogatives, he never departed from the pastoral notion that the Church is at heart inclusive and not exclusive, governed by the example of Jesus and only secondarily by the rules and mandates of institutional governance. Not everyone in his Church shares the same view. Father Richard Barrett, an agony aunt for *The Catholic Herald* with a fondness for Firbankian prose with its arch and decadent tone, delights in excoriating the wayward types who, in his opinion, deride tradition, dismiss authority, behave like French Revolutionaries, and invoke the "spirit of Vatican II" at the same time as they gleefully rummage about in the ruins of the old Church. The most destructive dissenters in the Church are what he terms "para-council theologians," a peculiar breed of theological second-raters chafing under the superior leadership of John Paul II. Barrett scornfully notes that the para-council theologians and opinion-makers are "always granted a simpering hearing by gushing journalists in the modern media." In his view

> . . . a chorus of para-council theologians has been assailing the people of God for 30 years now with what the council should have said. They announced Year One of the true Christianity that had been betrayed for the previous 20 centuries. Now taking over a parish say, after a para-council ideologue has had his or her runaround is frequently like being asked to preach Judaism at the headquarters of the SS. One bishop's secretary, renowned for his diplomacy, was told to move to a certain parish which had been dominated for 20 years by a para-council presider (they don't like being called priests) and was given two books to introduce to the parish—the Roman Missal and the Lectionary! The able secretary told me that what the people of God had been privileged (forced) to accept was "creative liturgy" (cultic exercises in egotism), "spontaneous testimonies" (how I became a saint in 24 hours), "demolition spirituality" (let me tell you why we have ruined the church your grandparents paid for), readings from the prophet Gibran (or how we can soothe the pain of a Christian upbringing), excerpts from the diary of Geri Spice (or why I am no longer a chico latino) and Eucharistic elements sponsored by Wonderloaf—all these are the hallmarks of the para-council.[41]

The Hume approach versus the Barrett approach highlights the challenge facing religious leaders. They can choose to find common ground in a multivalent universe or they can hanker for the restoration of an authoritative ecclesial model. This is putting the challenge in its starkest terms, of course, and the experience of the Church in a particular culture will vary not only in relation to other cultures but in relation to its own composite reality as well. But there are some issues that have acquired increasing urgency during the pontificate of John Paul II, and of these issues—priestly celibacy, seminary training, new models of ministry, national episcopal priorities versus universal Church priorities, intercultural and interfaith conflicts—none has been more vexatious for the pontiff than the role of women in the Church.

THE PONTIFF AND THE DISTAFF DILEMMA

Defining the role(s) of women in the Roman Catholic Church has been an ongoing task since the conclusion of the Council in 1965 and has proven one of the more durable and dynamic challenges facing the institutional Church. On the role of the feminine in spirituality—the special charisms brought by women to the Church, the noble tradition of service women have provided the Church over the centuries in terms of prophetic leadership, contemplative understanding, and scholarship—the Pope is ceaseless in his praise. He untiringly celebrates the dignity of motherhood, and, as previously observed, he attaches great importance to the role of Mary: "the Church sees in Mary the highest expression of the 'feminine genius.' "

Prepared in his numerous addresses, locutions, apostolic letters, and homilies to allow for as many adjustments as doctrine and culture will permit in finding new ways to employ the gifts of women, on the matter of ordained ministry he is immovable. The Pope has publicly reprimanded erring clerics and women religious who have advocated for change, exhorted bishops at *ad limina* visits (official quinquennial visitations to Rome by bishops from a region or country to meet with the Pope and the heads of his dicasteries) to actively discourage discussion about women and ordained ministry in any public forum, interrogated through his nuncios episcopal candidates inclined to take a soft position on the issue, and instructed Ratzinger to do his best to quash any expectation of change in the Church's teaching and practice regarding women and the ordained ministry. As a measure of his growing alarm, he issued in 1994 his Apostolic Letter *Ordinatio sacerdotalis* (*Priestly Ordination*) in which he unequivocally declared that the "Church has no authority whatsoever to confer priestly ordination on women," and also added that "this judgement is to be definitively held by all the Church's faithful." This was followed in 1995 with his Letter to Women, issued on the eve of the Fourth World Conference on Women in Beijing, and he used this occasion to once again remind women that their inadmissibility to the ministerial priesthood, the Church's constant teaching, is in conformity with the will of Christ and is in no way prejudicial to them:

> If Christ—by his free and sovereign choice, clearly attested to by the Gospel and by the Church's constant Tradition—entrusted only to men the task of being an *"icon" of his countenance as "shepherd" and "bridegroom" of the Church through the exercise of the ministerial priesthood*, this in no way detracts from the role of women, or for that matter from the role of other members of the Church who are not ordained to the sacred ministry, since *all* share equally in the dignity proper to the *"common priesthood"* based on Baptism. These role distinctions should not be viewed in accordance with the criteria of functionality typical in human societies. Rather they must be understood according to the particular criteria of the *sacramental economy*, i.e. the economy of signs which God freely chooses in order to become present in the midst of humanity.

Linked with the Pope's theology for signs in opposing any alteration to the Church's practice is his philosophical anthropology: "Womanhood and manhood are complementary *not only from the physical and psychological points of view*, but also from the *ontological*. It is only through the duality of the masculine and the feminine that the human finds full realization." By the conclusion of this letter—which he most cordially addresses to all the women of the world—the Pope outlines the special gifts the "genius of women" has provided the Church:

> From the heart of the Church there have emerged women of the highest calibre who have left an impressive and beneficial mark in history. I think of the great line of women martyrs, saints and famous mystics. In a particular way I think of Saint Catherine of Siena and of Saint Teresa of Avila, whom Pope Paul VI of happy memory granted the title of Doctors of the Church.

Eloquent though it is in its praise of women, there are many who are unpersuaded by its logic or comforted by its gentle paternalism. Joanna Manning, author of the best-selling 1999 broadside *Is the Pope Catholic?*, a work that is part polemic and part memoir, goes so far as to declare that "John Paul II has harbored a concerted effort to keep women in a second-class position within the Church." Although an extreme position, it does in great part reflect the attitude of many educated and professional women who cannot see why Rome's intransigence goes so far as to warn against even discussing the issue. Is it irrationalism, fear, or misogyny that drives Rome to refuse even to think about change?

There have been numerous instances of priests resigning their ministry in protest over the Church's failure to ordain women, of nun activists and academic researchers being disciplined by their orders or communities—usually under the direction of the Congregation for the Doctrine of the Faith—for teaching a position contrary to the officially held position, and of seminaries dismissing tenured faculty because of fears or misgivings concerning their adherence to orthodox teaching.

One of the most dramatic cases involving conflict between Rome and a public religious personality over women and ministry was the Dr. Lavinia Byrne case in Britain. For thirty-five years an active member of the Institute of the Blessed Virgin Mary (the seventeenth-century congregation founded by the proto-feminist Mary Ward), Byrne, a well-known and respected broadcaster, writer, and lecturer ran into difficulties with the Congregation for Institutes of Consecrated Life and Societies of Apostolic Life following the publication of her book *Women at the Altar* in 1994. In this work she categorically states that "the ordination of women to the priesthood is the logical conclusion of all the recent work of Catholic theology about women and, in particular, about the holiness of the baptised. It is not an aberration from what the Church teaches but rather a fulfillment of it." Naturally, this work found its way to the even more formidable Vatican Congregation, the "Supreme Congregation," the Congregation for the Doctrine of the Faith. In addition to challenging the Church's position on the ordination of women, Byrne inflamed the Roman authorities by speaking about the "empowering" effect of contraception for women. Not one red flag, but two. The Congregation for the Doctrine of the Faith's denunciation of the book resulted in the remaining copies being either stockpiled or burned by the American publisher.

Then, in 1998, the Congregation proceeded to inform the superior-general of Byrne's order that Sister Lavinia would be required to sign a public declaration assenting to the teachings of *Humanae vitae* and *Ordinatio sacerdotalis*. At this point in the drama, Cardinal Hume intervened on her behalf, informing the Congregation that she was a highly regarded person in Great Britain both in and outside the Catholic Church and that he was sure that the "Congregation will act wisely and with prudence and now leave the matter to rest. . . . Any other policy will be harmful to the Church in this country. Please accept my advice." It would appear for a time that the Congregation did precisely that and stopped putting pressure on her to sign the statement.

But Byrne was not satisfied. She objected that "the deal seemed to be that I had to keep silent on these matters," and clearly she had no intention of doing so. In January 2000 she chose to leave the Institute of the Blessed Virgin Mary and in her statement of departure, she concluded: "I hope to continue to lecture and broadcast and as well to write—and anticipate doing so without constantly feeling that my integrity is being called into question."

The politics of opposition represented by the Byrne case is complemented by the politics of consolidation represented by the Fessio case of 1987. Jesuit publisher and theologian Joseph Fessio, a disciple of Cardinal Ratzinger and who did his doctorate on the eminent theologian Hans Urs von Balthasar under Ratzinger at the University of Regensburg, was invited with Ratzinger's support to attend the 1987 Episcopal Synod on the priesthood as a "glorified secretary." But he was more than a secretary. He composed an intervention—a short position paper read by one of the episcopal delegates to the Synod—on women as acolytes or altar servers. He delights in telling the story about how as a lowly cleric he was able to outwit the U.S. delegation with its cabal of liberals—including the Benedictine Rembert Weakland and the much-admired cardinal-archbishop of Chicago, Joseph Bernardin—and produce a document much in keeping with the universal mind of the Church.

My sense was that Cardinal Bernardin was sympathetic to this idea of women acolytes being approved formally, and so when the discussion went in that direction he kind of led it in that direction; then, when there were objections from the Third World, saying, "Now, wait a second. Our people could never understand that: we get our vocations from altar boys, and our women aren't concerned about ordination for themselves. . . ." And so Cardinal Bernardin's response was, "Well, maybe we should make this a regional thing because in some countries it would not be culturally acceptable." Later, when we were having a coffee break I was sitting next to Francis Cardinal Arinze [a Nigerian prelate very high up in the Vatican] and I said, "Cardinal Arinze, you shouldn't so easily accept the fact that it's some kind of a cultural difference that makes Nigerians antipathetic to women acolytes. There are some deeper anthropological reasons which I think maybe Nigerians being closer to nature have a better view of." He said, "Oh, yes, well what would those be?" So I listed a few of these ideas that were on my mind. He said, "Could you write that down for me?" So I went off that afternoon and did so. I'll tell you one thing, the bishops work at those things and the periti work even more. I went off to the Hotel Columbus and there were some friends there with a tape recorder so I sat down and dictated this little paper which they typed up for me and I gave it to Cardinal Arinze. The next day, or two days later, he read what I had written and I guess he passed it around so that it became one factor, one element in the opposition which ended up actually ninety-five to five; ninety-five percent of the people voted against the proposition to have altar girls or to have women deaconesses studied, and just to drop the whole thing. I may have had a part in that.[42]

Fessio's was at best a pyrrhic victory in that through a combination of rubrical legerdemain, canonical nuancing, cultural adaptability, pastoral discretion, and episcopal prudence, girl and women altar servers can be found in local parishes and metropolitan cathedrals around the globe—including in Rome—with no official reaction or censure. The difficulty rests on the term "ministry," the notion of minor orders, and the conservative anxiety that it is the thin edge of the wedge.

Although he remains technically a Jesuit priest, Fessio has been largely marginalized by his order and his extreme theological perspective seen as unrepresentative of the Society of Jesus in most instances. The Vatican's concern over the appropriate role of women in the Church has been rendered more complicated by both the Byrne and Fessio cases—resignation from one's order does not mean disengagement with the

issues and apologetical overkill tends to exacerbate the polarization—
and there is very little evidence that the issue has been exorcized for the
third millennium.

JOHN PAUL AND THE LIBERATIONISTS

If John Paul's struggle with feminism is checkered and inconclusive, his
struggle with liberationist theology has been far more successful. Although
the liberationist critique is much broader than its original articulation in
the late 1960s and early 1970s would seem to imply, the open attitude
expressed by many of the early liberation theologians toward Marxism—
with their use of Marxist critical and methodological discourse and categories—generated deep concern in papal circles. In two very important
documents published by the Vatican in 1984 and 1986 respectively, the
Roman authorities sought to distinguish aspects of liberation theology that
were dangerous to the integrity of the faith from those that were compatible, liberationist concepts that were antipathetic to Catholic theology from
those that added insight to Catholic biblical and social thought. But Rome,
and in particular John Paul himself, remained uncompromisingly opposed
to priest-politicians as the priest and poet Ernesto Cardenal has noted
bitterly when the Pope came to Nicaragua in 1983:

> He came to Nicaragua and he spoke against the revolution before the
> 700,000 people who were there to listen to him, people who were both
> Christian and revolutionaries. The whole multitude protested the
> pope's attitude very strongly and did so to the pope himself, which
> clearly illustrates that the people of Nicaragua are with the revolution. If
> they had been against it they would have applauded the pope. It is the
> first time in modern times that the pope has been humiliated by an
> entire nation, and by an entire Catholic nation at that. . . . He tells the
> priest in Latin America not to become involved in politics when he
> himself does absolutely nothing but interfere with the political situation
> in Poland. In Panama he told the Panamanians not to go to armed strug-
> gle in order to liberate themselves, and yet in Poland he canonized two
> priests who engaged in an armed conflict with the Czarists. He had said
> that the struggle had been the road to sanctity for these two priests.[43]

John Paul's implacable opposition to clerical involvement in the political arena does appear selective rather than comprehensive, but his opposition to any kind of Marxist infiltration into the Christian vocabulary, even a hint of strategic collaboration or ideological convergence, is an opposition total and immovable. No controversy better illustrates the conflict of wills over differing ecclesiologies and pastoral strategies in the Latin American context than that between the Pope and the Brazilian Franciscan friar Leonardo Boff.

Boff's theological work had been an irritant for many years before the Vatican decided to clamp down on his increasingly progressive and liberationist writings. In March 1991 Boff received a letter from John Vaughn, the minister general of his order. The letter informed him that a canonical visitor had been appointed to take over Boff's responsibilities for the influential and popular Vozes, a Franciscan Brazilian publishing house, to review both the editorial and administrative policies of the publishing house, and to ensure that all its publications henceforward manifested "a theological and pastoral orientation in compliance with the Church's Magisterium." In addition, the visitor would arrange for a censor for all Vozes's publications and, in agreement with Boff's provincial superior, determine who would replace Boff as editor of the publishing house review, *Revista de Cultura Vozes*. The work that was principally responsible for precipitating this debacle was Boff's 1981 collection of articles, *Church, Charism and Power*, a work that boldly consisted of self-defined "explorations in militant ecclesiology." Ratzinger and Boff came head to head. The Congregation for the Doctrine of the Faith bided its time, put pressure on the Franciscan order and Brazilian episcopacy, and then struck full force in 1991. By this time, Boff had far fewer supporters among the Brazilian bishops, many of the Franciscan authorities had been either relentlessly badgered or subtly undermined, and new theological trends on the continent, both conservative and restorationist, combined to make the time propitious for direct Vatican action. A dispirited but not defeated Boff resigned both from the Franciscan order and the active ministry and published an open letter "to companions on the journey of hope" on June 28, 1992:

The fundamental purposes which have inspired my life will continue unaltered: the struggle for the Reign of God which begins with the poor; passion for the Gospel; compassion with those who suffer in this world; a commitment to the liberation of the oppressed; articulation of the connection between critical thought and inhuman reality; and the cultivation of tenderness for every created being according to the example of St. Francis of Assisi. The hierarchical church has no monopoly on evangelical values, nor is the Franciscan Order the only heir to Francis of Assisi. There is still a Christian community and an abundance of Franciscan friendship in which I can situate myself with cheerfulness and freedom. . . . There is undeniably a grave crisis within the contemporary Roman Catholic Church. Two basic approaches are violently colliding. The first believes in discipline, the other in the innate vitality of the historical process. The first approach believes what the Church needs is order. Accordingly, it places its priorities on obedience and universal compliance. The second approach believes that the Church must itself be part of the experience of liberation. Accordingly, it places its faith in the power of the Spirit at work in history and in the power of life to nurture the ever-present fecundity of the Church's millennial body. This latter attitude is embraced by important sectors of churches on the periphery in the Third World and in Brazil.[44]

Boff made the decision to serve as a faithful critic of the Church outside of the authority structures that define its ministry of governance. This is a decision that has been made by scores of religious women and men, religious superiors, priest-scholars, etc., who find that it is no longer possible for them to exercise their gifts while holding public positions of accountability in the Church. Byrne and Boff are but two of them. Quite reasonably, Church authorities have the right to expect loyalty from their officials and it is not an abuse of their power to adopt measures that ensure that that loyalty is appropriately exercised. But the role and procedures of the Congregation for the Doctrine of the Faith continue to be a cause of consternation in both the Church at large and in the Church's power circles. Disturbing stories about the investigative methods of the Congregation for the Doctrine of the Faith have been recounted by such eminent thinkers as the iconoclastic Ivan Illich, the Redemptorist moral theologian Bernard Häring, and the interfaith scholar Oblate Tissa Balasuriya. In August 1997 the Congregation issued its first revision of procedures and policies since the Curial reforms of 1971. "Regulations for Doctrinal Examination," as the text was known, strengthened the author's safeguards, "in consideration of the heightened sensitivity in this area characteristic of contemporary thinking." But the Congregation's priorities are ever firm and clear: "it can be said that the regulations constitute a noteworthy and valid effort to harmonize the indispensable demands of safeguarding and promoting the faith with respect for the rights of the faithful: The first cannot be given value to the detriment of the second." But as the internationally respected Irish moralist and theologian Father Enda McDonagh notes:

> . . . although there are some improvements on what we have heard about the Congregation's practice hitherto, one still has serious difficulties about it. First of all, in the opening statement of the most recent document about it published in the late 1990s the document says: "The Congregation for the Doctrine of the Faith has the function of promoting and safeguarding doctrinal faith and morals throughout the Catholic world." Now, where does it get this function? It is after all a Curial office, an administrative assistant to the Holy Father. Now, the function of promoting and safeguarding doctrine, faith, and morals throughout the Catholic world belongs to the College of Bishops, with the Pope as its head. But it's only in item number two of the document that it says of this fundamental pastoral responsibility, "and all pastors of the Church have the duty and right to exercise vigilance whether individually or gathered in particular councils." So it's first of all, I think, starting from the wrong end. We had a lot of problems with the old Index Librorum Prohibitorum or Index of Prohibited Books, which was abolished as late as 1966 by Pope Paul VI, and with the Holy Office of the Roman Inquisition, renamed the Congregation for the Doctrine of the Faith in 1965 as part of a reorganization of the Roman Curia. But still, in the end, all these Curial offices ought to be subject to the College of Bishops with the Pope as head, so then they can decide how it is to work.
>
> Now undoubtedly there are improvements in terms of, for example, the examination of the representative of the individual under scrutiny; you know, that representative has to be engaged in the discussion. But

taking the fundamental issue, it seems to me this ought to be a question first of all for the Pope and the College of Bishops and some episcopal group drawn from the pastoral bishops around the world.

The second thing you will think of is that the theological pluralism which is characteristic of the current Church ought to be represented in any group that operates on behalf of the College of Bishops because theology varies so much around the world. So this is the second element which is obviously not true in the document. We should have a serious international commission of theologians along the lines of the current International Commission of Theologians dealing with this. But of course the International Commission of Theologians, as many people have put it, has now become confined more or less to court theologians. Karl Rahner and Yves Congar, who could not be accused of being disloyal in any way to the Church, resigned from this Commission partly for this very reason, so I see great difficulties in the current operation.

I think there are further difficulties about it, too. One is that they ought to be able to distinguish between what you might call the exposition, which is expounding the doctrine of the Church as it has been established, and the exploration, which goes on in doctrines of the Church that are not so firmly established or are now under question, perhaps for the first time. There must be a lot more room for exploration in these matters.

One of the reasons that's given for this is that you have to think of the potential danger to the faith of the people in the Church. Well, what they don't consider at all is the potential danger to the faith of the people posed by their own operations. I think far more people have their faith hurt by some of these operations than have their faith hurt by some of the things that the theologians are saying. Now, I don't want to excuse theologians from responsibility. I think some theologians behave as if they were infallible themselves, which is also part of the difficulty. We can be very arrogant in certain respects and we have a sense of responsibility in responding to both our local church and the universal Church and indeed to the faith of the people. We can't, as it were, invent and then insist that these are the true doctrines of the Church. I think serious theologians don't do that. Still, there must be a broader recognition that the Church is always engaged in exploration. This then has to be referred to the faith of the whole Church, which is in itself in development anyway.

The distinction that McDonagh makes between exposition and exploration is critical in understanding the work of theologians and of the Magisterium. And nothing causes greater anxiety for the hierarchy of the Church, as well as for many of the faithful, than the matter of changes in Church teaching, no matter how nuanced and historically contextualized. But changes there have been and changes there will be.

IN THE FACE OF CHANGE

For instance, official Church teachings on slavery, religious liberty, monogenism, bishops as the sole administers of the sacrament of confirmation, procreation as the only primary end of marriage, as well as numerous other examples indicate that changes in authoritative teachings by the Magisterium are possible and have occurred.

Walter Principe, late professor of theology at the prestigious Pontifical Institute for Medieval Studies in Toronto and a past president of the Catholic Theological Society of America, wrote compellingly of the need for change:

> Changes in church teaching can and will occur in our own culture in response to new questions raised by our history. Think of discoveries concerning evolution, problems of ecology, population growth or decline, immigration of peoples from around the world, the meeting of eastern and western spiritualities, advances in medicine and genetics, the impact on our very ways of perception and learning made by cinema, television, videotapes, computers, modems, [the Internet], etc. These influences mean that we cannot simply repeat the Gospel message in the same way as in the recent past. New problems must be faced; new opportunities must be used; new insights can enrich our expression of the Gospel. . . . Another way in which church teachings come to be modified is through the reception or non-reception of such teachings by the whole People of God. It has long been taught that one

test of church teachings is the action of the Holy Spirit in all Christians leading them to discern what is truly of divine revelation. In the past the errors of Arianism were rejected by the people even when secular rulers and some bishops accepted them; what was perceived as a rejection of the divinity of Christ was overcome by the devotion of the Christian faithful to Mary under the title of *Theotokos*. Many point today to the widespread rejection by Catholic married couples of the official teaching against contraception in every case as a possible indication of nonreception that may indicate the need for a more nuanced teaching. Base communities in Latin America, the women's movement, the call by many of the faithful for various reforms in the church are seen by many as the working of the Holy Spirit in the People of God that may result in changes in official church teachings. . . . Our partial grasp and expression of the divine Mystery must vary from age to age and from culture to culture because God intervenes in every moment of our history and in every part of the world. Changes—never contradicting what has been truly taught in the past—are inevitable in church teachings.[45]

The key dilemma for the Church is the challenge of reconciling the *fact* of change with the *doctrine* of unalterable truth. How do Church leaders, theologians, jurists, and other specialists on matters ecclesiastical provide public acknowledgement of the reality of change in Church teachings and at the same time hold to the belief that the faith is both continuous and constant? For the Roman Catholic Church, the power of the Magisterium to define and protect the teachings of the faith is indispensable. But it is not an arbitrary power without limits or conditions attached to its exercise. A *theology of fidelity* is not incompatible with a *theology of dissent*; a *ministry of exposition* is not irreconcilable with a *ministry of exploration*. But a culture of silence exists within Church authority that often prevails over the prophetical impulse to speak forthrightly, a culture so deadening that the great lay thinker Baron Friedrich von Hugel once wrote critically of that *éminence grise* of modern Catholic thought, Cardinal Newman, in a letter to the cardinal's biographer, Wilfrid Ward:

I cannot but feel, more strongly than formerly and doubtless quite finally, one, to my mind quite grave, peculiarity and defect of the cardinal's temper of mind and position. His, apparently absolute, determination never to allow—at least to allow others—any public protestation, any act or declaration contrary to current central Roman policy, cannot, simply, be pressed, or imposed as normative upon us all. For, taken thus, it would stamp Our Lord himself, as a deplorable rebel; it would condemn Saint Paul at Antioch as intolerable; and censure many a great saint of God since then. And certainly this way of taking things can hardly be said to have done much good or to have averted much harm.[46]

Newman's native discretion and prudential way of operating clearly provoked the baron, and with some cause, but Newman, as we have already seen, was a sharp critic of Roman abuse. He just preferred a different way of expressing it. Still, the need for Church leaders, particularly those who are the chief advisers and collaborators of the Supreme Pontiff, must feel free to speak their minds in a manner of "public protestation" should such an imperative arise. There are historical precedents, one of which is provided by Robert Markus, emeritus professor of medieval history at the University of Nottingham, who justifies a papal change of view when he identifies a letter written by Pope Pelagius II in the 580s:

"Dear brethren, do you think that when Peter was reversing his position, one should have replied: We refuse to hear what you are saying since you previously taught the opposite? In the matter [now under discussion] one position was held while truth was being sought, and a different position was adopted after truth had been found: why should a change of position be thought a crime by this See which is humbly venerated by all in the person of its founder? For what is reprehensible is not changing one's mind, but being fickle in one's views. Now if the mind remains unwavering in seeking to know what is right, why should you object when it abandons its ignorance and reformulates its views?" Remarkable words, not the less so for having been written for a pope by a deacon who was to succeed him within a few years as Pope Gregory the Great.[47]

It is possible to be outspoken and rise in the hierarchy, but there is frequently a cost. Institutional pathology, spiritual timidity, a misplaced sense of obedience, an exaggerated deference to authority—a particularly Catholic malady—and fear of being excluded from the community, all contribute to a climate of unholy reticence that can only be truly shattered by charismatic leaders who rise above the primadonnish and theatrical to achieve a status of genuine integrity. History provides a handsome, if short, list of such figures. But for some theologians and religious thinkers, like Gregory Baum, the question of leadership and ecclesial dissent has to be understood in the larger context of institutional governance itself:

> I think that the Church at the moment is really quite ungovernable. You know that there are studies in the sociology of industry where you have a company that becomes so big that it can't be run anymore. First, you have a board that runs a company and then it becomes so big that this board simply can't do it anymore. In other words you can figure out in quantitative terms that so many decisions have to be made that this number of people can't do this and, therefore, what is needed is reorganization. It seems to me that the Catholic Church, at the moment, is non-functional in its organization and, therefore, even without any highfalutin' spiritual liberal ideas, any kind of consultant on organizations would say, "This is simply impossible. You have to decentralize. You have to delegate and decentralize. You need a different system."

It is not likely that John Paul II will agree with the McGill professor that we need a different system, but he cannot avoid facing the serious political and ecclesial problems that confront an institution like the Vatican: the struggle for the local voice in an homogenizing universe, the perils of unchecked globalization, the extirpation of Aboriginal cultures, meaningful inculturation, controlled decentralization, and universal leadership in a time "disjoint and out of frame."

John Paul argues in his blueprint for the new era—*Novo millennio ineunte*—that it is possible to hold together no matter how scattered, to cohere no matter how disparate, for "the unity of the church is not uniformity, but an organic blending of legitimate diversities." The Church must become "the home and the school of communion." This notion of a "spirituality of communion," among other things, calls for the continued reform of the way the Church operates—the Roman Curia; the organization of

Episcopal Synods; the functioning of national episcopal conferences. And once again the current procedures for appointing bishops and the kind of criteria used to determine the best episcopal candidates cry out for reform. John Wilkins, editor of *The Tablet*, recalled a conversation he had with a senior Scottish archbishop:

> Archbishop Keith O'Brien of St. Andrew's has voiced strong concern over the growing number of rightwing bishops. "A number of bishops are more rightwing than previously, and if you have more rightwing bishops in the Roman Curia then you can be assured that there will be more rightwing bishops appointed worldwide in the future. As a result, the movement for reform in the church has certainly slowed down a very great deal in recent years." There is nothing wrong, certainly, with the appointment of conservative bishops; conservatives see things that progressives don't. There's a lot wrong, however, with second-rate conservative bishops, as indeed there is with second-rate progressive bishops. I suspect, indeed I am quite sure, that church historians in the future will conclude that the appointment of bishops is one of the most questionable and problematic features of John Paul II's reign. Some time ago there came into my hands as Tablet editor a copy of the questionnaire that is sent out to people when they are asked about specific candidates for the episcopate. It stressed orthodoxy, as you would expect. After all, a bishop is a guardian of orthodoxy. It also stressed loyalty and fidelity to the Holy Father. It insisted on the observation of the general norms on ecclesiastical dress, stressed that the candidate's views must be sound on the ministerial priesthood, sexual ethics, marriage, social justice, the priestly ordination of women, etc. Nothing wrong per se with any of that. But what you don't get from this document of scrutiny, as far as I can see, is much sense that candidates should also be judged on their ability to be Vicars of Christ in their own dioceses. These are criteria for "yes men," courtiers at the papal court, "safe" bishops.[48]

But change in the Vatican itself is subject to the same features of inertia, quiet resistance, and competing proprietorial interests that define every other major institution secular and religious. One of the great founders of sociology, Max Weber, has spoken of charisma as a function of the inter-play between the leader and the led. The kind of psychic conditions that existed at the time of the election of John Paul II in 1978 and that have nurtured his remarkable connectedness with the most diverse of cultures no longer exist to the same degree and in the same way. Weber also tells us that charisma is evanescent and that once a leader has been long installed in his position, he becomes "routinized" and swallowed up by the struc-tures and priorities of the bureaucracy. It is safe to say that the latter has not happened to John Paul II. He has successfully eluded the seductive securities of the bureaucracy by opting for a life as much away from head office as at home. The wandering pastor touches down only when he has to. He has spurned the comforts of routine for the vagaries and *frisson* of world travel and evangelization. But those psychic conditions that Weber speaks about—bubbling at the surface in the dying days of the Pauline pontificate—are now themselves spent.

New conditions exist. In the afterglow of the Jubilee celebrations an anxious Church waits for new directions, a revitalized papacy, and a new wave of internal reforms to help it face an increasingly needy but uncom-prehending world.

2

Health Care and Education: The Perils of Secular Society

During the deliberations of Vatican II (1962–1965), the Council Fathers insisted that the Church must always be in a state of renewal; as a result, the Latin phrase that echoed throughout the Council chambers and that has since formed a kind of rallying cry for those smitten by Vatican II is *Ecclesia semper reformanda*. Still, the authors of that phrase could hardly have anticipated the nature and extent of the reformation the Church would undergo throughout the dying decades of the twentieth century. Although the most obvious signs of change were quickly visible both in the liturgy and in the seminary, the transformation of the Church's role in health care and education is equally dramatic, especially so since these two ministries provide the most tangible representation of the Church's message as it is expressed in the visible world, both in word and in deed. No small point, first of all, since from a purely pedagogical point of view, good words without good works have always been seen to constitute a hollow form of evangelization; and, of equal import, Vatican II placed the Church firmly within the flow of human history, responsive to the joys and the hopes of humankind engaged in the give and take of the modern world.

CATHOLIC HEALTH CARE

The unseemly ripping of Quebec society from the comfortable clerical womb of the nineteenth century provides a dramatic example both of the

Church's and of society's transition from a rural/traditional to a post-Enlightenment/urban society. Almost overnight, during the late 1950s and early 1960s Quebec was transformed from a Catholic-centred society that balanced its government's books through the labour of love provided gratis by legions of priests, sisters, and brothers toiling in that province's hospitals and schools into a virtually post-Christian and certainly anticlerical society that relies instead on government bureaucracy to care for the minds and bodies of its citizens.[1] Although Quebec does obviously represent a special case—aren't all cases special?—the province's rush to secularization and technocratic specialization is hardly unique in our post-Enlightenment and post-industrial world. Indeed, Reginald Bibby sees it as a mirror image of the Canadian scene in the twentieth century,[2] and it is surely a direction that has been accelerated by the laissez-faire economic attitudes inherited from the Thatcher/Reagan era, attitudes that fly in the face of Catholic social philosophy by diminishing the role of government in caring for society's weakest members and by sacrificing the human rights of individuals on the altars of financial profit and unrestrained global business interests. One needs to ask, therefore, can Catholic institutions survive in such an atmosphere? Can the for-profit approach to the delivery of such defining services as health care and education leave any room for religiously inspired participation?

ISSUES CONFRONTING CATHOLIC HEALTH CARE IN THE UNITED STATES

The Quebec situation also underscores one of the key practical issues facing Catholic institutions at the turn of the century. Because Catholic hospitals, schools, and universities have been so dependent for their survival on the donated salaries of sisters, brothers, and priests, how can these institutions survive in an environment depleted of vowed religious and in an atmosphere, therefore, where these institutions must provide their employees with the living/saving wage traditionally espoused by Catholic social teaching? Indeed, few religious are still working in the fields of health care and education—50 percent of the CEOs in U.S. Catholic hospitals were professed religious in 1980, but by 1995 that number had shrunk to 15 percent[3]; professional interests of religious under vows have changed dramatically since Vatican II, their numbers have been decimated, and so few religious are now professionally qualified for specialized careers that it is becoming increasingly more difficult to appoint even the few religious who are interested in pursuing these ministries. In such a climate, it is difficult to be optimistic about the future of Catholic institutions as they were known for much of the nineteenth and twentieth centuries.

Reflecting on the national scene and reacting to a *National Catholic Reporter* special on Catholic health care in the United States, Richard McCormick concludes that: "As it becomes more and more difficult for Catholic hospitals—founded not to maximize profits but to serve—to survive, so it becomes more difficult for any caring or decent organization to make it, economically."[4] Speaking to the bishops of the United States and doing so in her capacity as president of Catholic Health Initiatives, Patricia Cahill stressed the passion for lower costs coupled with better service means that "The days of the stand-alone Catholic health care facility or any stand-alone health care facility, are over."[5]

In the United States, the well-spring for the for-profit initiative, the tension between Catholic health care and private care has been clear for some time. As a result, throughout the 1990s that country's bishops insisted that health care is a human right, not a commodity, and as such it must be provided equitably to all citizens of the United States; the Church has an unambiguous evangelical mandate to care for the sick and to comfort the dying; the profit motive is essentially antithetical both to the equitable delivery of health services and to the needs of the underserviced and underprivileged since it puts the interests of the shareholder above the interests of the sick.

The profit motive, the bishops argued, tends to marginalize those who cannot afford proper health insurance; it tends to centralize in the name of efficiency, closing hospitals and creating huge bureaucracies that are not sensitive to local needs; it abbreviates hospital stays and accentuates less costly home care in ways that are not always in the best interests of the patient or of the family members who are forced to assume responsibilities for which they are too often personally ill-equipped; it tends to minimize treatment in the interests of fiscal accountability; it tends to minimize referrals to specialists, seeking instead to find cheaper means of treatment—even group diagnoses for similar symptoms are reported to be on the horizon; it undermines the patient/physician relationship by dehumanizing the individual from patient to line item on a ledger and by putting the financial interests of the doctor in apparent conflict with the medical interests of the patient; it discourages volunteering; and ultimately it increases prices to augment the bottom line.

So, medical ethicist Dennis Brodeur poses the question: "Do we want Wall Street companies dealing with managed care?" He cautions that there are those who "would turn over all health care to the market, and that means the profit is measured by the services they don't provide."[6] Cardinal Joseph Bernardin put the question another way: "When the provider is at financial risk for treatment decisions, who is the patient's advocate?"[7] As for insurers of medical care, their obvious target group is the healthy—Bernardin points out that, in 1994, 40 million people were uninsured in the United States, 50 million others were underinsured, and in Illinois alone approximately 86,000 individuals were losing their insurance coverage each month.[8] In its rush to maximize growth, reduce costs, and enhance market share, the corporate U.S. is creating huge health care conglomerates that consume not just other for-profit hospitals, but not-for-profit (and Catholic) hospitals as well.

Speaking in his capacity as president of the Catholic Health Association in the United States, John Curley, Jr. argued the incompatibility of investor-owned health care with the not-for-profit, Catholic model when he insisted:

- First and foremost, our church ministry sees itself as a sacrament, an unconditional sign of God's compassionate presence; investor-owned chains see themselves as commercial enterprises like ball-bearing manufacturers.
- Our church ministry sees health care as an essential human service; investor-owned chains see health care as a commodity to be exchanged for profit.
- Our church ministry is driven by the desire to care for people and to serve communities with a preferential option for the poor and vulnerable; investor-owned chains are driven by their need to produce quarterly dividends and a return on equity.

- Our church ministry expects its executives to transform Gospel values into health care initiatives; investor-owned chains expect their executives to achieve a positive bottom line.
- Our church ministry is committed to community accountability; investor-owned chains are accountable to remote shareholders.
- Our church ministry respects the sanctity of each human life; investor-owned chains usually provide services that deny the sanctity of life.
- Our church ministry uses profitability as the means to address the needs of the people; investor-owned chains use health-care needs as the means to achieve profitability.[9]

In fact, the figures do show that in the United States the commitment to the poor and the provision of services for the underinsured are impressive components of the not-for-profit health care system. The huge profits that the investor-owned system delivers to its shareholders are often redirected to those in need by the not-for-profit hospital.[10] Arthur Jones compares the 2.7 percent of annual revenue that the Catholic hospitals provide for those in need with the 0.6 percent made available by the for-profit system,[11] and yet there are many who have serious doubts about the survival of the Catholic health care system.

As a survival tactic, Joseph Bernardin and others have argued for the creation of Catholic health care coalitions that would establish their own efficiencies and, as a result, ensure the continuation of this essential service as an alternative to the for-profit juggernaut.[12] In fact, collaborations of this sort have begun to take place, and some of the resulting structures are huge both in the volume and the variety of services they provide and in the profit they produce: Arthur Jones estimates that the $3.9 billion 1993 revenues produced by the Daughters of Charity eclipse the entire budget of the Vatican nearly four times over.[13] According to Patricia Cahill, in 1997 there were some 625 Catholic hospitals in the United States, about 10 percent of the national total, caring for approximately 16 percent of the population; when one adds the nearly 700 Catholic long-term care facilities, the total revenue generated by the Catholic health care system in the United States in 1996 was a staggering $45 billion.[14] Still, Bernardin worried that in their dealings with one another, Catholic hospitals sometimes tend to be competitive rather than co-operative,[15] and Patricia Cahill, speaking in her former position as the health and hospitals director in the Archdiocese of New York, paints a picture of administrative jealousy, mistrust, and a penchant for non-co-operation that, paradoxically, too often throws these same institutions into the collaborative embrace of a non-Catholic entity.[16] Sometimes, of course, the Catholic coalition simply cannot compete with its for-profit competitor.

Many Catholic and other denominational hospitals and health care providers have been incorporated into the for-profit system. Perhaps the most celebrated case to date involves the Jesuit-sponsored St. Louis University Hospital, which succumbed to the Tenet Healthcare Corporation on February 28, 1998. Faced with growing deficits and the need to maintain the facility as a teaching hospital, committed to the principles of Catholic health as enunciated by the bishops of the United States,[17] and determined to remain an inner-city facility in a city where business was fleeing to the outskirts, the board of St. Louis University Hospital turned first to the local Catholic systems and then to Tenet as potential purchasers. Justin Rigali, archbishop of St. Louis, objected to the proposal, arguing that regardless of the arrangements the board might strike with Tenet, the hospital's Catholic nature could not survive a for-profit takeover. It was, he noted, a disastrous direction in the country and a line needed to be drawn in the sand; moreover, the sale would be contrary to Canon Law and would require a Roman approval that had not been solicited. It was a local, national, and ecclesial issue.[18] Bernard Law, the chair of the bishops' Pro-Life Activities Committee, applauded Rigali's stand, considered the proposal a blow to the Catholic identity of the institution, and noted that "Leaders in Catholic health care, as well as the bishops of the United States, are one in our conviction that we should not yield our institutions to for-profit corporations."[19]

Lawrence Biondi, the Jesuit president of St. Louis University, responded to the criticism, defending the university's historical role in caring for the poor and upholding the ideals of the Catholic tradition in health care; he also pointed out that the hospital's board had approached both Catholic consortia, SSM Healthcare (administered by the Franciscan Sisters of Mary) and Unity Health System (administered by the Sisters of Mercy), neither of which began to meet the Tenet proposal with respect either to purchase price (the difference exceeded $100 million), equipment renewal (Tenet provided for an influx of twice the cash flow in half the time frame offered by the Catholic groups), or even with respect to charity care. In the board's judgment, without the cash flow guaranteed by Tenet, St. Louis University Hospital could not continue its teaching ministry in the various areas of professional care in which it specialized, nor could it provide the up-to-date equipment essential to a teaching hospital. The proposed sale to Tenet was, therefore, reviewed and received the blessing of the Society of Jesus in St. Louis as well as in Rome; in addition, though defining operational conditions were attached to their approval, no objections were raised either by the prefect of the Congregation for Institutes of Consecrated Life (Cardinal Eduardo Martinez Somalo) or by the prefect of the Congregation for Catholic Education (Cardinal Pio Laghi); Tenet agreed to abide by all the conditions presented to it, including adherence to the bishops' "Ethical and Religious Directives for Catholic Health Care Services"; and Archbishop Rigali could do naught but concur.[20] As a result, the proposal was consummated and St. Louis University Hospital continues to serve as one of the five Catholic teaching schools in the United States. John Curley, president of the U.S. Catholic Health Association, provides a cautionary note on what he sees as the predatory behaviour of the big chains: he warns that the for-profit chains will say whatever needs to be said and promise whatever needs to be promised to accomplish a takeover, and in the end it is the viability of the Catholic hospital as such that is being held for ransom.[21]

Legalities met. Immediate issues solved. But the long-term issue of the viability of the Catholic health care system in the United States must remain an open issue. And the prognosis cannot be optimistic.

The situation in the United States is, in a sense, exactly the opposite of what occurred in Quebec following the Quiet Revolution—with the rapid withdrawal of government support for the health care sector in the U.S., the poor and the underserviced are increasingly dependent on the denominational delivery of health care. Unfortunately, this reversal comes at a time when the ability of the churches to operate in that arena is increasingly problematic.

ISSUES CONFRONTING CATHOLIC HEALTH CARE IN CANADA

If our high-tech, enlightened, and entrepreneurial world is a challenge to the Catholic health care facilities of the United States—and it is—that challenge is even greater in Canada where the difference in population does not provide for the same possibilities for the extensive networking that is at least theoretically possible in the U.S. In addition, Canada's health care is delivered under a universal and comprehensive Medicare program, although it is a program that is experiencing increasing stress as the free-market ethos of the United States creeps inexorably into the cabinet chambers of provincial governments "from Bonavista to Vancouver Island."

Since the funding of Canada's hospitals is the responsibility of the federal and provincial governments, there are no tax concessions to support pro bono or subsidized medical care as there are south of the Canadian border, but limitations imposed by the government purse can be just as debilitating as the profit motive that quickens big business. So, while many Catholic hospitals in Canada are donating their outdated medical equipment for use in the Third World, these same Canadian hospitals are struggling to keep pace with the successive generations of high-tech hardware that have succeeded it. As the CAT scan and MRI become increasingly irreplaceable within the modern medical world, only those facilities that are heavily subsidized by government are able to acquire, operate, and maintain the latest technological marvels; alternatively, for-profit institutions are beginning to fill the gap, even operating cross-border fee-for-service facilities as part of the North American Free Trade Agreement and the globalization of our economies. In an effort to reduce costs, attract expertise, and provide a more efficient delivery system, therefore, hospitals are under mounting pressure to rationalize facilities by merging institutions under a single governing body and reduce the number of acute-care sites. As Catholic hospitals lose their independent boards, they will find it increasingly difficult—perhaps even impossible—to remain Catholic in more than name, and inevitably there is a tendency for the role of the Catholic hospital to shift from acute care to long-term care, an area already crowded by the for-profit institution. It is a world in which only the most fit will survive.

As the Catholic hospital in Canada struggles to remain true to its mission, tensions do arise, especially over the Church's position on abortion, birth control, and homosexuality. Some of these tensions are real, others are the simple product of ignorance or prejudice. In the mid-1990s, for example, the Conservative government in Ontario created the Health Services Restructuring Commission (HSRC) as an arm's-length body charged with the task of rationalizing the delivery of health care within the province's hospitals and armed with the legal power to implement its determinations. By law, not even the provincial government could overrule its activities. When the HSRC opted to close the sole public hospital in Pembroke and to consolidate health care delivery on the site of the city's Catholic hospital, the local citizenry were up in arms, arguing that they were about to lose local access to services to which they had a right, services like abortion facilities. Ultimately, the matter went before the courts and the HSRC directives were upheld. For her part, Minister of Health Elizabeth Witmer took the private position that the government could not guarantee that any hospital in the province would offer any or all medical services. She and her party have repeatedly gone on record as supporting the Catholic hospital as a source of sensitive care provided in a setting that is driven by a Christian philosophy rooted in a vision of social justice.[22] In a Toronto address to the Catholic Health Association of Ontario, for example, Witmer assured her audience not only that her government understood the mission of the Catholic hospital, but that it fully supported it. Assuring the members of CHAO that Premier Michael Harris has again "declared his support of Catholic governance structures and their essential role in quality health services for Ontarians," Witmer went much further, confirming both support and comprehension:

> We fully respect your mission to provide holistic health care. And we fully appreciate your devotion to, not only the physical aspect of healing, but also the emotional and spiritual aspect, in keeping with the Catholic mission. We respect your philosophy that spirituality is a key factor for healthy living and a vital aspect of human development. And we acknowledge and support your mission. . . . You have worked with all governments to ensure that policies and programs affecting Catholics reflect the necessity to balance health care with social

justice. And, throughout the years, you have embraced and effected profound change.[23]

When the same Commission consolidated a number of hospitals in the Toronto area, leaving St. Michael's Hospital as a major supplier to one of its constituent groups, the gay community, that community was outraged, fearing that their needs, and especially the needs of the victims of AIDS, would be dealt with prejudicially. This despite the fact St. Michael's Hospital had played a leading role in the treatment of AIDS. At the same time, the demise of the neighbouring Wellesley Hospital meant the potential withdrawal of major abortion and related counselling services from an inner-city area. *Toronto Star* columnist Michele Landsberg put the case for community concern in its starkest terms, comparing the actions of the HSRC to the nefarious activities of the Inquisition. In her opinion piece, entitled "St. Mike's Religious Rules Undemocratic," Landsberg argued that with the consolidation of the two downtown hospitals, Wellesley and St. Michael's, onto the Catholic site, St. Michael's "rushed to announce that it would veto abortions, vasectomies, tubal ligations, and other birth control services—unless such permission was given on an individual basis by the religious rulers of St. Mike's."[24] For Landsberg, it was a matter of Catholic values versus public trust in which Catholic values were the determining factor in a hospital supported by public funds. "How," she challenges, "can this hospital justify taking over the assets of another public hospital and promptly cancelling services the public needs, wants and is entitled to?" Not an easy question on which to satisfy a populace with practical demands and little sympathy for specifically denominational postulates articulated in an abstract concept like "Catholic mission."

It is, in fact, a question not unfamiliar to Catholic theologians. Richard McCormick, for example, has argued that in our pluralistic society it is incumbent of the administration of Catholic hospitals to review seriously the matter of material co-operation and to review exactly those questions that Landsberg has raised.[25] For its part, the National Conference of Bishops in the United States is clear and uncompromising. Its "Ethical and Religious Directives for Catholic Health Care Services" states as a normative principle that "within a pluralistic society Catholic health care services will encounter requests for medical procedures contrary to the moral teachings of the church. Catholic health care does not offend the rights of individual conscience by refusing to provide or permit medical procedures that are judged morally wrong by the teaching authority of the church,"[26] and that refusal extends explicitly to the principle of material co-operation.[27]

As for the specific charges of St. Mike's Roman Catholic homophobia, Dr. Philip Berger, a prominent Jewish physician with a long-standing history of working with the gay community, rejects the accusation outright. Berger points to the leading role St. Mike's has played in serving the gay community, and asks: "So how is it possible this is a homophobic, bigoted institution?"[28] The issue is heated, divisive, and much debated. Tony DiPede, the co-chair of the People with AIDS Foundation, remained unconvinced. Responding to Berger's defence of St. Mike's, he noted that "St. Mike's is a religious institution performing a secular duty funded by the public purse and in conflict with its essential philosophy of the dignity of gays and lesbians."[29] The Catholic Church, we are often reminded, is not a democracy, yet it must exist in harmony (and even in consort) with societies that are unsympathetic and often hostile to its moral code. It is called *realpolitik*.

In our complex multicultural and pluralistic societies it is essential that the Church find a way to reach out with true compassion to those who are suffering or marginalized while still retaining its own sense of itself as a counterwitness to the prevailing social ethos. The Vatican's November 23, 1994 *Charter for Catholic Health Care Workers*, the U.S. bishops' November 17, 1994 *Ethical and Religious Directives for Catholic Health Care Services*, and the 1991 *Health Care Ethics Guide* issued by the Catholic Health Association of Canada, for example, are uncompromising in the area of sexual medical issues, even in cases of potential pregnancy following rape. It is an ethical position not widely shared by a large percentage of Catholics in Canada and the United States, and it is a position that surely makes compassionate counselling difficult for a victim of rape who, in conscience, does not accept the Church's determined conviction, who may not even be Roman Catholic, and who has nowhere else to turn for assistance in a time of severe need.

Richard McCormick notes that, in 1984, 21 percent of all surgery performed in the United States was done so on an out-patient basis; by

1998 that percentage had almost quadrupled to 75 percent.[30] This same trend is underway in Canada and perhaps it will solve the dilemma of selective reproductive services; at the same time, it may also render the traditional hospital obsolete. Whatever the solution—and the status quo will become less and less tenable in smaller centres with limited health care facilities—McCormick cautions that "Some entities within Catholic health care may gain the whole world. . . . Will they also suffer the loss of their soul?"[31]

THE MISSION OF CATHOLIC HOSPITALS

For a secular society that worships efficiency and unencumbered individual freedom, the logic of the situation is unassailable. Why should government funds be directed to smaller religiously based institutions that view the world from their own limited ethos when consolidation into larger units would be more efficient, more procedurally inclusive, and more cost effective? In addition, weren't Catholic hospitals founded in the first instance to care for Catholics in a society divided along religious lines? And haven't those considerations been relegated to the dustbins of history? Are Catholic hospitals relevant in the twenty-first century? These often-asked questions are not always easy to address. To argue that the mission is based on the healing ministry of Christ is the only honest response, but to state the case is to risk the implication that there is a lack of compassion at the heart of the secular institution, a case that no one wants to make. And yet there is a difference. Time and time again patients turn to the Catholic hospital as their caregiver of choice, and they do so because they sense the difference. Ours, however, is a materialistic world for which numerical formulae provide the only compelling form of argumentation. How does one quantify the "healing ministry of Christ"? Satisfaction is certainly a good and noble sentiment, but one does need to pay the bills, attract the experts, and purchase the most current costly equipment. The "Sign of Hope" that Cardinal Joseph Bernardin celebrates in his October 1995 pastoral letter on health care does not have that practical ring, which is the only authentic touchstone for many in the democratic and utilitarian West.

Richard McCormick tries to address some of these practical issues as they exist in the context of the United States. In his "The End of Catholic Hospitals?" McCormick notes that in 1998 the Catholic health care system in the United States included some 542 hospitals, fully 10 percent of all non-federal hospitals, but he foresees the potential loss of at least one-third of these in the short term and the very real potential for loss of Catholic identity over the longer term. McCormick worries about the ability of the not-for-profit not simply to serve the poor and underprivileged, but to survive in a world where health care has become a business that is driven by the market considerations of efficiency, bottom line, competition, ability to pay, and customer satisfaction; a system in which the patient has become the depersonalized, dehumanized object of service and in which hospitals are forced into competition for paying customers and into mergers simply to survive in the competitive environment. In such a context, McCormick argues, the Catholic hospital too often becomes indistinguishable from the for-profit, and even pastoral care is at risk since its services do not obviously contribute to the bottom line. Catholic hospitals seem to be headed the way of mom and pop's corner store in the world of Costco, Wal-Mart, and big box marketing. The juggernaut would appear to be unstoppable.

Jesuit Californian Steve Privett picks up the same themes, but adds a different (and typically Jesuit) point of view that combines practice with theory and that sees the provision of necessary service as more important than who offers that service:

I've just got back from El Salvador. They're trying to privatize health care there nationally and the consequences are just horrendous. It looked almost to be a fait accompli except that the FMLN won the last congressional elections. This would mean, for example, that people with broken arms don't get them fixed. It would go from something like $265 to $380 just overnight. It's horrendous. I would expect that there would be similar consequences here, absent some kind of national health insurance. It seems to me that the bigger issue here—the future of Catholic health care is an issue, okay—it seems to me that the bigger issue is health care for everybody and how that's going to be addressed. Now who delivers that health care is a whole other question. If there's room in a national system for Catholics to deliver that because they can deliver it better or differently but as efficiently but at the same cost, then there's room for it, but I think that unless the United States comes to grips with the fact that 23 percent of this country has nothing, that seems to me to be the issue.

Privett gets to the nub of the issue when he asks the real question: What have Catholic hospitals got to offer as Catholic hospitals? Can they offer health care differently? Can they offer health care just as efficiently as the private sector? Privett surely asks the right questions while McCormick casts a pragmatic pall over future possibilities.

Bruce Antonello, chair of the Catholic Health Association of Ontario and CEO of St. Mary's General Hospital in Kitchener, Ontario, addresses Privett's issues from a Canadian perspective; and unlike Richard McCormick who readily admits that he is inclined toward pessimism—and hence he intentionally draws his doomsday words from the mouths of others—Antonello is more naturally inclined toward optimism. And why shouldn't he be? His hospital has survived a near-death experience at the hands of the Health Services Restructuring Commission. It is a death blow that he, his board chair Lloyd Wright, and previous board chair David Graham were prepared to face rather than sacrifice Catholic identity to a forced merger in the name of corporate efficiency. Arguing for an independent governing board in an atmosphere in which forced integration was the watchword, Wright reasoned: "If we have no control over programs or services, how can we maintain control over our mission or values, and make sure programs reflect those values?"[32] Unlike other Catholic hospitals in Ontario, many of which were forced to merge with secular institutions to form single governing boards, St. Mary's emerged with its board of trustees intact, but with the directive to co-operate with a joint executive committee to rationalize services with its neighbouring hospitals and with a good number of the local citizens unconvinced of the need for separate administrative structures.

Drawing on a impressive breadth of experience, Antonello reflected on the past, present, and future of the Catholic hospital in Ontario, its mission, and its viability:

The first hospitals in this province and in this country were Catholic, with the sisters starting facilities in Quebec City, Montreal, and Ottawa. But there has been and there continues to be some continual pressure on our continued existence, especially with the advent of Medicare since prior to that there was a definite and obvious need for Catholic hospitals, with their priority for the poor, the underserviced, and underprivileged. With the universal funding of hospitals and other services, it hasn't been as obvious to other observers as to why there should be Catholic hospitals. They wonder if we aren't all doing the same things. In the last several years, driven by the thesis that bigger is better, there has been a real push by governments to regional authorities and homogeneity in governance. So, in my view, there has been a real threat to the continued existence of Catholic hospitals. There has, therefore, been a need for an organization like the Catholic Health Association of Ontario to make the case for us to continue the work in which we are engaged throughout Ontario.

Although several Catholic hospitals in Ontario have been redefined into long-term care roles, those with a strong history of acute care have survived the Health Services Restructuring Commission and are equal partners in their communities. I think that in most instances the hospitals that have remained have in fact become stronger by expanding their services and assuming new responsibilities. Does stronger mean stronger as Catholic hospitals, or just stronger as hospitals?

Our approach, at least since I've been involved with this organization, has been that it is not as important to consider what you are doing as how you are doing it. Through the mission that the Sisters of St. Joseph have created and evolved over time for the St. Joseph's Health Care System of which we are a part, and through the spirit of the mission of our hospital, which is a statement of our own values and beliefs, we believe that we do things differently. We've changed our role several times and have been chameleons to some extent, being able to change as it is necessary and appropriate to remain relevant in our local situation. For example, after a great deal of debate and soul-searching, we rationalized the obstetrics and pediatrics components of our service to the Grand River Hospital, the cross-town secular facility, in 1989.

That was a very difficult decision on our part. Obstetrics and pediatrics had been part of our services since day one and we estimated that there had been up to 100,000 babies born at St. Mary's over the years—we were the more prolific hospital in terms of obstetrical services until the late 1960s and into the 1970s when things started to shift and the demands for postpartum tubal ligations were on the rise and the sizes of Catholic families were reducing, as they were in the rest of society. One thing led to another. On the basis of our beliefs, we weren't able to provide members of the community with the breadth of reproductive services which they wanted and demanded; so, we had to make the very difficult decision that if governments were pushing for rationalization of services—as they were and are—that in a two-hospital town such as this if we were going to be a monopoly through an amalgamation of services, we had to be able to provide what people wanted and demanded. We couldn't do that, so we reluctantly gave over that role to the other hospital. We were then able to change our direction and become quite a force in the community in adult medicine and surgery. So, we have changed over the years and we are in the process of considering even more change in what we do, but we like to think that even though we have limited the spectrum or range of programs we provide for whatever we're doing, it's how we do it and not what we do that's important as a Catholic organization.

There's no doubt that there has been a movement toward secularization of health care, but we are constantly on guard against any movement away from our Catholic organizations. At the same time, when you bring it down the level of the individual, I've had so many people—people of political power and influence—who have told me that in their personal experience they have felt they have received better care at Catholic hospitals, Catholic hospitals located farther afield than across Ontario. So, while there is that mob mentality, if you like, toward non-denominational homogeneity, there still is among the power brokers an appreciation, for the most part, for what we do and how we do it. Can you ascribe that to size? I'm not sure. We've got very large Catholic hospitals and several smaller ones, but we get the same sorts of feedback about the way in which people care for patients and their relatives no matter the size of the organization. Is it geographical? I don't think so.

Again, anecdotal and hard to define as they are, we get the same kinds of stories coming back from people who feel that they've received a better level of caring within our facilities. Admittedly, most of us aren't able to judge whether the level of medical and nursing care is more competent at one place or another, but we do know whether or not we like the care we receive. We know whether people are caring in the application. Our patient feedback consistently tells us as organizations that people feel more comfortable and more fulfilled in the care that they get in our Catholic hospitals.

As far as Catholic identity is concerned, there is no doubt that the depletion in the numbers of religious working in the medical field is a real issue for us. So, how does St. Mary's maintain its Catholic identity without the involvement of nuns and priests in the hospital? On the one hand, we attempt to grasp the last vestiges of the sisters' involvement, but at this time we do not have any sisters working on a day-to-day basis in the hospital. We do have a very strong tie to the St. Joseph's Health Care System, which is governed by a board of directors mostly populated by Sisters of St. Joseph's; so there is this chain of mission which comes from the board of directors of the system, through our individual boards, down through me as the CEO of the hospital, and through all of the employees that work here. We try as best we can to continue that presence because history and culture are important and the symbolism is important to remind people of where we came from.

Several years ago we tried, I think successfully, to capture the values and beliefs upon which the Sisters of St. Joseph founded this hospital and upon which they operated it for the last seventy-five years. By developing a statement of mission—and by including the owners, the staff, physicians, patients and their families, and neighbours around the hospital in its composition—we were able to get into words what we thought were the underpinning values and beliefs that made this place what it is and we then put that statement on the wall all over the place and said, "Look, when we do things as a physician, as a nurse, as an administrator, or as a volunteer, we should have this mission at the heart of what we do." Many organizations celebrate people who come up with cost-saving ideas; we celebrate those who live the mission. When we make major policy decisions, we are generally challenged by at least one board member: "How does this wash with our mission? It may be good financial decision-making, but is it in keeping with our basic values and beliefs?" So, how does a denominational hospital differ from a non-denominational hospital? In my view, we give people the latitude, the opportunity, to think about mission in an open way.

Many of us did begin as a result of specifically Catholic philanthropy, but Catholic hospitals in this province and right across the country are ecumenical in just about every way. We don't hire Catholics: we hire qualified people. In the hiring process we try to judge whether the people we hire are in keeping with our own values. We attract volunteer board members. We don't ask them what their religion is, but we do ask them to subscribe to our mission in the decision-making process in which they are involved. We hire good people and we make it clear that these are the values and beliefs that we have and here are some of the things that the Roman Catholic Church believes in; then we ask those that work with us—be they physicians, board members, employees, volunteers—to fulfil their respective functions in accord with our mission.

I do worry about what we are going to do when we don't have the visible sign of connectedness to the Catholic tradition through the founding congregation of sisters. The demographics suggest that in not too many years there will not be any Sisters of St. Joseph involved in St. Mary's; in fact, they, like other religious orders, may decide they are not going to continue in their sponsorship role at all. The question then is: How do we as laypeople continue the work they've done for some seventy-five years of providing Catholic-based health care? It probably helps in understanding where we come from and some of our beliefs to have a Catholic CEO, but it is not a policy requirement. In fact, of the six organizations that are in the St. Joseph's Health Care System, three if not four of the CEOs are not Roman Catholic.

We're at a watershed point in our history right now. I support our Ontario Minister of Health, Mrs. Witmer, in calling for a national debate on where we are going to go as a nation with our health care. After many years of Medicare, the time is right to look at the forces that are being exerted on the system and try to make a future out of what has happened. There is no doubt in my mind that our aging baby boomer population, a group that is probably the wealthiest in the history of the world, a group that now and in the future will have even more political clout, is a group that will likely not be satisfied with a system that will not allow them to "buy up" with respect to their health care. I think we have a great deal of work to do to try to fashion the kind of groundswell of political power with that same group and with others feeling, as we do as Canadians, that we have to care for those less fortunate. So there is this dichotomy where I want to buy better health care for myself, but I also want to make sure that Sally down the street has good health care too. I think we as Canadians are in a unique position in the world where we've all been acculturated to the notion that we will provide equitable care, but at the same time the world is changing. Globalization is dictating that people think differently, without boundaries, and now a good number of people in Canada are wondering why they can go tomorrow to Buffalo to get an MRI but in Canada they have to wait three months and they can't buy that same service here. I think that somewhere in the midst of that thinking there can be some compromise that will serve everybody well—differently, perhaps, but well nonetheless.

Strangely enough, I think that there might be some additional opportunities for Catholic health care in the future. As I mentioned earlier on, it seems to me that there is absolutely no doubt in anybody's mind prior to universal Medicare of the worth of Catholic hospitals as a significant part of the system since they were hospitals which had a bias to serve the poor and underprivileged. When Medicare put everybody on a level playing field, some of that obvious need for our kind of thinking disappeared. It seems to me that in the future we may be back into that situation where there will be people who will fall between the cracks if we go to a semiprivatized system; there will be a need for somebody to pick up the unwanted patients—those that don't add to your bottom line. It may be that Catholic hospitals and other denominational hospitals will have a brighter future than they have a present.

Concern for the underprivileged, of course, is not limited to those living in our backyard. The St. Joseph's Health Care System has for a number of years been involved in offshore work, primarily in developing countries: Romania when they had their major crisis, Russia after the fall of the Iron Curtain, the Caribbean, Uganda. . . . The idea in all cases was to attempt to help developing countries and those not as well off as we are to help themselves: providing them with supplies and equipment, human resource expertise, medical expertise, in some cases bringing patients with specialized conditions back to Canada for treatment, in many more cases sending over biomedical technicians, anesthetists, and other medical professionals to train and teach their colleagues in other countries techniques and bring them up to at least some state of leading-edge technology and expertise. So, there is quite a rich heritage that we've developed. When we buy equipment for hospitals as part of our province-wide group purchasing agreements, we ask if there is equipment which is still in good working order and which can be salvaged and sent to other countries. We assess whether that technology can be sustained in those countries—the Third World and other developing countries are littered with good intentions. You have to be very selective because in those countries if the equipment doesn't work in a month or so, there is no one there to repair it. You need to take care in selecting and customizing the aid that you give.

On the level of personnel, some of our people are very involved in justice issues. One of our doctors has recently been given an award for his work with Physicians for Global Peace and one of our nurses regularly spends her vacation working in an eye clinic in South America where she sees all manner of problems. The St. Joseph's Health Care System is working to provide opportunities for local health care providers to get involved in any number of ways—not everybody has the desire to go oversees to do volunteer work, but they may provide pro bono work for patients who come to our hospital for treatment not available in other countries. In Hamilton, a number of physicians have become involved in care as a direct result of the work the sisters have done.

In short, one might say of Catholic hospitals, as one might say of Catholic schools, that they are institutions with a clear difference, institutions at the heart of which beats a philosophy of community born in the council halls and meeting rooms of Vatican II. Lamenting the imminent demise of Bon Secours Hospital in Beaconsfield, Buckinghamshire, and the imperilled state of others, such as St. John and St. Elizabeth in north London, *The Tablet* sees Catholic hospitals in England falling by the wayside as medical insurers look for the most cost-effective way of providing their service in an increasingly competitive marketplace, a marketplace where the insurers sometimes are also owners of competing facilities. In such a system the work of the Bon Secours Sisters and of the Catholic hospital is cast aside, as is the charitable work that benefits from the "profits" of such institutions. *The Tablet* concludes that "Anyone who has ever visited a Catholic hospital knows that it can provide something a little different."[33] *Vive la différence* carries no coinage.

Bruce Antonello's observations provide impassioned and eloquent testimony to a system whose raison d'être is distinctive at heart, a system based on commitment to the essential human dignity of each member of society, a system rooted philosophically in the provision of service and not in the search for profit. It is a service that society desperately needs, and it is one that faces an uncertain future. As Antonello notes, there was a time in the immediate past when Catholic values with respect to health care reflected the national conscience of Canada, just as Bernardin argues that in many ways these same principles at one time inspired the Declaration of Independence and the Constitution of the United States.[34] The ubiquitous consumption of the profit motive, however, has profoundly altered our view of ourselves, our view of government, and our view of society. Lamenting the Canadian sellout of Medicare in particular and of the caring society in general to the profit motive, Dalton Camp reflects on Neil Postman's thesis in his *Technopoly* (New York: Vintage, 1993) that "the United States is not a culture but merely an economy."[35] It would be difficult to shape a more succinct reflection of the antithetical attitudes of the culture of Catholic health care and the consumer approach to human well-being.

CATHOLIC EDUCATION: AN ENVIABLE HERITAGE/
A MODERN VISION

Mater et Magistra: "The Catholic Church has been established by Jesus Christ as MOTHER AND TEACHER of nations. . . ."[36] When good Pope John began to write the seventieth-anniversary encyclical to commemo rate the publication of Leo XIII's 1891 *Rerum novarum* (*Of New Things*), the cornerstone of the Church's social teaching, he reflected quite naturally on the time-honoured images of the nurturing Church, Church as mother and Church as teacher, a Church whose teaching mandate, like its health care apostolate, is concerned with the immediate and the ultimate well-being of the human person, physically and spiritually, in time and beyond time. "Go forth and teach all nations. . . ." (Matthew 28:19). This emphasis on the teaching Church springs quite naturally from the Gospel representation of Christ as rabbi, as teacher; the common epithet for Christ in Old English is, accordingly "Se Lareow," which in modern English translates as "teacher" or "dispenser of wisdom." It is with this in mind that Cardinal G. Emmett Carter, Canada's pre-eminent Catholic catechist and educational theorist, recommends that classroom teachers imitate the instructional methods exemplified by the Teacher: teach through love and teach through story, teach by action and teach by analogy.[37] Similarly, the Society of Jesus's decision to centre its educational direction on education for justice flows from the deliberations of the Jesuits' Thirty-second General Congregation and is rooted in the Teacher's example, in his deeds and in his discourses.[38]

The Church's early and abiding interest in education has always had both a practical and a theoretical component. Augustine of Hippo's late fourth-century *De doctrina christiana* (*On Christian Doctrine*),[39] for example, contains not merely an early example of a manual for effective preaching (an *ars praedicandi*), but a practical translation of Cicero's rhetoric for use by the Christian as both an exegetical and a predicatory (preaching) tool—little wonder that *De doctrina christiana* became a handbook for the pedagogical content of much of the poetry of the high Middle Ages. Boccaccio, for example, turns to it expressly,[40] and Chaucer (his fourteenth-century contemporary) does so implicitly, since for them, as it was for many a medieval poet, poetry was an effective means for delightful instruction.[41] Augustine had explained that the effective homilist would follow classical Ciceronian form and, hence, his composition of the classical characteristics of fine discourse—*docere, delectare, movere* (*flectere*)—teach, please, move—teach your audience in a pleasing way and you will enhance your ability to alter their behaviour for the better. Old and Middle English homilists, as a result, incorporate poetic forms into their discourses and some of the more imaginative went so far as to shape their homilies as pure poetry.

Poetic narrative provided the pleasurable medium for instructive story and Chaucer's Pardoner blends the poetic and homiletic traditions by noting that the unlettered love a good story since it helps them to remember and to repeat the inherent lesson; and hagiography—the crafting of the life of the saint—is, of course, the homilist's response to the time-honoured and biblical penchant for teaching by storied example.[42] Bede's early eighth-century codification *De schematibus et tropis*[43] (*Concerning Schemes and Tropes*—a catalogue of the classical rhetorical modes whereby word order and the hidden meanings within the words themselves can be used for effective composition) springs from motives not dissimilar to Augustine's. It is intended to defend the stylistic sophistication of the Bible from the attacks of its critics, but it is also a textbook for students at Bede's monastery at Jarrow and as such it introduces the Christian era to the rhetorical techniques practised by the classical masters, techniques that the text catalogues for practical purpose. And since the homily, in all its forms, was essentially a teaching device, the form and content are in fact studies in effective pedagogy. Hence the medieval refrain—*praedicare id est docere*—to preach, that is, to teach. Alanus de Insulis's twelfth-century *Summa de arte praedicatoria* (*Compendium of the Art of Preaching*), for example, provides detailed hints on how to adapt one's discourse to the interests of the audience. All of which is to suggest that examples of the medieval Church's instruction manuals for effective pedagogy—the *Didascalicon*[44]—are legion and provide living witness to the unbroken life of the teaching Church.

The Church's role in the development of the medieval cathedral school and of the university system in Western culture is well known. Medieval texts like Bonaventure's *Reductio artium ad theologiam*[45] (*The Leading Back of the Seven Liberal Arts to Theology*) record the medieval churchman's efforts to put the treasury of all practical and theoretical knowledge at the service of the Church in an effort to lead humankind back to God. The seven liberal arts, which are the object of Bonaventure's attention, constitute the source of all knowledge: the trivium: logic, rhetoric, and grammar; and the quadrivium: arithmetic, music, astronomy, and geometry. Since, by definition, the seven liberal arts embrace the totality of the intellectual and practical modes of knowing, to the medieval schoolman it followed by necessity that observation of the tangible world and reflection within the world of the mind ought all to focus on the ultimate end of human existence. These are educational postulates within the Catholic tradition that run in an unbroken continuum into the modern world. It is important to understand the world around you, not solely for its own sake but for a higher good. It is a thesis that separates Catholic education from its secular counterpart in the post-Enlightenment world.

Not surprisingly, therefore, the roots of modern education as we know it were cultivated within the medieval and renaissance Church: education as a system was an invention of the Society of Jesus, the Jesuits, in the late sixteenth century. Formed as a counter-Reformation movement, the Jesuits were a group of learned men dedicated to the defence of the Catholic faith who put themselves at the service of the Pope, ready to go wherever they were needed anywhere in the world. And wherever they went, their commitment to learning and teaching accompanied them. It was a commitment that was wholly appropriate to a religious organization founded in the intellectually tempestuous period unleashed by Martin Luther.

In 1540 the fledgling Society of Jesus was a small band of university-educated devotees led by Ignatius of Loyola. The Jesuits (as they were quickly christened) bound themselves constitutionally to an educational apostolate and their mandate expresses their educational interest in a practical manner, a manner that echoes generations of exhortations on the art of effective preaching/teaching: "Above all things let them have at heart the instruction of boys and ignorant persons in the knowledge of Christian doctrine, of the Ten Commandments, and other such rudiments as shall be suitable, having regard to the circumstances of persons, places, and times."[46] Because the Jesuits were prepared to carry their missionary work anywhere in the world, they needed a teacher's manual, a practical handbook to codify purpose, curriculum, classroom manner, and the like. The *Ratio studiorum*, the "rationale for studies," was first adopted by the Society in 1599 to serve just these purposes; with the *Ratio* was born the first standardized educational system as such.

John Padberg, the director of the Institute of Jesuit Sources in St. Louis, at St. Louis University, explains the purpose of the *Ratio*:

The *Ratio*, to put it in its simplest terms, was a handbook on how to teach. But it's much more than that. It was basically a handbook that grew out of the experience of Jesuit teaching and a very rapid expansion of Jesuit teaching in the last years of Ignatius's life and for a few decades after his death. By the 1580s, the then general of the Society, Father Claudio Aquaviva, decided on a way to gather that experience and almost to codify it into a manual of practice whereby adequate teachers might learn from good teachers, and good teachers might learn how to become excellent teachers. As a result, first and foremost, the *Ratio* is a manual of practice on how to conduct a class, what courses were to be taught year by year by year in the Jesuit schools, what classroom method was to be like, what books were to be used, what authors were to be treated. . . . One of the things that's most important to remember about Jesuit education falls within the purview, the ambit, of the *Ratio*, and that is that it was the first organized system of education in the Western world. It was so in two ways. First of all, you could go from Montreal, for example, in Canada to Monreale in Sicily, or you could go from Cuzco in Peru to Krakow in Poland and have the same Jesuit education—an international system where people could easily move from one place to another. For example, Edmund Campion, after leaving England, coming to the continent, joining the Society, taught briefly in Rome, then taught in Prague, and from there was called to go to England. He could do that because there was a coherent uniform system throughout all of the Jesuit educational enterprises. The internal system was such though that year-by-year, step-by-step, students entering a Jesuit school could progress in an orderly and intelligent manner from the lowest classes up to the highest.

Another noteworthy aspect of Jesuit education that has its contemporary variations in Catholic and state schools is its rootedness in human experience. As Padberg points out, it provides both training for employment and social utility as well as for a more noble purpose.

At the beginning of one of the trial editions of the *Ratio*—and remember, it grew out of the tried and true experience of the Jesuits—Diego Ledesma, who is one of the Jesuits' great educational theorists, was asked why Jesuits had schools. In response, he gave four reasons which are pretty well, it seems to me, the same kind of reasons for which Jesuits would run schools today. He said, first of all, that Jesuit schools provide a way in which people can effectively, practically, earn a living; that is, there is a practical reason for education. Secondly, they provide for the right governing of society and the proper making of law and public affairs. In other words, there is a social reason for education. Thirdly, he said that Jesuits have schools because they provide (I'm using his baroque term now) for the ornaments, splendour, and perfection of the rational nature of man. In other words, there is the liberalizing effective end of education. Finally, he said, and this is almost a quotation although I don't have it in front of me, "What is most import is that education helps lead humankind, men and women, most securely to their last end, God, our Lord." In other words, there is a religious motive for the Jesuit educational enterprise. So, you've got a practical, a social or civic, a cultural or liberal, and a religious motive for Jesuit education.[47]

As if to reinforce the logical legitimacy of these observations, Andrew M. Greeley and Peter H. Rossi's 1966 *The Education of Catholic Americans*[48] explores the viability of Catholic education in the United States by examining the nature of its religious education, the commitment of its graduates to the Catholic Church, the socialization of its graduates, preparation of its graduates for the workplace, and the impact of the principle of change espoused by Vatican II on attitudes toward school, society, and Church. Greeley would return to these questions and the issue of institutional effectiveness some ten years later. Indeed, they are at the heart of the matter since these are the issues that point to a theory of education that is essentially and universally Catholic, an educational theory that is decidedly different from its secular counterpart.

The Church's initial and enduring interest in education has generated a noble tradition to offer the modern world, a consistent and developing tradition, a practical yet lofty view of humankind and of the purpose of the educational endeavour as such. In his 1929 encyclical letter, *Divini illius magistri (On the Christian Education of Youth)*, Pius XI promulgates the first significant papal articulation of the Church's role in education in modern times. Although there are impressive echoes of a distinguished inheritance, the encyclical letter is, unfortunately, characterized by a triumphalist tone—a tone that the Church shed as it emerged from Vatican II—coupled with a catechetical concept of education that informs too many of today's churchmen and a moderate proportion of the laity; it is a tone that dogs us still. Pius XI puts his case in bold terms: "first of all education belongs pre-eminently to the Church, by reason of a double title in the supernatural order, conferred exclusively on her by God Himself: absolutely superior therefore to any other title in the natural order."[49] The logic of the hierarchical worldview enshrined in Pius XI's observation leads naturally to his noting of the Thomistic declaration that "the father is the principle of generation, of education and discipline and of everything that bears upon the perfecting of human life."[50]

Although Pius's attitudes toward his Church and its educational apostolate are a reflection of the 1917 Code of Canon Law in which canon 2319 threatened parents with excommunication if they exposed their children to the "risk of perversion" within the non-Catholic school—indeed the attitudes are sufficiently widespread to have been endorsed in a U.S. episcopal decision to withhold absolution from non-compliant parents[51]— neither the tenor of Pius's assertions nor their anthropology would survive the deliberations of the Second Vatican Council, which would bury, at least for the short term, the centuries-old distinction between the *Ecclesia docens* and the *Ecclesia discens*.[52] According to the former—the *Ecclesia docens* (the teaching Church)—the ecclesiastical hierarchy is the teaching body, whereas the laity and (usually) the lower clergy constitute the *Ecclesia discens* (the learning Church). The first is the deposit and dispenser of knowledge, of teaching, the second is the recipient thereof. Although the conciliar concept of the People of God and its preference for broadly based consultation were in practice to replace the instructional rigidity inherent in the notion of the *Ecclesia docens* and the *Ecclesia discens*, and although there is at least a more transparent effort within the Vatican to consult on some issues, the preconciliar concerns about the inflexibility of the Magisterium, the Church's teaching office, is a sticking point even today. This is particularly the case when the Church is confronted with reasoned arguments by Catholic educators and other educated Catholics who would rethink the Church's position with respect to issues related to sexuality and ministry, arguments that, for the most part, are met with hostility and closure.

Pius's perception of education as such, and especially the pedagogical process, are equally problematic. He quotes Leo XIII approvingly, even with admiration, when he incorporates Leo's "pithy sentence" into his own encyclical: "Greater stress must be laid on the employment of apt and solid methods of teaching and, what is still more important, *on bringing into full conformity with the Catholic faith*, what is taught in literature, in the sciences, and above all in philosophy, on which depends in great part the right orientation of the other branches of knowledge."[53] (The italics are ours.) The Pope's notion of "teaching methods" is exactly the kind of contrived indoctrinational approach to teaching and learning that has rendered Catholic education suspect in the minds not only of its non-Catholic critics but of Catholic educationalists as well. In such an approach, where is the basis for intellectual excitement? Where is there room for objective analysis? Where is there room for individual discovery and personal growth? Where is there room for honest and reasoned differences of opinion? Emmett Carter puts the case clearly when he argues that "every child must learn for himself. And that is why, no matter how great the truth with which we are dealing, we must respect always the individuality of the human mind." To which he adds: "we must avoid the ready-made solution. In the schools of philosophy which dot the Catholic world there is a procedure which may be described as the 'thesis technique'. . . . It is as though we are told: 'Here is the thesis. The truth has been found for you. There is no need for you to look any further; simply understand what these other people have thought, and you will have wisdom.' "[54]

The process, Carter argues, is not only anti-intellectual; it is psychologically anti-Thomistic since the assimilation of knowledge "must come through the self-operation of the individual involved."[55] In an earlier book Carter had made a similar point when he noted that "It is a great temptation for the master to take what he has learned, to reduce it to a capsule, and to think that it can be assimilated like a pill. It is in a sense the easy way, but again it is the mistaken idea that one generation can do the work for another."[56] Logically, therefore, Carter insists that "The teacher who loves children and desires to awaken in them the appreciation of virtue, love of truth, and awareness of the problems of life, with a desire to arrive at something of a personal solution, is the teacher who will make the greatest contribution."[57] Not only are Carter's educational values at odds with the long-standing concept of the *Ecclesia docens* and *Ecclesia discens* implicit in Pius's assertion, but they would find little sympathy with many contemporary politicians and educational pragmatists for whom the purpose of education is indoctrination of a different sort, indoctrination into a social economy rather than into a denominational culture.

Carter's perspectives on education and educational theory are wholly consonant with the thinking that would permeate Vatican II some few years after the publication of his educational theories. *Dignitatis humanae* (*Declaration on Religious Freedom*), for example, explains that "It is in accordance with their dignity as persons—that is, as beings endowed with reason and free will and therefore privileged to bear personal responsibility—that all men should be at once impelled by nature and also bound by a moral obligation to seek the truth, once it is known, and to order their whole lives in accord with the demands of truth. . . . The inquiry is to be free, carried on with the aid of teaching or instruction, communication, and dialogue."[58] In their document on education, *Gravissimum educationis* (*Declaration on Christian Education*), the Council Fathers presented a theory of education that was thoroughly consistent with their views on human dignity. They teach, for example, "that children and young people have a right to be encouraged to weigh moral values with an upright conscience, and to embrace them with personal choice. . . ."[59] At the same time, the Council extends the theoretical scope of Catholic education so that it closely resembles the approach outlined hundreds of years earlier by Diego Ledesma: it assumes a social responsibility that extends beyond the narrowly Catholic perspective.

Ledesma's tone and the vision had been light years beyond those apparent in Leo XIII's assertions and sound much more like Good Pope John in his wish to be the mother and teacher to nations: "As a mother, the Church is bound to give these children of hers the kind of education through which their entire lives can be penetrated with the spirit of Christ, while at the same time she offers her services to all peoples by way of promoting the full development of the human person, for the welfare of earthly society and the building of a world fashioned more humanly. . . .

By virtue of its very purpose, while it cultivates the intellect with unremitting attention, the school ripens the capacity for right judgement, provides an introduction into the cultural heritage won by past generations, promotes a sense of values, and readies for professional life."[60]

Not only were subsequent Roman statements on education to be shaped by the thinking of the Second Vatican Council, as we shall see, but so was the Code of Canon Law, which was revised in 1983. The Code, therefore, reiterates the above principles when it asserts that "Education must pay regard to the formation of the whole person, so that all may attain their eternal destiny and at the same time promote the common good of society" (Canon 795). As a result, care is to be taken so that students develop a "sense of responsibility and a right use of freedom, and be formed to take an active part in social life" (Canon 795); moreover, a proper education, according to Canon Law, is one that is in harmony with the consciences of the parents (Canon 799).

PRE-UNIVERSITY CATHOLIC EDUCATION IN THE UNITED STATES

The principles embodied both in *Gravissimum educationis*, the education document issued by Vatican II, as well as those embedded in the body of documents produced by the Council, have had a profound and consistent effect on a good deal of the educational outlook of the Church, at least in theory. These principles, for example, fully inform *The Catholic School*, a 1977 information statement issued by the Sacred Congregation for Catholic Education, which begins by locating the document squarely within the context of the Council.[61]

Accordingly, *The Catholic School* explains the mission of the school as the "development of the human person" and the "formation of the whole man." Consistent with the teachings of Vatican II, the Sacred Congregation for Catholic Education envisions the Catholic school as presenting its specific Christocentric message within a pluralistic context, as providing its own positive contribution to the cultural dialogue, and doing so for the betterment of human society. To which the document adds the crucial conciliar observation: "Moreover, in this way she helps to promote that freedom of teaching which champions and guarantees freedom of conscience and the parental right to choose the school best suited to parents' educational purposes." Freedom and proselytism are, of course, polar opposites; yet critics of Catholic education have often accused the Church of intellectual rigidity and its educational system of indoctrination. It is important to note, therefore, that the Sacred Congregation explicitly rejects any "one-sided outlook" that could be seen as proselytism, noting that "This can happen only when Christian educators misunderstand the nature and methods of Christian education." On the contrary, meaningful education must provide an engagement with familiar real-life situations, must, in fact, do so "as a matter of duty" so that any school "which merely offers pre-cast conclusions hinders the personal development of its pupils."

In a directive that is clearly at odds with the counsel of Pius xi, *The Catholic School* cautions: "It would be wrong to consider subjects as mere adjuncts to faith or as a useful means of teaching apologetics." Each student, therefore, must engage society as it is and must develop an ethical perspective to enable that student to choose freely and intelligently for the betterment of the individual and of society. Accordingly, the subject matter is of lesser importance than the instructor and the lived example of that instructor who teaches "in imitation of Christ, the only Teacher" and who teaches "not only by word but by every gesture. . . ." In the hands of the Catholic teacher the world becomes the spoken expression of the Creator and the school becomes "a community whose aim is the transmission of values for living." All these attitudes are variously articulated throughout the ages in the thinking of Augustine of Hippo, Bonaventure, Alanus de Insulis, and the medieval homilists, Hugh of St. Victor and the *Didascalicon*, as well as being expressed in the pedagogical theory enunciated by Diego Ledesma and Gerald Emmett Carter. They are attitudes, however, that needed to be recast in contemporary form since they had been lost in the anti-intellectualism that had become an unfortunate part of the Church's life at the end of the nineteenth and for a good part of the twentieth century.

The Catholic School is a landmark of sorts in the history of Catholic education and captures the essence of Vatican ii in its enunciation of contemporary and traditional Catholic thought, including the thorny issue of Catholic identity within the school. In many ways, this question of identity is the nub of the problem since the devil is always in the detail and it is the detail that leaves itself open to interpretation. Hence, there are bound to be tensions between individual institutions and individual bishops, and between individual bishops and individual teachers. As a result, the perspective is clear: "Where difficulties and conflicts arise about the authentic Christian character of the Catholic school, hierarchical authority can and must intervene."

Intervention, as we shall see, can sometimes seem, at least, to give the lie to the theory. In the Vatican's *The Religious Dimension of Education in the Catholic School*, one is struck not only by the condescending tone but also by the legalistic caveat by which the call for collaboration is immediately qualified: "The church, therefore, is willing to give lay people charge of the schools that it has established, and the laity themselves establish schools. The recognition of the school as a Catholic school is, however, always reserved to the competent ecclesiastical authority."[62] Is this is the basis of true community, of a partnership rooted in trust and mutual respect? When talking community and co-operation, one does not bludgeon with legalities, technically accurate though they may be.

The educational principles enunciated by Vatican II have formed an effective call to action and have been repeated in various forms since reflection on the Council's thinking began to be taken seriously with the study and publication of its documents. At the Thirty-second General Congregation of the Society of Jesus, for example, the Jesuit Order took a specific and inspired option for the poor. As Doug McCarthy, one-time novice master for the Jesuits in their house of formation in Guelph, Ontario put it:

... with the Thirty-second General Congregation [which met from December 2, 1974 to March 7, 1995] we left the courts of the kings and moved into the courts of the poor, and unless we remain in the courts of the poor and do our ministry from there, we are not going to meet the needs of the time. I know that there are people who can't do that, who can't move to the courts of the poor. I don't think we can get the message across without being there. I think we have to be on the margins of society to be able to speak to the mainstream of society. We can't speak to a mainstream society living the way mainstream society lives. I don't think we are heard. We have no credibility, we have nothing to say if we're in the mainstream. So, we have to go to the courts of the poor. I don't mean just the financially disadvantaged here. We have to be with them and they will mould our message for us. Until we do that, I think we will plod along, keeping our institutions going and meeting needs and doing good work, but not meeting the hunger in the way it has to be met.[63]

The educational imprint of the Thirty-second General Congregation and the thrust that McCarthy describes with such passionate commitment have clear implications for the educational apostolate at all levels of Jesuit education. Moreover, it is a direction that is wholly consonant with the Church's traditional approach to health care, as well as with the Council's assertion that special attention be given to promising students from developing countries, especially students "of slender means."[64] The Thirty-second General Congregation detailed the implications:

- We must be more aware of the need for research and for theological reflection, carried on in a context which is both interdisciplinary and genuinely integrated with the culture in which it is done and with its traditions. Only thus can it throw light on the main problems which the Church and humanity ought to be coming to grips with today.
- Greater emphasis should be placed on the conscientization according to the Gospel of those who have power to bring about social change, and a special place given to service of the poor and the oppressed.
- We should pursue and intensify the work of formation in every sphere of education, while subjecting it at the same time to continual scrutiny. We must help prepare both young people and adults to live and labour for others and with others to build a more just world. Especially we should help them form our Christian students in such a way that animated by a mature faith and personally devoted to Jesus Christ, they can find Him in others and having recognized Him there, they will serve Him in their neighbor. In this way we shall contribute to the formation of those who by a kind of multiplier-effect will share in the process of educating the world itself.[65]

Whether it be at its secondary schools at Stonyhurst or Jamaica, or its universities at Fordham, Santa Clara, or San Salvador, the Jesuits have tried to live that vision. For their efforts many have died, most notably the six Jesuits at the University of Central America in San Salvador who believed implicitly that universities should be a centre for social reconstruction. For UCA president Ignacio Ellacuría, the incarnation of the preferential option for the poor is essential to the raison d'être of the Christian university. Enfleshing that principle does not mean the abandoning of academic excellence since without academic excellence, the university could not play a useful social role. For him, the university has a responsibility "to provide science for those who have no science; to provide skills for the unskilled; to be a voice for those who have no voice; to give intellectual support for those who do not possess the academic qualifications to promote and legitimate their rights."[66] His convictions cost him his life.

But Vatican II has not only placed its imprint on Jesuit education as such; it has had a dramatic effect on education within the Catholic world. Sociologist Andrew Greeley has documented the Catholic ethos in the United States, the success of the Catholic school system there, and in particular its impact on the poor in the United States. In *The Catholic Myth*,[67] Greeley develops his thesis that the underlying difference between Protestant and Catholic can be explained in terms of the Catholic Imagination as being essentially sacramental, a vision that promotes community over individuality, a social concern for the poor and suffering rather than a sense that one's well-being is an individual responsibility. The vision of school as community and the conviction that the school provides a community at the service of the poor is central to the conciliar document *Gravissimum educationis*, with the Jesuit determination flowing from the Thirty-second General Congregation, as well as the documents from the Sacred Congregation for Catholic Education, which emanate from *Gravissimum educationis: The Catholic School, Lay Catholics in Schools: Witnesses to Faith*, and *The Religious Dimension of Education in a Catholic School*.[68]

Greeley is enthusiastic about the Catholic school system in the United States from virtually every perspective—commitment to the faith, assistance to the poor and underprivileged, tendency to return to the faith, reception of sacraments, upward mobility socially, increased wealth, advancement to graduate studies, attitudes toward the role of women and their role in society, attitudes toward marriage and sexuality. All of these findings, he explains, were thrust upon him—he did not enter his study of Catholic education in the United States with the expectation that the Catholic school was so overwhelmingly successful.

In *The American Catholic: A Social Portrait*, Greeley lists as one of the great myths of U.S. Catholicism the notion that parochial schools are substandard, that they do not prepare their graduates for success economically, and that they do not instil appropriate lifelong Catholic values. In fact, Greeley devotes three chapters of detailed sociological analysis (augmented by copious charts and an impressive array of figures) to document the effectiveness of the Catholic school in the United States and the willingness of Catholics to support the educational enterprise. Not surprisingly, therefore, he is dismayed to discover that his enthusiasm is not shared either by nuns and priests who are no longer interested in the educational apostolate or by the episcopacy who seem also to have lost their passion for Catholic education; as a result, new schools are not being constructed and the future looks bleak indeed. In his earlier jointly authored study of Catholic education, *Catholic Schools in a Declining Church*, Greeley concluded quite bluntly that "It seems that only a handful of Catholic theoreticians are prepared to defend the continuation of Catholic schools."[69] As a result Greeley concludes that unless those in leadership positions can find another means to integrate the Catholic youth of the United States into the Catholic community and into Catholic institutions, "the continuing decline of the proportion of the Catholic population in Catholic schools will inevitably lead to a diminished level of Catholic commitment in the years ahead."[70]

In the meantime, inner-city schools in the United States, like inner-city hospitals, are moving to the suburbs and abandoning the hostile inner core to the denominationally based institutions and usually to the Catholic Church, which has established both a skill and a reputation for dealing successfully with the urban poor. And the need is staggering. Bruce S. Cooper notes, for example, that 65 percent of live births in the large cities of the United States are to unwed mothers under the age of eighteen, and that these babies have a briefer life expectancy than that of children born in the world's poorest countries. He points out that in New York City scarce resources were recently being redirected from classroom essentials to the purchase of some 2,300 pairs of handcuffs to assist in the maintenance of order within the primary and secondary school system.[71] But the dogged separation of Church and state in the United States, coupled with a traditional racism and economic neoliberalism, has left the Catholic educational system to fend for itself financially. School closings have become a way of life in the United States, with the Catholic school population declining by 43 percent between 1965 and 1980 and an additional 18 percent between 1980 and 1989;[72] and between June 1990 and June 1994, 435 U.S. Catholic schools closed their doors, while cities such as Boston, New York, Philadelphia, and Chicago had already experienced dramatic decreases both in their Catholic schools and in their Catholic school populations.[73]

As Catholics in the United States become increasingly successful economically, they have tended to meld into the social mainstream, complete with its individualistic and materialist ethic; at the same time, the lack of social acceptance that differentiated the Catholic population and spurred it to develop its own institutions has eroded just as surely. Indeed, there is an increasing tendency for Catholics to join the mainstream pre-university educational system, and a dramatic increase in non-Catholic teachers and non-Catholic students within the Catholic system as the postconciliar school reaches out to the poor and marginalized. At the same time, with the dramatic decrease in church attendance—71 percent participated in the liturgy weekly in 1963, but only 40.5 percent did so in 1990—the ability of the parish to support the urban poor has itself become more problematic; it is a financial problem exacerbated by the fact that the increasingly prosperous suburban Catholic does not feel a philanthropic commitment to the urban poor or socially marginalized.[74] Indeed, the urban poor have given up on the public education system in the United States, so that cities like Cleveland and Milwaukee have turned to a voucher system through which some students can bypass the public educational system and enrol in a Catholic or other Christian school. It is an approach that is not without its own controversy, but it is also an approach that underlines the need for an alternative, value-based educational system.[75]

PRE-UNIVERSITY CATHOLIC EDUCATION IN CANADA

In Canada, where various forms of government support for Catholic education at the provincial level differentiate the Canadian from the U.S. experience, Ken Westhues, a sociologist at the University of Waterloo, argues that the rush to secularization and the creeping convergence of the Catholic public system of education with the public secular system do not bode well for the future of Catholic education as a meaningful alternative. And unlike Greeley's studies in the United States, Westhues's research suggests that the near convergence of the Catholic and public systems of education in Canada is such that there is simply no appreciable difference in moral values or social achievement between Catholic graduates of both systems.[76] The best we can hope for from the Catholic school in Canada, he argues, is a forum for the transmission of Catholic social values and, perhaps, a lived example of those values in the operation of the Catholic school—or maybe a movement away from integration and full government support as it exists in Ontario to the establishment of more privately run Catholic schools like those in British Columbia and Manitoba (and the United States). Yet, in an earlier study of Catholic education in Canada, Westhues had concluded that without public legitimation of the educational system, coupled with the financial support that accompanies that legitimation, there was very little support for Catholic education.[77] It is a conclusion that seems to be borne out by recent history.

At the close of the twentieth century, provincial governments were taking action to reverse constitutionally entrenched educational rights for Roman Catholic and Protestant minorities, viewing these rights as being either discriminatory or parochial in a multicultural and post-Christian society. The thesis has, in fact, been tested at the United Nations where a November 5, 1999 ruling by the UN Committee on Human Rights supported a petition by a Toronto-area Jewish parent, Arieh Waldman, who had argued that Ontario's support of Catholic students discriminated against him as a Jew as he was faced with a $14,000 annual expense for the education of his two children in a Jewish day school. (The same UN Committee refused to hear a second petition by a group of Ontario citizens who had argued that government support of any religious school was illegal and discriminatory.) Faced with the Committee decision, the government of Ontario declined to respond, noting that its position was supported by the Canadian constitution and that the United Nations finding was exhortative but non-binding. Supporters of religiously based education—which includes Ontario's bishops—have not let the matter die, however, and the United Nations was continuing to exert pressure on Canada as late as July 2000 to end its practice of discriminatory funding. For the time being, however, the Canadian government notes that education is a matter of provincial jurisdiction, and the provincial government seems resolved to abide by its current practice of providing full funding only to Catholic schools as a matter of constitutional right.[78] As if to underscore the fluidity of the situation and the unpredictability of the political mind, in their 2001 spring budget the Ontario Conservatives seem to have completely reversed their tack by including a provision that would provide full funding for all private schools. It has proven to be an explosive suggestion that the Catholic community fears may well revive the public debate over the cherished constitutional protections enjoyed by the Catholic population.

In Newfoundland, however, the constitutional gamesmanship over the privileged funding traditionally accorded religious schools seems to have come to an unhappy but perhaps inevitable conclusion. In that province generations of support for denominational schools run variously by the Roman Catholic, Pentecostal, Seventh-day Adventist, and an integration of Presbyterian, Anglican, United, and Salvation Army churches were swept away at the behest of Roman Catholic Liberal premier Brian Tobin, who petitioned the Roman Catholic prime minister in Ottawa, Jean Chrétien, to amend Newfoundland's constitutional guarantees of provincial support for religious education. Although a delegation from the Canadian Conference of Catholic Bishops was prevented from appearing before the joint Senate-House of Commons committee studying the proposed constitutional amendment, Newfoundland's Catholic bishops did take to the trenches in a losing cause, and the Catholic population did not come to their aid in a 1997 provincial referendum, which sealed the fate of the denominational school in Newfoundland.[79] Despite the high-profile lobbying by the religious bodies involved in the schools issue, merely half the eligible voters took the time to visit a polling booth for the September

5 referendum, and of those who did, approximately 54 percent supported the government's position to alter the constitution. Accordingly, on December 15, 1996, following protracted debate and a number of subsequent resolutions in the federal Senate, the House of Commons voted 171 to forty-one in favour of the constitutional amendment to Term 17 of the conditions under which Newfoundland had joined the Canadian federation in 1949. Years of rancour and pockets of turmoil have not altered either the facts or the precedent.[80]

In Quebec, the historically and constitutionally entrenched Catholic and Protestant school boards also came under attack when the separatist Parti Québécois, led by Premier Lucien Bouchard, moved to amend Section 93 of the Canadian constitution to alter the denominational guarantees concerning religious education afforded to the Roman Catholic and Protestant communities, providing in their place linguistically based structures for the English- and French-speaking components of the Quebec community. In abandoning constitutional guarantees that had been in place for 131 years, Quebec's bishops accepted the government's legislative provision within its 1988 Education Act that denominational schools would be available where the demands of the Catholic population warranted them. On April 15, 1997, by unanimous vote, the federal House of Commons passed the necessary constitutional amendment and the deed was done. As Senator Anne Cools observed during the debate, the federal motion provided for the "extinction of constitutional rights to denominational education" in Quebec.[81]

In the meantime, the rest of Canada looks on and the equal funding rights that the Catholic schools of Ontario achieved in 1984 after decades of diligent lobbying appear already to have become time-dated, especially with the gutting of the powers of local school boards and the centralizing within the minister's office at Queen's Park of all authority for curriculum, finances, and conditions of teacher employment. Westhues's conclusions with respect to the inevitable educational revolution that would move the Catholic school from the public to the private realm in Ontario might well come to pass without the need to post a single government declaration to that effect.

A similar restructuring that threatened the Catholic educational system in Alberta in the mid-1990s provides the template for both a concern and an opportunity in Britain at the turn of the century. It is clearly possible for governments to support in principle what, willy-nilly, they do not support in fact. Indeed, Ontario's Progressive Conservative governments (under Bill Davis in 1984 and Michael Harris in the latter half of the 1990s) have supported Catholic education in an aggressive and politically unpopular fashion. Bill Davis's dramatic reversal of decades of opposition to equal funding of Catholic education from junior kindergarten through second-ary school has often been credited with the defeat of his government in the following year's provincial election, which effectively terminated decades of successful Conservative management, though the fact that in his law office Davis has framed and displayed a Donato *Toronto Sun* political cartoon on the issue would suggest that he has no regrets.[82] For his part, Premier Michael Harris has not only extended the funding initiatives of his Conservative predecessor, but has supported the constitutional rights of Catholic separate schools before the courts, including their rights to discriminatory hiring by giving preference to qualified Catholic teachers.

There have been other dramatic victories. It was a red-letter day for Catholic education, for example, when, on December 18, 1997, Justice Robert Sharpe of the Ontario Court's General Division ruled with respect to Section 136 of the Education Act that the hiring of Catholic teachers was essential to maintaining the distinctive nature of the Catholic school. It is a decision that was appealed to the Supreme Court of Canada by the Ontario Secondary School Teachers' Association, where an October 1999 decision upheld the ruling of the lower court, refusing to hear the appeal.[83] At the same time, in light of Premier Harris's observation that what the province needs is more doers and fewer thinkers, one has cause to worry about the perceived relevance of value-based education in an increasingly pragmatic world. In the long run, issues centre on curricu-lum and the concomitant ability to establish a vital Catholic ethos, while providing professional accountability to a centralized authority that may well be speaking a different language.

The political events of the 1990s were completely unanticipated by Westhues, whose 1976 study of the Catholic educational system in Canada[84] assumed that the difficulty of changing the constitutional guaran-tees enjoyed in various Canadian provinces was one of the few protections provided for a system that was already in deep trouble. Political inertia, he reasoned, would be the best ally for the Catholic school. Indeed, a comparison of the situation outlined province by province in Westhues's 1976 study and the scene at the turn of the century provides a dramatic illustration of the rate of decline and the very real threat to continued viability. One of the elements Westhues included in his definition of the Catholic school centred on significant control exercised by bishops, priests, or religious; not only would one be hard pressed in the year 2000 to find such a situation, but in his *Catholic Schools in a Declining Church* Andrew Greeley argues that the hierarchy should get out of the business of education, noting that for those who fear lay control, Canada provides a living example of how to do it.[85] Furthermore, the creeping secularization that Westhues had noted as being deleterious to the continued existence of the system has accelerated as the individualist and economic ethic of the post-Reagan/post-Thatcher era becomes ever more entrenched.

Westhues's argument that the privatization of religion contains within it a concomitant rejection of publicly supported sectarianism as it is expressed in a separate school system is surely being put to the test in Canada at the turn of the millennium. The aftermath of the constitutional change in Newfoundland suggests that there are limited possibilities for those willing and able to make the financial sacrifices required.[86] In addition, Westhues's suggestion that the success of the Catholic school could be a regional phenomenon springing from the popularity of a local bishop or from influential clergy might well be documented inversely since the scandal at Mount Cashel in Newfoundland and the spate of sexual revelations that have haunted religiously based education throughout Canada within the Roman Catholic, Anglican, United, and Presbyterian denominations, just as the many instances of scandal in Ireland and Australia have undermined clerical authority and respect for the Church in those countries. Ultimately, the system can continue to exist in something like its present form if it can garner the active support of a Canadian citizenry that is increasingly pluralistic in its religious makeup, increasingly secular in its values, and increasingly pragmatic in its educational goals. Catholic educators and Catholic parents might well wonder whether the apathy apparent in the Newfoundland referendum might be a harbinger of things to come as other provinces respond to the growing pressures to re-evaluate their educational structures.

PRE-UNIVERSITY CATHOLIC EDUCATION IN ENGLAND

Although the Catholic school system in Britain is uniquely British, its development is not wholly unlike that of its counterparts in the United States and in Canada, being rooted in interdenominational tension, enjoying steady growth, achieving enviable success, and facing an uncertain future rooted as it is in an increasingly secular society steeped in neoliberal economic values. England's dual system of Church and state schools, originally Anglican and state, dates to 1833, and, as such, predates the appearance of contemporary Catholic education.[87]

The modern Catholic school in England can trace its beginnings to the Elizabethan penal laws and the persistence of the recusant population in finding a way to educate its young within the Catholic tradition, even if that meant sending them to Europe for their schooling. The Jesuits' influential Stonyhurst in Lancashire provides an historical example of just such an institution, born as it was in European soil in Elizabethan times and transplanted home in better days. Those better days began with the Roman Catholic Emancipation of 1828, followed shortly thereafter by the 1847 decision to provide a level of government funding to Catholic schools and by the subsequent founding of the Catholic Poor Schools Committee.

The restoration of the Catholic hierarchy in 1850 provided a form of denominational legitimation that resulted in the growth of Catholic schools. Henry Manning, the cardinal-archbishop of Westminster from 1865–1892, championed this development by proclaiming that the building of schools should take precedence over the building of cathedrals. As a result, Manning reached out to embrace England's working class in a manner wholly unlike the approach adopted by the established Church, the Church of the realm. While the Church of England catered to the aristocracy, Manning was taking up arms for the poor, attacking the Industrial Revolution, and deploying his teaching sisters to establish schools to educate the working classes. This the sisters did with admirable zeal, building an effective system from the pennies donated by the Catholic working class. Eventually, the Education Acts of 1902 and 1944 moved the Catholic school from the educational periphery to the mainstream of society in England and Wales, providing both respectability and financial support, thus spawning a dual system of schools involving Church and county.

The late twentieth-century social developments in both the United States and Canada were also evident in England, however; with the economic integration of the Catholic population, with the rapid development of a pluralistic culture, and with the disappearance of an enemy to be kept at bay, Catholic parents found the sectarian separation of their children less imperative than their forebears had. Then, with the passing of the 1988 Education Act, the British challenge in no small way paralleled that facing Catholics in Ontario. The proposition was for provision of Grant Maintained Schools with centralized control rather than the local autonomy previously available, an offer that came complete with tantalizing financial incentives. There is for Britain a lesson to be learned from the ongoing and constantly debated dilemma for Catholic educators in Ontario subsequent to the full funding provisions of 1984, which has centred on the need to be different, to be different in a way that is identifiably Catholic; without a distinctively Catholic approach to education, one would simply have two separately funded public systems, with all the apparent financial inefficiencies such dualism would seem to include. It is, in effect, the Westhues dilemma.

Additional developments in England at the end of the century, though much feared—the pages of *The Tablet* reflect the angst—throw down the gauntlet: compete professionally and administer locally, with the financial and philosophical support of Westminster as long as standards are maintained. Christopher Storr's *Tablet* article, "Don't let's miss this opportunity," of May 16, 1998 (620–621) spells out the challenge. Storr poses a series of relevant questions, questions that have a familiar ring for Catholics in Ontario: "Will the Church be capable of meeting the challenge of providing denominational, distinctive education of even higher quality than now?" Many skeptics of a traditional bent in Ontario saw the open arms of government as a thinly disguised effort to smother through homogenization; Ontario Catholics, as a result, continue to ask the basic questions about differentiation: ethos, teacher training, lived example, governance, and measurable parental support for the Catholicity of the institution as such.

England's successes, like those in the United States and in Canada, can

be found on the level of academic achievement and service to the underprivileged (although the underprivileged in Canada are more likely to be
personally disadvantaged rather than socially so). And although the
Catholic school does struggle with its traditional impulse to serve the
wealthy—as it still does in Britain, the United States, Canada, and even in
Jamaica—it also has an enviable reputation for working with the poor. It is
a reputation that has been part of Catholic education in Britain from the
restoration of Catholicism to social legitimacy in the nineteenth century, a
reputation it was gaining even as it found ways of serving the wealthy.
While the prime minister and his wife, Tony and Cherie Blair, register
their two sons at the London Oratory School, and as their daughter
claims one of the limited spaces at Sacred Heart in Hammersmith, other
Catholic families parry for limited spots for their children; at the same
time, Catholic parents of financially deprived children collect grocery
stamps and engage in fund-raising activities to provide the "extra" educational tools necessary for schools located in poor areas of the city.

There is a tension in the system, a tension that reflects the reality of
English society. An *Observer* poll, for example, rated four Catholic
secondary schools among the top ten in England in its 1998 survey,
"consistently exceeding the national average" since the inception of the
league table;[88] yet, it is the concern for the marginalized that wins the
more constant accolade and that helps to define the Catholic nature of the
institution. In a Mass of thanksgiving to mark 150 years of Catholic education through the Catholic Poor Schools Committee (today's Catholic
Education Service), Cardinal Basil Hume outlined five principles to
which the Catholic school ought to attend: an introduction to a spiritual
life, the teaching of the basics of the Catholic faith, fidelity to the ethos of
the Catholic community, concern for children with special needs, and the
formation of Catholic teachers as shapers of youth—he does not empha-
size national averages.[89] As for the spiritual effects of the Catholic school,
which Hume notes as the primary objective of the Catholic school, the
benefits seem to be present, but marginal at best, with the most consistent
and most compelling influence on the young being the example provided
by the home environment.[90]

Of course, one might make similar cases for the Catholic school in the
United States or Canada, but one of the unique responses to the challenge

facing a value-based education in England and Wales is the joint school. A form of practical ecumenism, the experiment often takes the form of a Catholic and Anglican collaboration, though that is not the only model. As Terence McLaughlin notes, the jury is still out on the success of the experiment.[91] The co-operative approach to religious education clearly has the potential to foster ecumenical and interfaith understanding even while allowing students the opportunity to reflect on and grow in their own faith. Still, inherent in the joint school is the question of critical mass, the numbers of teachers and students required to ensure that students attain a healthy understanding of their own religious heritage. And there is, of course, the possibility that the questioning of one's faith and the testing of its teachings in light of the faith of others could lead to rejection rather than reaffirmation. For some, where ignorance is bliss, 'tis folly to be wise.

The celebrated test of the efficacy of the joint school is the much-publicized and hotly debated example of St. Philip's in Birmingham, which the Fathers of the Birmingham Oratory moved to close rather than operate what was for them no longer a Catholic institution, given the interdenominational and multireligious makeup of its student body and given that the Roman Catholic component had shrunk to under 30 percent. Yet, by all accounts, St. Philip's provided a model incubator for social understanding, racial tolerance, and interfaith dialogue.[92] According to David McLoughlin, theologian and chaplain at Newman College, University of Coventry:

In the city, St. Philip's was seen as a centre of excellence. It was a Catholic college, self-confessedly in its history, its ethos, its atmosphere. The theology department there could regularly take away fifty young people on retreat once a term and they had 300 youngsters doing theology. There's no equivalent in any of our other colleges around the blessed country with that number of students doing theology. So to think of it as a centre where Christian theology was not being done seriously is nonsense. But its greatest strength was that it was an academic community where there seemed to be negligible racial tension between Muslims, Afro-Caribbeans, and the Irish-English basis of the community, so it was a model for the rest of the city. It also gave young men and women, especially from the Afro-Caribbean community, an access to good quality higher education, which is rare in our city. It was precisely offering the sense of a community in which all cultures, all races and religions are respected, even though what drove the institution and what underpinned that respect was a particular religious vision of the world, Catholic Christianity. Now, it seems to me that it is precisely that quality of Catholicism which is linked to our being a world Church. There is no other Christian community that has that dimension to it in the same way that we do. We're used to working with multiple cultures and cross-cultures across language barriers and so on. Now that universal perspective has to be manifested at the local level, and one of the ways we do that, precisely in the inner cities, is in such schools where increasingly perhaps the Catholic children will be the minority group. But we still need to provide that quality of community life both for the future of our society and, in a way, as a witness to what the Church is.

The question of St. Philip's, as both its governing body and its critics agree, hinges on the definition of the Catholic school as such. For well-known Catholic educators Michael Walsh and Gerry Hughes, St. Philip's represents the essence of what the Catholic school should be: a public witness based on Gospel values, a leavening influence, a sign of the Church's commitment to human rights and a respect for other faiths. For them, number crunching and recourse to law don't quite cut it.[93]

There are some dozen or more examples of the joint school in England and Northern Ireland. In an impressive, instructive, and well-documented study of Britain's Roman Catholic and Anglican schools, past and present, Priscilla Chadwick selects two for detailed analysis: St. Bede's joint Anglican/Roman Catholic school, Redhill, Surrey, and Lagan College, Belfast. Chadwick's title, *Schools of Reconciliation: Issues in Joint Roman Catholic-Anglican Education*, makes the point: ecumenical co-operation is not only possible, it is a socially responsible as well as a religiously responsible route to follow. One of the lessons of the late twentieth century, she argues, is that unity does not necessitate uniformity; indeed, diversity is an enrichment within the Christian tradition, not an enfeeblement. The Anglican school, therefore, with its self-image as the official educational organ of the state and the Roman Catholic school with its traditionally sanctioned role as defender of the true faith have much to learn from each other. Together they are stronger, and together they can help not only to reconcile past differences but to build a better, more Christian society. The test, for Chadwick, is in the tasting, and *Schools of Reconciliation* provides an enticing fare.

If future directions in Catholic education look promising, and in many ways they surely do, the Achilles heel is in the question of critical mass: How many teachers committed to their faith are necessary to assure the denominational integrity of the institution? As Britain approached the end of the century, the challenge was clear. One estimate noted by Chadwick suggested that one-third of the secondary school teachers in the Catholic classroom were non-Catholic and that the number of Catholic teachers was decreasing dramatically.[94] Statistics provided by Terence H. McLaughlin, Joseph O'Keefe, s.j., and Bernadette O'Keeffe with respect to the United States, England, and Wales are even more troubling. Their research shows, for example, that the percentages of non-Catholic teachers within the publicly funded Catholic schools of England and Wales has escalated, over roughly twenty years, from 9.8 percent to 12.1 percent in the primary schools, and that nearly half (41.4 per cent) of secondary school teachers are non-Catholics.[95] Within the independent Catholic schools, some 43.5 percent of the teaching component was non-Catholic in 1994. Nor is the definition of critical mass within the student body easily defined: at St. Philip's the numbers had declined to the point where the governing body felt the school was no longer Catholic. In the case of St. Augustine of Canterbury, a joint Roman Catholic-Anglican school, necessity became a peculiarly inverted mother of invention when the local governing body decided that it had become possible to attract sufficient Catholic students to obviate the need for a joint school and moved to dissociate itself from the Anglican association, thus becoming a homogeneously Catholic school. The Catholic Church in England obviously needs to come to grips with the contrary messages inherent in the conciliar call to ecumenism and the Code of Canon Law's concern for the exclusively Catholic school as such.[96]

This, in a sense, begs the question. When explaining the decision to disestablish St. Augustine of Canterbury from a joint to a singularly Roman Catholic school, Father Mark Stock, the executive director of the arch-

diocesan schools commission for Birmingham, insisted in *The Tablet* that
the resolution had nothing to do with ecumenism; rather, it had to do with
the legal necessity of using diocesan money to provide "Catholic education
where possible." Vincent Nichols, the archbishop of Birmingham,
endorses Stock's assessment and expands on it: "The preference must be
for the establishment of a school in which the full scope of the Catholic
vision of human growth and education, the full life of the sacrament of the
Church and the desire by all in the school to contribute to the handing on
of faith, can find expression."[97] Yet, as Priscilla Chadwick assessed the
situation, St. Augustine's was using an approved Roman Catholic religious
education curriculum, was keeping the official English holy days of obligation, supporting Catholic charities, and sustaining a vibrant Catholic chaplaincy: the joint Anglican-Roman Catholic structure would seem to have
been a value-added arrangement.[98] The question as to what constitutes
Catholic education is obviously the knot crying to be untangled. How
many Catholic teachers? How many Catholic students? How do you
define a Catholic teacher or a Catholic student? Do liturgies define
Catholicism? Does the presence of an ordained chaplain? Is catechetical
instruction essential, and is it preferable to the more objective, more inclusive provision of religious education? And can these elements be provided
better in a homogeneously Roman Catholic context? Does the Anglican-
Roman Catholic dialogue of the joint school dilute or nullify the Catholic
nature of the school? Is ecumenical or interfaith exploration in an educational context in harmony with or antagonistic toward the contemporary
Roman Catholic agenda? Does the inculcating of traditional Catholic
teaching take precedence over the formation of a more just society?

These are difficult questions, especially since, as Chadwick demonstrates, parental motives for pursuing Catholic education may differ
wholly from episcopal intentions. Many parents, including many who are
not Christian, choose Catholic schools because they see them as a major
bulwark against the essentially liberal humanistic ethos of their secular
counterpart; others do so because they value the human face of the institution, or the perception of discipline, or the academic excellence, or the
prestige that accompanies so many of the Catholic institutions, or simply
as a matter of geographic convenience. In many cases, as Chadwick notes,
there is a perception that the catechetical approach is too religious, too

rigid, and not a few students would prefer a more secular, more intellectually open atmosphere.[99]

In fact, many of the parents who send their children to Catholic schools are not themselves committed Catholics; as a result, they are looking for something in the school that is very different from the view expressed either by Canon Law or the local bishop. That there is no consensus in Britain about just what the characteristics are that distinguish a school as Catholic[100] is hardly surprising—consider the varied and sometimes intemperate reactions to Joseph Bernardin's proposed Common Ground project designed to define the Catholic touchstones shared by U.S. Catholics of the religious left, right, and centre. The joint school is, however, a distinctively British experiment that invites local forms of organization as a means of responding to the racial, social, economic, and religious context in which the school is located. It is a school born of local circumstances rather than springing from the universal abstractions that tend to inform the documents spawned by Vatican dicasteries. It is, in a sense, the flip side of the Ontario conundrum with respect to mission and apparent lack of differentiation; in addition, the joint school begins to address the ubiquitous contemporary question of Catholic identity without inviting the oft-repeated suspicion of the establishing of Catholic ghettos or reintroducing the triumphalistic and long-held preconciliar declaration that outside the Catholic Church there can be no salvation: *Extra ecclesiam nulla salus.*

PRE-UNIVERSITY CATHOLIC EDUCATION IN AUSTRALIA

As is the case in the United States, Canada, and England, the history of the Catholic school in Australia is also born of religious turmoil, springing as it does from Catholic efforts to reinforce the faith of the fatherland—Ireland—reacting to the imposition of the stamp of the established Church of England, the Church of the country whose policies of deportation populated the fledgling colony and whose penal laws suppressed the faith of the disproportionate number of Irish deportees.[101] Here, too, the school system was an early success. So, when J.J. Mol, a sociologist and a non-Catholic, examined the Australian Catholic school in its postconciliar heyday, he ought not to have been surprised to find the lasting impact the school has continued to have in the development of a committed denominational membership. Mol's concomitant discovery of practising Catholics tolerant of other religious traditions, however, is a surprising one for a study conducted in the late 1960s and born in the heat of interdenominational strife.[102]

Since their arrival in September 1791, the Irish Catholics constituted the lower class of Australian society. Destined to live in poverty as they had in their home country, and as had also been the case in Ireland, they shared a sense of disaffection with their English overlords. Manning Clark captures the perception when he refers to the squalor of their condition and the superstition, "the stupor and ignorance" instilled in them by their priests, their conviction that "although the Protestant boys had gained the day, they would not gain the night,"[103] that though power and wealth were in the hands of the Protestant English, it would be the Catholic and Irish who would be rewarded at the end of the day. Though the fault lines were more strikingly religious in Australia than they had been in Canada, Canada's two solitudes, English and French, were replicated in the English and the Irish in Australia, the God-given Anglican heirs to liberty and prosperity and the priest-ridden Gael whom divine will had relegated to a life of poverty. Although Edmund Campion does document notable examples of Catholic/Anglican co-operation, he also provides ample evidence that the Catholic/non-Catholic cultural divide formed the basis of an inherent antagonism whose competing interests, Manning Clark argues, would ultimately help to shape the Australian educational system as being free, secular, and public, and which would press the Irish to support Australian federation as one means of reducing the influence of the English. A symptom of the situation: the influential (and Irish-born) cardinal-archbishop of Sydney, Patrick Francis Moran, for example, maintained that May 24 should celebrate neither Queen nor Empire but Australia.[104]

The Church and Schools Corporation of 1825 placed the responsibilities for education in the hands of the established Church and the English élite, a decision that put them at odds with the Irish Catholic population as well as with the Methodist and Presbyterian minorities. Later nineteenth-century efforts by governors Richard Bourke and George Gipps to provide educational opportunity for the Anglicans, Catholics, and Presbyterians without denominational discrimination served the colonies no better, since religious suspicion ran too deeply in New South Wales and Van Diemen's Land for ecumenical co-operation to take root; as a result, by mid-century a centrally funded national educational system had evolved that included Anglican, Catholic, and secular components.

In south Australia, on the other hand, denominational influence and its attendant interreligious squabbling were not nearly so problematic, and, as a result, by 1851 education was formally established as an essentially secular undertaking within a non-denominationally Christian context. Ultimately, governments were confronted with Roman Catholic insistence on their uniquely Catholic educational context, with Anglican bickering between High and Low Church adherents, and with Presbyterian, Baptist, Methodist, Congregationalist, and Independents rejecting any appeasement to the Roman Catholics or Anglicans, favouring instead state support for a secular system of education. As a result, by 1872 state governments in Australia began to pass legislation from which sprang its long-standing philosophy of education as being free, secular, and public. It was not a palatable direction to the Irish Catholic population who were convinced by the entrenched Catholicism of the day and the authoritarian pronouncements of the ecclesiastical hierarchy that the public school was an impediment to proper human development. Campion, for example, quotes Brother H.B. O'Hagan's speech at the dedication of a Christian Brothers' school in Balmain in 1887 in which O'Hagan reflects the self-confident educational philosophy of the day: "Our main objective shall ever be to teach our pupils to value above all things their eternal salvation, and to secure this by faithfully and steadfastly adhering to the faith of their fathers."[105] Australia's Catholics, therefore, pursued their own system of education separate from Protestant and separate from state, a system that for the most part served the working-class Irish Catholic, a system financed by the generosity of the Catholic population and the freely donated teaching services of numerous congregations of sisters, brothers, and priests, many of whom were Irish. (By 1910 there were in excess of 5,000 teaching sisters in Australia's classrooms, some of whose stories Edmund Campion sketches in his *Great Australian Catholics*.[106])

Although the dedication of this phalanx of religious instructors was exemplary and the Catholic population was determined that the building of the local school should take precedence over the erection of places of worship, the actual educational enterprise itself often left much to be desired. Catechetical education was essentially a rote exercise. Articles were to be learned, not explored. "To be Catholic meant to be obedient to the law. Catholicism was a religion of law."[107] It was a noble project, even if it was rooted in an aggressive turn-of-the-nineteenth-century triumphalism. Campion quotes one enthusiastic Redemptorist haranguing an ecumenical congregation in 1894 about the errors of other faiths and the refusal of absolution that would accompany the registration of their children in state schools, a penalty that had been decreed by a plenary council convened in 1885 by Cardinal Patrick Francis Moran, who was well known for his disdain of Protestants, an attitude eclipsed perhaps only by the archbishop of Melbourne, Daniel Mannix.[108]

Pope John XXIII's opening of the windows within the Vatican with the beginning of Vatican II in 1962 captured the tenor of the times and echoed the developing sense of openness in society in general, certainly in Australian society. The triumphalist Church of the past was now engaged with the world and was reaching out to other faiths. As a result, when faced with the increased costs associated with operating a modern school, the Catholic population was becoming both more multicultural in its composition and more ecumenical in its outlook. Catholics were now willing to reach out to the state for the infusion of financial support that would be its life's blood. If state funding was essential to the survival of the Catholic educational system, a promise of financial aid to Catholic schools was also a means to carry the Liberal Party of R.G. Menzies—and his non-Catholic confreres—to victory in the 1963 elections, a victory that established the basis for the Commonwealth Schools Commission of 1974 and the resolution of the Catholic Question. By 1974, however, the percentage of Catholic children in Catholic schools was in a virtual free fall and stood at only 17.4 percent in 1972. At the same time, the financial backbone of the system—the donated services of sisters, brothers, and priests—had collapsed from 95 percent of the teaching body in 1950 to 10 percent in 1984.[109] Not only is the faith of the fathers being revisioned, but so is the system of education that had been erected to secure its continuation.

Australia, like the rest of the post-Christian West, is in the grip of a secular culture in which priesthood and sisterhood are no longer valued— the ranks of Australia's priests and nuns are in dramatic decline. There is no small irony in the fact that at a time when Catholic education is arguably at its apex; when numerous books and articles are being published to analyze its history, nature, and contribution;[110] when it is needed most as an alternative voice within an acquisitive, narcissistic, and secular society; when it has self-consciously striven to embrace the best of a long historical tradition, and to realize the promise of its more recent conciliar tradition that it is most in jeopardy. Its old antagonists are now as time-worn as its own triumphalistic past; contemporary Catholicism has new challenges to face and different means with which to face them. The Catholic school provides an alternative vision, a counter-witness, and a better way for those who would have ears to hear. Joseph Bernardin observed that the Catholic school is "the fault line of the church's dialogue with the world"; and Emmett Carter has characterized it as "one of the last remaining supporters of Christian teaching and moral values in the world."[111] As with the future of the Church itself—as in a sense it always has—the future of Catholic education as a real alternative to the secular humanist model depends wholly on the will of those who are convinced that its future is worth the sacrifice.

History teaches us that every era presents its own demands and provides its own solutions. Today's challenges and today's Church are dramatically different from those with which our forebears had to contend during the twentieth century. Whatever its future and whatever its form, Catholic education, like the Catholic Church itself, will continue to address the needs of the times, and of one thing we can be certain: neither the Church nor its educational apostolate will be dominated by the ecclesiastical inner circle, which has governed both with the awesome authority of an exclusive educated elite since the high Middle Ages. Power and authority are no longer the prerogative of the few, nor are the knowledge, professional expertise, and commitment so vital to both the Church and the educational apostolate in the twenty-first century. The days of simple memorization, unquestioning assimilation, and reflex repetition are long gone; gone too are the simple obedience and docile Catholics encouraged by the pedagogy of an earlier time. Twenty-first-century problems really do demand twenty-first-century solutions. And problems there continue to be. As Priscilla Chadwick's *Shifting Alliances* reminds us with respect to the English dual system of educational funding and as do the various legal challenges that highlighted Canadian Catholic education in the 1990s, the enemies of the Church school are at the gates—they are determined and organized. The future of the educational apostolate lies squarely in the hands of the Catholic community; it is theirs to sustain and theirs to squander.

CATHOLIC COLLEGES AND UNIVERSITIES: TENSIONS WITH THE VATICAN

For the past century and a half, the hierarchy of the Roman Catholic Church has viewed the educational system as a means of sheltering the faithful from a hostile environment as well as a vehicle for assuring the continuation of the faith of the fathers. Indeed, the Vatican document written in preparation for the 1990 Synod of Bishops to be held at the Vatican noted that from its earliest days the Church defended her right to establish her own schools since these schools "must always serve as a source of vocations, as surroundings for formation and as a place of preparation for the work of the apostolate."[112] Until the close of the twentieth century, they had been singularly successful in achieving those objectives. The postsecondary apostolate has, however, been a very different matter, and it is to the postsecondary level of Catholic education that the Church must look for the heart of the leadership in the Church now struggling to be born, for the university produces the professional and intellectual classes, which in turn will provide most of the teachers, writers, parish assistants, parish administrators, lectors, and committee members who will be instrumental in shaping and invigorating the Church of the future as well as transmitting the essence of the Church of the past. Indeed, the Vatican's Apostolic Constitution on Catholic Universities, *Ex corde ecclesiae*, reinforces this very point when it elaborates on the university's "Service to Church and Society."[113]

Still, the fact of the matter is that few Catholic bishops have experienced a true university education, especially beyond the baccalaureate degree, having been trained in the academic cocoon of the seminary; those who have pursued a postseminary education have almost always done so within the sheltered and academically rarified confines of the Roman university where traditional pedagogical approaches still prevail: write, assimilate, regurgitate. The Canadian bishops suggest that they understand the dynamic quite well when, in an unpublished preparatory document for the 1990 Synod of Bishops called to deal with the Formation of Priests in the Circumstances of the Present Day, the Canadian bishops observed of the Vatican's approach to seminary training: "The document is frozen in a philosophy of education that should be challenged: on the one hand, professors who are omniscient, and on the other hand, candidates who are ignorant. In reality, adult formation usually takes place in an atmosphere of collaboration, which contemporary adult education approaches are defining more and more clearly." Rome's is the traditional catechetical approach, the pill of knowledge, as Cardinal Emmett Carter has characterized it.[114]

Although attitudes certainly vary from national council to national council, as well as from bishop to bishop, there is a widespread conviction that many appointees within the ecclesiastical hierarchy, as a result, are suspicious of the academy where open debate and the need not merely to state a position but also to defend it are the hallmarks of intellectual development. Hence, George Bernard Shaw's often-quoted observation that the term "Catholic university" is a contradiction in terms, and hence the lingering suspicion prevalent on many campuses that what Catholic universities are engaged in is a form of catechesis—traditional Catholic indoctrination—and not university education at all. Yet the recognized interrelationship between faith and reason is almost as ancient as the Church itself. Indeed, in a recent address to the Jubilee of Men and Women of Learning, John Paul II observed that "Faith is not afraid of reason. They are like two wings on which the human spirit rises to the contemplation of truth. . . ."[115] Although many—maybe even most—bishops do acknowledge that there is, and there needs to be, a healthy tension between the Catholic university and the Catholic hierarchy, there is often a huge gap between the concept and its actualization. When push comes to shove, the hierarchy tends to be very clear about where it wants ultimate authority to be placed.

Indeed, during the last quarter of the twentieth century, the attitudes of retrenchment that were so pronounced within the Vatican did much to reinforce the justified skepticism concerning the role of the Catholic university. The list of professors, thinkers, and writers who have fallen prey to Rome's scrutiny under the watchful leadership provided by Pope John Paul II and his prefect for the Church's teaching office, the Sacred Congregation for the Doctrine of the Faith, Cardinal Joseph Ratzinger, has been unequalled since the intellectual witch hunts initiated by St. Pius x in his modernist crusades during the early years of the twentieth century. Some names come readily to mind: Charles Curran of the United States,[116] Edward Schillebeeckx of Belgium, Leonardo Boff of Brazil, and Hans Küng of Germany. The list also includes, among others: Tissa Balasuriya of Sri Lanka; Anthony de Mello of India; Paul Collins of Australia; Lavinia Byrne of England; André Guindon of Canada; Matthew Fox, Barbara Fiand, Roger Haight, Carmel McEnroy, Robert Nugent, and Jeannine Gramick of the United States; Gustavo Gutiérrez of Peru; Luigi Lombardi Vallauri at the Catholic University of the Sacred Heart at Milan; Belgian Jesuit Jacques Dupuis at the Gregorian University in Rome; Luigi Marinelli, a retired Vatican official; Bernard Häring of England; and Ivone Gebara of Brazil. The Vatican has even appointed an Italian bishop to oversee the publications of the Society of St. Paul. Most of the above are (or were) either priests or sisters.

Indeed, many well-educated priests have assured us that in today's climate it is generally acknowledged that only the foolhardy would venture into Catholicism's ethical and moral minefields where intellectual exploration is overtly discouraged and where the traditional and dichotomized roles of the *Ecclesia docens* and *Ecclesia discens*—the teaching and learning Church—which were discredited as such at the Second Vatican Council are now the order of the day. One is reminded of Morley Callaghan's novel *Such Is My Beloved* in which Father Dowling reacts to a university student's confession by quizzing: "Are you sure you're not getting your notions from authors of books? Are you sure your reading doesn't tend to destroy your faith?"[117] There is here a suspicion of the written word, which prompted Paul IV to introduce the Index of Forbidden Books in 1557, a catalogue of proscribed texts whose reading carried with it the threat of excommunication and whose 409-year history ended only in 1966 when Paul VI concluded that the Index was incompatible with the commitment to individual intellectual responsibility, which was an overarching tenet of Vatican II. Paradoxically, a peculiarly anti-intellectual strain runs deep within the institution that introduced the university to Western culture. It is the kind of intellectual suspicion that not so long ago prompted the administration of St. Peter's Seminary in London, Ontario, to keep the writings of modern philosophers under lock and key.

Father Jim Wahl, a Resurrectionist priest and scholar who is a professor of law and Church history at St. Jerome's University in Waterloo, Ontario, laments that in today's climate many priests are afraid to speak their minds openly, not just in the classroom but even in the pulpit. For his part, the late Richard McCormick, Jesuit and one-time professor emeritus at Notre Dame University, sees a possible shift in emphasis from Paul VI's concept of persuasion to a current one of coercion. McCormick's sentiment echoes Wahl's, though McCormick takes the point one step further, arguing that not only is coercion the enemy of openness, but it undermines the papal Magisterium: "If bishops are not speaking their true sentiments, then clearly the pope is not able to draw on the wisdom and reflection of the bishops in the exercise of his ordinary magisterium. When this happens, the presumption of truth in papal teaching is weakened because such a presumption assumes that the ordinary sources of human understanding have been consulted."[118] In addition, McCormick reasons, the "frosty" atmosphere, as Bernard Häring had characterized it, will inevitably muzzle the theologians, especially on sensitive issues, and one more source of insight is discarded.

Rosemary Radford Ruether agrees with this analysis, arguing that the climate of fear Rome is creating is intended not simply to silence those under direct scrutiny, but to silence all creative thinkers, "to create an atmosphere of fear where none dares lift his or her head in criticism of authority."[119] With this in mind, Ruether develops a sixfold series of "Survival rules for those under scrutiny by the inquisition" and concludes her battle plan with the summary exhortation, "Don't let the bastards get you down." Then, as an augmentation of what was now widely perceived to be an inquisitorial atmosphere, on February 25,

1989, the Congregation for the Doctrine of the Faith published a proposed Profession of Faith in *L'Osservatore Romano*, an oath of fidelity intended to be taken by various ecclesiastics holding offices specified in Canon 833, including rectors of Catholic universities and teachers of disciplines dealing with faith or morals. The firestorm that ensued centred mostly on the clause: "With firm faith I believe as well everything (*ea omnia*) contained in God's word, written or handed down in tradition and proposed by the church—whether in solemn judgement or in the ordinary and universal magisterium—as divinely revealed and calling for faith (*tamquam divinitus revelata credenda*)."[120] A pretty inclusive prescription, this. The Vatican intention is clear and the pressure for uncritical conformity unrelenting. One is reminded of Blessed Pius IX's bland contention that God "has constituted the Church the guardian and the teacher of the whole of the truth concerning religion and moral conduct"[121] and, at the same time, one has to wonder both who the Congregation for the Propagation of the Faith includes in its definition of "Church" and, given its narrow approach to the intellectual life, how that Church as *Ecclesia semper reformanda* is to engage in the process of constant reformation envisioned by Vatican II.

Then, apparently growing uncharacteristically sensitive to the international groundswell of criticism triggered by its inquisitorial and anti-intellectual predilections, the Vatican Congregation for the Doctrine of the Faith proclaimed a new set of procedures to be followed in the examination of theologians found to be potentially in error. Promulgated on August 29, 1997 and published in the September 11, 1997 issue of *Origins*, the new procedures were intended to be more open and more in keeping with the usual dictates of natural justice: the possibility that the accused could be accompanied by an advocate or an adviser, with provision for face-to-face meetings with members of the Vatican Congregation. Commenting on the "loss of nerve" that is characteristic of the modern scene, theologian Enda McDonagh agrees that there are "some improvements" in the new procedures, but he is quick to add that "one still has serious difficulties."[122]

Jesuit theologian Jon Sobrino, nonetheless, tries to tackle the role of theology within the university setting, noting that it is the role of the university to examine theological truths and not to defend theological orthodoxy. As a result of its rigorous scientific examination, the university has the potential to explain and to defend orthodoxy, but that is not its intellectual starting point. For Sobrino, "the university offers the possibility of a scientific theology more open to truth and less subject to vested interests: it offers the possibility of 'declericalizing' theology."[123]

Henri Goudreault, the late bishop of Labrador City-Shefferville, quotes Christ's exhortation that "The truth will set you free," noting that it is sometimes said that theologians scandalize people who lack their academic sophistication. "But very often the truth is bothering. It is painful to adjust to the truth. Should we have stayed with the 19th-century exegesis in scripture in order to avoid shocking or scandalizing people? Many people felt ill at ease, at first, and expressed their concern, but finally they were liberated and capable of progressing because of the new exegetical approaches and principles."[124]

The liberating character of truth, however, seems to have been far from the minds of Joseph Ratzinger, prefect for the Sacred Congregation for the Doctrine of the Faith; Angelo Amato, vice-rector of the Salesian University in Rome; and Fernando Ocáriz, vicar general of Opus Dei, as they crafted *Dominus Iesus*, Rome's statement on "the unicity of the church" and the Church's role in God's plan as forming "an indispensable relationship with the salvation of every human being."[125] By defining Catholicism as the only true road to salvation—salvation is available to non-Catholics by virtue of a special grace, which has "a mysterious relationship to the church"—and by designating other religions as "gravely deficient," the authors of *Dominus Iesus* have set out to stem theological explorations in ecumenical or interfaith dialogue. In the authors' minds, such explorations are inimical to the inherently unique role reserved for the Roman Catholic in the salvation of humankind. Rome has drawn one more line in the sands. It is a line that calls for "firm belief," a line necessitated by the "relativistic mentality" and the "mentality of indifferentism" characteristic of modern society, a line expressly intended to establish parameters for "theological reflection"—a reflection that *Dominus Iesus* directs at "bishops, theologians, and all the Catholic faithful" but which, in his "Letter to Bishops' Conferences," Ratzinger expands more generically to include "Catholic universities" as well.[126] Turn-of-the-century triumphalism. There is no hint here of a pilgrim Church in a humble search for perfection, no hint of an imperfect Church in a state of constant reformation. *Dominus Iesus* is cast in the uncompromising preconciliar tone of the *Ecclesia docens*.

Luke Dempsey, an Irish-born academic and Dominican priest, has assumed a number of teaching and administrative assignments, including one in the shadow of the Vatican at the Dominican Order's St. Thomas Aquinas University. While Dempsey has enjoyed his Roman assignments and has felt no sense of professional censorship, his defence of Rome is at the same time an implicit acknowledgement of a lack of both intellectual excitement and of an encouragement for innovation. For Dempsey, teaching in Rome was no problem: "It's true that they don't like ambiguous formulations, but one never feels haunted, so to speak. You adjust. You adapt to the situation. I wasn't conscious of any kind of tension in that regard. My own formation after all was in the Thomistic school. You know that Virtue Theology has become popular again, as it happens. It was popular at the time I was a student and although it might be formulated quite differently, and although the philosophers have made a great contribution, but for all that it is the same stuff. So it is in a sense fairly familiar territory."

Jesuit Steve Privett was the president-designate of the University of San Francisco when he offered his observations on several of the points of view noted above:

My generic response is that people who are most passionate about the Catholic tradition many times understand it least. They don't know the richness of the tradition; they don't know the breadth of the tradition. They're talking nineteenth-century Vatican I formulations and they're defending formulations. That's their idea of tradition. I think that would be the end of Catholic education. I think it has to stay open. It has to stay engaged in a significant way with the other, however one defines that.

I think that it is really crucial to say what you think if you want other people to tell you what they think. It's about engaging people with integrity. We have to get comfortable with tension and if you try to collapse the tension between the teaching Church and the thinking Church—not that those are two inseparable entities—but I would characterize the university as the place where the Church thinks out loud.

That's how Theodore Hesburgh talks about it. That's a whole different agenda from the one I'll have if I'm an administrative person in the Church: then my concern is order; or if I'm a prophetic person in the church: then my concern is challenge. Those points on the tradition I think are always going to be in tension and to try to collapse the tension does a disservice to the other two points on the circle. So I would expect that the bishop is not going to be real happy with what's going on in terms of gay-lesbian couples and their relationships. We're going to disagree and it's going to take a couple of hundred years probably for that tension to get resolved into some kind of practice or formulation that everybody agrees is reasonable and really captures what we're about. It took 300 years to figure out who Jesus was. I don't think it's any great surprise that it's going to take us a long time, and in the meantime it's a little difficult to be there as this stuff develops, but I think we're going to have to get comfortable with that. My hope is that the bishops will come to see that too, that we don't serve the Church well by functioning as the defender of whatever formulation gets articulated by those persons who have responsibility for keeping order in the institution. That's not our responsibility.

THE INITIAL STRUGGLE TO DEFINE THE CATHOLIC UNIVERSITY

There have, in fact, been over three decades of ongoing international dialogue to try to determine exactly what a bishop's legitimate responsibility is on the Catholic postsecondary campuses within his diocese. The concept of a statement on the Catholic University in the Modern World was agreed upon at the 1965 meeting of the International Federation of Catholic Universities (IFCU) in Tokyo, after which formal discussions began at Kinshasa in 1968, continued in Rome in April 1969, and became part of and integral to subsequent deliberations of IFCU, which began in 1971 with four regional conferences, one in Kyoto, Japan, a second at Wisconsin's Land O' Lakes in the United States, another at Grottaferrata, Italy, and a fourth in Caracas, Venezuela.

Subsequent to those four sessions, an additional meeting was organized at Grottaferrata to synthesize the results from the four separate conferences and hence to produce the Grottaferrata document, an IFCU text that was submitted to the Sacred Congregation for Catholic Education and to all Catholic universities worldwide in preparation for a meeting to be held in November 1972. That meeting took place within the Synod hall in the Vatican from November 20–29 with representatives present from twenty-three countries during which they produced a joint statement on the Catholic University in the Modern World. Although the document as such did not form the official policy of either the Sacred Congregation for Catholic Education or for IFCU, it is a groundbreaking twenty-eight-page statement outlining the nature of the Catholic university, its objectives, governance, and relationships with external bodies.

The document addresses the need for the university community to demonstrate the inherent harmony between faith and science, "to contribute to the solution of the pressing problems of the day," to provide a coherent set of values for those engaged in the contemporary quest for meaning, to promote ecumenism, and to build an intellectual community centred on a "respect for the intellectual life, for scholarly research, and also for religious values." While recognizing the teaching authority of the Church with respect to matters of doctrine and accepting the need for vigilant bishops to bring to the attention of an offending party any danger to the "orthodoxy of the people under their pastoral care," the paper makes it clear that such recognition "does not of itself imply the right of the Hierarchy to intervene in university government or academic admin-istration." That is, administration of the university is an internal matter. Any attempt at direct external interference with internal administrative issues that would compromise the professional autonomy of the institu-tion would be simply unacceptable. The document reasons that "A Catholic university today must be a university in the full sense of the word, with a strong commitment to and concern for academic excellence. To perform its teaching and research functions effectively a Catholic university must have true autonomy and academic freedom. . . . This freedom is limited by no other factor than the truth which it pursues."

VATICAN INTERVENTION IN THE CATHOLIC UNIVERSITY DEBATE

Despite the fact that the Grottaferrata document was the product of joint deliberations, and that IFCU itself grew out of the expressed wish of Pius

XII and the Sacred Congregation for Catholic Education in 1949, the pronouncement was not embraced as an official agreement, and for its part the Vatican was intent on developing a set of documents that would resolve any lingering ambiguities by clarifying the nature and responsibilities of the Catholic postsecondary institution as Roman Catholic. To that end, John Paul II promulgated *Sapientia christiana* (*Apostolic Constitution on Ecclesiastical Universities and Faculties*) on April 15, 1979. *Sapientia christiana* was addressed specifically to ecclesiastical faculties and universities:

> ... which is to say those [Catholic postsecondary institutions] concerned particularly with Christian revelation and questions connected therewith and which are therefore more closely connected with her mission of evangelization.
>
> In the first place, the church has entrusted to these faculties the task of preparing with special care students for the priestly ministry, for teaching the sacred sciences and for the more arduous tasks of the apostolate.

Indeed, there are various institutions internationally that were erected by and that grant degrees in the name of the Holy See; for these institutions, Rome wished to "set down by law" those "Things which are necessary and which are foreseen as being stable." Given the ecclesiastical nature of these institutions and the immediate practical relationship of the mission of the specific type of university in question with the institution of the Church, *Sapientia christiana* was received in relative tranquility. But Rome was not done. *Sapientia christiana* asserts that "All teachers of every rank must be marked by an upright life, integrity of doctrine, and devotion to duty . . .", a provision that might well seem appropriate in a seminary or in a pontifical institution, but to translate that prescription into a university setting within a civil structure is quite another matter altogether. Yet this was the course which the Vatican set for itself subsequent to the promulgation of the Apostolic Constitution on Ecclesiastical Universities and Faculties, *Sapientia christiana*.

The process by which Rome was about to proceed was an apparently consultative one, but in preparation for these discussions the Vatican had added a few arrows to its quiver by issuing a revised version of Canon Law in 1983 that contained some eight items (807–814) dealing with the Catholic university. The most contentious are located in Canon 812, which demands a mandate from the "competent ecclesiastical authority" for any theologian teaching theology within a Catholic university, and Canon 810, which was a clear application to the non-ecclesiastical setting of a norm prescribed for those institutions falling directly under Vatican overview; namely, "In Catholic universities it is the duty of the competent statutory authority to ensure that there be appointed teachers who are not only qualified in scientific and pedagogical expertise, but are also outstanding in their integrity of doctrine and uprightness of life. If these requirements are found to be lacking, it is also that authority's duty to see to it that these teachers are removed from office, in accordance with the procedure determined in the statutes." Quite a change, considering that the 1917 Code was completely silent on the matter of Catholic colleges and universities, legislating only with respect to schools and seminaries. It is worth noting, as a result, that the rather general directive of the revised Canon Law with respect to those teaching in a Catholic school is limited only to teachers of religion and is, therefore, much more restrictive than it is in its subsequent reapplication to faculty members under the employ of a Catholic college or university. Canons 804.2 and 805 direct specifically that "The local Ordinary is to be careful that those who are appointed as teachers of religion in schools, even non-catholic ones, are outstanding in true doctrine, in the witness of their Christian life, and in their teaching ability . . . and if religious or moral considerations require it, [he has] the right to remove them or to demand that they be removed."

The first draft of the Roman directive on Catholic universities appeared in 1983, roughly coincident with the publication of the revised Code, and a second draft (the "Schema") was distributed to all presidents of Catholic universities worldwide in 1985. After intensive debate on the national level resulting in some 650 replies forwarded to the Congregation for Catholic Education, the Vatican issued a second draft document and invited representatives to attend a meeting in Rome scheduled for April 1989. Yet another draft appeared in advance of a final session in Rome to be attended by a small delegation to craft the final document. Nonetheless, both Canons 810 and 812 appear in the footnotes of Rome's ultimate declaration, so that when the Apostolic Constitution on Catholic Universities, *Ex corde ecclesiae*, was promulgated on August 15, 1990, the offending Canons 810 and 812 became the fuel for a firestorm that has yet to subside.[127]

That the need for a mandate should become a cause of concern within the Vatican is not surprising, especially given the official judgment of the Sacred Congregation for Catholic Education that the Grottaferrata document "does not give to the responsibility of the Professor and the Research Scholar in the field of theology an attention that is proportionate to the developments that the document gives to freedom of research and of teaching. This is why the Sacred Congregation, while fully cognizant of the value of many things treated in the text about the relations between the University and the Hierarchy of the Church, still judges it necessary to propose an amended text for certain paragraphs."[128] The official Vatican Observations on Grottaferrata reflect extensively on the role of the theologian and are particularly sensitive to the question of external interference, seeing it as a matter of last resort when legitimate "self-governance of the university community . . . is not effective." Even then, the intervention has to do only with theological matters, calls for the providing of information, and excludes direct or indirect intervention in the university's affairs. The application of Canon 812, which appears in footnote 49 of *Ex corde ecclesiae*, therefore, provides for an intrusion that goes well beyond what was envisioned even by the Vatican in the historical development both of the Apostolic Constitution on Catholic Universities and in the logical progression of Canon Law as it moved from discussing schools to its provision for the Catholic university.

Ex corde ecclesiae consists of two segments, a philosophical discussion of Identity and Mission followed by an outlining of General Norms, prescriptions for practical application on the local scene. The analysis of Identity and Mission is thoughtful, sensitive, and expansive—it is the fruitful product of a collaborative undertaking grounded in the insights of Vatican II with respect to human dignity, individual freedom, and personal responsibility. While recognizing the academic freedom appropriate to scholars in accord with the principles and methods appropriate to their particular area of expertise "within the confines of the truth and the common good,"[129] *Ex corde ecclesiae* adds that "If need be, a Catholic

University must have the courage to speak uncomfortable truths which do not please public opinion, but which are necessary to safeguard the authentic good of society." One might wish, of course, that the same critical principles might apply to the speaking of uncomfortable truths when they relate to the ecclesiastical society as well as to the civil society.

Unfortunately, *Ex corde ecclesiae* not only consists of two segments, it consists of two segments that do not fit well together. Although the Norms are meant to apply to local situations and are to take "into account the Statutes of each University and Institute and, as far as possible and appropriate, civil law," and although the Norms acknowledge the need to respect the freedom of conscience of each member of faculty as well as academic freedom in research and teaching, nonetheless, Rome decided to take a stand with respect to Canons 810 and 812 and to do so in a manner that is wholly out of character both with respect to the previous consultative process and with respect to the first half of the Apostolic Constitution itself.

Looking at *Ex corde ecclesiae* in its most positive light, its development and promulgation—especially the process of developing the Ordinances for the local application of the Norms at the individual national level—have generated a healthy debate both at the national and international level with respect to the nature, purpose, and administration of the Catholic university, a debate that has generally resulted in better understanding and respect not only among Catholic institutions but also with the national conferences of bishops. It also spawned international conferences such as the one held at Georgetown University in April 1993 whose proceedings were later published by that university's press.[130] At the same time, numerous articles on the nature of the Catholic university began to appear in publications such as the Association of Catholic Colleges and Universities' *Current Issues in Catholic Higher Education* (its winter 1994 issue, for example) and the topic has been addressed regularly at the Association's annual meeting. IFCU, of course, has also taken up the cause and Cardinal Pio Laghi, prefect of the Congregation for Catholic Education, has given a number of talks at various formal gatherings of academics, such as the address he provided on October 4, 1991 at St. Anselm College in Manchester, New Hampshire, to mark the first anniversary of the promulgation of *Ex corde ecclesiae* or the 1994 address to the international meeting of IFCU in the summer of 1994.

The pages of *Origins* began to carry fairly regular articles on the Catholic university; books such as Theodore Hesburgh's *The Challenge and Promise of a Catholic University* (University of Notre Dame Press, 1994), *The Present and Future Challenges Facing Catholic Universities* (St. Paul University in Ottawa, 1989), and Alice Gallin's *Independence and a New Partnership in Catholic Higher Education* (Notre Dame University Press, 1996) began to appear; articles multiplied dramatically in the Catholic press.

For the conservative Catholic, the directions were a long overdue formula to re-Catholicize the church's wayward universities, which had made their peace with secular society; for the academic, the directives were a cause for concern.[131] The dialogue has been both essential and healthy. But from a negative perspective, the process has fostered an ever-growing cynicism about the centralization of power in Rome and the relevance of Vatican opinion to the local scene as well as surfacing once more the radical difference in perspectives embraced by Catholics with divergent views of the Church.

The United States' National Conference took the composition of that country's Ordinances seriously indeed. Debate was protracted and there was no effort to conceal the anxiety that gripped many of the country's campuses. After much discussion and a detailed presentation at the annual meeting of the Association of Catholic Colleges and Universities, the proposed U.S. Ordinances were sent to Rome and a copy was published prematurely in *Origins* on November 28, 1996. The original U.S. Ordinances were quite general and did not address some of the thorny issues—such as the mandate—to the satisfaction of the Congregation for Catholic Education. Rome returned those Ordinances for serious revision.[132] The National Conference of Catholic Bishops resumed its task under the continuing chairmanship of Bishop John Leibrecht of Springfield-Cape Girardeau, Missouri, and a thoroughly revised document was sent to Rome subsequent to its approval by the National Conference of Bishops on November 17, 1999. (The draft was published in *Origins* on December 2, 1999.)

Finally, on May 3, 2000 the Congregation gave its approval (with modifications) and the document appeared in *Origins* on June 15, 2000 with the note that application was scheduled for May 3, 2001 after a year-long implementation period. The 1999 document bears very little resemblance to its 1996 predecessor, being detailed and historical. Some of the potentially inflammatory issues were qualified with conditional terminology: "The university president should be a Catholic," for example. With respect to the mandate and Canon 810, the Ordinances are explicit: "Catholics who teach the theological disciplines in a Catholic university are required to have a *mandatum* granted by competent ecclesiastical authority." This section of the document, however, is a well-developed one and contains a number of conditional clauses: "The *mandatum* should not be construed as an appointment, authorization, delegation or approbation of one's teaching by church authorities. Those who have received a *mandatum* teach in their own name . . ."; "the *mandatum* should be given in writing. . . ."; "a *mandatum*, once granted, remains in effect wherever and as long as the professor teaches unless and until withdrawn by competent ecclesiastical authority." The implementation process is underway, ending nine years of debate, composition, and concern. The United States' Ordinances are the first to receive formal Roman approval anywhere. As for their impact, the jury is still out.

Jesuit Steve Privett, the newly appointed president of San Francisco University, synthesized the opinions of many when he observed shortly after Rome's acceptance of the U.S. Ordinances:

I hope they just let sleeping dogs lie. The bishops clearly caved in to Rome. That's no big secret. Rome made this a loyalty test and that's why the vote was so lopsided. Some of the bishops wouldn't know a university from a post office, but they just vote the party line. I think that everybody is hoping now that because there is this two-year period when we're supposed to figure out what will happen, nothing is going to happen and that the conversation will continue and that we'll probably both come to a better understanding of the issues and challenges that are faced by the parties involved in this thing and, coupled with one major change in Rome, we're hoping that this will go away. I think that it's done a positive thing though here in the sense that it has forced people to look at the relationship, look at the conflictual areas and ask, "Are we the source of those conflicts, or is that just inherent in being a university? What does it mean to be Catholic? And so on." So I think it has provided some clarity. We're not reductionists. You can't say, "This is where the Catholic character lies. It's right here, or it's right here, or it's right there." I think we've got a much richer concept of what constitutes a Catholic university and I think that the Ordinances in particular have served as a catalyst for that conversation.

I do think that there are some fundamental contradictions between the Ordinances and *Ex corde* myself. I think they don't hang together. It's classic Roman nonsense. You have the fairly solid stuff up here in *Ex corde* and then you try to codify it and you already know what you want to codify, so you don't really reference the document except as a proof text and then you get into trouble.

For Fordham sociologist Jim Kelly, the process mirrored the practical give-and-take quest for down-to-earth solutions that is characteristic of his nation's approach to problem solving. As for *Ex corde ecclesiae* itself, it is a much-needed document that required a specific application to the political and social realities of the cultural environment of the United States. Kelly explains:

I think it starts off with a serious issue. If the university doesn't retain some sense of Catholicism as a vital, intellectual presence, what good is it, frankly? I mean, it's no good to anybody. That would be the worst of pre-Vatican II—sort of a tribalism, safe jobs for people; it's a ghetto approach which violates Catholicism and violates the intellectual life. So you start off with the Pope, once again, or the Vatican, with a clear sense of a problem and, I think, a clear sense of responsibility. Identity is important, this is a precious heritage, and we don't want to squander it just in terms of making bucks or keeping up with the rest of the culture, a culture which isn't so hot after all. But *Ex corde ecclesiae* comes out in its abstract form and it doesn't really cover all of the historical details of all of the churches incarnate in different nations. The American presidents got it and said, "Now wait a minute. First of all, you have to think in terms of the metaphors available to you." The first American thought is Washington D.C.—big government, bureaucracy. They don't know us. The second American thought is, "We have the best Catholic college system any place. Those guys don't do anything for us. What have you done lately?" The third thing is, "All right, let's sit down, have some beers, get in a back room, and talk it over." They get together. They find one document, and lots of these fellows are still Irish Catholics who come from labour backgrounds: they realize that they're going to have to give something later on in these discussions. They go back and forth. There's a fury in the media, and those few Catholic senates that took note of the Vatican document made sure that everybody knew they weren't parochial and tribal, and they had independent minds. And then, at the end of it, it's a footnote. And it's not a problem.

The late Henri Goudreault was a former rector of St. Paul University in Ottawa and was archbishop of Labrador City-Schefferville. Given his personal background and experience, Goudreault brings a particular insight to the relationship between the Church and the university. While he does allow for the Church's intervention when a Roman Catholic institution fails to fulfil its mission, intervention that should follow prescribed internal procedures, what Goudreault brings to the issues is a point of view that moves beyond the questions of power that drive the Norms to encouraging co-operation and collaboration—he uses words like "support," "encourage," "inspire," and "help" in describing the appropriate role of the hierarchy, a role to be played "in compliance with and respect for the rules governing the institution."[133] Goudreault's perspective represents the desirable outcome Privett has in mind.

Like their colleagues south of the border, the Canadians also took the call to action seriously, beginning with a consultation with St. Paul University's highly respected canon lawyer, Frank Morrisey, O.M.I., in the fall of 1990. Morrisey counselled an expeditious response and provided a detailed interpretation of the document. As a result, the Association of Catholic Colleges and Universities in Canada set to work and by fall 1992, it had prepared its first draft of the Ordinances in consultation with the Canadian Conference of Catholic Bishops, which duly forwarded the document to the Congregation for Catholic Education that November. Rome's request for refinements followed early in 1994, raising some detailed questions with respect to the wording and looking for more clarity on several issues, including the mandate, and pointing out that "Provision should be made for the prescription of Canon 810 concerning removal. . . ." By year's end, the Canadians had prepared their response, addressing all of the issues raised by Laghi. In 1997, Rome asked for additional clarification, raising some new points for clarification and returning to the issue of the mandate. The Canadian presidents debated the material, and compromised on most issues, including the mandate; they then sent their recommendations back to the Canadian Conference, which, in turn, passed them on to Rome with its accompanying recommendation. And there it lies, as of this writing, though the Vatican wheels continue to turn, ever so slowly.

In Australia and in England, however, the bishops have opted for a wholly different route from their North American colleagues. Peter Sheehan, vice-chancellor of the Australian Catholic University, explains that the bishops of Australia have adopted an essentially wait-and-see attitude toward *Ex corde ecclesiae*, reasoning that Rome is far away and that Rome cannot react intrusively to what it does not have in hand. Not that the Catholic nature of the Australian Catholic University can reasonably be called into doubt, but the prescriptions of *Ex corde ecclesiae* are simply not perceived as being helpful in furthering the enviable relationship that already exists between the Catholic university and the Australian hierarchy. In England, on the other hand, the bishops have responded, but they have opted for a generalist approach to the application of the Ordinances. The vagueness of the document prepared by the bishops of England and Wales is in some ways reminiscent of the broad brush approach attempted by the conference in the United States in its first (abortive) draft response. In both cases, the fond wish is clearly that at the end of the day it will be a footnote, a long-forgotten document gathering dust in some inconspicuous corner cabinet.

Michael Coughlan, principal of Trinity and All Saints College in Leeds, explains:

. . . the bishops have taken a fairly relaxed view of *Ex corde ecclesiae* in the sense that they don't regard the Catholic institutes of higher learning in this country as being typical in the sense that they are not directly responsible to the Church; nevertheless, they are sponsored by the Church and they carry the name Catholic and because of that they take the view that there ought to be some input. It's mainly through the trusteeship. Of course, the actual property is owned by the Church. They take an interest through making appointments to the Board and the bishop is chair of the Board and the superior general of the Sisters of the Cross and Passion is the vice-chair. When we appoint anybody to theology, the bishop has a representative on the appointment committee. The bishops' conference undertook to write our Ordinances, but I'm not sure if I can put my hands on it. They did share it with us. They responded in ways in which the Catholic colleges profess their Catholicity in recruitment, in the ways in which they include Catholicity in their mission statement and the ways in which they take into account Catholicity in the appointment of their staff. The bishops drew up the Ordinances—there was a collaboration. We have a close working relationship. A relaxed relationship. I understand that they sent the Ordinances to Rome in advance of their second to last *ad limina* visit [a regularly scheduled meeting of a nation's bishops "within the thresholds of the Vatican"] some five or seven years ago and that it was not entirely satisfactory; it was revised for their last *ad limina* visit and no serious problems were raised.

North American and British attitudes toward *Ex corde ecclesiae* are obviously oceans apart.

Brian Ray, the president of Newman College in Birmingham, and David McLoughlin, theologian and chaplain at Newman College, describe their bishops' response to *Ex corde ecclesiae* as conservative. McLoughlin explains:

Our bishops at the moment are careful because they don't accept actually the lines that are coming from Rome on all kinds of issues. Education would be one concerning which they think Rome does not understand the English situation. On questions such as divorce and remarriage Rome doesn't understand the situation in a cultural way. Nor is it willing to face the theological thinking necessary for ways forward. With respect to our bishops at the moment, unfortunately, the present group have allowed themselves to be browbeaten by Rome. It's partly to do with the fact that too many were trained there and some of them simply have too much respect for Rome as such. Some of them have not been able to take on board that they are the key figure in the local church and they as a body are the natural teaching body in these islands.

The administration at Newman clearly does have its concerns. The College has a reputation as a fairly independent provider of professional training for teachers and young people whom it is training to take their positions in a pluralistic English world. Clearly, they do not wish to be seen as some sort of Catholic ghetto and would be seriously compromised by any directive from Rome that might foster such a misperception.

Bernie Porter, sister of the Society of the Sacred Heart and rector/CEO of Roehampton Institute London, with which Digby Stuart College is affiliated, puts a different gloss on the episcopal attitudes toward the Roman directive. Commenting on her archbishop's concerns about the formal relationship that Digby Stuart College has formed with the Roehampton Institute London, she muses that "Their anxiety is about us moving further into a secular world because they feel that *Ex corde ecclesiae* doesn't count at Roehampton Institute London. Which is true—it doesn't, because we're not a Catholic university. So the struggle is between autonomy versus belonging to a secular society." It's a cautionary observation worth a reflection with respect to all Catholic colleges and universities that have established formal administrative alliances with secular universities, as they have in various formats in both Britain and Canada.

While it is clear that Roman Catholic postsecondary institutions in the United States, Canada, England, and Australia do have much in common, it is also clear that they differ dramatically by virtue of their unique cultural and historical situations, their particular relationship with their episcopacy, with their governments, and with their national university environments.

CATHOLIC COLLEGES AND UNIVERSITIES:
STRATEGIES FOR SURVIVAL IN A PERILOUS ENVIRONMENT

Rome's sabre-rattling is not the only cause for concern facing the Catholic postsecondary institution. Catholic colleges and universities must contend with a wide range of difficulties that are rooted in the very nature of the modern secular society and that threaten their very existence. There is, for example, a growing public and political interest in practical education rather than the more theoretical and arts-based curriculum characteristic of most Catholic postsecondary institutions. In addition, the Catholic college and university can no longer rely on financial support from societies that place a decreasing emphasis on formal denominational identification or even on religious values. The catalogue of challenges is indeed a daunting one: the rapidly increasing cost of delivering quality education at the post-secondary level, coupled with the almost total absence of the unpaid teaching staff of priests, nuns, and brothers whose presence at one time ensured a balanced budget; the difficulty of assuring Catholic identity in an environment where it is almost impossible to attract and retain a critical mass of qualified staff who are familiar with and supportive of the social, theological, institutional, and (or) educational aspirations of the Catholic tradition; the apparent lack of interest in denominationally based education as such on the part of prospective students; and students' concern about the "coinage" of a degree from a denominationally based postsecondary institution in a highly competitive market.

Recent studies in the United States have raised some of the alarm bells. The most compelling of these was published by James Burtchaell, c.s.c, in 1998. Entitled *Dying of the Light: The Disengagement of Colleges and Universities from Their Christian Churches*, Burtchaell's analysis traces the secularization process of numerous postsecondary U.S. institutions of varying denominational backgrounds and inevitably raises concerns about the ability of other colleges and universities to retain their religious identities in a modern secular society. Richard Hughes and William Adrian have set out to map possible strategies that institutions might use to stem the tide. Their 1997 *Models for Christian Higher Education: Strategies for Success in the Twenty-First Century* provides some fifteen case studies drawn from a variety of denominationally sponsored colleges and universities. Despite the intentions of the editors, the end product is hardly encouraging. The Roman Catholic examples fail to take into account the decimation of the teaching orders that have founded and staffed the approximately 229 Catholic postsecondary institutions in the United States associated with the Association of Catholic Colleges and Universities; at the same time, the authors link the maintenance of Catholic identity with these orders, document the inability of most denominations to attract students to their institutions, find that Catholic students constitute a significant proportion of the student body in many of the non-Catholic institutions, and note that in any event most students are not attracted to these institutions because of their denominational character. In addition, no mention is made of the Jesuit presence on the university scene, even though twenty-eight institutions are currently sponsored by the Jesuit Order and even though the Jesuits themselves have serious concerns about the future viability of their colleges and universities.

Reflecting on whether Jesuit higher education is facing a sunset or a sunrise, Charles L. Currie, the president of the Association of Jesuit Colleges and Universities, tackles the issue of Jesuit higher education.[134] Although Currie is prone to be optimistic, he tends to focus his observations on the Jesuits' well-established emphasis on "faith that does justice" and their effort to promote mission through chaplaincy; while he acknowledges the problems created by the declining interest in vocations to the Order, he places his hope in engaging the laity through the Spiritual Exercises and the proactive effort to hire to mission. What Currie does not do is wonder out loud whether the critical mass does in fact exist within the professoriate to maintain twenty-eight Jesuit universities and to retain them as Jesuit. During our scores of interviews with Jesuit educators, everyone with whom we spoke was convinced that Jesuit postsecondary education is in for a major shakedown. Steve Privett's reflections are representative:

The future of Catholic universities clearly does not rest with the Jesuits—there aren't any. There are thirty people in doctoral studies right now. That's over a six-year period and there are twenty-eight universities. The future of Catholic universities is going to lie in our ability to enlist and engage colleagues in a way that they come to be as enthusiastic about what we're doing as we are and that the vision, or the ideals, or the values are communicable, are transferable. I think we ought to stop focusing on this Jesuit control model and start saying—we have in fact started—that we need to figure out how one works collaboratively. And I think we need to acknowledge very frankly that this didn't start out of conviction. It started out of necessity. We ran out of Jesuits. We are forced to co-operate with laypeople. I think that now in hindsight we say, "Well this isn't a bad thing." I think we went into it saying, "This is a bad thing. We've got to keep deans and vice-presidents, and so forth." We kind of defined key positions. I think most of us are probably over that and are saying, "Okay, well we may have gotten forced into it, but that doesn't make it not a good thing and it's about time we wake up and realize it." So, I think that Catholic universities are going to be pretty self-conscious about their identity in the sense that they are reflective, strategic, and deliberate—not narrow, parochial, and exclusive. And I think that trying to be and act that way is going to be a challenge, particularly in this environment, which is so nervous about orthodoxy which wants such a clear formulation for everything. That just doesn't wash in the university.

I think that the future for all Catholic universities, with the possible exception of Notre Dame, is quite precarious financially unless something gives. Unless somehow we are able to develop these large endowments. . . . Right now the tuition at Santa Clara is about $20,000 a year. Sixty-eight percent of our kids are on financial aid. Nineteen cents of every tuition dollar goes to financial aid. Tuition is going up ahead of inflation and has for the last six to seven years. So, even I, who am not a financial person, can project that out for the next ten years and it's pretty scary.

I don't think that the future of Catholic education is by any means solidly ensured just on the financial level. One can talk about the values and the vision and all the rest, but if you don't have the dollars . . . unless there's some break such as federally financed money that's transferable . . . I think everybody's living in the hope that something like that is going to happen. Kids are leaving law school with $100,000 debts, and I think that the average debt at Santa Clara University is about $30,000. Either we're going to become very elite—that is to say, we're going to educate wealthy people's kids who are too dumb to get into the U C system—or we're going to have to come up with some fancy figures to be able to maintain ourselves. That's just straight tuition. Then you add technology, salaries, and all those kinds of factors and it's not a promising future.

Given the difficulties Catholic colleges and universities face in various countries, one would think that forming alliances would be the logical direction to head in, to cut costs, promote joint research, and develop innovative programs. For their part, the Jesuits have their own internal alliances, the Association of Jesuit Colleges and Universities. What does Privett think of the Association as a collaborative means on which to build for the future? Is the Alliance one in name only, or is it a functional alliance among the various Jesuit institutions?

I think the level of co-operation is minimal. We tend to be more competitive than co-operative. For example, we don't have a common alumni bank anywhere. It just seems obvious to me that everyone hands over their alumni list so that can be centralized to be used for everything from political lobbying to fundraising. Mind you, I'm not president yet, so I haven't been part of their discussions, but I don't think that universities want to give up their alumni lists to some kind of common bank. The University of San Francisco and Santa Clara University do nothing together. I've told Santa Clara president, Paul Locatelli, that when I take over the presidency at San Francisco we could seek out speakers and share the costs—there is very simple stuff we could do and do not do and I think that's a challenge we have not risen to. USF is starting to co-operate with California Institute for the Arts, so the Institute does all the studio work and USF does the classroom and the students can have their degree from the California Institute or USF. We have the same arrangement with an architectural school. USF has a lot of alliances and it seems to me that doesn't affect costs, but it definitely affects the richness of the experience at the school and can provide more options. I think there are other alliances like that we can form, but I think that most small Catholic colleges won't be here in ten years, frankly. I think the challenges are just formidable.

As for co-operation . . . There was a program called Western Conversations, which convened about twelve to fifteen faculty from the western Jesuit universities to talk about value issues. That ran over a two- or three-year period. People liked the experience, but I would characterize it as a kind of discrete experience. There wasn't a lot of spillover that I can see. We meet nationally in groups: deans of arts and sciences, vice-presidents, and various presidents meet three or four times a year, so there's a lot of exchange of ideas, but I don't know that

that's been institutionalized in any programmatic way. We're beginning now to explore the possibilities of distance learning and we have a person hired nationally to work with all twenty-eight of us, or the twenty-five of us who have bought into the idea. That would be the first co-operative piece which somebody could point to. We have a program in China. We're starting a program for all the Jesuit universities in El Salvador which will start in September—a one-semester immersion program for students. So there is just the beginnings of some of that stuff, but they tend to be add-ons as opposed to core activities.

LOOKING TO THE FUTURE

Given that education in Canada is a provincial matter, the nature and structure of Canada's Catholic colleges and universities can vary markedly from province to province; in addition, since most of Canada's Catholic colleges are either federated or affiliated with a secular university—the route being pursued by the few Catholic colleges still remaining in England—political arrangements and program development can vary dramatically from institution to institution even within a given province. Moreover, although all of Canada's ten provinces except for Newfoundland could at one time boast the existence of at least one Roman Catholic postsecondary institution, only seven provinces can now make that claim, with Newfoundland, Prince Edward Island, and historically Catholic Quebec having none, while Ontario has seven and Saskatchewan and Alberta have three each. Most of these institutions are quite small, St. Francis Xavier University in Antigonish, Nova Scotia, being the largest, a stand-alone university with a full-time student population of only 3,500. Most of the remaining sixteen colleges and universities are federated or affiliated with a secular university or are otherwise integrated into a larger university context and, as a result, one needs to ask whether any of these has the faculty component or student body to resist the contemporary rush to large, integrative structures or the relentless secularization of North American society.

Efforts at forming any association other than the loosely structured Association of Catholic Colleges and Universities in Canada have so far been futile as most institutions have neither the energy nor the inclination to establish formal alliances with sister colleges. At the same time, the federated/affiliated structure has been enormously helpful, providing access to library resources, social and athletic amenities, a wide range of professors and classes, and a host of medical, computing, statistical, and related resources, and a respected university degree that the smaller institution simply could not make available to its students. For their part, the colleges add an intimacy to the larger institution since they are more human in scale and more person-centred in their raison d'être. Their continued existence, however, is precarious at best and, given their structural dependence on the goodwill of their secular hosts, their potential ultimate assimilation either in fact or in function into the secular monolith is surely quite likely. It would be a mistake to equate physical survival with survival as meaningfully Catholic centres of learning.[135]

As for the situation in England, Michael Coughlan, principal of Trinity and All Saints College in Leeds, notes that in the 1960s there was a rapid development of Catholic colleges as they rushed to train teachers during an expansionary period.

But in the seventies, what had been the rapid expansion of teacher education during the sixties became a rapid contraction of teacher education and whereas in the early seventies there were nineteen Catholic colleges of higher education involved in teacher training in England and Wales they were reduced to about six, I think, by the end of the decade, four of which are subject to *Ex corde ecclesiae*: Heythrop, Newman, St. Mary's, and Trinity and All Saints are the only free-standing colleges. There is a Catholic presence within Roehampton Institute and there is a Catholic presence within Liverpool. Those which survived were the ones which saw the writing on the wall and began to diversify.

Given the dramatic depletion in the number of Catholic university colleges in England, one might conclude that their existence was in jeopardy and that inventive means of ensuring their future would need to be devised. The colleges have set out to identify themselves clearly as university colleges and have begun to establish relationships with secular universities, primarily as a means of assuring academic credibility. Trinity and All Saints University College in Leeds, as a result, hired Michael Coughlan away from the University of Wales where he had been a senior university administrator, and has worked to become a meaningful part of the University of Leeds; Newman has established strategic alliances with the University of Coventry, severing its previous relationship with the University of Birmingham since Coventry provided a more propitious academic arrangement—and since the University of Surrey with which St. Mary's Strawberry Hill and Digby Stuart at the Roehampton Institute London are associated is too distant geographically.

On the question of a Catholic college consortium, Michael Coughlan has decidedly mixed feelings.

There is a constantly recurring debate on this both at the bishops' level and at the principals' level, and not just concerning the Catholic institutions but the Christian institutions on an ecumenical institutional basis. I come from the University of Wales with the experience of the federal university and possibly have more insights on how that works than some people do and I think it would have to be a federal institution in this country. I'm not convinced that there is a lot to be gained from that, given the distances there are between the institutions. It would have to involve Heythrop, which is the main postgraduate research element, and then St. Mary's, Newman, ourselves, and possibly Liverpool Hope, though they may wish not to be involved because they are not distinctly Catholic. I'm not sure there is a lot to be gained.

We did explore in some depth over the last couple of years the possibility of a northern federation of Christian colleges. We are the only Catholic institution up north, but there are a number of Anglican colleges and of course there is also Liverpool Hope, which is an ecumenical institution. The idea of an ecumenical northern university hasn't got very far because people have too many separate agendas. There is also an anxiety about what the cash value would be for students in the employment market of a degree from a Catholic or Church institution. I think that in this country there would be a great deal of conservatism about the idea—a degree from the University of Leeds or a degree from the University of London has much more attraction for students than a degree from a Church institution, but I'm quite prepared to look seriously at any proposals that might be put forward. In the University of Wales—to take it as an example—when I was there, there were five campuses and there was a university registry which was coordinating the five and the budget for the university registry was greater than the entire budget for University College London. So there are significant costs and they were given an additional grant for this over and above what they were given for student funding. I do not see that the present government is in a mood to do that. So we would have to meet the additional costs ourselves and the financial pressure could be decisive. And we can't look to the bishops since the bishops haven't put money into Catholic higher education since the late 1980s.

Brian Ray, the principal of Newman College in Birmingham, England, takes a very different approach to the question of co-operation. In his mind, co-operation is essential to the future of Catholic postsecondary education in England.

I think that without some integrated sort of structure it is going to be very difficult. Without it, I think that Newman is vulnerable. St. Brendan's College at Bristol is vulnerable, too. It's a wonderful sixth form with 2,000 students and the spectrum of courses the students take is just wonderful. It's one of many colleges of its sort and it's another part of the infrastructure. It seems to me that we've got the infrastructure in place already with the further education colleges. There are several in the London area; others in the Lancashire and Manchester, Liverpool area; and there are others on the west coast—Middlesborough. So, you've actually got an enormous network where you could do a lot of the things we want to do, and much of it could be done without the students leaving home. Students could complete teachers' training there, and those places could also become postgraduate centres where you actually provide things not just to train teachers, but to provide training beyond what we are doing at the three colleges—I tend to say three because Digby Stuart at Roehampton is so integrated into that institution, and even though the rector and CEO of Roehampton is a sister of the Sacred Heart, Bernie Porter, the continued Catholic identity of Digby Stuart is a difficult issue. I've been pushing very hard for this and I've got one person with me at the moment, Arthur Naylor from St. Mary's. We're very keen to work together because our size is such that the practicalities of operating with strategic alliances with other institutions is quite attractive. We have 1,050 full-time students and 400 part-time students, but we've also got all the administration and we're running that with a fairly small structure so that the load on the administration—vice-principal, bursar, vice-principal of administration—is just enormous and then you have the load on the director of programs who has this plethora of programs. The reality is that it would be much better if we worked with other institutions and we're talking to not only St. Mary's but also Trinity and All Saints, but St. Mary's are immediately enthusiastic to try to work together. If we had Newman and St. Mary's, that would give us 3,000 to 3,500 full-time students and probably about 1,000 part-time—you could push yourself into a larger critical mass. If Trinity and All Saints were involved, you'd be up to about 5,500 full-time students and 2,000 to 2,500 part-timers.

The time is right in many ways because of the changes which have taken place in national structures during the 1990s. We have clearer ideas about what constitutes a standard program for an undergraduate degree or for a postgraduate degree and that means that institutions can collaborate on the basis of agreed currency, if you like, in relation to their courses. I think that the start that needs to be made is purely on the practical level. We're just starting to do that with St. Mary's Strawberry Hill and School Experience, for example. I can see that with the Internet and student mobility and a number of other things over the next few years, what you could get is a change in the way students perceive things so that you could spend some time on one campus and some time on another. Now that could get quite complicated, but it's the kind of thing people are going to have to start thinking about very carefully. Last September we had the Microsoft professor of information technology talking to us about the global university and the kinds of things that are possible. It seems to me that if you don't take advantage of these possibilities, you're going to lose your opportunity. All the things are in place to allow us to do that.

As for Digby Stuart College at the Roehampton Institute London, they're not at all interested. Digby Stuart is fundamentally integrated into

Roehampton, so much so that Roehampton holds the contracts of Digby Stuart faculty; still, one-time deputy principal Frances Speckman, who thinks the arrangement is the correct one for Digby Stuart, says flatly: "I know that there have been discussions about a Catholic university, and those sorts of things, but certainly it wouldn't be something that I would be terribly excited about. I think we've got our work cut out as we are." At the same time, Speckman does observe that "small and delicate, you're definitely vulnerable."

David McLoughlin adds a different perspective to the dynamic, observing that the present climate of postmodernity actually favours diversity. He notes that England is in a unique situation in which the Catholic community would be ready to accept, without suspicion, so high a profile a Catholic initiative as a national college or university. The Achilles heel for such a project, it would seem, is the credibility that a newly established Catholic university might have from the perspective of providing positive contributions to the field of research. One has to wonder, for example, whether it is possible for a teachers' college within the Catholic tradition to advance critical scholarship when so much of their energy might be directed rather to the more technical and pedagogical (even catechetical) rather than the intellectual. Newman's vice-principal, Pamela Taylor, does see a real problem with a training program whose emphasis is clearly not on the honing of critical skills.

> If you looked at teacher education when it was called teacher education five or six years ago, then the argument would have been that that was the way teacher education was going: there was a recognition that what you had to involve teachers in was intellectual debate, getting inside their own subject discipline, beginning to understand the nature of the cognitive structures within their own discipline. There has been, over the past five or six years, a very radical shift in the nature of teacher training and because of that teachers are now seen much more as technicians. There is a great demand for subject knowledge, but it is subject knowledge at a level which is described as the equivalent of A-Level, which is the level of the seventeen- or eighteen-year-old's examination which students take to go into university.
>
> So there is at one level a tremendous load now on intending teach-

ers, on what they have to acquire in terms of knowledge and skills and attributes, but at the same time there is a kind of downgrading of the intellectual challenge. The curriculum is so packed with the things that they have to prove that they are able to do that it is much more difficult to give students the time to reflect, to ask the real questions about the subjects they're interested in, follow through the real lines of intellectual inquiry. As a result, I think there is some suspicion in the university community as a whole as to whether institutions which are predominantly teacher training institutions—and they are now rather seen as training rather than education—whether they can hold their own in the university sector. A big issue for many of the colleges in Britain is whether they obtain university status or not, and the definition of that is that they are a mature, self-critical academic community. Our strength lies in the fact that because we're developing joint honours degrees, and because we've got masters' degrees developing, we've got faculty who are particularly interested in particular areas of research and that inevitably is going to strengthen our claim to be part of the university sector. We've also got people who are building their own research networks and they're achieving recognition in their own field and that will enable us to make the claim for university college status.

But how realistic is the academic vision for the future? David McLoughlin has his doubts.

The real tension is that the sheer amount of basic work, the building up of skills, that the staff have to be involved in on a daily basis actually undermines any real serious ongoing research that they might do themselves except in the particular areas they might be providing—they might be able to reflect on that. And so, while we can sustain putting together the M.A. programs at the moment, it would be difficult to see at the present level of student intake how we could actually creatively sustain them in the long term. The M.A. programs even at the university are always going to be small and we get funded in terms of the mass numbers of students we get, so there is just not the financial resources to push the way of masters programs at the moment and to free people up to do the sort of ongoing work they need to do to sustain that. I think I've seen, especially in the English Department, people almost oppressed by the sheer amount of work they have to do at this basic skill level, which of course is great in terms of enabling these young people to get the necessary skills for their work, but professionally for the members of staff themselves, they're not going anywhere with it. Their own subject knowledge is not expanding. They're becoming very skilled educators of educators, but in terms of their specific subject areas, it's a problem.

Arthur Naylor, the principal of St. Mary's Strawberry Hill, agrees that diversification became essential in the late 1960s; he also points out that working in a collaborative structure comes naturally to him, given his Scottish background and the collaborative approach to education that is part of the Scottish mindset. And, for him, the time is right for a more collaborative approach to university education. Collaboration is, after all, a form of diversification. In England, Naylor reasons, one can seek to be more distinctive in terms of what the Catholic population is trying to do than one could in Scotland or Northern Ireland because in England "what Catholics do is seen as being a contribution to the common good. Whereas in Scotland where you've got separate schooling, things that you do might be seen as in some sense promoting your Catholic identity, be seen as being divisive in a way you wouldn't in England." For Naylor, the matter is clear. To return to the past is not an option; to look to the future without some form of co-operation among the country's Catholic colleges would be perilous, yet there is no apparent movement in this direction.[136] David McLoughlin explains the English atmosphere and the current opportunity more poetically by observing that the postmodern world values diversity. And, paradoxically, collaboration is diversification since a Catholic university would provide a distinctive voice within the postsecondary world.

Without a doubt, the most imaginative and the most promising approach to Roman Catholic postsecondary education is to be found in Australia where a disparate group of Catholic teachers' colleges and training centres for nurses have banded together to form the Australian Catholic University. Although the desire to form an Australian Catholic university had been a long-standing one, the Australian Catholic University was ultimately born of necessity, driven by the restructuring of the postsecondary educational system under the direction of John Dawkins. The array of small Catholic colleges was no longer viable. A new and dramatic direction was required if Australian Catholic postsecondary education was to survive the impetus for change.

Australian Catholic University, ACU, took its first breath on January 1, 1991 at which time the federal minister responsible for Employment, Education, and Training formally recognized its independent existence, under the sponsorship of La Trobe University of Melbourne, which served as its initial guarantor of academic standards. As a result, ACU has received federal funding from the outset—some $51 million Australian in 1995. And by most measurements, the university has done very well indeed. Under the able and congenial direction of ACU's first vice-chancellor, Peter Drake, the fledgling university began actually to achieve what many outside Australia have implicitly characterized as the logistically impossible. Eight relatively small Catholic teachers' colleges strung along Australia's east coast effectively united through the use of modern technology and the willingness of faculty to see themselves as part of a national system that may require some travel and a willingness to innovate.

ACU began with eight separate sites whose campuses were located variously along the eastern seaboard and southeastern tip of the country: Ballarat (Aquinas), Brisbane (McAuley), Canberra (Signadou Dominican College), Melbourne (Christ and Mercy), and Sydney (Castle Hill, MacKillop, and Mount St. Mary). The eight sites were reduced to seven with the closing of the campus at Castle Hill, and further rationalization in Melbourne has reduced the number to six with the merger of the two campuses in the suburb of Fitzroy. The concept is exciting, the initiative bold, and the potential more than promising. By 2000 ACU could boast in excess of 10,200 student enrolments in the faculties of Arts and Science, Education, Health Sciences, and the sub-faculty of Theology, all of which was supported by an academic full-time equivalent staff of 496 and a support staff of 407. Clearly, institutions that were vulnerable as small colleges now enjoy promising possibilities as part of a much larger university.

To service its students, ACU has augmented its library holdings by integrating its seven campuses through a UNILINK system and students are

encouraged to borrow widely within the collaborative borrowing structure. Administratively, the individual holding the post of principal and
vice-chancellor is supported by three pro-vice-chancellors with specific
responsibilities assigned variously for Academic Affairs, Quality and
Outreach, and Research, and each of the three faculties is administered by
an academic dean, none of whom is on the same campus. Telephone,
Internet, video-conferencing, Open Learning, and travel all combine to
put a human face on the faculty and the administration, to reinforce the
sense of institutional identity, and to explore contemporary avenues for
program delivery. ACU is an impressive fusing of traditional Australian
mateship with the Catholic commitment to community, which extends
beyond Australia's borders. The university has an active International
Education Office whose director (who was Tony McKittrick at the time of
this writing) is energetically establishing student and professional contacts
throughout the Pacific Rim and North America with an eye to academic
collaboration, student exchange, and study-abroad possibilities.

The task of pulling all of this together appears to be an impossible one.
Indeed, the dean of the Faculty of Arts and Science, Peter Carpenter,
concedes that at first blush it does look impossible, but commitment and
co-operation can overcome any number of obstacles.

Although it's a curious animal, the Faculty of Arts and Science, in seven
campuses and four political jurisdictions, it actually works. It actually
works. And it works because we've had marvellous leadership at the head
of school level. The schools deliver the Faculty's courses locally and
we've had an almost fathomless amount of goodwill from staff. There have
been difficulties, but we've had an extraordinary amount of goodwill.

The bottom line for those in doubt, says Frank Maloney, foundation
professor of Theology and head of the sub-faculty of Theology, is a matter
of survival and self-interest. "Let's pull together on this, because if we
don't, you're going to lose. I think that because of excellent managerial
practices, even those who have not got what they want are beginning to see
that the federalist more national model is the one that gives them strength."

ACU is clearly a concept with broadly based support—support from
faculty, staff, and the bishops of Australia, who have been generous both

philosophically and financially. Indeed, ACU has earned its support, having been carefully conceived and carefully fostered. Its objectives are both comprehensive and specific: "(1) To establish, operate, maintain, and promote, as part of the mission of the Roman Catholic Church, the Australian Catholic University in accordance with the beliefs, traditions, practices, and canonical legislation of the Roman Catholic Church, and by doing so to promote culture and the development of the human person; (2) To foster and promote education, scholarship, and research and, through the education programs of the university, provide and promote preparation and continuing development of persons inspired by Christian principles who will be capable of assuming positions of responsibility in the Church and in society."

The commitment to scholarship is important since, in the long run, both the credibility of the institution as a university, as well as the quality of the service it provides to its students, to society, and to the Church will depend on the professional qualifications of its faculty. As a result, ACU is clear about its "rigorous and critical approach to scholarship, characterized by intellectual honesty, academic excellence and freedom of investigation." ACU, as a consequence, can point to a number of scholars conducting research and publishing in areas that are consonant with the mission of the university as well as other academic pursuits such as the joint sponsorship of the International/Australian Conference, "Religion, Literature and the Arts." The Faculty of Theology in 1998 had a subfaculty component of thirty-eight academics, twenty-eight of whom hold a Ph.D. in universities from all over the world. As Frank Maloney points out, "I've got a really classy team. You've only got to see the local journals and see who're writing the theological articles and who're doing the serious book reviews. They're all ACU people." Hallmarks of an up-and-coming university.

At the same time, as Robert Gascoigne, head of the School of Theology at Sydney, points out, ACU is a publicly funded university operating under government guidelines, which forbid denominational discrimination even in the hiring of faculty for the teaching of theology. In addition, theology is located administratively within the Faculty of Arts and Science and, as such, signals the university's intention to provide a meaningful academic dialogue among the various disciplines that constitute the Faculty. As is the case in German universities where theology exists as an object of serious study in its own right and does so without any taint of indoctrinational intent, theology at ACU is an integral but intellectually independent discipline springing from a Catholic and Christian milieu. ACU's approach to the study of theology will, by definition, be different from that undertaken in privately funded Catholic universities such as those in the United States. In an unpublished paper, "Theology at Australian Catholic University," Gascoigne sums up the approach of the subfaculty:

> As a public university in the Catholic tradition, ACU is committed to the belief that the espousal of a specific religious tradition can live in harmony with an affirmation of the academic values of free inquiry, and the ethical foundations of a pluralist society. Much contemporary discussion in the humanities emphasizes the role of tradition in shaping the kinds of questions we ask and the perspective we bring to the task of enquiry. . . . It is part of ACU's mission, expressing its own constitutive tradition, to affirm the importance of the spiritual dimension of existence and to ask questions, and shape reflection, in a way which recognizes its role. This choice of emphasis does not imply an interference with the academic freedom of particular disciplines. Rather, it affirms that particular forms of reflection and inquiry are important and fruitful.

It is still too early to declare the future of the Australian Catholic University experiment an educational success. Indeed, while lauding ACU's staff for their "caring approach" and the generally friendly and informal atmosphere of the university's classes, the 1996 *Good Guide to Australian Universities* rates ACU poorly in a number of areas, including prestige and research performance, noting that "Research and graduate teaching are in their infancy."[137] But ACU stands as a sign of hope in a troubled time. ACU provides an alternative voice, an avowedly Catholic institution that takes seriously its mission to pass on a hallowed tradition, to prepare a thoughtful and informed citizenry to work for the betterment of both the civil and ecclesiastical societies. Indeed, recent planning sessions have moved beyond the question of structure and organization to the core question of Catholic identity, the heart of the Catholic university.

It would be difficult indeed to unearth a commentary on the Catholic university that does not reflect either expressly or implicitly on George Bernard Shaw's insistence that the phrase is a contradiction in terms; such commentaries inevitably proceed to discuss each of the two words, "Catholic" and "university." With respect to the latter, one needs to recall that the Reformation and the Enlightenment hastened the demise of the great Catholic universities of the Middle Ages and were the unintentional forebears of the seminary as the arena for theological learning, not theological education. Seminaries by their nature have specialized in passing on a tradition, not examining it, and not exploring innovative means for making that tradition meaningful for our times. It is the task of the university to provide the opportunity for analysis, for assessment, for the discovery of new knowledge, and for the development of minds capable of making prudential judgments. There is a place for rote learning, but it is only a small part of the educational process. Universities ought not to be engaged in the catechetical enterprise as such. Too many bishops and too many dedicated lay Catholics have celebrated catechetical institutes as if they were centres of learning rather than schools of instruction.

Many Catholic universities in the United States, Canada, England, and Australia have developed truly effective chaplaincies, inspirational liturgies, and enthusiastic Christian communities. In England in particular there has been an exemplary emphasis on wedding the chaplaincy with the educational program. For Michael Hayes, academic and chaplain at Digby Stuart College, Roehampton Institute London, the fusing of the two is a self-evident necessity: "We are an academic institution and I've never thought that the chaplaincy should be separate from that. For me it's a question of engagement. The chaplain needs to engage the students in the teaching of courses." University chaplaincies are lively places, the seedbed for the Church that is to come. Without the Catholic university, who will ask the searching questions? The implications of the priority of labour over capital, the preferential option for the poor, the inherent dignity of the human person, the principle of subsidiarity, and a host of other issues at the heart of the Catholic tradition need to be expounded, explored, and applied to civil and ecclesiastical societies in an effort to build a better world and to assist in the reformation of still imperfect institutions. Should the conscience of the nation, the national soul, emerge from the boardrooms of big business and the research laboratories of transnational corporations? Indeed, without the Catholic university, who will be prepared to advance such issues? How and where will basic Christian principles be tested, refined, augmented? Surely not in the huge secular, technological, postsecondary professional schools that are fast becoming the darlings of our secular, post-Christian culture.

One wonders the extent to which the Catholic preoccupation with schooling, from junior kindergarten or kindergarten through secondary school, with its attendant fiscal problems as well as with its strong emphasis on education as catechetical inculcation has affected both the episcopal and to some extent the Catholic lay vision of the role of the Catholic university. It seems to be a truism in England and the United States that postsecondary institutions that see their role as transmitters of the tradition are viewed most favourably by a good number of the countries' bishops: Steubenville in Ohio, U.S.A., and Maryvale in Birmingham, England. Because institutions such as these are arguably cast more in the seminary than the academic mode, they provide a comfort level for those who are wary of the academic ethos. But no age can do the work for another, and a vibrant Church must necessarily be populated by inquisitive minds and a desire to find new ways of understanding ancient truths.

Departments of education in both Australia and England have accepted the Catholic university as a valued addition to the well-being of society, institutions worth supporting. It would be an ironic twist of history if those Catholics who do not appreciate the value of a sound Catholic academy discover its importance only when it is too late, only when today's Catholic universities and colleges have gone the way of the great Catholic universities of the past when a mistrusting civil society viewed them with suspicion. The Catholic Church needs the Catholic university if it is to be true to itself as an ecclesiastical body constantly engaged in the necessary act of reformation—*ecclesia semper reformanda*—and society needs the Catholic university as an alternative voice, perhaps a dissident voice, as it struggles to build a better world. The Church needs its institutions, its hospitals, and its centres of learning as a formal means of evangelization; that is, as vehicles for incarnating the Christian message in a post-Christian and rampantly secular society. Society needs Catholic institutions as visible signs of our innately human capacity to extend our vision beyond the merely sublunary interests that have so captivated the post-Enlightenment imagination.

3

And the Greatest of These Is Virginity:
Sex and Marriage

While clashing with his mother over his loss of faith and centring the discussion on the Blessed Virgin Mary, Stephen Dedalus, the hero of James Joyce's *A Portrait of the Artist as a Young Man*, remarked that "religion was not a lying-in hospital."[1] Dedalus had made his way through the fire and brimstone hell of a sexually repressive Catholicism epitomized in the angst of a high school retreat, a retreat from which he had dutifully emerged determined to mortify each of the senses—the senses, the retreat master had assured his teenaged charges, being the gateway to sin. Then, having toyed with thoughts of a religious vocation, Dedalus reluctantly rejected the religion that shaped him, a religion that demanded an obeisance he ultimately could not provide. As a result, he consciously turned his back on the dispassionate theological abstractions and the traditional Catholic suspicion of physical pleasure, which were significant components of his Jesuit formation and which he found inimical to his artistic temperament; instead, he set out on a course of self-discovery rooted not in philosophy or theology but "in the reality of experience."[2]

Dedalus's particular quest and his particular questioning anticipate in imaginative form the plight of contemporary Catholics who have concluded in ever-swelling numbers that religion is not a lying-in hospital, that traditional Catholic celebrations of the virginal and its persistent denigration of the sensual do not speak to their own experience of life or of married love. Gone are the days when philosophy and theology were the mysterious preserve of a clergy who received unquestioned adulation; gone are the days when title brought with it both a reflex for respect and for submission; and gone are the days when a celibate elite could dictate marital behaviour on the basis of deductive argument proper to the ecclesiastical library but at odds with the inductive evidence garnered through lived human experience. Indeed, the Church's prescriptions with respect to sexual behaviour are now more often seen as expressions of arcane power than of genuine religious solicitude—one is reminded of the dramatically visual scene in the National Film Board of Canada's "Behind the Veil" in which a stream of grey-haired men in cassocks flows from a Vatican synodal session, a quizzical image of those celibate and male sexagenarians who issue doctrinal formulae meant to regulate the sensitive behaviour of husbands and wives.[3]

There was a time when mysterious words and complicated definitions brought with them a concomitant sense of power, power entrusted to an exalted elite exercising positions of authority. In today's society there is a suspicion of those who would wrap themselves in a confusion of words, and in today's society the respect that accompanies power relates to merit rather than to title. Too often, power has been abused. In fact, several critiques of clerical sexual abuse have centred on questions of power, its use, its misuse, and its abuse. Cardinal G. Emmett Carter, archbishop emeritus of Toronto and a student of psychology and the cross, has spoken often and frankly about clerical power. Carter views the cleric's penchant for power as the natural filling of the vacuum created by the vow of chastity:

To give responsibility means to relinquish authority to some degree. Authority in Catholic circles is for the most part in the hands of religious (priests, brothers, nuns). Religious are formally dedicated to a life of chastity. Now there are three fundamental human drives: (a) the preservation of self, (b) the propagation of the species, (c) the will to power. Celibacy involves the repression of the second of these. What is more natural than to expect that this repression will take the form of a transfer of drive at least in some degree and that the will to power will be proportionately strengthened? Besides, parenthood is the normal means of satisfaction for the drive to power. Since that is impossible for the celibate, he tends to concentrate on the power given to him by his position. Religious are notoriously jealous of their rights, privileges, and prerogatives.[4]

Carter extends his thesis to the next logical step, arguing that as a means of solidifying this quest for power, it is to be expected that clerics will all too often surround themselves with yes-men, a phenomenon that Carter observes is all too evident both nationally and internationally. Those of us who have followed developments at the Episcopal Synods in Rome will have seen all of these inclinations in action, including the reflex will to please the Seat of Power, a reflex that is an obvious and unfortunate by-product of the contemporary drift toward what several have termed "popalatry." It is a penchant neatly encapsulated in the synodal observation of Cardinal Paul Zoungrana, the African regional representative to the 1990 Synod of Bishops, who opined before the Pope and the assembled Synod fathers: "It [the Synod] is for us a chance to affirm our fidelity to you and our attachment to your person, especially in certain difficult hours."[5] And one thought that the purpose of the Synod was at least consultative, since it is apparently not to be deliberative! Celibacy becomes an impetus for the will to power; both popalatry and certain Vatican manifestoes concerning marital intimacy are today widely viewed as just that—manifestations of power. As a consequence, the Vatican is often seen as being out of touch both with the Roman Catholic faithful as well as with the scientific and professional communities, and even at times with its priests. This splendid isolation is expressed most especially in issues relating to human sexual behaviour and marital intimacy.

This isolation follows quite naturally from a tradition that is philosophical and abstract in its origins and that was translated into a Christian discourse by men who were for the most part celibates steeped in philosophical propositions. At the root of Roman Catholic theological expression, for example, there lies a teleological view of the universe, a sense of order that is presented as a reflection of the mind of the Creator Himself. St. Thomas Aquinas, thirteenth-century Dominican philosopher and quintessential Catholic theologian, translated Aristotle's theory of causality into the Christian West and in doing so introduced a wholly Christian perception of the well-ordered cosmos. Aquinas's famous demonstrations for the existence of God, for example, is rooted in the theory of causality and spring from this sense of order. This same notion of a hierarchical universe also accounts for the Church's dogged defence of the divine right of kings, even when the rest of the Western world had moved on to more democratic political structures. It is, of course, a view of reality that defends the Vatican's own political operations even to our present day and it is also a sense of order that argued quite rationally that the terra firma that the Creator had shaped for the human pilgrimage was by definition a geocentric one, no matter what scientific observation might say about the matter. More importantly for our present purposes, it is a hierarchical view of the universe that has historically denigrated the physical, the female, and the marital states as inferior to the spiritual, the male, and the virginal, no matter what experience may witness to the contrary. The more divorced from matter, the more perfect; the Most Perfect being totally removed from matter. Even though over the course of time Rome has grudgingly come to accept the fact that the sun (rather than the earth) is at the centre of our universe, it is moving even more grudgingly to re-evaluate the hierarchical status of the physical, the feminine, and the conjugal.

Christian views of the sensual and of womanhood have been intimately at one since their intimacy was first explained by the Philosopher (that is, by Aristotle) some 350 years before the birth of Christ. Proceeding in the first instance from his observation of the natural world, Aristotle posited as his philosophical starting point concerning the relationships between man and woman the premise that woman is misbegotten, a mutilated male. Fusing his scientific and philosophical conclusions with his theory of causation, Aristotle reasons in his *On the Generation of Animals* that man's contribution to the generative process is an active one (man acts as efficient cause to infuse into the new being the spiritual life principle, the formal cause, "the principle of soul") whereas the female's contribution is both passive and material (she provides the matter for the semen to work upon and acts therefore as a hierarchically inferior material cause). Aristotle explains: "While the body is from the female, it is the soul that is from the male, for the soul is the reality of a particular body."[6] By definition, the efficient activity of the male is divine in its nature and the role of the female merely material, since "the first principle of the movement, or efficient cause, whereby that which comes into being is male, is better and more divine than the material whereby it is female" (II, i). Hierarchically speaking, therefore, it follows quite logically that the contribution of the female to the act of generation is by definition inferior to that of the male. "Thus while it is necessary for the female to provide a body and a material mass, it is not necessary for the male, because it is not within the work of art or the embryo that the tools or the maker must exist. While the body is from the female, it is the soul that is from the male, for the soul is the reality of a particular body" (II, iv).[7]

Aristotle's philosophical principles were subsequently Christianized by Thomas Aquinas in the thirteenth century and have since become an operative component of contemporary Western culture; indeed, they continue to have their influence within the Vatican even today. Thomas Aquinas (saint since 1323), Angelic Doctor (since 1567), patron saint of Catholic schools (since 1879), thirteenth-century Christianizer of Aristotle, teaches in his *Summa theologica* (Ia q. xcii art. 1) that "the active power of generation belongs to the male sex, and the passive power to the female" and "as regards the particular nature, woman is defective and misbegotten, for the active force in the male seed tends to the production of a perfect likeness in the masculine sex."[8] By extension, given their respective hierarchical roles and the relationship of each to the hierarchy of soul/body, spiritual/material, reason/sense, it follows by reason and flawless logic that woman's relationship to man is by nature one of inferiority: "For good order would have been wanting in the human family if some were governed by others wiser than themselves. So by such a kind of subjection woman is naturally subject to man, because in man the discretion of reason predominates."[9] And by that very God-given reason, it follows that "When all things were first formed, it was more suitable for the woman to be made from the man than (for the female to be from the male) in other animals. First, in order thus to give the first man a certain dignity, so that just as God is the principle of the whole universe, so the first man, in likeness to God, was the principle of the whole human race."[10]

Aquinas's demonstrations for the existence of God centre on causality, primarily on efficient cause; that is, on attributes of maleness. Given his own Greek roots, it was entirely natural for St. Paul to explain in his first letter to the Corinthians, chapter 11: "I would have you know that the head of every man is Christ; and the head of the woman is the man; and the head of Christ is God." It is possible to construct an immensely impressive logical edifice if one proceeds in step with the consequences of one's principles; in this particular case the first principles were based on an observation of nature that is scientifically questionable by modern standards and an understanding of the mechanics of human reproduction, which we now know is simply quite incorrect. It is, nonetheless, a logical construct with wide-reaching consequences. The film "Behind the Veil" for example, notes that in the year 900 at Macon, France, an episcopal conference affirmed by a majority of one the proposition that women have souls, with the less Romanized Celts providing the requisite numerical support to carry the thesis. This same train of thought can lead to contemporary *cris de coeur* such as Sister Kevin Bissel's "I don't think the church regards women as human beings. I don't know why they bother to baptize us."[11]

Aristotle's love of wisdom begins with observations of nature, which quickly become consumed by his philosophical ruminations. Within the Christian tradition, the musings of the Greeks create a tension between deductive and inductive reasoning; that is, between what one can conclude from pure reason as opposed to conclusions that can be gleaned from scientific or human experience. It is in essence Stephen Dedalus's dilemma. One is reminded of the cleric who sat in judgment of Nathaniel Hawthorne's Hester Prynne, "a great scholar, like most of his contemporaries in the profession, and withal a man of kind and genial spirit. This last attribute, however, had been less carefully developed than his intellectual gifts, and was, in truth, rather a matter of shame than self-congratulation with him. There he stood, with a border of grizzled locks beneath his skull-cap; while his gray eyes, accustomed to the shaded light of his study were winking, like those of Hester's infant, in the unadulterated sunshine."[12] Divorced from the natural world, yet pontificating on it. It is a long tradition with several strands, but all leading inevitably to the Church's current teachings with respect to the senses, to women, to marriage, and, in some ways, to priesthood.

What is one to make, for example, of the late seventh-century penitential of Theodore—a handbook designed to be used by confessors in determining the gravity of one's sins in an effort to make the penitential punishment fit the crime—when it prescribes that a man who persists in "unnatural intercourse" (that is, sex in other than the missionary position) is to do penance "as one who offends with animals"?[13] (Medieval literature often gives women animal characteristics, especially characteristics of a sensual and tactile sort.) Or what is suggested by a penance for adultery that stipulates: "If any layman begets a child on another's wife, that is, commits adultery, violating his neighbour's bed, he shall do penance for three years, abstaining from juicy foods and from his own wife, and so shall his guilt be wiped off by the priest"?[14] Thomas Aquinas pointed out some years later that there is an explanation for the generation of woman, that "defective and misbegotten" being: she, rather than the "perfect likeness in the masculine sex," is the result of "some external change, such as that of a south wind, which is moist, as the Philosopher observes."[15] Woman is sentient, animal. In Milton's seventeenth-century *Paradise Lost*, Adam recognizes Eve's relationship when he observes of his Helpmate that Nature "at least on her bestow'd / Too much of Ornament, in outward show / Elaborate, of inward less exact. / For well I understand in the prime end / Of Nature her th' inferior, in the mind and inward Faculties" (VIII, 537–542).

Aristotle's relegation of the female role in the generative process to material cause implicitly associated woman with the physical, and hence with the sentient, with body. Anthony Kosnik explains that when St. Paul cautions the emergent Christian communities about inclinations toward the flesh, his concept of flesh embraced all of the temporal order and was not limited simply to body in opposition to soul;[16] early English writings regularly assigned to woman that same extended role as she became the symbol of flesh, of those transitory objects that distract man on his spiritual journey. Early in the eighth century, for example, writing in his *Ecclesiastical History of the English People* (I, xxvii), the Venerable Bede, respected English scholar, records a late sixth-century exchange of correspondence between Pope Saint Gregory (the Great) and Augustine of Canterbury who, while on his mission to Christianize the English, wrote to the Pope to ask his advice on a number of issues that were troubling him. He wondered, for example, whether a man who suffered a loss of sperm during a wet dream might receive Holy Communion, or if he were a priest whether he might celebrate the Eucharist. Gregory responded that "all sin is fulfilled in three ways, viz. by suggestion, by delight, and by consent. Suggestion is occasioned by the Devil, delight is from the flesh, and consent from the mind. For the serpent suggested the first offense, and Eve, as flesh, was delighted with it, but Adam consented, as the spirit, or mind."[17]

Geoffrey Chaucer's spokesperson for the Christian tradition in the Middle Ages, the simple country Parson, makes a similar point by relating for his fellow Canterbury pilgrims the story of Adam and Eve as an explanation for the origin of sin. The Parson reasons: "There may ye see that deedly synne hath first suggestion of the feend, as sheweth heere by the naddre [snake]; and afterward, the delit of the flessh, as sheweth heere by Eve; and after that, the consentynge of resoun, as sheweth heere by Adam. / For trust wel, though so were that the feend tempted Eve, that is to seyn the flessh, and the flessh hadde delit in the beautee of the fruyt defended, yet certes, til that resoun, that is to seyn Adam, consented to the etynge of the fruyt, yet stood he in th'estaat of innocence."[18]

In a similar vein, Chaucer translates Boethius's sixth-century *Consolation of Philosophy* and in so doing reiterates the all-embracing association of women with flesh and all things passing, whereas men he continues to associate with reason. As he renders Boethius's Latin into Middle English, Chaucer provides both translation and interpretation, so that in the poetic segment with which Book Three concludes, Chaucer explains that, when Orpheus casts his eye back on his beloved Eurydice as he redeems her from Pluto's hell, in looking back on Eurydice, Orpheus has set his eye on temporal things and hence loses all. "For whoso that ever be so overcomen that he fychche his eyen into the putte [pit] of helle (*that is to seyn, whoso sette his thowhtes in erthely thinges*), al that evere he hath drawen of the noble good celestial, he leseth it whan he loketh the helles (*that is to seyn, into lowe thinges of the erthe*)."[19] As a consequence, Chaucer's Parson refers to the lecherous kissing of a woman rather like the kissing of a hot oven, the undertaking of a fool "for the mouth is the mouth of helle. . . ." Is it any wonder, therefore, that Chaucer's Chauntecleer should conflate the Johanine *in principio* with the story of Adam and Eve to croon of womankind: *"In principio, mulier est hominis confusio"* (In the beginning, woman was the confusion of man)? Indeed, as Chauntecleer perches beside his Pertelot, when he sees the beauty of her eyes and feels the warmth of her sides, all reason escapes him—woman is depicted as the death of reason and her body as the downfall of man. (An encapsulation of Plato's concern about the body as an impediment to undistracted rumination.)

Aquinas explains the divinely ordained role of woman (I, q. xcviii, art. 1) by commenting on the first Genesis story's depiction of woman as help-mate: "she was not fitted to help man except in generation, because another man would have proved a more effective help in anything else."[20] Woman's role, in Aquinas's eyes, is a purely sexual one. Clearly, woman was created "not, indeed, as a helpmate in other works, as some say, since man can be more effectively helped by another man in other works, but as a helper in the work of generation."[21]

The medieval Christian view of body, woman, and sense is further compounded by the persistent depiction of the body as an impediment, a prison for the soul. In his *Confessions of a Catholic*, ultraconservative U.S. Catholic Michael Novak takes direct aim at the concept, denying the existence of what is a well-established dualism. Novak insists that "Christianity is not about the soul, or in any case not the soul alone. It does not regard this body as a prison, a cage, a corruption."[22] Would that Novak's assertion were more than defensive rhetoric. Plato makes frequent reference to the relationship of body and soul as prison and captive, mentioning it in his "Phaedo," "Phaedrus," and "Cratylus."[23] In fact, Walter Kaufman recalls Plato's citing of the ancient wordplay whereby the body (*soma*) is the soul's tomb (*sema*), a wordplay that Kaufman notes was a favourite of the Orphic sect.[24] Given the enormous influence Plato and the Neo-Platonic philosophers had on the development of Christian thought, it was quite natural that English literature should be replete with references to a telling image that translated comfortably into the Christian tradition. For the Anglo-Saxon, death was both the great equalizer and the constant companion. Extant Old English poetry, therefore, not only contains a sardonic poem that modern editors have entitled "The Grave," but it also has in its corpus two "Body and Soul" poems in which the soul complains bitterly to the decaying body in imagery suggestive of body as jailer and soul as captive. The soul laments its plight: "thou hast bound me with cruel hunger and fettered me in the torments of hell. I dwelt within thee; encompassed by flesh I could not go from thee, and thy evil desires thronged upon me. . . ."[25] In the high Middle Ages, Chaucer's Second Nun prays to the Virgin Mary:

> And of thy light my soule in prison lighte,
> That troubled is by the contagioun
> Of my body. . . .[26]

Renaissance writers show a repetitive fondness for the image of the imprisoned soul, perhaps the best-known example of which is Andrew Marvell's "A Dialogue between the Soul and Body." Marvell begins his poem in a dramatic and engaging style typical of the metaphysical poet:

> O who shall, from this Dungeon raise
> A Soul inslv'd so many wayes?
> With bolts of Bones, that fetter'd stands
> In Feet; and manacled in Hands.
> Here blinded with an Eye; and there
> Deaf with the drumming of an Ear.
> A Soul hung up, as 'twere, in Chains
> Of Nerves, and Arteries, and Veins.[27]

In similar vein, Richard Crashaw, who was a subcanon at Loreto when he died in 1649, introduces his celebration "To the Infant Martyrs" with the exhortation,

> Goe smiling soules, your new built Cages
> break[28]

and Thomas Traherne's opening lines of "Hosanna" recapture the image:

> No more shall Walls, no more shall Walls confine
> That glorious soul which in my flesh doth shine.[29]

That William Shakespeare was also familiar with the image as it had been canonized over the ages is clear in *King John* when King Philip banters:

Look, who comes here! A grave unto a soul;
Holding the eternal spirit against her will,
In the vile prison of afflicted breath.[30]

But it is no doubt Jesuit poet Gerard Manley Hopkins's "Caged Skylark" with its echo of the Old English kenning and its overarching vision of man's spirit being caged like a bird eking out its dreary existence that is best known to modern readers. The style of Hopkins's lyrical meditation unites past with present in a way that bespeaks a sense of tradition, a tradition in which the body is an encumbrance for a soul meant to fly to loftier heights:

As a dare-gale skylark scanted in a dull cage
Man's mounting spirit in his bone-house, mean house dwells. . . .[31]

The sampling is sufficient to illustrate both an image and an attitude, an image that bespeaks an attitude. Despite Michael Novak's protestations to the contrary, ours is a tradition that has not celebrated but has instead denigrated the physical. Chaucer's "Tale of Melibee" nicely outlines in simple allegorical form the medieval Christian sense of body as the source of sin, of the five senses as the gateways of the devil. And so it is that 700 years later and as part of an unbroken tradition, the preacher of Stephen Dedalus's high school retreat sketches a graphic depiction of a hell in which each of the senses is tormented since it is the senses that have consigned the soul to the torments of the netherworld. Joyce's homilist warns his charges: "Every sense of the flesh is tortured and every faculty of the soul therewith: the eyes with impenetrable utter darkness, the nose with noisome odours, the ears with yells and howls and execrations, the taste with foul matter, leprous corruption, nameless suffocating filth, the touch of redhot goads and spikes, with cruel tongues of flame."[32] For his part, Stephen Dedalus reacts as generations of Christians have been taught, by mortifying the body: "mortify"; i.e., "to make dead."

James Joyce, Geoffrey Chaucer, the Old English and Metaphysical Poets, the range of writers quoted and to be quoted provide important voices in what Joyce's Stephen Dedalus would term the discovery of "the uncreated conscience of my race." Given a legacy in which both classical and Christian philosophy as well as the literature of the Western world have associated woman with the material and sensual, and the sensual with an incarcerating evil, what attitudes will have been inculcated willy-nilly into generations of Christians with respect not only toward womanhood but also toward marriage? What does the Venerable Bede's paraphrase of the Pauline acquiescence with respect to concupiscence mean both with respect to marriage and to woman when he quotes Pope Saint Gregory's advice "Let him that cannot contain himself, have his wife"?[33]

Although Aquinas's universe relegates woman to a hierarchical position inferior to man's, he does not wish this natural inferiority to be taken as a licence for abuse. While examining the second creation myth, therefore, Aquinas concludes (I, xcii, art. 2) that "it was right for the woman to be made from the rib of man. First, to signify the social union of man and woman, for the woman should neither use authority over man, and so she was not made from his head; nor was it right for her to be subject to man's contempt as his slave, and so she was not made from his feet."[34] There is, Aquinas notes, another significance to Eve's birth from the side of Adam: "there is a sacramental reason for this. For by this is signified that the Church takes her origin from Christ."[35] (This point is not inconsequential when considering the role of woman in the ecclesial hierarchy.)

Consistent with his other uses of scholastic thinking, Chaucer turns to his Parson to translate the teachings of Aquinas into the realm of the imagination and hence to introduce it to the secular household. While discussing the virtue of chastity as a remedy for lust—a hierarchically threefold chastity relating in descending order from virginity, through widowhood, and marriage—the Parson argues that it would be egregious for women to have more than one head (that is, more than one husband), as the marriage between Christ and his Church will bear witness. The Parson continues his disquisition: "Now comth how that a man sholde bere hym with his wyf, and namely in two thynges, that is to seyn in suffraunce and reverence, as shewed Crist whan he made first womman. / For he ne made hire nat of the heved of Adam [he did not make her from Adam's head], for she sholde nat clayme to greet lordshipe. / For ther as the womman hath the maistrie [mastery], she maketh to much desray [disarray] . . . certes, God ne made nat womman of the foot of Adam for she ne sholde nat been holden to lowe, for she kan nat paciently suffre."[36] (A comment relevant not just to Church teaching with respect to domestic society, but one that also extends to the rationale for an exclusively male priesthood.)

Both Aquinas and Chaucer have taken Paul's interpretation of the second creation story and provided their own augmentation. Paul's first letter to Timothy (2:12–13) had admonished: "But I suffer not a woman to teach, nor to use authority over the man: but to be in silence. For Adam was first formed; then Eve." It is an argument that Chaucer's Wife of Bath sets out to turn on its head in a satirical tour de force that documents the wide gap between philosophical abstraction and lived experience. Indeed, Chaucer's Clerk—a student of philosophy and lover of Aristotle—returns to the fray with a tale intended to prove the validity of the schoolmen's logic, and in so doing demonstrates once more the folly of divorcing experience from philosophical reflection. In classical satirical style, Chaucer accepts the thesis at face value and has the Clerk present a story of an ideal wife, Griselda, whose obedience to her husband is total: she accepts his proposal of marriage on his terms, promising never to say nay when he says ye, nor ever to hint at her displeasure with so much as a grimace. Griselda understands her divinely ordained role as it is filtered through the Middle Ages: "a kind of friendly and genuine union of the one ruling and the other obeying."[37]

Griselda's relationship with her husband is a satiric representation of the divinely ordained marital contract as it is described by St. Paul and Aquinas. Not only does the relationship echo Paul's advice to Timothy, but it also recalls the hierarchy constructed by Paul in his first letter to the Corinthians: "But I would have you know that the head of every man is Christ; and the head of the woman is the man; and the head of Christ is God." Griselda's submissiveness to her husband, therefore, is an allegorical representation of man's obedience to God and that of the wife to her husband, the image of divinity within the marriage union.

The Clerk's tale outlines the classical-medieval thesis of the well-ordered and divinely shaped universe in which man images God in domestic society, and does so in a way only a clerk could conceive of it. It is a wholly male-dominant perception of reality conceived in the abstract and it is greeted with a hearty guffaw at the conclusion of its telling since its thesis simply does not square with reality. The poet has the ability to test the dominant philosophy in the crucible of everyday living in a way the philosopher is not equipped to do. One is reminded of the allegorical debate in Chaucer's *Parliament of Fowls* in which the cuckoo, the image of the priestly clerk, advises the assembled that the remedy for the discord that has developed in the pairing of the fowl is lifelong chastity: "Let ech of hem be soleyn al here lyve!"[38] It is an otherworldly piece of advice that is greeted with general derision and accusations of outright hypocrisy. Monty Python's Twistian extravaganza "Every Sperm Is Sacred," a Broadway-like sketch from "The Meaning of Life," is a lighthearted broadside at the teachings of *Humanae vitae* on birth control cast in a style that owes a good deal to Chaucer, as does a good bit of Pythonesque satiric humour, and suggests that the gap between dictum and practice is by no means a recent construct. If only Milton's poetry implied a sense of humour, one would put his Eve's first words to Adam into the same category rather than accepting them as a Puritan perpetuation of the Aristotelian and Pauline traditions:

. . . O thou for whom
And from whom I was form'd flesh of thy flesh,
And without whom am to no end [i.e., I have no purpose], my Guide
And Head. . . ." (*Paradise Lost*, IV, 440–443)[39]

Thinking such as this has reached effectively into contemporary Western society. Take, for example, Elizabeth Elliott's insistence: "Scripture makes it very plain that sexuality is a paradigm of a relationship which exists between Christ and His Church. And because it is a pattern of a heavenly mystery it should not be tampered with. . . . I believe the feminist movement is a form of rebellion against God, because God is the one who arranged distinct roles for men and women."[40] Is it any wonder that Nora, the heroine of Henrik Ibsen's *A Doll's House*, should slam the door on her husband and her past, with her husband's admonitions ringing in her ears, "Can you understand your place in your own home? Have you not a reliable guide in such matters as that?—have you no religion?" For Nora, Torvald's time-honoured plea rings hollow: "This is how you neglect your most sacred duties. . . . Before all else you are a wife and a mother." To all of which Nora responds: "I don't believe that any longer. I believe that before all else I am a reasonable human being just as you are—or, at all events, that I must try to become one. I know quite well, Torvald, that most people would think you are right and that views of that kind are to be found in books. I must think things over for myself and get to understand them."[41] Nora first slammed her door in 1879, but as Elliott reminds us, for many, even today, the ancient hierarchies still stand.

There is an unbroken line from Elizabeth Elliott that one can retrace through the Christian tradition to St. Paul and before him to Aristotle, one which establishes clear attitudes toward women, men, and their respective marital roles. There is an inevitable consistency to this vision as it helps to shape the Vatican's attitudes with respect to sexuality.

THE THREEFOLD HIERARCHY: VIRGINITY, WIDOWHOOD, AND MARRIAGE

The Christian sense of hierarchy mirrors the soul/body perspective that runs inexorably through the Church's thinking concerning sexuality, marriage, and priesthood. According to the medieval order with respect to human relationships, there was a threefold hierarchy of virginity, widowhood, and marriage that became well established in the early Middle Ages, appearing as a leitmotif in much of the homiletic literature throughout the Old English period. The closer one's relationship to the physical, the less perfect the relationship. In his *Adversus Jovinianum* ("Against Jovinian," 1, 3), Saint Jerome relates each of these states to the seedgrain of Matthew 13:8, which brought forth an abundance of a hundredfold, sixtyfold, and thirtyfold. Ælfric "the Grammarian," late tenth-century abbot of Eynsham, England, and a prolific homilist, makes use of Jerome's exegesis on a number of occasions, including his discussion on virginity (*De virginitate*) and his Homily on the Purification of Mary. His comments with respect to the least of the three rewards, the thirtyfold reward associated with the married state, is explicit in its attitude toward marriage and sexuality, and reflects a perspective on the marriage bed to which we will return. Ælfric explains: "Those who rightly hold their marriage vow, and at permitted times, and for the procreation of children, have carnal intercourse, shall have a thirtyfold meed for their discretion. He who will satiate his libidinousness as often as he lists, shall be compared with the beasts and not with men."[42]

All of these sentiments are repeated by Chaucer's Parson at the close of the fourteenth century in his discourse on the sin of lust when he notes that there is "the hundred fruyt" for those who remain virgin, a phrase he says he has translated from the Latin text and its reference to the "*centesimus fructus*."[43] This preference for virginity over the married state is a long-standing one. Augustine's *De bono coniugali* and *Holy Virginity* are directed against the teaching of Jovinian, a late fourth-century monk who argued against the elevation of virginity over marriage, an argument that garnered sufficient support among cloistered nuns and monks to merit papal condemnation.[44] For Aquinas, unsullied virginity is the more perfect option since the perpetual celibate is "immune to the flame of concupiscence" (IIa, IIae, q. 152, art. 1).

Aquinas amplified his argument concerning the superiority of virginity over the married state (IIa, IIae, q. 152, art. 4), encapsulating Augustine and reasoning that Christ had selected a virgin for his mother and that Christ himself had remained virginal. Virginity, Aquinas posits, is a divine good and by its nature superior to a merely human good, just as the contemplative is superior to the active; virginity pertains to the good of the soul in accord with the contemplative state, whereas marriage relates to the good of the body and the corporal multiplication of the human race—man and woman join in matrimony and live by necessity cognizant of the good of this world as St. Paul had pointed out in his first letter to the Corinthians 7:33–34. So, when John Paul II argues in his statement on marriage, *Familiaris consortio*, that the virgin state is the most perfect, he is following a well-established tradition, as unwelcome as his words may be for many a married person. John Paul II reasons: "Virginity, or celibacy, by liberating the human heart in a unique way, 'so as to make it burn with greater love for God and all humanity,' bears witness that the Kingdom of God and His justice is that pearl of great price which is preferred to every other value no matter how great, and hence must be sought as the only definitive value. It is for this reason that the Church, throughout history, has always defended the superiority of this charism to that of marriage, by reason of the wholly singular link which it has with the Kingdom of God."[45]

These attitudes toward the virgin state have been much studied and are well known. They represent not only an escape from the world and an expression of the *contemptus mundi* that is an unhappy component of our Christian heritage, but they also represent an attitude toward sexuality that is essentially negative. St. Jerome's letter to Eustochium in 384, for example, was written to reassure her in her decision to live under the vow of virginity. Marriage and married women, he says, have their place, though there are certain disadvantages, such as pregnancy, crying babies, the need to manage a household. . . . To which Jerome adds that his purpose in writing to Eustochium is to show her that she is "fleeing from Sodom" and that, like Lot's wife, she should not look back.[46] These are, perhaps, not unexpected sentiments given the context of Jerome's letter; however, his correspondence to Furia, written in 394, paints an even more negative picture of the married state. Writing to urge Furia to remain a widow now that her husband has died, Jerome urges her not to imitate the dog who has returned to its vomit or the freshly washed sow to its muck; Jerome wonders if Furia is worried that the line of Camillus will be cut short, or whether her father will be deprived of "a brat of yours to crawl upon his breast and soil his neck with nastiness."[47] The life of the widow, however, will not be an easy one. Since the widow will recollect past pleasures, she will need to take care to mortify her body so as to live a chaste life: "she must quench the fire of the devil's shafts with the cold streams of fast and vigil,"[48] eschewing fine dress and rich food, being a woman who is "dead while she liveth." As one might expect, therefore, medieval lives of the saints are populated not only with the heroic example of virgins under siege but also with the chaste ministrations of virtuous widows, such as she who "chastely" cares for the bones of Saint Edmund in Ælfric's hagiographic recounting of Edmund's death, miracles, and cult.

If virginity and widowhood are to be most prized, then what of marriage and sexuality? At one point in her long preamble to her tale, Chaucer's caricature of the woman of the world, of sexuality, temptation, and unrestrained libido, the Wife of Bath (five times a widow), exclaims; "Allas, allas, that evere love was synne!"[49]—the sinfulness of sexuality is suggested by Ælfric's comments above, but it too is an attitude with a long history, a history that states that the pleasure associated with the sex act is sinful. This sinfulness is explained to Augustine of Canterbury at the end of the sixth century when Pope Saint Gregory notes that a man who has had intercourse with his wife may not enter the church without washing, and even then he may not enter it immediately out of respect. Bede records the exchange in his *Ecclesiastical History of the English Nation*, including Gregory's explanation: "Nor do we, in so saying, assign matrimony to be a fault, but forasmuch as lawful intercourse cannot be had without the pleasure of the flesh, it is proper to forbear entering the holy place, because the pleasure itself cannot be without a fault. For he was not born of adultery or fornication, but of lawful marriage, who said, 'Behold I was conceived in iniquity, and in sin my mother brought me forth.' For he who knew he was born in iniquity, lamented that he was born from sin, because the tree in its bough bears the moisture it drew from the root. In which words he does not call the union of the married couple iniquity, but the pleasure of the copulation."[50] Hence the medieval schoolman's attitude toward the genitalia as the *partes inhonestae*, a perspective satirized by the Monty Python team in their reference to "the nasty bits."

Viewpoints such as these are implicit in St. Augustine's thesis that if Adam and Eve had not sinned in the Garden, copulation and childbirth would have taken place without physical desire, but rather would have been modulated by the human will: no concupiscence, no shameful appetites.[51] Although Aquinas rejects the contentions of some of the Fathers of the Church, such as Gregory of Nyssa's notion that without the Fall procreation would have taken place without a sexual embrace as is the case with the angels, Aquinas is inclined to Augustine's perspective, save that Aquinas acknowledges the existence of pleasure as inherent in the sex act and argues that without the sin of Adam and Eve, pleasure would have been curbed by reason. This, says Aquinas, is what Augustine really meant: he was not excluding sensual pleasure, just its intensity, "the ardour of desire and the restlessness of the soul."[52] However one interprets Augustine's ruminations, it is difficult indeed to find in his words a celebration of sensual pleasure or even an exoneration of it; indeed, Augustine's own wayward youth and his heated encounters with "the slimy lusts of the flesh and the bubbling froth of puberty" left him anything but a dispassionate commentator on the relationship between the sexes.[53]

Chaucer's Parson avoids the extreme rhetoric that Augustine was inclined to employ; nonetheless, the Parson concurs on the central point, explaining that there are two ways to control the "movings of the flesh"— chastity in widowhood and chastity in marriage. Matrimony, he points out, has the effect of replenishing Holy Church with sound lineage as well as of "cleansing fornication," "for that is the ende of mariage and it chaungeth deedly synne into venial synne bitwexe hem that been ywedded."[54] Sex is for procreation, not pleasure. As Ælfric had noted in his late tenth-century homily for the dedication of a church, it is sinful for a man to eat more than his body requires or to enjoy his wife more often than needs be for the procreation of children that: "he oftor wifes bruce. donne he do for bearnes gestreone."[55] Philosophical food for satire. So it is that Chaucer pokes fun at the Church's elevation of procreation over the sinful pleasures of the flesh when, in his "Nun's Priest's Tale," he sets up the lusty barnyard cock for his fall from grace on Friday, Venus's day (vendredi; i.e., Venus's day)—Venus, whose prescriptions for love Chauntecleer had embraced as a devotee, for whom sex was "more for delit than world to multiplye" (v. 3345).[56]

Attitudes such as these are often found in the medieval penitentials and provide an insight into early Christian sexual teaching, which is neither sensitive nor healthy; attitudes such as these could, in fact, only be the product of a reclusive clerical rationality. Take, for example, the advice for confessors to be found in the tenth-century Old English penitential of Pseudo-Ecgbert. In Theodoric's penitential, confessors are advised how married couples ought to conduct themselves before God. It counsels that Holy Books teach what each of the faithful is to do when he brings home his bride. According to these texts, the newlyweds must first maintain their sexual innocence for three days and three nights, and then on the third day they must attend Mass, but without taking the Eucharist, and afterwards they may consummate their marriage before God and the world, as their need may be. In addition, each must conduct his marriage so as to remain chaste during the forty days and forty nights of the holy Easter season and all of Easter week and every Sunday, Wednesday, and Friday. And every righteous woman must maintain her chastity three months before childbirth, and after childbirth she must hold herself chaste for forty days and forty nights, whether the child born be male or female.[57] For the convenience of the confessor, the penitentials take care to prescribe appropriate penances for many of the above offences, including penalties for women who enter the church during their time of "impurity" or before the forty-day period of purification.[58]

THE "CONSTANT TRADITION" FROM LEO XIII TO JOHN PAUL II

These attitudes toward human sexuality, domestic relationships, and the underlying concept of a divinely conceived hierarchical structure as shaped during the early and high Middle Ages were transmitted without substantial change into the twentieth century. Pope Leo XIII's *Arcanum*, an encyclical on Christian marriage issued on February 10, 1880, does nonetheless break some new ground. There is, to be sure, the tradition-ally ingrained notion that it is the naturally divined role of women to fulfil their marital obligation and to "minister to the pleasures of men":[59] for those who cannot contain the fires of concupiscence, it is better to marry than to burn; as flesh of his flesh and as daughter of Eve, it is also the wife's lot to be both subject and obedient to her husband whose God-given role it is to command while it is hers to obey, though successions of popes have insisted that such a subjugation is not without due respect for honour and dignity. The husband has the additional obligation to bring up the children "in the discipline and correction of the Lord." At the same time, Leo talks about equal rights for husbands and wives, and, although he does place primacy on the begetting of children "for the Church," he expands more traditional notions with a touch of sensitivity, adding: "Not only, in strict truth, was marriage instituted for the propagation of the human race, but also that the lives of husbands and wives might be made better and happier"—an observation with which even Augustine would have agreed since he saw the good of marriage "not . . . solely because of the procreation of children, but also because of the natural companion-ship between the two sexes. Otherwise, we could not speak of marriage in the case of old people, especially if they had either lost their children or had begotten none at all."[60]

Unfortunately, however, Leo's principal target in the composition of *Arcanum* is more political than familial. Leo is concerned about political developments at home and abroad, the detrimental impact of various Socialist and Communist governments on the Christian family, the after-effects of the French Revolution (the Pope refers to it as that "conflagration in France"), the ever-increasing lack of respect for public order, the enfeebling of legitimate authority, growing demands for individual rights, and the widespread judgment that nothing is "so unbearable as submission and obedience." It is therefore time, Leo argues, for the state and the Church to work hand in hand, for "when the civil power is on friendly terms with the sacred authority of the Church, there accrues to both a great increase of usefulness." The happy and stable household that the Church can foster is good for the state: "From such marriages as these the State may rightly expect a race of citizens animated by a good spirit and filled with reverence and love for God, recognizing it their duty to obey those who rule justly and lawfully, to love all, and to injure no one."

Leo's *Arcanum* is an unflatteringly politicized statement that repeats many of the traditional hierarchical attitudes concerning husbands and wives long canonized by the Church, but adds to that thinking both a sense of partnership and personal well-being in a tone that is generally absent from earlier, more tightly argued teachings. For the translation of traditional thinking into turn-of-the-twentieth-century perspectives, however, one ought also to consider Leo's famous 1891 social encyclical, *Rerum novarum*—Leo's groundbreaking reflections on Communism and liberal capitalism. For example, in *Rerum novarum* Leo reiterates the Church's attitudes toward virginity as the superior charism, noting that an individual is free to choose either "the counsel of virginity given by Jesus Christ, or to bind himself in the bonds of matrimony."[61] At the same time, to his repudiation of child labour and the imposition of sweatshop conditions on bodies and minds that are not sufficiently mature, Leo adds that women, too, are unsuited for certain trades, "for a woman is by nature fitted for home-work, and it is that which is best adapted at once to preserve her modesty, and to promote the good upbringing of children and the well-being of the family."[62]

If *Arcanum* was a response to a particular context, so was its immediate successor, *Casti connubii*. Not only were there external and non-Christian pressures being exerted on the traditional Christian marriage in the early twentieth century, but attitudes within the Christian Churches themselves had begun to change. In 1930, at the height of the Great Depression, the Anglican Church's Lambeth Conference confirmed by a vote of 193 to sixty-seven the proposition that prospective parents might feel a justifiable moral duty to limit the size of their families. While accepting this possibility, the Conference argued that such parents ought, however, to make such decisions in the light of Christian principles—they ought to exercise abstinence and self-control. Other means may well be morally acceptable, however, provided that they, too, were pursued in a manner consonant with traditional Christian morality and not for selfish reasons, luxury, or as a matter of convenience. Centuries of sexual teachings with respect to the procreative and unitive ends of marriage had been breached and Pius XI was quick to respond. *Casti connubii*, "Of Chaste Wedlock," was promulgated on December 31, 1930. Its title, the first two words of the Latin text, tells it all.

Noting that matrimony was not instituted by man but by God, Pius quotes with approval Leo XIII's attitudes toward virginity and marriage, and, with respect to the latter, he makes it very clear that "To take away from man the natural and primeval right of marriage, to circumscribe in any way the principal ends of marriage laid down in the beginning by God Himself in the words 'Increase and multiply' is beyond the power of any human law."[63] (As John Paul II argues concerning the ordination of women, some things are simply beyond the ability of mere humans to regulate.) Implied in the Pope's quoting of the Genesis directive to "Increase and multiply" as authority for his regulation is the codicil "in every instance" and implied, too, is the inclusion of the restriction "and the sole purpose of sex is exclusively to facilitate the divine directive to increase and multiply." These are implications that the text will not sustain.

Although Pius XI's insistence that the primary end of marriage is the procreation of children is wholly consistent with centuries of Christian teaching, his quoting of Genesis or his like-minded predecessors is hardly convincing evidence for his position, nor is his insistence on the assurance of the Council of Trent that God will provide, that "There is no possible circumstances in which husband and wife cannot, strengthened by the grace of God, fulfill faithfully their duties and preserve in wedlock their chastity unspotted." Nor is it necessarily reassuring to be told by the apparent source of power within the Church that "Christ constituted the

Church the guardian and the teacher of the whole truth concerning religion and moral conduct," or that a religious authority is necessary to enlighten the intellect and direct the will as well as to strengthen human frailty, and that "Such an authority is found nowhere save in the Church instituted by Christ the Lord."

The main problem, Pius argues, is "unbridled lust." To rein in this vicious inclination, Pius urges an adherence to the divine plan, a plan, as Augustine described it, in which the lower should be subject to the higher: just as man is subject to God, so the flesh must be subject to man. There is here no concept that God's plan may well have included sexuality for an end that includes more than the procreative. Pius presents the problem as one of lust and a lack of respect for God's intention in ordering the universe. Pius's attitude toward sexuality and human behaviour is all too clear in his enumerating of the convictions of those who would argue for the use of birth control: (1) "they are weary of children and wish to gratify their desires without their consequent burden"; (2) "they cannot on the one hand remain continent nor on the other can they have children because of the difficulties whether on the part of the mother or on the part of family circumstances." In response to which Pius argues that birth control is "intrinsically against nature," that birth control is "intrinsically vicious," and that there is an uninterrupted Christian tradition to back him up. We would surely be the recipients of fewer lectures on "unbridled lust" if the authors of Roman documents had experiential knowledge of the human reality that the real pleasure of the sexual embrace is in giving pleasure to one's spouse or if they understood the interpersonal covenant that is conceived in a loving act of sexual intimacy. Blanket assumptions about humankind's headlong rush into a hedonistic nirvana do justice neither to the human condition nor to the nature of marital love.

Other uninterrupted traditions with divine sanction to which Pius refers include the primacy of the husband and the "ready subjection of the wife and her willing obedience," the hierarchical ordering of things by which "man is the head, the woman is the heart, and as he occupies the place in ruling, so she may and ought to claim for herself the place in love." It follows from God's intention in establishing this natural order, therefore, and despite the contrary teaching of Leo XIII, that it is wrong to assert that "the rights of husband and wife are equal" (par. 74), that it is

against the nature of things to suggest that "woman even with the knowledge and against the wish of her husband may be at liberty to conduct and
administer her own affairs"—to which he adds, judgmentally, "giving her
attention chiefly to these rather than to children, husband and family"—
for "this false liberty and unnatural equality with the husband is to the
detriment of the woman herself, for if the woman descends from her truly
regal throne. . . ." Because universal assertions such as these and abstract
philosophizing such as this fly in the face of real human experience, they
no longer command the uncritical respect of legions of even the most
committed adherents to the Catholic faith.

Writing in his weekly *Record* column, Frank Morgan, a United Church
minister in Kitchener, Ontario, reflected on an event that took place on
Parliament Hill in Ottawa on October 18, 2000. On that day the Canadian
government formally unveiled the statues of the Famous Five, the five
most prominent women in Canada to lead the struggle for women's equality under the law. Morgan searches the Bible for attitudes of inequality
and finds none. He does, however, find them within the Christian tradition. Morgan casts his eyes on his bookcase, to pictures of his wife, his two
daughters, and his two granddaughters, and, noting that like the Christian
thinkers who had determined over the centuries that women were not
equal to men, he points out that he, too, was raised in an all-male environment. From all of this, Morgan concludes that now he has his own famous
five to help provide a better outlook on the world for him, and, he
suggests, "His Holiness would write better encyclicals if he had a wife and
two daughters looking over his shoulder and checking up on his public
opinions."[64] Both Dionysius and St. Alphonsus Liguori would applaud
Morgan's conclusion since both spoke out on marital issues in their day,
and both insisted that they would not do so without first consulting
married couples.[65] Mary Kenny, noted Catholic journalist, would also
agree with Morgan. From her perspective, the Vatican in general, and
John Paul II in particular, simply does not have its feet on the ground
when pontificating on marital issues.

I think anybody who is married or has been married is likely to have a
much more sour view of marriage. I think, again, paradoxically, that
celibacy—this is true of the present Pope—is what has kept this ideal of

marriage. He's so idealistic and romantic about marriage, isn't he? Maybe they're too high, those ideals. But I think once you have been married, once you are in a marriage, your view of marriage becomes much more banal in a way. The French have a good verb for that— *balaniser*, "to make banal."

When Good Pope John threw open the windows to allow some fresh air to blow through the Council chambers at the Second Vatican Council, he unharnessed the whirlwind. Not only did the Council Fathers in general begin to take a more compassionate view of the marital relationship, but they even began to talk in more holistic language about the human person. *Gaudium et spes*, the conciliar *Constitution on the Church in the Modern World* promulgated on December 7, 1965, speaks in terms of a union of body and soul in which the body is to be viewed as "good and honourable," though it has suffered the wounds of sin. Despite Leo's assertions in *Arcanum* about the wounding of legitimate authority and about the inflaming of minds "with a reckless spirit of liberty"—in the case of woman, Pius preached about a "false liberty and unnatural equality" in *Casti connubii*—the Council Fathers depicted liberty as essential to questions of human dignity, insisting that "Only in freedom can man direct himself toward goodness." Freedom also implies certain fundamental rights and abominates discrimination of all sorts, whether based on "sex, race, social condition, language, or religion."

Part II of *Gaudium et spes* concentrates on problems of "Special Urgency" including matters relating to family. Referring to the domestic society as "this community of love," the Council Fathers continue their examination of joy and hope in a consistently compassionate tone that is so often absent from the more juridic and philosophical texture so characteristic of Vatican pronouncements. In *Gaudium et spes*, conjugal love is not only life-giving with respect to its procreative purpose, but "these actions signify and promote that mutual self-giving by which spouses enrich each other with a joyful and thankful will." Nor is the marital relationship posited on a happy subjection of wife to husband; rather, the unity of marriage will radiate from the equal personal dignity of husband and wife." While the begetting of children remains the "supreme gift of marriage," in the eyes of the Council Fathers, it is not the only purpose of marriage, nor are these other purposes hierarchically inferior to it. As a result, the usual directive to "increase and multiply" is followed immediately with the qualification: "Hence, while not making the other purposes of matrimony of less account . . .", the Council taught that the couple should be ready to co-operate with the Creator to enlarge the human family. At the same time, the couple is counselled to take into consideration their welfare and that of their children, both those born and those who might one day be born, and they ought also to regard both their material and spiritual circumstances as well as their own social situation. The picture of the family as it is presented throughout this section of the document might in many ways be an idealized one, but there is none of the harshly judgmental tone that was characteristic of *Casti connubii*; so, when Paul VI decided not to deal with the question of birth control at the Council, the Catholic community might have been forgiven for anticipating a more compassionate response than had been forthcoming in *Casti connubii* once Paul's special commission submitted its review.

For their part, the Council Fathers had concluded their deliberations of the birth control question by noting the principles at issue: the nature of the human person, the nature of human acts, the need to retain a sense of self-giving, of being open to procreation "in the context of true love," and the need for the Church's teaching authority to declare that the regulation of procreation is not blameworthy as it interpreted the divine law. And consistent with the Council's teaching on conscience both in *Gaudium et spes* and in *Dignitatis humanae*, the matter is ultimately a matter of informed conscience, of weighing the issues and coming to the right decision; hence, "With docile reverence toward God, they will come to the right decision by common counsel and effort." *Gaudium et spes* teaches, it reasons, and it respects its readers—it does not proclaim. Fresh air indeed. The tone is more evangelical and less monastic; in addition, the emphasis has begun to shift from sexuality as function to sexuality as fusion, to a more holistic view of the human being as a sexual person, from marriage as bond to marriage as relationship. In light of all of these considerations, the issues that the commission was to study would appear to be open to debate, interpretation, and to the benefit of renewed reflection in light of contemporary advancements in the realms of human and scientific knowledge, especially with respect both to our understanding of human psychology and to the proposition that the birth control pill did not artificially interfere unnaturally with the process of human reproduction.

England's Cardinal Heenan reflected the mounting anticipation among the Catholic population when he observed in his 1966 Trinity Sunday pastoral letter that the Church needed to remain current in its teachings. Given his role as a member of the Paul VI's special papal commission, Heenan seemed to be preparing the faithful for new directions in the Church's teaching on sexual issues when he proceeded to explain: "Physical science has revealed new facts about nature. Medicine and psychology have made discoveries about human life itself. Although truth remains the same, our knowledge of it is always increasing. Some of our notions of right and wrong have also undergone change."[66] So, as a result of mounting pressure within the European Church in particular,[67] in response to the persistent urgings of Cardinal Leo Josef Suenens of Malines-Brussels, and in preparation for the anticipated United Nations and World Health Organization conference called to deal with issues relating to population control, in March 1963 Pope John XXIII established a pontifical commission to study the matter of regulating human reproduction. Pope John clearly expected that the commission's findings would be available for deliberation before the conclusion of the Second Vatican Council, which was in fact also the expectation of the majority of the Council Fathers. This commission was unusual in that it included representation from well beyond the usual clerical community, including the voices not only of lay and medical experts on the science of human reproduction, but also of demographers, psychologists, lawyers, and a broad range of other professionals,[68] and eventually it also provided for the voice of thirty-four lay members among whom were married couples and six women. By 1965 the commission had swelled from an original core of six to fifty-eight. Notwithstanding the fact that Paul had expanded the representation of its membership beyond that established by John XXIII, with the death of Pope John and the accession of Paul VI the commission's activities were no longer destined for the Council hall, nor, indeed, were they meant to be available for public scrutiny. This penchant for secrecy is a well-established component of the Vatican modus operandi; delegates to the 1987 Episcopal Synod in Rome, for example, were cautioned that "it would be gravely sinful for them to show the list [of propositions] to anyone or to photocopy it."[69] The commission's deliberations dragged on.

The UN/WTO conference came and went. Then, in April 1967 the commission's report was leaked. Another year passed. Finally, on July 26, 1968, Pope Paul's long-awaited encyclical letter was promulgated. Catholic liberals were dismayed, traditional Catholics reassured. Despite the promise of the Council and the tone of the conciliar documents to which *Humanae vitae* makes reference—*Gaudium et spes* gets special mention—the tone of *Humanae vitae* is a retrenchment, a step back into the all-too-familiar Vaticanese. Though eminent historian David Knowles judges the document to be "solemn and magisterial, yet intensely personal and compassionate . . . perfectly clear and simple,"[70] his point of view is a decidedly minority one. Although the list of the encyclical's addressees begins with the usual hierarchical cast of clerical eminences and tapers finally to the "faithful and to all men of good will," the approach and the terminology characterize a document that was hardly meant to speak to these lesser sorts, who are, nonetheless, the apparent topic of discussion. What, for example, is the lay Catholic to make of an explanation such as this: "To justify conjugal acts made intentionally infecund, one cannot invoke as valid reasons the lesser evil, or the fact that such acts would constitute a whole together with the fecund acts already performed or to follow later, and hence would share in one and the same moral goodness"?[71]

Rather than offering a well-crafted argument addressed to the laity in a language to which they might easily respond, the authors opt instead to employ an array of rhetorical phrases meant to impress and implicitly to command compliance: "It is . . . indisputable," "as no one can deny," "manifested by the constant teaching of the Church," "as interpreted by its constant doctrine," "the teaching authority of the Church has frequently declared," "The Church is coherent with herself." But the documentation itself does not tend to support the lofty rhetoric. For example, the "indisputable" fact that Jesus constituted the apostles as his "guardians and authentic interpreters of all the moral law, not only, that is, of the law of the Gospel, but also of the natural law which is also an expression of the will of God" is substantiated by reference to Matthew 7:21: "Not everyone who says to me, 'Lord, Lord,' shall enter the kingdom of heaven; but he who does the will of my Father in heaven shall enter the kingdom of heaven."

Not a very convincing justification, especially given the importance of the point. The argument of the Magisterium is, after all, based on a theory of natural law reinforced by scripture, and the authors insist that faithful adherence to the magisterial teaching on natural law is "equally necessary for salvation." (The term "Magisterium" is introduced in sections 4 and 6 of *Humanae vitae* and underlines the fact that Paul had taken the matter out of the hands of his commissioners—a widely representative professional group—and given it instead to the members of his Curia under the direction of conservative Cardinal Alfredo Ottaviani of the Holy Office, men who could be counted on to put things right. In Paul's mind, this was a necessary step after the sixteen specially appointed bishops he had inserted into the proceedings *in medias res* in an effort to put a Vatican stamp on the findings of the commission after it had failed to produce the advice he had expected. Consultation Roman style.

The Magisterium, whose advice the Pope had accepted in putting his signature to *Humanae vitae*, notes quite candidly that it is in no way constrained by the decisions of the papal commission, and that, in any event, the Magisterium was bound to make its own examination of the topic. Furthermore, the Magisterium argued that the recommendations of the commission were not unanimous (it does not acknowledge that almost all of the commission's membership favoured change), and that some of the criteria used by the commission in coming to its conclusions were not consistent with magisterial teaching, which had been "proposed with constant firmness." (Redemptorist Bernard Häring, a moral theologian and a member of the commission, is one of many who suggest that in fact the tradition is neither constant nor firm.[72]) Given guidelines such as these, one would have to wonder what it was the commission was supposed to do, other than confirm the "constant" teaching that had preceded its deliberations. When, however, the commissioners were prepared not only to recommend new directions, but even to cast doubt on the theory espoused in *Casti connubii*, Pope Paul apparently decided to seek advice more to his liking.

John Marshall's *Tablet* article "Inside the Commission" provides a first-hand account of the proceedings, including the makeup of the commission, the nature of its deliberations, and the process leading to the vast majority of the commission members' conclusion that "the intrinsic evil of contraception could not reasonably be demonstrated"—only four members were opposed to the recommended change in the Vatican's position.[73] But the Pope and his small coterie of advisers would have none of it. Not only did Paul's Magisterium reaffirm that "each and every marriage act must remain open to the transmission of life," but it proceeded to include in its scope and within a single paragraph birth control, abortion, and sterilization as being apparently equally culpable morally, thus leaving "recourse to the infecund periods" as the only acceptable means for planning the size of one's family since intercourse during the infecund periods was faithful to the "natural rhythms" of human reproduction, as Pius XII had previously taught. The convoluted resolution carries with it what Stephen Dedalus's friend Lynch would have dubbed "the true scholastic stink."[74] All of this despite the fact that the original commission had produced evidence to show that it was the experience of many Catholic families that not only was the rhythm method not in accord with nature, but that it was frequently detrimental to harmonious marital relationships.

Evidence such as this was available from a number of sources, but was certainly submitted to the commission by two of its members, Pat and Patty Crowley, co-founders of the Christian Family Movement. In the end, despite (or perhaps because of) the philosophical trappings in which the encyclical is shrouded, the argument itself is not convincing to the vast majority of the Catholic faithful, especially not convincing to those to whom it is ultimately addressed—the married Roman Catholic—so that what *Humanae vitae* requires of the Catholic spouse is more an act of faith than an intellectual conviction; that is, the traditional proposition that faith and reason are intimately interconnected is seriously eroded both in the argument and in the acceptance of the argument.

Humanae vitae, therefore, provides one more example of the age-old conflict between the cloistered study and life as it is lived in the wider world. One is reminded of the conclusion drawn by Ian Hutchens, the protagonist of Morris West's *Moon in My Pocket* (an early novel published under the nom de plume Julian Morris). Agonizing over his call to become a Christian Brother, Hutchens struggled with the ubiquitous conflict between experience and the "desiccated pedantry of studies";[75] Hutchens's conclusion was certainly shared by West, as it has been for many a Catholic: "Study is not experience. Academics are no substitute for life—nor scholarship—even mellow and rich scholarship—either."[76]

When the Magisterium admitted, with a case of colossal understatement, that "It can be foreseen that this teaching will perhaps not be easily received by all," it blamed this lack of reception on society's "modern means of propaganda" rather than the format of its own message. Not only is *Humanae vitae* loaded with its own ecclesiastical hyperbole, but it also inclines toward a denigration of the human capacity for selfless marital love, opting instead to issue warnings about human weakness, selfish pursuits of pleasure, and the debasing of women. Where, in all of this, is there any recognition of truly loving couples facing hard decisions in their everyday lives? Where in *Humanae vitae* is there either sensitive understanding or compelling argument addressed to "all men of good will" in support of a "constant" and "coherent" directive from Rome? Is it any wonder that *Humanae vitae* has been accepted by very few avowedly Catholic couples committed to living their lives in harmony with basic Gospel values rooted in the principles of Christian love?

It is no secret that *Humanae vitae* has not been widely embraced by the vast majority of practising Catholics. Robert Kaiser records the embarrassed and even hostile reaction it received from both large numbers of bishops and clergy,[77] and Andrew Greeley has concluded that support for the encyclical among priests in the United States has fallen,[78] a perspective reiterated by Garry Wills in his *Papal Sin* and by many others, including Australian historian and broadcaster Father Paul Collins[79] and Donald Cozzens, author of *Changing Face of the Priesthood*, both of whom relate the pain many priests experience in trying to represent a Roman directive that most parishioners simply do not accept.[80] Cardinal G. Emmett Carter of Toronto recalls that when the papal nuncio, Emmanuele Clarizio, brought the news of the encyclical to him, he introduced the topic with an apologetic: "I am very sorry but here is the pope's statement." Carter notes that he and the three other Canadian bishops present at the time "promptly dropped everything else we were doing and poured over the encyclical. It was with a certain sense of dismay that we read the vital passages in it. He had clearly taken a position that was contrary to the majority of his own Commission. We felt that this was going to be a major problem."[81]

Neither Carter nor the Canadian bishops were prepared for the message before them. Consider, for example, Paul VI's encyclical in light of a 1964 confidential report emanating from the Canadian Catholic Conference in response to a questionnaire from Rome and written at a time when the sale of contraceptives was still illegal in Canada.[82] The bishops reported that, for Canada's priests who were working dutifully to teach Catholic sexual doctrine faithfully, the exercise was frustrating indeed, and that from a theological perspective Catholic sexual teaching was running from the extreme of a seminary pedagogy that had not changed in fifty years, to the much more liberal teachings of contemporary Catholic theologians who were inclined to argue for a rather generous leeway on questions relating to the control and regulation of birth. As for the bishops themselves, they confessed that they too were suffering the frustration of not knowing exactly what the Church's teaching was, while among the Catholic population in general the use of contraceptive devices was estimated to range, even then, from 50 to 80 percent. Yet, with respect to sexual morality, the bishops concluded that there was no overriding moral problem, aside from the use of contraception.

Their advice to Rome was characteristic of the Canadian conference. The bishops counselled the adoption of a more pastoral approach than the Vatican's well established preference for simple pontificating in terms of moral right and wrong. They also quote, with apparent approval, the assessment of one of their members who had argued that the Church's formulaic approach to sexual issues, centering on what is forbidden and what is permitted, is both painful and dehumanizing. What was needed, the bishops concluded, was a clear and concise statement from Rome, since the current confusion was causing great concern both for priests and laity alike. Moreover, this confusion, the bishops lamented, was having the unfortunate side effect of calling into question the very teaching authority of the Church and the legitimacy of the natural law. Given the tenor of the times, Canada's bishops cautioned that Rome's statement must be sympathetic in its tone and comprehensible in its diction. It must address the needs of the modern world, including problems relating to population as well as the economic and psychological issues with which the average person must contend. At the same time, Rome's penchant for esoteric philosophical vocabulary ought to be replaced by the more colloquial language spoken by the average person in the pew—the teaching must be readily adaptable to the pulpit, to the confessional, to the classroom.

The ultimate message of *Humanae vitae* is certainly clear, but sensitive it is not, comprehensible to the average person it is not, adaptable to the confessional or classroom it is not. As for the diminution of respect for the teaching authority of the Church, virtually every serious Catholic scholar has concluded that the determining argument that swayed Paul VI to put his name to *Humanae vitae* had to do with retention of the continuous tradition and the potential loss of authority that would accompany the taking of a new direction. It is ironic, therefore, that the effect of promulgation has been exactly the opposite, a decrease in respect for Rome's teaching authority and a feeling that both it and its insistence on a theory of natural law are in fact out of touch with reality. *Humanae vitae*, in other words, has become the perfect catalyst for the promotion of a mature Church, a Church in which individual members assume responsibility for making informed decisions, taking into account their own situation and the directives of the Church. And if the individual is convinced that the Church is out of touch with reality and that its directives are ill-conceived, there is little doubt how most will choose. Thus was born the much-debated term "cafeteria Catholic."

British neurologist John Marshall, who was an original member of the six-person papal commission, points out that most acts of intercourse are naturally non-procreative and that in fact nature intended them to be so. With this in mind, he tries to paraphrase a Roman syllogism on the subject. "By what moral principle are men and women forbidden to make intercourse, for good reason, what nature at other times makes it? Because it shows 'contraceptive intent'. But are not couples who deliberately choose non-procreative acts showing 'contraceptive intent'? No, because they are not interfering with the nature of the act of intercourse. So, we go round the circle again."[83]

Many would argue that when Pius XII gave Rome's blessing to the rhythm method, he was, in effect, showing his own support for "contraceptive intent" since the clear intention of the rhythm method is to engage in coital acts whose intention is contra conception. As a result, Roman Catholics no doubt more readily than non-Catholics have been conditioned to appreciate the layers of satire at the heart of Monty

Python's "Every Sperm Is Sacred" or to relate to Adam Appleby's frustrations and his wife's miscalculations in David Lodge's novel on Vatican
Roulette, *The British Museum Is Falling Down*. More's the pity, first of
all because the old museum did not have to fall down and secondly
because, as John Marshall points out, there is a social need for a clear and
respected moral voice, a voice that begins with a sensitive understanding
of human love and that challenges Christian couples to make their love
one with the divine. But, regrettably, the Catholic Church has created a
vacuum of leadership in this area because of its rigid adherence to apparently negative attitudes toward sexuality and married life.[84] Greeley
concludes that the organizational Church has suffered dramatically as a
result of the encyclical, that its administration is a shambles, that people
are leaving the Church in large numbers, that both the priesthood and
sisterhood are in decline, that financial donations are taking a beating,
and that *Humanae vitae* is the primary culprit.[85] He recalls a conversation with Cardinal John Cody on the topic, which Greeley says took
place while Cody was archbishop of Chicago and which Cody says never
took place at all. For his part, Greeley insists that Cody told him that the
Holy See has expectations about the kinds of comments members of the
hierarchy can make about Roman encyclicals, but "I have a hard time
sleeping at night because of the terrible harm that goddam encyclical is
causing in my archdiocese."[86] Yet the affirmation of *Humanae vitae*'s
teachings has become one significant element of the litmus test applied to
any who would be bishop.

THE AFTERMATH OF *HUMANAE VITAE*

Although the workings of the commission, like many of Rome's consultative gatherings, were intended to be conducted under a veil of absolute
secrecy, the findings of the commission were widely anticipated as a result
of the April 1967 clandestine publication of the *Pontifical Commission on
Population, Family, and Birth* (1964–1966) in *The Tablet* and *National
Catholic Reporter*. So, when the magisterial report was finally promulgated some two years after the commission had submitted its findings to
the Pope, the groundswell of disappointment and resistance was simply
too dramatic to be ignored. Bishops' conferences scrambled to reassure

the laity, often counselling them that an informed conscience was to serve as their guide. Such indeed had been the recurrent theme that ran through the commission's report, arguing the case for responsible parenthood by reasoning that parents "will make a judgement in conscience before God about the number of children to have and educate according to the objective criteria indicated by Vatican Council II."[87] In this light, the commission defines the marriage of husband and wife as a union of love and refers to sexuality in this relationship as life-giving, finding sexual intercourse morally objectionable when it is "spoiled by egoism or hedonism," but concluding that with new knowledge and a better understanding of marriage, biology, sexuality, psychology, infant mortality rates, the nature of womanhood, and demographics, the commission favours the "regulation of conception by using means, human and decent, ordered to favouring fecundity in the totality of married life and toward the realization of the authentic values of fruitful matrimonial community."[88]

For the commission, the heart of the matter lay in the concept of fruitfulness and an expansive understanding of the concept of life-giving. And, the commissioners reason, "In such a conception the substance of the tradition stands in continuity and is respected."[89] Unlike *Humanae vitae*, the terminology of the commission report is clear and the tone sensitive. The commission has not only taken into account the progress of human understanding, but in so doing has given the Vatican a means to make a responsible redefinition of its position in light of new knowledge and in a manner consistent with Gospel principles. Cardinal Carter and his fellow bishops had good cause to be dismayed and the papal nuncio good cause to be apologetic.

Like bishops around the world—bishops from countries such as West Germany, Austria, Scandinavia, France, Brazil, and the United States— Canada's bishops felt duty-bound to respond. When the Canadian bishops gathered in Winnipeg in September 1968 for their annual conference, therefore, they used the opportunity to draft a response for the Canadian Church, a response that was quickly christened *The Winnipeg Statement*. Carter, who had functioned as the author of *The Winnipeg Statement* by putting to paper the thoughts of his fellow bishops and the *periti* present, explains that "Our statement was definitely meant to indicate to the people of Canada that if they found, as we anticipated, and God knows history has proven us to be correct, that they couldn't follow the directives of the encyclical, then they were not to consider themselves cut off from the Church. We were trying to create a situation wherein Catholics would not feel that they were alienated from the Church although on the issue of birth control they could not follow the teaching of the Pope." These were heady times. Carter even recalls finding his hotel suite broken into in an apparent attempt to pirate the draft document.

Like many other communiqués of this sort, *The Winnipeg Statement* begins with an expression of solidarity with the Pope, but proceeds to assure the Catholic faithful that "In all activity a person is bound to follow conscience faithfully"[90] and counsels confessors to assure penitents who have exerted an honest effort to act in accord with the directives but have been unsuccessful in those efforts that "whoever honestly chooses that course which seems right does so in good conscience."[91] (It is the same position the bishops had adopted in their presentation to the House of Commons Standing Committee on Health and Welfare: On Change in the Law on Contraceptives when rather than oppose any change to prohibition of contraceptives, they argued for the rule of conscience both for individuals and for legislators.[92]) It is particularly noteworthy that in a meaningful reversion of the traditional hierarchical approach to dialogue, as an admission that the bishops understand that consultation on marital issues properly begins with the laity and extends secondly to those with whom the laity consult directly, and as a sign of their sincere intention of expressing their solidarity with the faithful, the bishops make clear the need for future dialogue, a dialogue with the laity, priests, and bishops.

The question of conscience was addressed again in the Conference's April plenary assembly. While not backing away from their September position, the Canadian bishops were much more prescriptive, making it perfectly clear that the Magisterium is the authentic teaching authority of the Church and that individuals must consider the teaching of the Magisterium in the formation of conscience; indeed, one must approach magisterial teaching with respect and openness, with a desire to assent to those teachings.[93] Obviously, the matter was both complex and quite unwilling to go away. As a result, the April 1969 clarification served as a preamble to the comprehensive examination of the formation of conscience issued on December 1, 1973 in which the Canadian Conference of Catholic Bishops defines the dynamic Christian conscience as one in which individuals assume personal responsibility to both community and Church: "Persons in this category feel a responsibility for a progressive search and striving to live out a life ideal according to the mind of Christ."[94] The concept of the dynamic Christian conscience flows from the conciliar teaching on human dignity, the freedom of the individual to make properly informed choices, choices that are based on a knowledge of and an adherence to one's faith in a God who yearns for the salvation of all, and choices for which one needs ultimately to accept full personal responsibility. Behind it all was the mind of John Henry Newman as expressed through the mind and the pen of Gerald Emmett Carter. Not everyone was pleased, either with the bishops or with Carter. Conservative Catholic Anne Roche Muggeridge, for example, wrote two scathing attacks on the Protestantizing of the Catholic Church, zeroing in on both the bishops in general and Carter in particular. The titles of her two books, *The Gates of Hell: The Struggle for the Catholic Church* (1975) and *The Desolate City: The Catholic Church in Ruins* (1986), certainly capture the perspective. They are a far cry from the tone of Ed Sheridan's *Love Kindness!: The Social Teaching of the Canadian Catholic Bishops* in which the documents are reprinted.

THE 1980 SYNOD ON THE FAMILY—AN OPPORTUNITY LOST

With the announcement that the 1980 Synod of Bishops meeting in Rome would centre its deliberations on The Role of the Family in the Modern World, those who were looking for a more contemporary, more sensitive approach to the respective and mutual roles of husband and wife decided to prepare for the debate. Determined to help shape a more pastoral approach to the matter, the U.S. and Canadian delegations met at Notre Dame to map their strategy. For his part, G. Emmett Carter published a regular column in *The Catholic Register*, providing general briefings before, during, and after the Synod. On September 6, 1980, Carter argued that there must be no negative voice coming from Rome, no laying down of the law, but a recognition of the pain that exists in many Christian families "who are not abstractions, but tangible, vibrating, human beings caught up in the problems of human relations in all their stark dimensions."[95] In today's society people want to know the why of things; they do not want prescriptions. As a result, the Synod "will have to make a heroic attempt to tell them 'why' in the most beautiful, most positive, most cogent presentation available to us."[96] The Synod, Carter insisted, "cannot afford to use the methods of the past. Our people will not accept ready-made solutions or absolutes . . . our responsibility of leadership is to teach people through their lived experience."[97] Carter tackled the traditional issues one by one, arguing, for example, that it is time to jettison the traditional Christian notion that marriage is a sop for the weak, an antidote for concupiscence, and by its very nature inferior to virginity.[98] His reports from the Synod hall are upbeat, and on November 1 he suggested he was convinced that the time was right for updated teachings and new insights, adding that "The old bromide that the Church is supposed to teach that couples should have as many children as physically possible is not only absurd but hopefully passé."[99]

On November 8 he argued that the Synod needs to communicate its message in the language of the times and it must recognize the agony of the times. As a result, it simply is not sufficient to tell married couples that they are obliged to live by the Church's teaching on contraception under the pain of sin; rather, "We have to reach into the resources not only as God's loving design expects, but to the new technologies, a more personalist view of human love . . . We have to leave the ideal plane, the level of doctrinal principles without denying either, and enter into a more concrete order of moral understanding and compassion."[100] These are brave and appropriate words.

On November 15, Carter was making a plea for the Synod as an exercise in collegiality. The Synod, he argued, ought to be deliberative, not simply consultative. His has not been a lone voice. During an interview he had with us on February 24, 1989, for example, Bill Ryan, past provincial superior of the English-speaking Jesuits in Canada and general secretary to the Canadian Conference of Catholic Bishops, confided that the level of dissatisfaction with the proceedings at the 1987 Episcopal Synod held in Rome to discuss "The Vocation and Mission of the Laity in the Church and in the World" had reached the point where action was required: "The level of frustration was so high that we had to do something and I suggested a motion of non-confidence in the plenary session. It was a question of how the Secretariat handled the propositions. We had an early morning meeting on this, and we went around the room: all agreed. Chiasson agreed that he would do it." The *Toronto Star* headline for October 30 announced: "Canadian Bishops Angry, Bitter Over Synod."[101] When the *Star* reporter asked Donat Chiasson, archbishop of Moncton, what the Canadian bishops would take back to Canada, he replied: "Nothing, except perhaps . . . the conviction that the Church is lived at home." The official response from the Canadian delegation was more diplomatic, but very clear nonetheless, noting that "the Synod seemed to hear only faintly the cries of a world spinning into the twenty-first century" and urging that the Synod ought to become "as was originally intended, an effective instrument of episcopal collegiality." For those of us who have attended several of these synodal events, the criticisms form somewhat of a leitmotif.

When the Canadian and U.S. bishops as well as the bishops of England and Wales arrived in Rome in the fall of 1980, they brought them high hopes for a pastoral Synod cast in the language of the people and based on practical experience.[102] As the president of the Canadian Conference, Henri Légaré, pointed out in his September 30 intervention, "the Church is truly in a pilgrim state . . . connected in history" and, as a result, one needs to take history and experience into account while still holding sacred the indissolubility of marriage. For their part, the bishops of England and Wales conducted a National Pastoral Congress in Liverpool from which they prepared their position for the upcoming Synod and whose thinking they summarized in the Congress's report entitled *The Easter People*. Delegates to the Liverpool meeting had voted 93 percent in support of the proposition that "There is widespread lack of understanding and disagreement amongst Catholics about the present teaching on contraception" and 81 percent in support of the statement that "The Church's teaching on marriage is at an impasse because of confusion, uncertainty, and disagreement over contraception, which affects the whole sacramental life of many Catholics."[103]

Francis X. Murphy suggests that consultation at the grassroots level had been widespread internationally and the process of consultation with the laity had generated real hope for change, change that he argues neither John Paul II nor his close advisers were prepared to tolerate. The Vatican, therefore, micromanaged the proceedings, inserting Cardinal Joseph

Ratzinger into the role of relator and making it clear that an affirmation of *Humanae vitae* was what was expected.[104]

When Archbishop John Quinn of San Francisco rose to speak of contraception, of the non-reception of the teachings of contraception within *Humanae vitae* both on the part of the priests and of Catholic spouses, therefore, the fox was in the henhouse. Many episcopal delegates also rose to outline the practical problems they were facing on the home front and explained the increasing need for families to be better planned. England's Cardinal Hume spoke of the need to listen to the voice of the people as a resource for theological reflection, to take into account that the outright ban on artificial contraception prescribed by *Humanae vitae* was a source of great suffering for many, suffering that could not be dismissed as either moral weakness or human frailty. Imagine, therefore, the frustration that many a devoted bishop must have experienced in reading the Secretariat's summary of the proceedings as they are contained in the final message of the Synod.[105] The Synod is seen to rejoice that so many are willing to live decent lives in difficult times while others opt for lives bent on pleasure and acquisition—the tone becomes the familiar Vatican voice, the reiteration of platitudes centring on God's plan for married couples, the need to overcome our human weakness and live up to "the demands which Jesus Christ makes of us," the consolation that the Church is "fully aware of the frailty of our common human condition," and that we need humbly to open up our "soul before God as a sinner before the saving love of Christ." For this the Church surely did not need 200 bishops spending four weeks in Rome or a year's preparation consulting with their people!

Robert Blair Kaiser muses that the intention of the Canadian and U.S. bishops' request for a re-evaluation of the Church's stated position on birth control was naive in the extreme. The bishops ought to have known, he suggests, that "Pope John Paul II was not ready to re-evaluate anything. Nor would he let others try."[106] Kaiser also insists that John Paul had his mind made up in advance of the Synod, a perception of his Synods that the authors of this book are inclined to share.[107] Perceptions, of course, are at least in part within the eyes of the beholders. Kenneth Baker, the editor of the *Homiletic and Pastoral Review*, for example, saw the synodal exercise as a healthy exchange of ideas whose conclusions ought to be translated into pastoral action back home. As for the Quinn intervention, Baker notes that Quinn retracted his questioning of *Humanae vitae* by labelling it media spin, though Baker protests somewhat quizzically that he thinks the media could be forgiven for interpreting Quinn as they did.[108]

Familiaris consortio, John Paul II's apostolic exhortation on the Christian family, pronounces the final word on the 1980 Synod since it purports to embrace the thinking of that Synod's participants.[109] In it, the Pope insists that the Synod Fathers have expressly reconfirmed the teachings of *Humanae vitae*, including the sections relating specifically to contraception and the regulation of birth. As a result, speaking on their behalf, John Paul II specifically asks theologians to work in consort with the hierarchical Magisterium "to commit themselves to the task of illustrating ever more clearly the biblical foundations, the ethical grounds and the personalistic reasons behind this doctrine . . . to render the teaching of the Church on this fundamental question truly accessible to all people of good will. . . ." The use of artificial contraception, the Pope argues, is a selfish act because through its use the spouse has been placed in a position of "not giving oneself totally to the other" and he adds a little later that "the function of transmitting life must be integrated into the overall mission of Christian life as a whole, which without the cross they cannot reach the Resurrection." Natural contraception "by means of recourse to periods of infertility" is recommended in lieu of artificial contraception, because in this way spouses are not only respecting the procreative and unitive purposes of sexuality but they are acting in accord with the divine plan and hence "they 'benefit from' their sexuality according to the original dynamism of 'total' self giving, without manipulation or alteration." Clearly, the Pope does need some help to render his teaching "accessible to people of good will"; yet, these moral truths, the Pope implies, represent the clear and unanimous thinking of the members of the Synod.

Although *Familiaris consortio* provides a philosophical and theological recapitulation of the usual biblical and papal prescriptions (some ancient, some not so ancient) about the marriage of man and woman serving to mirror the union of Christ and his Church, about the superiority of celibacy and the complementarity of man and woman, about the procreative and unitive purposes of sexuality, John Paul brings his message clearly into the late twentieth century. There is in the document the recent

Roman penchant for buzz phrases like "contraceptive mentality," "consumer mentality," and "anti-life mentality," and even the contemporary reflex to blame the media for all our woes since he suggests that it is the media that have become the shapers of conscience.

At the same time, *Familiaris consortio* does speak to contemporary issues, having much to say about social justice (a particular concern of John Paul II), even talking about the rights of children and recommending a detailed charter of family rights. There is in addition an effort to shape a new anthropology that retains a semblance of the traditional teaching on complementarity while at the same time trying to come to grips with more modern efforts to provide a more enlightened voice on the equality of man and woman. Setting Pius XI aside, John Paul II argues that both husband and wife are educators of their children, even providing for a public and professional role for women as long as they are not compelled to work outside the home. This new role, the Pope adds, must not be at the expense of woman's "femininity" or "in imitation of the male role." As for the husband, though he now shares the educational responsibilities with his wife (an explicit advance over Pius's directive in *Casti connubii*), it is still his responsibility to "ensure the harmonious and united development of all the members of the family" and he will do so "by exercising generous responsibility for the life conceived under the heart of the mother."

John Paul's interlacing theory of solidarity does move him somewhat off the old mark with respect to the time-honoured Christian anthropological perspectives of men and women, husbands and wives, parents and children, but it is still too often a vision constructed on philosophical abstractions that have more recently been superseded both by experience and contemporary scholarly insight. Ruminations about the family as a "community of love," about the "royal priesthood" of mother and father, and marriage as a "communion of persons" are lofty and welcome philosophical reflections often expressed in enthusiastic and warm words, but when the going gets tough, so does the prose and the receptivity of the message. The conclusion drawn by a respondent to a recent questionnaire about natural family planning (NFP) no doubt strikes a chord for many a married Catholic: "Ethically, the difference between NFP and contraception is so small. Why are we bothering about it? This is actually a debate about church authority."[110] In the eyes of many a Catholic,

Rome's dogged adherence to ancient thinking despite more modern insights and scientific advances is a matter of ecclesiastical power, not of Gospel principle. Rome has a long way to travel indeed if it is to "render its teaching accessible to people of good will"—it will, as G. Emmett Carter suggested, have to dig much deeper into its resources to explain its position if its message is to be received by Catholic parents.

FROM CONSTANCY TO KINDNESS: LIFE-GIVING RELATIONSHIPS

As John Marshall has suggested and as Jack Dominian has demonstrated time and again, other more human, more humane, more informed, and more helpful approaches to the marriage relationship are indeed possible—approaches that are wholly consonant with the teachings of the Christian Church. For his part, Jack Dominian brings to the discussion years of work as a marriage counsellor, a consultant psychiatrist, the founder and director of the Marriage Research Centre in London, England, and as an author of numerous books on the nature of marriage including *The Capacity to Love, Christian Marriage*, and *Proposals for a New Sexual Ethic*.

Predictably, Dominian's starting point differs dramatically from the Vatican's. His is a much more positive view of human sexuality and, ultimately, of the human person and the nature of human relationships. Working for the Catholic Marriage Advisory Council in London, Dominian began his work thoroughly imbued with traditional Catholic teachings with respect to the primary (procreative) ends of marriage and the secondary (mutual help and the remedying of concupiscence). But he soon discovered that something was wrong with the theory. He discovered that the grace of the sacrament simply was not sufficient to prevent marriage breakdown. As a result, "Little by little, I formulated the view that the principal feature of marriage was relationship. The second conclusion was that the language of primary and secondary ends, the language of the church for nearly a thousand years, was mistaken and should go."[111]

Dominian's altered perspective is nicely summarized in his observation that "every sexual act gives life to the couple and on one or two occasions gives new life."[112] Sex is about relationship, a relationship of love, of sealing that relationship and giving it new life. To put one's emphasis on procreation as the primary end of marriage is, therefore, not only to miss the point but to misunderstand the role of sex in the fostering of the marital relationship. As a result, the Vatican's thesis concerning society's penchant to trivialize sex is misguided. "The trivialization of our age," he insists, "is not that of sex but of persons, who, in the name of rights and freedoms, are sanctifying the partial, the transient, the incomplete, the shallow and who ultimately place each other constantly on the sacrificial altar of the disposable. The evil of our day is disposable relationships. . . ."[113] People, Dominian reasons, are, by nature, sexual beings, and the sexual relationship between a loving couple is the best way to "sustain, heal and grow in the life they give to each other." Procreation itself is but one life-giving element within the coital experience.[114] It is important, therefore, to begin to dismantle the hierarchy's position concerning the procreative and unitive ends of marriage, the hierarchy of *Casti connubii*; the Council Fathers took some guarded steps in this direction at Vatican II, according to Dominian, without doing violence to the reputation of the Church.[115] For Dominian, marriage is about love, and it is from this love that all else flows. The insistence on procreation as the primary end of marriage, therefore, misrepresents the nature of marital love and is a potential obstacle to its fruition. And so, Dominian concludes, based on the confirmation of his professional experience, that "It is about time that the Church's preoccupation with procreation gave way to reality."[116] In discovering one another, married couples experience the divine in their own lives, they experience in their own homes what it is to live a Christian life. This, Dominian suggests, is the cornerstone for the re-evangelization of Western society.

Despite his divergent views, Dominian notes that with a single instance in 1976, no bishop has taken exception to his writing, a fact he explains by noting that he is a dedicated Catholic with a strong love and affection for the Magisterium and the Church. Despite this affection, however, he can see both the strengths and the shortcomings in the Church. Dominian explains that even at an early age he realized that with respect to its teachings on sexuality and marriage, the Church's theories had been developed by male celibates who were preoccupied with suppressing their own sexual impulses and whose principal concern was quite naturally the development of theory supportive of the single state. For these reasons, Dominian set out quite consciously to explore the mysteries of marriage and sexuality, and hence to add an informed Catholic layperson's point of view to the heretofore rather one-sided discussion,[117] which no doubt explains why Jack Dominian's message is so radically Christian, and yet it is so much more easily embraced by so many than is the traditional theory promulgated by the Vatican.

Although Peter Stanford describes their book as "sort of frivolous," in what is itself a statement both of the times and of their thesis, Kate Saunders and Peter Stanford dedicate their *Catholics and Sex: From Purity to Perdition*[118] "To the people who spoke out to us but couldn't give their names." An avowedly liberal view of Catholicism within the Catholic tradition, *Catholics and Sex* sees the contemporary Church, the Church of the people rather than the hierarchy, as dissociating itself from a disabling tradition: times have changed, but the institutional Church has not changed with them. Moreover, they argue, the Church's view of sexuality is neither biblically based nor rooted in the reality of the human condition; it springs instead from a misinformed and misogynistic perception of womanhood and of woman's sexuality. Former editor of *The Catholic Herald*, Peter Stanford has written several books of a religious and Catholic nature including a biography of Cardinal Basil Hume in which the cardinal muses wearily: "I don't think that our role is to be custodians of sex. I think sex looms too large in people's thoughts about Catholicism, after all we have far more interesting things to talk about."[119] Despite the cardinal's protest and even Peter Stanford's, as Stanford himself reflects, sexuality as it is presented within the Catholic tradition is not only a crucial issue both individually and socially but that message is being generally ignored largely because of the Church's unwillingness to locate itself within the realm of lived experience. A 1992 survey published by the *British Journal of Family Planning* reported a mere 3 percent of young people in England believed that premarital sex was wrong and nearly half of the respondents were no longer virgins at age sixteen.[120]

The tone of *Catholics and Sex* is flippant, but what is going on in a sense is that people's lives are actually being destroyed. I suppose that one of the hopeful things that I thought about in doing the research is that when we went to talk to sixth formers in particular—seventeen- and eighteen-year-olds—is that they weren't as hung up. I remember sitting with this group of seventeen- and eighteen-year-old girls and saying to them, "What does the image of the Virgin Mary mean to you?" And they all looked sort of puzzled. Of course, if you said to someone of my generation "What does the image of the Virgin Mary mean to you?" it was all to do with those ideas of purity. I don't think those ideas are being pushed as hard in Catholic schools any more. So, I think you've got a rising generation, certainly in the developed world, of people who have a completely different approach to Catholicism and sexuality. They don't grow up with the same kind of burden of guilt which perhaps we grew up with, but there's something lost in that. You gain something in that you become like everybody else, but you lose something as well. Although I feel very critical of individual things that the Pope says, I do actually think that at the end of the day these things are important. These are not things which should not have a moral import put on them; I just think that you have to think very carefully what it is. Teaching authority has to rest on a kind of consent. . . . We live in a democratic world in which we have come to think that for better or for worse democracy is the best form of social organization—all other systems have now failed—and it has all sorts of flaws, but that's the system. And I think that for Pope John Paul and the hierarchy of the Catholic Church to try to put forth what I think are often very important messages—difficult messages and unpopular messages, but very important messages—that teaching authority has to be buttressed by something. It has to be buttressed to a certain extent by ideas of democratic accountability and democratic input. I'm not suggesting that we should have a great election for who's the Pope, but I think that what the Church has to do is to try to appear in some way to be listening to what people are saying. So, you have ludicrous situations like the one here in the Archdiocese of Westminster at the moment where the Vatican has now taken five or six months pondering over who is to be Cardinal Hume's successor. Now they actually could have told us on the day he died who it was they wanted, because they had clearly worked it out. So why have they taken five or six months? It's not because they're consulting people because you'd be hard pressed to find anyone in this country who's been consulted. It's because they want to give the show of listening to people, so they've learned to a certain extent that you have to pretend to be listening to people. And so the Pope goes travelling around the world and he says, "I've met all my far-flung flock," but he never listens to what they say. He just goes and sort of lectures, so there is a show now. It's not that they don't understand the principle of democratic accountability because they give the show of doing it, but of course they take no notice at the end of the day.

The bishops have no interest to find new directions in sexuality. It's all too difficult really. I don't know how universal this is in the Catholic Church, but I think you end up with two entrenched positions. You've got the Vatican saying "This is what we've got to say and we're going to carry on saying it and we'll say it until we're blue in the face" and on some level they realize that there is an inherent popularity in giving a black-and-white message on moral questions since some people want that sort of approach. And I think that the black-and-white message tends to be put over in the wrong places, but I think there is an attraction for that. And then you've got the English bishops who think, "Well, we are actually a kind of minority faith and we live in a fairly secularized society"—I mean Britain has the highest rate of teenage pregnancies in Europe now—we live in this kind of society. How do we work within that society? Effectively they've chosen to keep their head down.

When I was writing the book on Hume, I asked him about this and he said that it ill-behooved him to talk about sexuality because he had very little experience of it himself, which I thought in some ways was a very wise thing, but in other ways was a complete cop-out in that he was a prince of a Church which says a lot about that and indeed has damaged very many people's lives in this particular country as well as across the world, and also, it's a complete lie. Of course, he knows about sexuality. He's a human being. I mean, this idea that somehow priests put on a cassock and forget about those kinds of sexual urges is nonsense, and as we've discovered it's palpable nonsense because they're busy having mistresses, and children, and boyfriends, and schoolboys and whatever. They are sexual beings and I think that it's not just at the level of the English bishops, the hierarchy, that they don't want to talk about or explore sexual issues—and they've extended that bound to all sorts of other people. So, back in the late sixties you had people like Hubert Richards and Charles Davis resigning their posts and leaving the priesthood and ultimately marrying because they wanted to explore those issues of sexuality and Cardinal Heenan didn't want them to do it. He basically chucked them out. He couldn't bear it. Even now the Vatican recently criticized Jack Mahoney who is the English bishops' favourite resident theologian in some ways (he's at King's College, London) because he suggested in a very gentle way that the teaching on sexuality and contraception may not be right.

I mean, Hume and Worlock together tried very hard. They had a national pastoral congress in 1980 and I think they did it sincerely. They gathered all these Catholics together to listen to their opinions and the opinion was very much that this teaching is misguided and very damaging. Then they went to Rome and Worlock gave a very straightforward talk which was completely ignored and Hume gave that rather elliptical thing about "I have a dream and all the signposts have been changed," which no one knew quite what it meant. There was a wonderful picture of John Paul at the time sitting there kind of scratching his hair. And that was Hume's genius in a sense because for nice liberal Catholics like me, I thought "Oh yes, Basil Hume understands what sort of dilemmas we all have and he's sort of voicing them," but for the Vatican, he said it in an oblique enough way that no one knew what he was getting on about: "Very spiritual, very clever. We don't know what he's talking about, but it all sort of seems fine." So in that sense the English Church has tried in a very gentle way to progress the agenda, but the Vatican said no and started clamping down on people like Jack Mahoney. So the bishops said, "Let's just keep out of it altogether. Let's not bother with that." So, they won't even talk about it. When they're pressed, they will come out with nicely mild liberal sentiments; so Basil Hume, when he talks about gay Catholics, will condemn homophobia, for instance—which is obviously a bit rich coming from the Church given that the reason we have anti-gay laws in any Western democracy has to do with the Christian influence so that actually the notion that the Church condemns homophobia when actually it is the great generator of homophobia. . . . It is against natural law. And where does natural law come from? Thomas Aquinas. The Church pushed all these things forward and now is saying that society shouldn't be doing them.

There are certainly many who would agree with Stanford, including theologians. Charles Curran is no doubt the most celebrated of their number. In correspondence dated July 25, 1986, Joseph Ratzinger, cardinal prefect for the Vatican Congregation for the Doctrine of the Faith, formally informed Curran that he was no longer "suitable nor eligible to teach Catholic theology."[121] Curran had found himself in disagreement with the ordinary Magisterium, Ratzinger's Congregation, on questions relating to sacramental marriage, abortion, euthanasia, masturbation, artificial contraception, premarital intercourse, and homosexual acts and had argued that his dissent was with non-infallible teachings only and was therefore, properly speaking, responsible dissent. In response, Ratzinger insisted that "submission of intellect and will" is also required for teachings of the ordinary Magisterium as well as to teachings of the Pope or college of bishops when they "enunciate on faith or morals when they exercise the authentic magisterium, even if they do not intend to proclaim it as a definitive act."[122] In other words, no dissent whatever from positions taken formally by the teaching authority of the Church will be tolerated.

Other Catholic theologians as well have been caught in the Roman dragnet. One of them, Canadian theologian André Guindon, succumbed to the ravages of a cardiac arrest while he was under formal investigation by the Vatican. Guindon, an Oblate priest, was the darling of the Catholic liberals in Canada and the *bête noire* of the conservatives, so much so that when he died on October 20, 1993 the rector of St. Paul's University in Ottawa where Guindon taught received a phone call from a local Catholic rejoicing in Guindon's passing. It was Guindon's *The Sexual Creators* that had been the catalyst for his personal conflict with the Vatican, especially his attitudes toward premarital sex and his concept of gay fecundity, the extension of relational love and intimacy beyond the procreative act, arguing as he did that surely for every Christian love is "the basic law of human relationship."[123] Speaking at a May 1993 Toronto meeting of the Coalition for Concerned Canadian Catholics, Guindon suggested that for most Catholics sexuality is guided by a magic formula overseen by a God "who has created something ugly in us and is waiting to punish us for using it."[124] Guindon's reaction to Rome's review of his research? "This church doesn't belong more to

Cardinal Ratzinger than to myself. I've been a Catholic all my life, I've had heart attack after heart attack trying to do my job well. This is my church, why the hell should I leave?"[125]

Guindon was the author of three books, *The Sexual Language: An Essay in Moral Theology*,[126] *The Sexual Creators: An Ethical Proposal for Concerned Christians*, and *Moral Development, Ethics and Faith*.[127] The tone and content provide a wholly readable theological vision for matters of human concern ranging from human fertility, to masturbation, to homosexuality and premarital sex. At the heart of Guindon's thinking is an embrace of "an authentic orthodoxy" that is rooted in Paul Ricouer's concept of sexuality as a language that bespeaks tenderness. As a result, Guindon builds his theology of sex on a series of principles, among which there is: (a) "fidelity to the great, living Tradition";[128] (b) a conviction that moralists have laboured under a "powerful and pervasive sexual taboo" that has inhibited their ability to apply the basic tools of their science to issues of sexual morality and have opted to apply infallible codes of obligation in place of the human capacity for making informed moral decisions;[129] (c) an approach to truly human relationships posited on tenderness rather than rationality, on the equality of the sexual partners that enhances the sexual relationship;[130] (d) a deep conviction to the thesis that "the radical meaning of human sexuality is to create loving bonds";[131] (e) a determination that our sexual attitudes and our sexual behaviour are inherently enculturated; (f) a resolve that no ethically principled "stand for life" can ignore the basic human, physical, social, and environmental needs of the child-to-be.[132] Guindon's detailed and scholarly study led him to the rejection of the academic approach pursued by the Magisterium in drafting *Humanae vitae* and the prohibiting conclusions at which the Magisterium arrived. As a result, Guindon concluded that "I do not believe that, as a Catholic theologian, I have to hold and teach a papal position which I cannot understand, which is not an object of faith, and which is not a precept falling under the moral virtue of obedience."[133]

Although Paul VI's commission on the regulation of birth would have been in essential agreement with most of what Guindon had to say, a good bit of it was apparently at odds with *Humanae vitae*. As a result, his delation to Rome was inevitable and a visit from Joseph Ratzinger's representatives a virtual given. Yet, no one would deny that the thinking of Augustine, Aquinas, Leo XIII, or Pius XI was influenced by their own particular history as well as of the historical-sociological contexts in which they wrote.

Indeed, although the Church insists on its constant tradition, it also ignores the fact that much of Augustine and much of Aquinas has been quietly put to rest because it is no longer relevant or, indeed, accurate in light of today's insights. It is surely fair to ask if new insights might cause the Church to modify or amplify its current thinking. It is equally fair to wonder how that might happen if any voice deemed to be dissident is censured and silenced. In fact, *Humanae vitae* concludes with a series of appeals that, although looking for affirmation and support, also implies a willingness to adapt to changing positions where that is possible, appeals to public authorities, to Christian husbands and wives, to doctors and medical personnel, to priests, to bishops, including an appeal to men of science that "by pooling their efforts they labor to explain more thoroughly the various conditions favoring a proper regulation of births."

Significantly, there is no appeal to theologians. The implication would seem to be that the authors of *Humanae vitae* are intent on shoring up the theological position taken by the Magisterium, not on adapting traditional theological thinking to the contemporary context. Yet, the reference to "men of science" is taken from *Gaudium et spes* and is excised from a context in which the Council Fathers make a much broader appeal than its appearance in *Humanae vitae* would suggest; indeed, the context for the quotation within *Gaudium et spes* openly calls for a multidisciplinary approach to expanding our understanding and not a rationalizing of traditional prescriptions. The relevant section of *Gaudium et spes* notes that in promoting the values of married and family life and in the provision of "those helps and necessities which are suitably modern . . . the Christian instincts of the faithful, the upright moral consciences of men, and the wisdom and experience of persons versed in the sacred sciences will have much to contribute. Those, too, who are skilled in other sciences, notably the medical, biological, social, and psychological, can considerably advance the welfare of marriage and the family, along with peace of conscience, if by pooling their efforts they labor to explain more thoroughly the various conditions favoring a proper regulation of births."[134] In short, the Council Fathers seem to be appealing to the very cross-section of professional Catholics rejected by the Magisterium in formulating its own conclusions in the composition of *Humanae vitae* and their reference to *Gaudium et spes* has been ripped from its original context in order to make a point not intended by the authors of the conciliar document.

Indeed, the next section of *Gaudium et spes* deals with questions of faith and culture and, in so doing, refers both to theological principles and to the secular sciences, psychology and sociology in particular, as vehicles for assisting the faithful "to live the faith in a more thorough and mature way."[135] Moreover, this particular section of *Gaudium et spes* concludes with a plea to teachers in seminaries, colleges, and universities to collaborate with experts in other fields of knowledge, stressing in a way that is wholly consonant with the writings of the Council Fathers that such experts must necessarily have the academic freedom to pursue areas of intellectual inquiry appropriate to their own areas of academic competence. In fact, such freedom, they argue, is indispensable: "In order that such persons may fulfill their proper function, let it be recognized that all the faithful, clerical and lay, possess a lawful freedom of inquiry and of thought, and the freedom to express their minds humbly and courageously about those matters in which they enjoy competence."[136] Without the freedom for scholars to pursue their various and appropriate avenues of investigation, we would be repeating the errors, inaccuracies, and even some of the absurdities of the past: errors such as the time-honoured proposition that the purpose of marriage is to serve as a remedy for male concupiscence; inaccuracies like Aquinas's understanding that the human embryo is fully contained as a homunculus in the male effluent and that the female functions essentially like an incubator—the existence of spermatozoa was discovered in 1677 and ovulation in 1827; absurdities like Aquinas's explanation that the conception of the female "comes from a defect in the active force or from some material indisposition, or even from some external change, such as that of a south wind, which is moist;"[137] convictions such as Augustine's that the having of children "is the sole reason that marriage takes place."[138]

It is clear that modern science unravels the mysteries of nature in a way that alters our perceptions materially—as Cardinal Heenan pointed out in his 1968 pastoral, modern scholarship has shed light on the nature of the homosexual person, which was simply unavailable to previous generations of theologians or even to the Magisterium. Surely the Church is best served if committed Catholic professionals of goodwill explore relevant issues of concern to society and to the Church and then make the results of their inquiries available to both Church and society for debate, for information, and for the formation of fully enlightened decisions, remembering always that human knowledge constantly needs to be tested, expanded, and perfected. Indeed, Aquinas himself was condemned by the University of Paris on March 7, 1277 for some twenty propositions based on his philosophy of nature, a condemnation that not even Aquinas's illustrious master, Albert the Great, was able to reverse.[139]

For his part, Guindon does not shy away from the difficult issues, nor is his thinking static. It evolves with research and new insights, though it remains essentially consistent. While it is certainly true that his later writing concerning homosexual relationships, for example, has evolved to the point where confrontations with Rome were inevitable, the same cannot be said for his thinking on the same topic in the 1970s, even though his basic thinking on the nature of relational love was more or less in place. In *The Sexual Language*, published in 1976, Guindon provides a detailed and scholarly analysis of the question of homosexuality from anthropological, sociological, theological, and medical perspectives, an analysis that is sensitive yet, one would have thought, not one that ought to have incurred the wrath of Rome. Guindon makes clear his own conviction that no one would willingly choose to become a homosexual. This, for a number of reasons. Not only are the lives of homosexuals torn by oppression, but too much is lost in the homosexual relationship since the relationship between a man and a woman is so fundamental, Guindon then concluded, that the sexual language itself is significantly if not completely eroded in a homosexual engagement. Even bodily postures during acts of homosexual intercourse are not conducive to physical intimacy and suggest a breakdown in human communication. Moreover, because the relationship is by definition a fruitless one, homosexual partnerships tend toward instability. Although there are those homosexuals who do develop a lasting and supportive relationship, Guindon argues that even in their case their emotional adjustment will never mature beyond "the canons of adolescent conduct."[140] Because the homosexual relationship by nature is non-productive and is not directed to the male/female human relationship intended by nature, it is defective from both the unitive and the procreative perspectives that form the core of the Catholic perspective on human sexuality, and by definition it cannot be called a mature sexuality but will "always represent a certain failure in the growth process."[141] The sexual language, he reasons, is intrinsically defective. Although recent studies tend to be sympathetic, according to Guindon, sympathy is what one would expect from those engaged in the "caring professions," but care for the victimized ought not to gloss over the real issues. As his thinking evolves, in *The Sexual Creators* Guindon does anything but gloss over the issues, and, as a result, he gains the unwelcome attention of Joseph Ratzinger.

No one would accuse Cardinal Joseph Ratzinger of glossing over the issues. "The Pastoral Care of Homosexual Persons" was circulated by his Congregation for the Doctrine of the Faith in 1986 as a pastoral guideline for Catholic bishops who have the responsibility of acting as the teaching authority in their dioceses. And, Ratzinger insists, it is the bishops' responsibility to teach the magisterial position fully and accurately, not ignoring it and not departing from it. For it represents the truth, a truth that is rooted in reason, illuminated by faith, and informed by science. And the truth is that homosexual actions, as opposed to homosexual inclinations, are "intrinsically disordered"; that is, homosexuality is in inherent opposition to the divinely ordained nature of sexuality as it is found in the theology of creation recorded in the book of Genesis. The word "disorder" appears five times within the text. As a result, "To choose someone of the same sex for one's sexual activity is to annul the rich symbolism of meaning, not to mention the goals, of the Creator's sexual design."[142] Homosexual activity as such, therefore, in the minds of the Congregation is not only disordered because not naturally life-giving, but in engaging in homosexual activity, the individuals "confirm within themselves a disordered sexual inclination which is essentially self-indulgent."[143] Apparently, sexual activity can be "other-indulgent" only when it contains the possibility of procreation. It is a consistent assessment in many ways—this penchant for seeing only pleasure where procreation is not the desired end of sexual intimacy—but it is an assessment with which many well-meaning Christians would certainly have some difficulty.

Thomas Gumbleton, auxiliary bishop of the Archdiocese of Detroit, is not quite as sure about our understanding of sexuality as is the Congregation for the Doctrine of the Faith.

You read what John Paul writes about marriage and it's so idealistic and mystical almost, but it's clearly accepting the human body, sex, and the pleasure that goes with it as all part of marriage. It's all part of deepening intimacy. Well, that evolution has happened. My point is that I can't predict what's going to happen, but I say two things to the homosexual community. One is that even in the human sciences we don't know enough about sexuality right now and how people integrate their sexuality into their personhood in the healthiest way possible. And I say every one of us has to struggle to do that, whether we're heterosexual in a marriage relationship or whether we're a celibate like I am. I have to integrate my sexuality with how I continue to grow as a human person. I can't repress everything or be self-destructive. I have to have friends, I have to have intimacy, and yet I'm committed to a celibate life. I have to struggle to do that. Well, homosexual people also have to figure out how sexuality integrates into life in the healthiest way possible, because ultimately what is morally right and morally good is what leads us to become the full human person God intends us to be. There aren't predesigned rules out there, nor do you have to jump through hoops that make you good. What God intended is that we become the full person that we have the capacity to become. Part of that is our human relationships that nourish us or nurture us as a person. If they're destructive, well then there is something wrong with them. They can't be wrong just on a human scale but, rather, morally wrong, too, because if you deliberately choose to be self-destructive, however much freedom there is in your choice, that is a moral flaw or defect.

And so I point out that through evolution we haven't come to the point of having a definitive understanding of everything that has to do with sexuality. The Church is still learning and we have to continue to learn. Part of this learning has to be from the experience of homosexual people. That's never previously been part of the content that the moral theologians put in the textbooks. They never drew out of the homosexual experience to say what is nurturing, what is life-giving, and what makes them free to be fully human, so we need their experience.

But then the other key thing is primacy of conscience. That's a very traditional part of Catholic teaching. The ultimate arbiter of what is right or wrong for you is the well-informed conscience. You have to consult scripture, the tradition, your own prayer life, take consultation with other people and try to discover what is right for you. Then, when you have made your choice in conscience, you follow that.

The latest pastoral that the United States Conference put out, called *Always Our Children*, had half a page in there on the primacy of conscience. First, we clearly set forth the teaching. Again, we're conserving so we're not going to jump way out in front. Then there was this section on primacy of conscience, which would have been helpful to the homosexual community. The pastoral said this is what the Church is saying, and yet in my life I have to follow my conscience. But then we pulled that. It's not in the final text, but I give it out. I share that with people. Or I've been to some colleges or universities where they have student groups that are trying to become accepted or in some cases they are accepted on campus. But their frustration is that the Church tells them, "It's okay to be who I am, but then you tell me that I can't act on who I am. That is frustrating and it's stifling to me."

So I talk about the evolution of the teaching and how no one knows how it's going to evolve and I also talk about the primacy of conscience. At least that gives an opening for people. They feel less alienated from the official Church even though they're not being affirmed and told it's okay to act on who they are. But within the primacy of their own conscience, they can act on who they are.

For Bishop Gumbleton, there is still much to be learned about homosexuality and intimacy within homosexual relationships. Nor is the nature of homosexual love a clear and settled matter for theologian and Catholic priest Enda McDonagh, who has had the opportunity to minister to the gay community and to learn from that experience:

While I was teaching in St. John's University in New York, I worked at a parish in Greenwich Village at the request of the pastor who had a very high percentage of gay men in his parish and, in fact, the head of his parish council was a gay man. At that time in the early nineties, maybe every couple of weeks, although the Catholic population was small, he would have an AIDS funeral in his parish. We were very concerned about this and we decided that we couldn't help without enabling them to help themselves in terms of their involvement in the parish.

So through our contact on the parish council, we established a routine whereby from nine o'clock until the eleven-thirty Mass every Sunday morning the presbytery was turned over to gay men who might or might not have HIV/AIDS. After a while we defined the task of this group, which was a very loosely organized group, people coming and going. The parish was quite active. While I was there, the task we asked them to consider, apart from practical things that might be done about HIV and AIDS, was whether one could be honourably gay and honourably Catholic—this sort of thing. And one of the most effective pieces of evidence I was introduced to was being taken by some of these gay men—gay women, lesbians, were much slower to come and that was another story—but being taken to some of the homes where you had one of the partners dying of AIDS. The kind of care—now this wasn't true of every couple any more than it would be true of heterosexual couples—but the number of couples where the attention and self-sacrifice of the healthy partner and the responses, loving and spiritual, of the partner who was seriously ill, was extraordinarily impressive. And I couldn't believe but that this was some manifestation of truly Christian love. I had to accept that there was true Christian love going on in this relationship, and in a number of relationships I saw.

Another interesting example was on Christmas night in this parish. Singing began at eleven o'clock and Mass began at midnight and we were out there in the sanctuary, of course, dressed up in our gear, watching all the people coming in during the singing of the various hymns. It is a very musical church. Some of the people from the Metropolitan Opera used to help out with the singing. But I saw one particular couple, gay men, very elderly and infirm, making their way up and we went to greet them afterwards. They had been together thirty-eight years. I doubt if there were many heterosexual couples in the church that had been together that long. Again, it was part of the kind of witness that you find in relation to these things. So unless we're prepared to listen to and work with that world, we won't come up with any satisfactory commentary on the morality of it.

Adding his voice to those who are prepared to stand and be counted and referring to John Paul II's formal millennial *mea culpa* for sins committed by the Church, Bishop William Newman, an auxiliary bishop in the diocese of Baltimore, added a further sin for which the Church ought to seek forgiveness, "the sins individually and collectively which the Church has committed against the gay and lesbian community."[144]

Certainly, the Church has not made it easy to serve the gay and lesbian community. The life's work of Jeannine Gramick and Robert Nugent, a School Sister of Notre Dame and Salvatorian priest respectively, has been dedicated to developing a better understanding of homosexuality and of the Catholic Church's teaching concerning it. As co-founders of New Ways Ministry in the suburbs of Washington, D.C., and the authors of two books, *Building Bridges: Gay and Lesbian Reality and the Catholic Church*[145] and *Voices of Hope: A Collection of Positive Catholic Writing on Gay and Lesbian Issues,*[146] they had established an active pastoral ministry for the gay and lesbian community. Their ministry had, however, attracted the attention of the U.S. episcopacy and ultimately of the Congregation for the Doctrine of the Faith. In their preface to *Voices of Hope*, Gramick and Nugent explain the founding of New Ways Ministry as a means of promoting justice and reconciliation between gay and lesbian Catholics with the Catholic community at large. Ironically, the preface ends with the aspiration: "We hope that this publication may provide motivation and encouragement for all those who still believe it is crucial to speak honestly and respectfully to each other" and among the various voices they include is that of Archbishop Raymond Hunthausen, one-time archbishop of Seattle, who observes some years before his unceremonious departure from Seattle: "I must say I await with great interest the findings of our theologians and the ensuing dialogue between them and the church's Magisterium."[147]

Voices of Hope consists of an eclectic collection of materials, much of which centres on questions of non-discrimination, and it includes in a single volume an array of primary documents issued by Rome, bishops' conferences, individual bishops, religious congregations and professional associations, Catholic newspapers, and the like from the United States, Canada, England and Wales, New Zealand, and western Europe. The Washington State Catholic Conference's *The Prejudice Against Homosexuals and the Ministry of the Church: Policy Document* is noteworthy for its detail and in some ways for its daring. The policy document deals squarely with the question of homosexual acts, for example, pointing out that we cannot judge the sinfulness of a homosexual's activity; we can only conclude that such activity "falls short of the ultimate norm of Christian morality in the area of genital expression."[148]

On the other hand, the Washington State Catholic Conference adds that prejudice against homosexuals constitutes a greater transgression against Christian moral norms than either homosexual orientation or homosexual activity. In addition, the Conference calls for the Church to foster ongoing research on its theological tradition with respect to homosexuality as well as research on possible means of combating prejudice against lesbians and gays.

Voices of Hope also includes the Archdiocesan Pastoral Plan of the Senate of Priests of San Francisco in which the Senate calls for a pastoral plan based not just on the teachings of the Church, but also on the findings of the social sciences and the lived experiences of gay men and women. At the same time, the Senate quotes the "Declaration on Certain Questions Concerning Sexual Ethics" issued by the Congregation for the Doctrine of the Faith in 1975 in which the Congregation cautions that because of "their kind and their causes, it more easily happens that true consent is not given" in the area of sexual activity.[149] It is a reflection that may help to explain the conclusions of a Dutch study, which found that 86 percent of the priests who responded to the survey advised homosexuals under their pastoral care "to accept their feelings and give their lives the form which they deem best"[150]—sinfulness, in other words, is a matter of personal conscience rather than all-encompassing decree.

Part Three of *Voices of Hope* includes a catalogue of often apologetic or explanatory, generally dismayed, and sometimes angry responses to an unsigned letter from the Congregation for the Doctrine of the Faith, a letter that is itself an all-encompassing decree rooted in the 1986 Letter to Bishops issued by the same Congregation. Entitled "Some Considerations Concerning the Catholic Response to Legislative Proposals on the

Non-Discrimination of Homosexual Persons," the Congregation seems to be advocating social discrimination as a means of protecting the traditional family structure. Although its author had obviously intended the correspondence to be kept confidential, New Ways Ministry released a copy of it to the press, along with its own analysis. The media throughout the Western world voiced their displeasure, and though several U.S. bishops did attempt to explain away the problem, Bishop Gumbleton captured the convictions of many when he concluded more frankly than most would: "I cannot in good conscience accept the statement as consistent with the Gospel nor can I justify implementing it."[151]

The uproar makes for instructive reading, but it cannot have been reading that pleased either the members of the U.S. Conference who had been attempting for some twenty years to convince Gramick and Nugent to openly confirm their acceptance of the Church's teaching on homosexual activity as it is outlined by the Congregation for the Doctrine of the Faith, nor can it have been well received by the Congregation itself. Failing in their repeated efforts to bring the two in line, the Congregation issued its formal condemnation on May 31, 1999 under the name of its prefect, Cardinal Joseph Ratzinger.[152] The Notification traces the history of their ministry and its conflict with the Church's doctrinal teachings with respect to the intrinsically disordered nature of homosexual activity as well as other deficiencies in their writings and pastoral practices as had been previously determined by a special Commission of inquiry. As a result, the Notification serves as formal notice that neither Nugent nor Gramick would be permitted to remain active in any pastoral capacity with homosexual persons and that neither would be eligible for any office within their respective religious communities for an unspecified period of time.

The issue of *Origins* in which the Notification appears reprints an article by Father Robert Gahl, Jr., which had appeared in the Vatican's official newspaper *L'Osservatore Romano* the day following its publication of the Notification. Gahl, a professor of ethics at Rome's Opus Dei university, the Pontifical University of the Holy Cross, traces the divinely established order with respect to human sexuality as it is expressed in Genesis and explains that homosexuality is "one of the many manifestations of the disorder in human inclinations introduced by original sin"—

the wounding of human nature as a result of the disobedience of Adam and Eve in abusing their freedom. Gahl points out that original sin is the remote cause, but that modern science has still to understand the phenomena that provide the immediate cause. Having explained the Church's teachings concerning the nature of the disorder, Gahl provides pastoral guidelines in keeping with Roman Catholic moral teaching, guidelines based on respect for human dignity, a frank admission of the sinfulness of homosexual acts, acceptance of one's condition, a joining of one's personal suffering with the cross of Christ, a personal acceptance of the teaching of the Church on the part of all pastoral ministers who must work under the guidance of the local bishop, and a clear separation from any group that supports gay lifestyles or would equate the homosexual lifestyle with that pursued by married couples or celibates. The same issue of *Origins* contains several episcopal explanations of the situation as well as a comment by Robert Nugent and Jeannine Gramick's religious congregations. If the accompanying explanations were meant to quell an impending cause célèbre, they have obviously fallen far short of the mark. Articles of condemnation have appeared in the press of many countries, Gramick has refused to acquiesce to pressure from Rome, and efforts to provide a pastoral home for the homosexual community within the Catholic Church have received a serious blow.[153]

The problems faced by both the Church and the homosexual community are encapsulated in two related events that took place in 1998 in Australia: one in Melbourne, the other in Canberra. In Melbourne, Archbishop George Pell refused a similar gathering of activist homosexuals Holy Communion at St. Patrick's Cathedral; in Canberra, Bishop Pat Power, an auxiliary bishop in Canberra Diocese, Australia, welcomed the group and commented: "I have to admit that at times the Church's teaching on human sexuality has been overly negative and there are times when it has been out of touch with human reality. Together we need to find new and better ways for the Church to enunciate its teaching on sexual morality."[154]

Eileen Flynn, professor of theology at St. Peter's College in Jersey City, New Jersey, suggests that there is good reason for the Church to engage in a dialogue with the gay community. She questions, first of all, whether it is appropriate to judge homosexual activities simply according to their objects (that is, on the activity divorced from its circumstances) rather than judging them as acts in their entirety, in light of the circumstances under which such acts are performed. This, she notes, is the proper basis for moral judgment. Lack of dialogue on this aspect of the homosexual act, she concludes, is a result of the current climate in the Church "in which questions go unaddressed for fear of reprisals."[155] Secondly, she recommends that until we have a better scientific understanding of homosexuality, the proper response for the Church would be to refrain from generalities that it promotes as certitudes and strike a more humble, more tentative posture. Finally, Flynn is not convinced that the Church's reference to Genesis as the touchstone for its thinking does justice either to the resourcefulness of the Creator or to the reading of scripture. In the meantime, the 1986 Congregation for the Doctrine of the Faith's Letter to Bishops, which is critiqued in *Voices of Hope*, has driven a wedge between the Dignity movement in the United States and many of that country's bishops, while Courage, a group that has received formal recognition from the U.S. Bishops' Conference as well as the Canadian bishops and the Vatican, actively works to help homosexuals live within the teachings of the Church and, apparently, even to "grow into heterosexuality."[156] There obviously is much to be done. The nagging question remains: Who will have the temerity to do it?

The Church's interest in the gay rights issue has always had at some level a concern about sustaining the sanctity of marriage. Certainly, there have been initiatives in several countries to provide equal status for homosexual and heterosexual unions. When, for example, Proposition 22 was added to a March 7, 2000 ballot in California as a means of limiting marriages to the union of a husband and wife, that state's bishops provided almost $300,000 in support of the initiative. In Vermont and in British Columbia the same question was raised as an equality issue, especially in relation to the provision of equal benefits, and in both cases the local bishops expressed their opposition;[157] in Vermont the issue was settled by establishing civic unions for gay couples rather than recognizing the relationship as a marriage in the traditional sense.[158] In Ontario, however, the matter has moved beyond the question of equal benefits to the level of theological debate since Brent Hawkes, a pastor at Toronto's Universal Fellowship of Metropolitan Community Churches moved in

December 2000 to solemnize the marriage of a gay and a lesbian couple by legalizing the relationships through the reading of the marriage banns within the Sunday services for three consecutive weeks. However, in the intense media attention that accompanied the event, the root of the debate in most instances centred not on theological but on social justice issues—the securing of equal rights extending to taxation, succession, company benefits, and the like—so that at least in the public debate the religious component of the marriage relationship seems to have been subsumed by the economics of legal unions.

The crisis facing the Christian marriage, however, cannot be attributed simply to the quest for equal rights by members of the homosexual community. In Britain, for example, there were fewer marriages in 1995 than at any other time since 1926, yet Britain had the second-highest rate of divorce of any country in the European Union and only 25 percent of its families consisted of the traditional mother, father, and children, whereas 20 percent were single-parent families.[159] 1998 figures in the United States indicate that only 26 percent of families were traditional in their makeup.[160] At the same time, the instance of cohabitation is so high in the United States—some 50 percent of the couples enrolling in marriage preparation courses are cohabiting—that the U.S. National Conference issued a detailed report analyzing the nature of the problem and outlining the pastoral implications of counselling couples who are living in such a relationship.[161] The report is detailed, comprehensive, frank, and thoughtful. It deserves to be studied.

More or less coincident with the investigation's publication, Archbishop Michael Sheehan of Sante Fe issued a pastoral letter reaffirming the Church's prohibition of premarital sex, urging chastity and self-control, recommending that cohabiting couples seek reconciliation through the sacrament of penance, and admonishing them to forego "conjugal pleasure" during courtship.[162] Unfortunately, not many of those couples will have been at Mass to hear the archbishop's letter being read, and, unfortunately, the archbishop has not moved intellectually beyond the simple notion of "conjugal pleasure," as if that were the sum total of the sexual experience. Effective pastoral initiatives are going to require more than a reiteration of well-worn platitudes. If the Church's message is going to get the hearing it deserves, the Church will have to learn to speak *with* the faithful rather than opting to speak *at* them. *The Church will also have to listen to the voice of women since its doctrine with respect to sexuality and marriage has been conceived and delivered whole blown solely from the minds of men.* For their part, not only are women becoming an ever-increasing presence on university campuses but they are becoming an increasingly significant percentage of lay students registered in programs in Catholic theology. In the fall of 1997, for example, the president of Regis College, the Jesuits' graduate theologate at the University of Toronto, reported that 65 percent of its student population were lay and, of that number, 58 percent were women.[163] Male-centred approaches to theological development are surely inappropriate in an age in which impressive numbers of women are studying theology and when the research of female academics is demonstrating convincingly that male and female attitudes toward the nature of the sexual experience are not one and the same; indeed, female academics are arguing that what men have defined as natural may be natural for men, but it is a decidedly one-sided masculine vision of what constitutes nature.[164]

One might argue, in fact, that the Church's persistent male-centred view of nature has been more harmful than helpful in promoting conjugal harmony. The institutional Church has too often devalued human love and the spousal relationship by viewing sex as an ideally practical or hedonistically pleasurable activity rather than as a relational one; at the same time, it has persistently described the male as the recipient of pleasure and the female as its provider. Moreover, it has defined the male as the dominant figure in the domestic society, the decision maker, the voice of reason, the one whose gaze is directed more on the world of commerce than of hearth; the female, on the other hand, has been narrowly defined as the affective element in the relationship, the heart of the home, the one described in the closing words of Vatican II as having "always had as your lot the protection of the home, the love of beginnings, and an understanding of cradles."[165] It is a dualistic structure that the bishops of Quebec have identified as one of the origins of those social stereotypes that have contributed to violence against women within the conjugal relationship.[166] It is an influence that Geoffrey Chaucer understood all too well when he depicted his Wife of Bath as being somewhat deaf, the result of a blow to the head visited upon her by her husband, a student of the Bible, who struck her with the very book that legitimized his action. In his presentation, Chaucer offers a sadistically humorous fourteenth-century affirmation that the ecclesiastical authorization the Church has provided for violence against women is a long-standing one; in that same context and as a further means of confirming the point, Chaucer refers to the threefold causes for men leaving their homes: nagging wives who will not be corrected, leaky roofs, smokey houses—sententious clichés derived from Proverbs, clichés whose ubiquitous coinage is suggested by their further appearance both in Chaucer's "Tale of Melibee" and William Langland's contemporary but West Midland *Piers the Ploughman*.[167]

Today's recognition of the rights of women, about which the Church has had so much to say but toward which it has contributed so little that is positive, carries within it the concomitant rejection of traditional dualistic structures. Women are no longer willing to be violated in their own homes. Priests are less inclined to counsel women to remain in abusive relationships or to suggest that they shoulder their inferior lot with a resigned passivity. Indeed, if the Church is to resume its rightful role as a moral voice championing the sanctity of the family, it might do worse than look to the bishops of Quebec as a model for listening to the stories, for weighing the experiences, and for responding with a pastoral insight that transcends the time-worn platitudes.

Divorce rates have increased dramatically in the Western world over the past few decades for any number of reasons: easier legal access to divorce, economic stability and social reconstruction, a systemic individualism and creeping quest for pleasure, a concomitant loss of religious commitment, and, indeed, woman's discovery of her inherent worth and her decision to play no longer the role of passive marionette. Yet, despite these quite radical revisions in social structures, human relationships, and the progress of knowledge, the Church's official position on separation and divorce has not been refined since the concept of indissolubility was first proposed by Augustine some 1,600 years ago. Nor is the institutional Church willing to review seriously its ban on the divorcee's right to receive the Eucharist despite a popular will to the contrary—such a review, for example, was recently recommended by some 96 percent of those attending a National Conference of Priests at Newman College in Birmingham. Instead, the Pope has noted that "Neither Scripture nor tradition recognizes any faculty of the Roman pontiff for dissolving a rati-fied and consummated marriage; on the contrary, the church's constant practice shows the certain knowledge of tradition that such a power does not exist."[168] This despite the fact that St. Paul himself supplied the origi-nal basis for exceptions to the law and that over the centuries various popes have in fact made timely concessions to this hard-and-fast regula-tion. And this despite the fact too that the Church has never suffered a shortage of skilled casuists or inventive masters of philosophical discourse, semantics, or syllogistic disquisition.

The issue, of course, centres on the word "ratified." For some the question of divorce is simple indeed—one is reminded of James Boswell's discussion with Samuel Johnson concerning a lady who had been divorced by an act of Parliament as a result of the abusive behaviour to which she had been subjected by her husband. Boswell records John-son's response in his diary for May 7, 1773: "The woman's a whore, and there's an end on't." Yet, modern psychology has surely demonstrated that life is in fact not quite so simple. In his *What Binds Marriage? Roman Catholic Theology in Practice*,[169] Timothy J. Buckley provides a detailed and compelling history of the theology of marriage and includes a discussion of acceptable contemporary pastoral options that could be used if only Rome were willing. One of the means Buckley discusses is the internal forum and the *sensus fidelium*, making it very clear that the interpretation of the validity of one's options depends principally on direction from Rome and the particular attitudes of the sitting pontiff. Quoting *Gaudium et spes*, Buckley argues that the Church has a respon-sibility not only to read the signs of the times, but to speak in an intelligi-ble language to the laity of every generation; in addition, Buckley quotes with obvious approval Bernard Häring's exhortation in a *Tablet* article to "let the Pope know that we are wounded by the many signs of his rooted distrust, and discouraged by the manifold structures of distrust which he has allowed to be established."[170] There is, Buckley agrees, a real possibility of two Churches, the institutional and the popular, each going its separate way. Buckley suggests that there is a need to examine the question of annulment, the theology of the marriage bond, and the insights of modern psychology from a contemporary theological and pastoral perspective and he wonders if we have here another *Humanae vitae* crisis in the making, a battle over power and authority. And if this is the case, who will be the winners?

Resurrectionist priest and professor of medieval law, James A. Wahl, has served as vicar judicial to the Diocese of Hamilton in Bermuda and certainly understands the politics of interpreting legal documents from an historical, personal, and Vatican perspective. He would find himself in essential agreement with Buckley.

I was full judge in the marriage tribunal where I served for three years. With a tribunal of this sort, the judge really runs the court: he can call the witnesses and be involved from top to bottom. This was 1978 to 1981, and so I began under John Paul I and continued under John Paul II. It was also just before the new Code of Canon Law, but we knew that there were changes coming—in the distinction between the primary and secondary ends of marriage, for example; the primary end was the procreation of children—the act had to be open to the procreation of children—and the secondary had to do with the community of life, partnership of life. That distinction is not there anymore. Many canonists talk about the partnership of life as included in the procreative element. They don't make that distinction anymore. This reading really took place primarily because of the advances we had made in the social sciences, psychology and psychiatry. There had been decisions coming out of the Rota from the late sixties which took into account the psychological makeup of the person, whether or not the person could actually form a partnership, a union, a common life as a partner. That kind of changed things because the old code from 1917 really didn't talk about things in terms of partnership so much as it did about procreation as the basis for marriage. This changed things. You married someone as wife and husband, not as mother, caretaker, that kind of thing. That had a lot to do with the psychological. And so that's why, for example, one of the great rows that began to emerge was the inability to form a lasting union at the time of the marriage. So all the questions and investigations really centre on the time of marriage and leading up to it. Now, sometimes things that happen after the marriage can, of course, lead one to investigate what went on before.

I am convinced that, given the North American and European

culture and given our very, very exalted theology of marriage, 75 percent of seemingly valid marriages—and I might even go higher—are not valid marriages because, if you ask the right questions, you can get the invalidating answer. For example, "Do you believe that marriage is for life? Yes or no?" They all say yes. "If, through no fault of your own, this marriage should break down, do you believe that you have the right to marry again?" The answer automatically comes back yes. That's invalidating.

One might reasonably conclude that we are well on our way to the creation of two Churches, one institutional and one popular, except that one would then have to define who is included in each. Certainly, most of the priests and many of the bishops we have interviewed are more clearly identified with what one would define as the popular rather than the institutional Church. And, although there clearly are other issues at work in the Church, the sexual ones are those that most clearly define the demarcation lines. Recent histories of the popes, notably *Saints and Sinners: A History of the Popes*[171] by English Church historian Eamon Duffy and *Lives of the Popes: The Pontiffs from St. Peter to John Paul II* by U.S. theologian Richard P. McBrien[172] document the rise, fall, and rebirth of the power of the papacy as well as the consistencies and inconsistencies of papal policy, including the sexual escapades of not a few popes. But, at the end of the day, the average well-intentioned Catholic is left wondering if the papacy might be a little less doctrinaire if priests, bishops, and popes really understood on an experiential level the role that sex actually plays in the everyday lives of an average loving couple. Edmund Campion discusses the Australian Church's resistance to the rhythm method in the 1940s and observes: "Always there lay in the background the priests' own troubled sexuality."[173] It is a bit of a refrain, this. Indeed, it is generally agreed that Augustine's own long-term illicit relationship and the son it produced ultimately had their own negative impact on one of Catholicism's primary patristic resources on questions relating to women, marriage, and sexuality (with respect to *Humanae vitae*, for example).

No person and no policy springs pristine from a vacuum. Yet, despite the fact that experience is the starting point for the Church's theory of natural law, and despite the fact that the shapers of the Church's official teaching are resources with their own personal and historical limitations, the lived experience of the laity is generally discounted in favour of the cerebral insight of aging celibates. Even the advice of lay and clerical processionals tends to be unwelcome. Is it any wonder that the Church's credibility in this area has been all but discounted? The exercise of absolute power begins to assume a certain absurdity when there are few who will bend to the rod. Surely by working together as Church we can create a dialogue that will foster a society rooted in Christian love and expressed through selfless partnership.

A. Richard Sipe is a psychotherapist whose extensive research into the question of clerical sexual abuse has led him to the certain conclusion that questions of power and sexuality are intimately intertwined in the teachings of the Catholic Church; moreover, the teachings of the Church are themselves often harmful both to the laity and to the priests. He refers, for example, to studies whose conclusions have prompted their authors to coin terms such as "ecclesiogenic neurosis" and "ecclesiogenic pathologies." The first of these disorders results from the tabooizing of frank and open discussion about sexuality, associating punishment and immorality with the sexual and erotic. Ecclesiogenic pathologies he defines as "those mental and emotional aberrations that are induced or fostered by Church teaching or practice."[174] Moreover, Sipe notes that since seminary training centres its concern on the vow of celibacy rather than on an understanding of sexuality as such, priests are ill-equipped to deal with either their own sexual issues or those of their parishioners. On the contrary, he suggests that graduates of Catholic seminaries are often impaired psychosexually and that many Catholic priests are sexual adolescents—though he characterizes the institutional Church as preadolescent in its psychosexual development.[175] Sipe observes that given the nature of sexual development associated with seminary formation, the confessional becomes (or became, when Catholics were more accustomed to frequent the sacrament) the lecture hall for the priest. In the confessional he became not only informed, but perhaps overwhelmed and possibly even jaded as he learned something of the frequency of masturbation, infidelity, homosexual activity, and other sorts of sexual carryings on that he had not even dreamed about, such as necrophilia or zoophilia. Given the inflexible and all-encompassing Vatican decrees on sexual issues and given the pastoral need for priests to deal with real individuals struggling with the Church's teaching while doing their best to lead a good life, is it any wonder that in their 1990 survey the bishops of the United States discovered that most priests who have been in active ministry from five to nine years have a low comfort level with Church governance and its moral teachings?[176] Or that fully one quarter of the newly ordained leave the priesthood within their first five years of active ministry?

When Rembert G. Weakland, the archbishop of Milwaukee, published his "Reflections for Rome" in an April 1998 issue of *America*, he was talking about his archdiocese, but he did so with an insight that could apply quite accurately to the Church in the most of the Western world. Weakland's comments provide a useful summary, therefore, of the present state of affairs and imply the attitudes that are destined to shape the Church of the future. On questions of sexual morality and married life, he reports:

> The largest group of Catholics in my archdiocese can be found in a kind of middle ground. . . . They seem to ignore much of the church's teaching on sexuality and just do not talk about it, especially about birth control. They use common sense, they say, in dealing with many of these problems, having long ago ceased believing that all acts of masturbation were mortal sins, having accepted gays as human beings to be respected and loved but having many doubts about so many aspects of gay lifestyle, being secretly sad that their children are living with partners before marriage but not wanting to break bonds with them. They are pro-life but stay clear of the organized pro-life movements; they adopt a stance that is much more related to the consistent life ethic.[177]

4

The Curse of Clericalism

THE HIGH COST OF CLERICALISM

The image of the cleric in the High Middle Ages is anything but a flattering one. Medieval imaginative literature and even the visual art of the period frequently depicted the medieval priest, friar, monk, nun, and quasi-religious functionaries such as the summoner and pardoner as morally bankrupt, sexually libidinous, and often inclined to cupidity. The medieval priest was, in fact, very often uneducated and all too often pursued the tonsured professions for their promise of a life of relative ease and artificial respect. Although the imaginative literature of the Middle Ages tends often to depict the medieval churchman as educated, that learning is often deployed in the literature as a means of personal advancement or a handy enhancement in the sexual conquest. Geoffrey Chaucer's Monk, Friar, Nun's Priest, Pardoner, and Summoner are stereotypical cases in point.

When the sixteenth-century Reformers set out to correct the corruption within the Christian Church by making the Bible available to the average church-going Christian and by establishing a priesthood of all believers, the Catholic Church dug in. Instead of universalizing the priesthood and empowering the laity, the Catholic Church moved to establish seminaries and hence to professionalize the priestly order; at the same time, the Council of Trent reinforced the perceptible power of the ordained cleric by requiring for the first time that all marriages be solemnized in the presence of a priest. The Catholic priest became a person apart, someone a little closer to God in the human hierarchy. This elevation of status and authority led inevitably to a heightened position of power. Clericalism, the abuse of the power of the priesthood, was destined to become the unhappy by-product. And if power comes with the pedestal, so does responsibility. Sacred trust demands a higher level of accountability. Breaches in trust will, conversely, lead to cracks in the pedestal.

The curse of clericalism, as Bishop Alexander Carter had characterized it in a 1971 intervention to a Vatican Synod of Bishops, is at the heart of the most troublesome challenge facing the Catholic Church in the twenty-first century. How does a Church whose sacramental character is at the core of its self-definition incorporate the laity into its clerical mindset? And how do its priests measure up to the lofty image the post-Reformation Church created quite intentionally for its ordained ministers?

To be sure, the Catholic priesthood does have its modern martyrs, like the six Jesuits murdered at the University of Central America in San Salvador in 1989 for preaching, in word and in deed, the preferential option for the poor espoused by Vatican II; or Martin Royackers, the Canadian Jesuit who was shot to death in June 2001 for daring to apply the co-operative principles of Pius xi's *Quadragesimo anno* (*On Reconstruction of the Social Order*) to those incarcerated by the inhuman poverty of a Jamaican ghetto. There are, in fact, many of the Church's ordained who have given their life's blood for the message of the Gospel. Nor have all of the priestly martyrs died a violent death; many have effectively laid down their lives for their friends by embodying the ideals of service and self-sacrifice on a daily basis in an inner-city parish, a high school, or one of a hundred different apostolates. Too often, however, today's educated clergy are unhappy replicas of their medieval antecedents. And too often the offence is traceable to an abuse of clerical power.

Clerical power is, of course, expressed in myriad forms in everyday parish life, but for more dramatic documentation of the exploitation of clerical power, one might point to the Winter Commission's report of sexual abuse by the clergy in Newfoundland, or to similar findings in the United States, Ireland, England, or Australia. However, recent revelations coupled with the Vatican acknowledgement of the widespread abuse of clerical power within the African Church ought to provide cause for serious reflection. As *The Tablet* reported in its March 24 and 31, 2001 issues, clerical sexual abuse has been confirmed in some twenty-three countries, but the African situation is the most persistent. Sexual abuse, even rape, of African nuns by priests has been well documented for years; yet, those who speak up are silenced while the Vatican does little more than turn a blind eye.[1] Priests are known to seek out nuns for sexual gratification, arguing that if the sisters do not comply, the priest will be forced to seek the favours of prostitutes and, as a result, run the risk of contracting AIDS. One superior-general who complained to her archbishop that twenty-nine of her sisters had been impregnated by priests was relieved of her administrative responsibilities and an alternative administration imposed by the archbishop. And while pregnant nuns are dismissed from their order to face a life of almost certain destitution and humiliation, the priests who have fathered the children are quietly moved to another parish, sent on retreat, or shipped abroad on study leave. The official explanation for the abuse is rooted in cultural perceptions concerning the status of the priest in African society, the relative roles of men and women in society and in the Church, the superiority that accompanies education and the inferiority that accompanies poverty and ignorance, the conviction that celibacy as sexual abstinence is a social convention peculiar to Western culture, and the perception that having sexual relations with many women is an expression of power and status. It is a structure of power coupled with a naive sense of obedience to male authority that is available to the impoverished African male in virtually no other form, since, as a candidate for the priesthood, the seminarian receives an education from the Church that would almost certainly be otherwise unavailable to him.

With status comes power. With power comes responsibility. And with responsibility comes accountability.

Although it may not be difficult to unearth similar stories in the industrialized West, social realities continue to shift. The priest is losing status in a society that has begun to idolize wealth and acquisition over religion and the mystical. Seminaries are closing. Ordinations are few. The pedestal is crumbling. Hardly a week goes by without some report about the crisis in the priesthood, about the closing of churches, about lay movements seeking to share power with a hierarchy reluctant to consider meaningful means of lay participation in the administration of the Church.

Although the curse of clericalism is surely in its death throes at the local level in the industrialized West, it is stirring in the modern seminary and it is enjoying something of a Roman renaissance. Yet, the future of the Church will almost certainly depend very much on the realizing of a meaningful priesthood of all believers. The challenge is clear: the cost of clericalism is high indeed.

A FRESH PERSPECTIVE ON THE CATHOLIC PRIESTHOOD

Vatican II's Dogmatic Constitution on the Church, *Lumen gentium*, refers repeatedly to the "royal priesthood" in which the laity participate by virtue of their baptism. It is a recurrent phrase in a number of the documents of Vatican II and it is terminology that is used even by Pope John Paul II when, for example, he envisions Catholic parents leading their family in prayer—and John Paul II is a staunch defender of the Catholic Church's more traditional approach to priesthood.[2] The Council Fathers, however, had something much more inclusive in mind than John Paul's family at prayer when they referred to the shared priesthood. They explain, for example, that "The baptized, by regeneration and the anointing of the Holy Spirit, are consecrated into a spiritual house and a Holy Priesthood."[3] In addition, the Council Fathers envision a shared infallibility in which all participate according to their respective calling: "The body of the faithful as a whole, anointed as they are by the Holy One (cf. 1 Jn. 2:20, 27), cannot err in matters of belief. Thanks to a supernatural sense of the faith which characterizes the People as a whole, it manifests this unerring quality when, 'from the bishops down to the last member of the laity,' it shows universal agreement in matters of faith and morals."[4]

While it is clear that ordination to the episcopal ranks marks the "fulness of the sacrament of orders,"[5] and that the sacramental priesthood represents a more perfect form of priesthood than that enjoyed by the laity since the consecrated priest is "united with the bishops in sacerdotal dignity,"[6] nonetheless the faithful are "in their own way made sharers in the priestly, the prophetic, and kingly functions of Christ."[7] There is here a *sensus fidei*—a sense of the faithful—that both recognizes the traditional hierarchical structure of the teaching Church and embraces John Henry Newman's sense of the essential role that the laity have to play in the life of the Church and its evangelical mission. The vision of *Lumen gentium* is consistently that of the People of God as a pilgrim people engaged in a common quest, a shared pilgrimage of renewal.

Although the ecclesiology adopted by the Council Fathers is in principle wholly divorced from the "pray, pay, and obey" mentality that characterized that of the preconciliar Church and produced a clear chasm between the inferior and superior roles to be assumed within the Church's hierarchical strata, there is no doubt that the levels of perfection conceived by the medieval Church and bequeathed to our modern times are still very much at work even within the enlightened thinking of the Council Fathers. The laity are admonished, for example, to look up to their priests and to "follow them as their shepherds and fathers"; the priest, therefore, is to show true leadership, "allowing them [the laity] freedom and room for action" while simultaneously serving as "strenuous defenders of the truth, lest the faithful be tossed about by every wind of opinion."[8] Indeed, the conciliar *Decree on the Ministry and Life of Priests*, *Presbyterorum ordinis*, depicts the priest as a man apart, one pursuing a higher calling and from whom more is clearly expected so that priests are described as "always going to greater lengths to fulfill their pastoral duties more adequately."[9] Superior status implies more exacting responsibility.

Cardinal Archbishop Emeritus G. Emmett Carter of Toronto attended the Second Vatican Council, having been consecrated bishop of London just as the Council was about to begin. Carter became a changed man, a changed Christian, and a changed ecclesiastic. He took to heart the logic of the Council's efforts to empower the laity and it has become something of a theme to which he has frequently returned these past few years. With this in mind, Carter has often elaborated on the three eras in the history of the Church as he sees them, and in his elaboration he places the emerging era, the millennium of the laity, into the context of Vatican II.

During the first of Carter's three eras, the foundational period, roughly the first millennium, the Fathers of the Church put in place both the intellectual and the institutional structures for the early Church whose ancestry they traced to the apostles. The second era—the second millennium more or less—is characterized by the rise of the religious orders, the Franciscans and Dominicans in the thirteenth century, for example, as well as the Jesuits in the sixteenth and a legion of religious congregations of priests and sisters in the nineteenth century in particular. Although the first era provided the framework for a privileged clerical caste, the second era truly is the millennium of the cleric, characterized not only by the spawning of religious orders and congregations but also by the dogmatic retrenchment of the Council of Trent and the pronouncement on papal infallibility promulgated by Vatican I in 1870. Carter is openly puzzled by some of the trends he sees in today's Church, but he does see clearly that there is today an opportunity for a revitalized Christianity.

And now we are turning to another era. And I always like to feel that we shouldn't have to be dragged into this era kicking and screaming. We should lend ourselves peaceably and willingly like good Christians to the grace of God and to the evolution of human affairs. I am reminded how Cardinal Bernardin went so willingly to his death. I've just read a book by Morris West, *A View from the Ridge*, which is his autobiography. It's a comment on the project of life and how we go through it, up hill and down dale, until we wind up on the ridge where we can see the whole pattern, the darkness on one side and light on the other, and how nothing remains for us at that moment but to cast ourselves into the hands of God. It's a beautiful idea. It's the kind of thing Bernardin did and it should serve as a pattern for us. We shouldn't have to be dragged into the new era kicking and screaming.

One of the interventions at the Council was by my brother Alex who talked about the decree on the laity. He said that this document was born in original sin, in the original sin of clericalism. He went on to develop the idea that we had misplaced the concept of the church and we had misplaced the revelation which Jesus brought us because we insisted on postulating that the only leadership in many areas had to be in the hands of the clergy, the priests, or the religious orders. We had neglected the leadership of the laity. All Christians were called to leadership, were called not only to receive but were called to give, to do things for other people. Doing things for other people is in many cases the role of leadership. We have to see where need exists and respond to that need. It's not only a monetary question. It's a question of assuming our Christian responsibility and sooner or later we will be called upon to make sacrifices, and we will be called upon to lead. Leading, in many ways, psychologically, has been misrepresented. When we fall into the trap of thinking of leadership only in terms of power, we miss the message of Christianity. Jesus was not a leader because he wanted power—he didn't want power. In fact, he never had power—he had power in the sense that he performed miracles: he helped the sick and the poor and the rest, but he had so little power that a group of rascals could put him to death. I think that may be a trap for this particular era. We must not think of leadership as power and therefore I am not suggesting that laypeople should become ambitious like politicians who want to lead because they want power. I'm talking about giving of oneself.

Leadership is not easy. Leadership is a sacrifice. In order to lead, you have to give up a lot of the things you might prefer to be doing. You have to abdicate your own tastes, your own preferences, your time, and you have to be ready to do something for other people. That is why I say that the layperson must not be seen as taking over the job of the priest. That's not what we're talking about at all. What we're saying is first of all through a meeting of forces that I'm not prepared to understand personally, the falling off of the number of priests and the falling off of their dominance, you might say, in the Church of our time is not something we should struggle against. We should simply say that this means that we all have to pitch in and work harder than we did before. Far from being a weakness, this should be a strength. I don't want to denigrate the priest in any way, but at the same time I believe that we are going to come out of the semi-darkness in which we find ourselves the better for the new light. If we hadn't had the Second Vatican Council, we would be much worse off than we are. But why did we lose vocations? Why have we been almost decimated after the Council? The Council should have been a light in the darkness. It should have been a sign of the leadership which was really beginning. The Council was the high point of my education in the Church. It changed my whole view of the Church. It changed my whole view of Christianity. Not that I was in heresy, but I had a great need of light and the four sessions I attended gave it to me. It was also a turning point in the history of the Church, a turning point that should have brought us greater strength and instead brought us a great deal of weaknesses in certain areas. I don't really understand why this came after the Council rather than before, but, however, I do think that this is a great challenge for the laity to assume their responsibility as Christians. We have to realize what it is to be a Christian, and it is not a question of power but rather to say that I am a Christian and therefore a giver, a giver of that which I have received.

Not a bad summary of the personal and political dynamics of the Catholic Church in the last half of the twentieth century.

Even as the Church was finding its wings within the first millennium, there were calls for renewal, such as the Great Benedictine Reform, which consumed a good part of the tenth century, and the Gregorian Reform near the end of the eleventh. Reformation has, in fact, been an ongoing project within the Catholic Church: as Vatican II declared with both candour and honesty, "the Church, embracing sinners in her bosom, is at the same time holy and always in need of being purified, and incessantly pursues the path of penance and renewal."[10] The Council of Constance (1414–1418), for instance, sought to end the crisis engendered by the Great Schism by providing for a conciliar form of Church governance—a *reformatio in capite et in membris*—a reformation both at the head and within the members; the Council of Trent (1545–1563) attempted to cauterize the wounds inflicted by the Reformation and in so doing reinforced the hierarchical ecclesiastical structure that the reformers were in the process of dismantling; Vatican I (1869–1870) reaffirmed the Tridentine victory of the ultramontanists by arming the besieged pontiff with infallible powers in issues of faith and morals; Vatican II (1962–1965) continued the process of reformation, attempting to find a role for the bishops, the priests, the laity, for non-Catholics, and even for non-Christians—unfinished work from Vatican I, and then some. And after all this, it is, as Carter says, a time to pitch in.

The preoccupation of the Councils during the second era in the history of the Church is clearly a question of power: from the global spiritual and political claims staked by Innocent III in the thirteenth century, to the ultramontane centralization of spiritual authority enshrined in the Bishop of Rome at Vatican I as an aftermath to the loss of the Papal

States, to the more expressly familial but still hierarchical vision of Vatican II. What is its source, in whose hands does it reside, and with whom should it be shared? A youthful G. Emmett Carter had observed that, given the renunciation of the human drive to propagate the species, the celibate "tends to concentrate on the power given to him by his position" and, as a result, "religious are notoriously jealous of their rights, privileges, and prerogatives."[11]

Clearly, the sharing of power envisioned by Vatican II and more recently by an experienced and pragmatic churchman like G. Emmett Carter is no simple reflex for a Church whose history and psychology suggest neither egalitarian nor democratic inclinations. And it is precisely this elevation of the clerical caste, its defined superiority, that has sometimes bred a sense of awe and admiration, but that has just as often been the source of both a healthy sense of skepticism and an ingrained anticlericalism. A Church triumphant whose public posture declares that it is the sole bastion of truth is an institution ripe for satire. The dramatist would speak of hubris and watch expectantly for the fall. Quite predictably, therefore, one need only glance at the songs of the medieval goliard, troubadour, or court poet to know that the cleric's misdemeanours have been the butt of satire, parody, and general high comedy for centuries. Indeed, the fabliau was developed as a medieval literary genre as a vehicle for poking fun at the follies of the wayward cleric, while the courtly love tradition with its sensual gardens and cult of the lady flourished as a parody of Christian values.

One needs, however, to put the parody, the satire, and the burlesque into context because despite the aggressive role the medieval papacy played in the political and religious domains, the Middle Ages provides an instructive laboratory for the study of a fruitful working relationship between the layperson and the ordained, one that has in many ways been replicated and even surpassed in our own time. While it is true that denigration of the wayward cleric was both a source of good fun and perhaps even a licence for libidinous lay behaviour, it was also a call for reform and a return to basic Christian values. Geoffrey Chaucer's Parson is a case in point. The simple, otherworldly country Parson defines the essence of the ideal priest, the one too seldom found in a world overrun by clerics—as Chaucer's Summoner and Friar exchange insults, the Summoner paints a vivid sketch of Satan with a swarm of honeyed friars (some 20,000 in number) nesting under his tail.[12] As a result, the Parson portrays the qualities the layperson expected to find in the ordained minister but too seldom did. Chaucer notes of his Parson that he provided a noble example, teaching first by his actions and then by word: the medieval dictum is to teach *in facto* and then *in verbo*, first by deed and only then by word. To which Chaucer asks the proverbial question, "If gold rusts, what will iron do?" That is, if the priest lives a sinful life, what can one expect of lesser types like the lowly layperson? It is a standard to which priests, bishops, and Pope are held to this day. But it is also a universal call to build a society firmly rooted in gospel values. Chaucer concludes his *Canterbury Tales* by inviting his audience to join him in acts of contrition and penitence, and he includes as his departing words his own confession as an author: an expression of remorse for anything he may have misspoken.

Chaucer's concluding remarks are important, too, for what they tell us of the relationship of the medieval poet to his society. By protesting that "Al that is writen is writen for oure doctrine [instruction],"[13] Chaucer allies the intention of *The Canterbury Tales* with St. Paul's clarification in his letter to the Romans (15:4), just as Chaucer's explanation of allegorical interpretation puts him squarely within the Augustinian tradition of biblical exegesis when Chaucer remarks of the Nun's Priest's allegorical tale: "Taketh the fruyt and lat the chaf be stille."[14] This is Augustine's advice in his influential manual for preachers, *De doctrina christiana*: When interpreting the Bible, take the fruit (the inner meaning) and let the chaff (the story in which the meaning is buried) be still. It is a direction adopted by Dante,[15] Boccaccio,[16] and other medieval poets as they shaped their art for the teaching of Christian morality. Many a medieval poet has taken to heart Augustine's instruction that the first-class homilist will hone his art so that it will teach, please, and move one's audience.[17] In fact, during the Middle Ages many homilists composed their homilies in pure poetry; conversely, both Dante and Boccaccio talk expressly about the hidden truths that lie within their imaginative compositions. That is, both the ordained clergy and the educated layperson share the responsibility of the medieval teacher of Christian morality, each according to one's talent.

A quick pilgrimage through representative medieval literature will make the point. Although there would no doubt be many within any given audience who would provide a knowing nudge at the recitation of any satirical song or recognize a local ecclesiastic in a particularly pointed parody, that same audience would also know that the purpose of satire is to expose a fault so that it might be corrected. As a result, both poet and audience in the Middle Ages would find common cause with the eighteenth-century English novelist Henry Fielding when he explains in his dedication to *Tom Jones*: "I have employed all the wit and humour of which I am master in the following history, wherein I have endeavoured to laugh mankind out of their favourite follies and vices." Furthermore, as Fielding observes in his preface to *Joseph Andrews*, characters are drawn from nature rather than experience and the intent is comic catharsis, to laugh at the foibles of humankind as an incentive for reformation.

Although some of the attacks recorded in *The Political Songs of England from the Reign of John to That of Edward II* are more tragic than comic, the intent is not simply to upbraid the clergy for what the poet perceives to be greed, lasciviousness, or generally benighted behaviour. Indeed, some of these poems could have been written by disheartened clerics themselves. Such is the case of a thirteenth-century Latin song—which is therefore the product of at least a learned lyricist if not a disenchanted priest. In this poetic analysis, the sin of avarice in society in general, and in the Church of Rome in particular, is imaged as a grasping miscreant. *Contra avaros [Against avarice]*: "The bishop loves a cheerful giver, and dares either right or wrong after the smell of a bribe. . . . The priest, whatever the dead or the living give, carries off to his fireside woman, he gives himself and all he has; he of the holy name and the equal mind, who meditates the law of the Lord by day and night."[18] Another Latin lyric from the same era, "A Song Against the Bishops," complains that "The clerical order is debased in respect of the laity; the spouse of Christ is made venal, she that is noble, common; the altars are for sale. . . ."[19] Sentiments of this sort abound. And there is in the criticism a yearning for a more perfect world. Some of the more extensive and bitingly satiric verses are to be found in the early fourteenth-century Anglo-Norman "Order of Fair-Ease"[20] and the "Satire on the Consistory Courts"[21] whose titles suggest their content accurately enough and whose topics could point to either clerical or lay composition. In something of the same manner, the Middle English "Land of Cockayne"[22] provides a thoroughly English parody of the paradisal setting in which monks and nuns eat, drink, and make merry—the reappearance of the irreligious order suggests the near generic nature of the motif. Clearly, since those who establish the standard are called to a higher degree of compliance, their inability to match word with deed is a natural source of comedic delight that might simultaneously issue implicit licence for the sinful behaviour of lesser mortals or, more likely, it might preach the need for a reformation of Church and society. Rust has stained both the gold and the iron.

William Langland's "Fair Field of Folk," which serves as a prologue to his *Piers the Ploughman*, a late fourteenth-century West Midland allegory, depicts a cross-section of society grasping for gain; on the plain among the tramps, beggars, and alcoholics one might also find palmers, friars, pardoners, priests, and bishops. It is a vision of society and of Church that causes the poet to conclude: "Indeed, I fear that there are many whom Christ, in His Great Consistory Court, will curse for ever."[23] In similar fashion, Chaucer's *Canterbury Tales* begins with a General Prologue to introduce the poem's audience to the hustle and bustle of medieval society, to a Knight and a Squire, a landowner and an inn-keeper, a Miller and Reeve, but also to a Monk who is a manly man and not much given to being cloistered, to a Prioress who lives a life in awkward imitation of the medieval court, to a Pardoner who preaches against avarice but is himself the epitome of the vice against which his homilies rail, to a Friar with a wandering eye and lecherous tooth. . . . It is a cast of sinners, a social microcosm, to which the humble Parson makes a call for repentance as the pilgrimage winds its final steps toward the shrine of St. Thomas à Becket.

So it is that Boccaccio riddles his *Decameron* with tales of faithless priests and nuns as well as grasping ladies and gentlemen; so it is that as Dante populates his Hell, he also includes popes and lesser ecclesiastics. Perhaps the two most unlikeable characters in Chaucer's *Canterbury Tales* are his Summoner and Pardoner, two agents of the ecclesiastical court who had previously been pilloried in "The Satire on the Consistory Courts." Chaucer's Pardoner (the dispenser of papal indulgences for the remission of the temporal punishment due to sin) is the subject of particularly pointed irony, since the sin of simony—the selling of ecclesiastical favours for personal gain—is among the lowest on the medieval scale; by the same token, the abusive sale of indulgences is castigated in Langland's

Piers the Ploughman and all serve as an ominous anticipation of the likes of Johann Tetzel, the German Dominican friar whose entrepreneurial-like passion for the peddling of indulgences incensed Martin Luther and led directly to the posting of his ninety-five theses on the door of Castle Church in Wittenberg on October 31, 1517.

So it is that poet and priest join hands to preach the Christian message in the Middle Ages—both of them "pitching in" and both of them in need of repentance. And so it is that John Gower's late fourteenth-century *Confessio amantis* is framed around the seven deadly sins, as Gower provides representative stories for each. In his prologue Gower observes that his stories will be more than the simple telling of a tale; there will be "Something to please, something to profit." He adds, moralistically, that the world is in a decaying state: "Its plight much worse than long ago." Gower's message, therefore, will centre on the need for love, since in his day "Love walks a stranger, and unknown." Even among the clergy, Gower laments, one will find a lack of love, and even signs of heresy. Ultimately, he makes a plea for a life of virtue, "Such as Christ taught when here below."[24] Chaucer, Gower, Dante, Boccaccio, Langland—all laymen engaged in the evangelical ministry and each contributing according to his talent.

The twentieth century has enjoyed an emergence of first-rate Roman Catholic writers whose imaginative fictions engage the Church and its teachings in realistic situations—writers like Morley Callaghan, Brian Moore, and T.F. Rigelhof of Canada; Graham Greene, David Lodge, Piers Paul Read, and David McLaurin of England and Wales (though McLaurin is an ordained priest); Morris West, Thomas Keneally, and Les Murray of Australia. Our contemporary era, like the Christian Middle Ages, is a time in need of evangelization, so there is room for cleric and the layperson to pitch in, to work together to introduce biblical precepts into our everyday affairs. Unlike the Christian Middle Ages, however, the modern world is hardly abuzz with swarms of clerics. Even the 1960s conciliar documents on the Church and on priesthood, *Lumen gentium* and *Presbyterorum ordinis*, speak of the shortage of ordained priests. If that shortage drew cautionary references in the 1960s, it rang alarm bells in the 1990s, and it is urging wholly new directions in the twenty-first century. Unlike the Middle Ages, where Gower's generalized image of the non-cleric was the rustic working in his field, the lay talent available to the Church today is highly educated, variously talented, often better trained professionally than the priest, and prepared to pitch in at levels of ministerial assistance that would have been unimaginable even a generation or two ago. The face of the Church in the twenty-first century is about to change dramatically as we enter the era of the laity. The question, as G. Emmett Carter characterized it, is whether we will enter the new era kicking and screaming, or whether we will do so like good Christians all willing to make the sacrifices inherent in the call to service.

THE ORDAINED MINISTRY

It is frequently observed that the Vatican's view of the married state is an impossibly idealistic one. Similar observations might be made about those who are called to priestly ordination. The ordained priest is indeed called upon to be a man among men, but he is also asked to present an otherworldly ideal, forsaking wife and family, personal self-interest, and many of the trappings of the material world in order to serve humankind as an *alter Christus* in a world not much given to religion and often much more appreciative of individualistic initiative than self-denial for an idealistic greater good.

Presbyterorum ordinis, the Second Vatican Council's Decree on the Ministry and Life of Priests, recognizes the potential for loneliness inherent in the priestly vocation and, in order to combat the "dangers" of so singular an existence, encourages the priest to establish some form of community life, sharing accommodations, meals, or finding time for social gatherings with other clergy (section 8). The loneliness, of course, results in no small measure from the Vatican's determination that the priesthood in the Latin rite should be reserved for those willing to live a celibate life. The Council Fathers do not dwell on the question of celibacy, but do explain that by virtue of their consecration through "the Holy Spirit and sent by Christ, priests mortify in themselves the deeds of the flesh and devote themselves entirely to the service of men. Thus they can grow in the sanctity with which they are endowed in Christ, to the point of perfect manhood."[25] It is, in effect, a definition of convenience. Did Christ become man and image the perfection of manhood by living a celibate life? Is the married state, therefore, an imperfect one and if so, as the Wife of Bath inquired so long ago, "to what conclusion / Were membres ymaad of generacion, / And of so parfit wys a wight ywrought?"[26] The Council Fathers do return to the topic (in article 16), noting the long-standing tradition of priestly celibacy (*Presbyterorum ordinis* says that the Church has "always" held "perpetual continence" in high regard) and recognizing that it is a discipline only within the Latin rite. While the Council Fathers state their support for the continuation of the tradition of clerical celibacy, they add rather idealistically that the priest should pray both in humility and perseverance for "the grace of fidelity. It has *never* been denied for those who ask"[27] (italics added). As the literature of the Middle Ages suggests, and as modern history confirms, the Church needs a more practical rationale for the denial of so basic a human drive.

But the priest is called upon to deny much more than the joys of marriage and family. His is a lofty call, indeed, one that both elevates and imposes. *Presbyterorum ordinis* articulates the responsibility in terms it admits are "ideal" while simultaneously depicting the sacrifices as every-day: "As rulers of the community, they [the priests of the New Testament] ideally cultivate the asceticism proper to a pastor of souls, renouncing their own conveniences, seeking what is profitable to the many and not for themselves, so that the many may be saved. They are always going to greater lengths to fulfill their pastoral duties more adequately."[28] One fulfils one's duties "more adequately" through a reflex selfless renunciation for the good of the many? The description sounds more heroic than adequate, yet it is an ample description of "fatherhood" properly embraced.

What sets the priest aside and elevates him beyond that of the layper-son, however, is not the degree of virtue to which he must aspire—all Christians, after all, are called upon to pursue a life in imitation of Christ—but the cultic powers that he has received as an ordained minister. *Presbyterorum ordinis* stresses the Eucharistic quality of the Catholic community, explaining that "no Christian community . . . can be built up unless it has its basis and centre in the celebration of the most Holy Eucharist."[29] Celibacy is a Church discipline peculiar to the Latin rite. It is not an essential requirement of ordination to the priesthood. Living in imitation of Christ is a prerequisite for any Christian. It is not peculiar to the ordained priest. However, only the ordained priest can act *in imitatio Christi* as presider at the eucharistic sacrifice. The shortage of priests to which the Council Fathers refer is, therefore, not simply a problem for the Church. No Christian community can thrive without the Eucharist—that is, without an ordained priest. And, as Donald Cozzens argues in his *The Changing Face of the Priesthood*, the priesthood is in fact in crisis. It is a crisis the hierarchy will not address since it is in a state of denial; it is a crisis that professionals outside the inner hierarchy will not address, because to study contentious issues relating to priesthood is simply "too threatening in the present climate of suspicion and mistrust."[30]

The ideal that the Council Fathers have outlined is a daunting one indeed. And there are many who have accepted the call. Many priests do live lonely and heroic lives, exemplifying the life of love captured in the words of the New Testament. Some of these men live in inner-city parishes ministering to the poor and forgotten; some have reached out to those suffering of AIDS when they were society's untouchables; some work in parishes whose membership has swollen to numbers impossible for one man to embrace. We have visited Canadian priests living and serving in the slums of Jamaica in circumstances few of us would have the courage to encounter; we have visited priests at the University of Central America in San Salvador, priests who volunteered to help fill the void created when their fellow Jesuits were brutally murdered for preaching and incarnating the Gospel of justice; we have visited priests in Nicaragua who were living in frightful circumstances in response to the call of Vatican II to foster a preferential option for the poor, priests who worked under suspicion from Rome. There are thousands of stories of heroism to be told. But there are too few priests, and despite the occasionally optimistic interpretation of statistical data, the priesthood is surely in a state of crisis.

When the Vatican announced that the 1990 Synod of Bishops scheduled to meet within the walls of Vatican City would deal with the Formation of Priests in the Circumstances of the Present Day, the topic and the timing seemed propitious—even Cardinal Joseph Ratzinger, in his opening address to the Synod, characterized the "huge drop" in vocations as being a crisis for the Church. "The Catholic Priest in the U.S.: A Demographic Study," an analysis commissioned by the bishops of the United

States, for example, projected a 40 percent decline in the numbers of active priests in the year 2005 as compared to 1966, and in that same year almost 46 percent of those priests still in active ministry will be fifty-five or older, with only 12 percent being thirty-four or younger.[31] Canadian statistics are equally alarming. Between 1970 and 1990 the number of diocesan priests had declined by 26 percent, and by 1987, 34 percent of Canada's priests had reached age sixty-five, with only 26 percent being younger than fifty. Estimates put the number of active diocesan priests under age fifty at 15 percent by the turn of the century.[32] In Quebec the numbers are even more alarming.

Not only were vocations to the priesthood in English- and French-speaking North America in an apparent free fall, but accusations of clerical sexual abuse of children were beginning to surface as issues of titanic proportions with the potential, if not to scuttle the Roman barque, then at least to leave it storm-weary. In Canada, the first stirrings of what became very troubled waters indeed were cast before an incredulous public in 1988 when the immensely popular Father James Hickey, principal organizer of the Pope's 1994 visit to Canada, was accused and subsequently convicted of pedophilia. Not only was the incident highly publicized, but with the publication of the findings of the commission he had established, the archbishop of St. John's, Newfoundland, Alphonsus Penney, stepped down in disgrace, condemned by his failure to act in the light of evidence available to him.[33]

Hot on the heels of the Hickey event, allegations of sexual abuse of children by the Christian Brothers at Mount Cashel Orphanage in St. John's became a Canadian cause célèbre whose national importance prompted the creation of an award-winning television docudrama, "Boys of St. Vincent," which centred on the efforts of two boys struggling to escape sexual victimization in circumstances virtually identical in nature to those reported of Mount Cashel. Commission findings pointed to an abuse of power and a failure to honour the responsibilities of a sacred trust. In addition, the Winter Commission, which had examined the Hickey allegations, recommended that the Canadian bishops review "fully, directly, honestly and without reservation questions relating to the problematic link between celibacy and the ministerial priesthood." In the meantime, Catholic Newfoundlanders have become sometimes skeptical and sometimes even hostile to the Church they embraced so affectionately until the light of public scrutiny began to reveal what had been hidden in its darkest corners.

Subsequent findings in Ontario, British Columbia, and elsewhere in Canada have further undermined the credibility of Vatican policy with respect to sexuality, the discipline of celibacy, the possibility of women's ordination, and the openness of a Church too often unwilling to listen. For their part, as has so often been the case, Canada's bishops as a conference have been exemplary. They have faced their Church's sexual scandals forthrightly, but they cannot undo the damage that has been done or easily restore the confidence that has been lost.[34] The concluding statement in the bishops' response, "From Pain to Hope," is a sign of understanding and acceptance worthy of any Christian serious about righting a wrong:

> Forgiveness is certainly not the easiest path the Lord has indicated to us. In cases of sexual abuse it can, at times, become confused with other paths erroneously called "the road to pardon." We must never forget, for example, that sacramental forgiveness can be used as a kind of security or a form of "cheap grace," to use Dietrich Bonhoeffer's expression. Nor should we demand premature forgiveness on the part of victims, particularly as a means of more or less silencing the demands of justice or concealing an unhealed wound.

Canada's bishops have never been known to hide behind platitudes, but have, on the contrary, been quite willing to speak their minds where matters of justice are at issue.[35] Their preparations for the 1990 Synod of Bishops, therefore, were typical of the Canadian Conference. Reacting to the Vatican's working document, the *Lineamenta*, the bishops needed to find scope to deal with the real issues. Rome's working paper insisted that the ministerial priesthood as such had been studied in the 1971 Synod and that the Congregation for the Doctrine of the Faith, Pope Paul VI, and Pope John Paul II had addressed any issues that have arisen since. The Synod was to deal only with the formation of priests; that is, the question of married priests, the discipline of celibacy, and the ordination of women were not up for discussion. These were topics the Canadians had raised at past Synods and which were, if not burning, then at least simmering issues on the home front. For the Vatican, it was sufficient to rule the nature of the priest out of order: the priesthood was a man's world, a world in which "chastity in celibacy for the sake of the kingdom" is a requirement—hence a certain "maturity" is essential to live the life of a priest in our "divided world." Thomas P. Rausch summarized his analysis of the *Lineamenta* by pointing to its weakness in understanding contemporary society or the world in which future priests will have to serve, the Vatican perspective of priesthood that provides the background for the preliminary document, and the clericalized concept of priesthood that is out of step with the needs of the modern layperson.[36] The *Instrumentum laboris*, the reworked *Lineamenta* that formed the working paper the delegates would take to Rome as a backdrop for their discussions, addressed none of these issues.

Under the circumstances, and given the history of Canada's bishops, their embargoed October 27, 1989 response to the *Lineamenta* was insightful, to the point, forceful, and practical. It criticized the advance document for being out of step with *Lumen gentium*, for resurrecting the past rather than "daring to create the future." It accused the Vatican authors of a lack of vision and an unwillingness to face frankly the reasons for the dramatic reduction in vocations to the priesthood, and it lamented the harsh and negative attitudes the Vatican had adopted toward the modern world. The Canadians asked the key question: "Will the Church accept being challenged in order to inculturate the Gospel today, or will it, guided by a strategy of dodging fundamental problems, isolate itself more and more from the contemporary world?" It is a question that Donald Cozzens raised some ten years later, having been frustrated with the Church's unwillingness to date to face the hard issues head on. But the Canadian bishops did not stop there. They argued that the Vatican document was focussed more on power than on service, and were dismayed that the Roman perspective "leaves little place for contemporary questions increasingly more urgent: a limited-time ministry, ordination of married men, ordination of women. . . ." The Canadian bishops asked the questions that increasing numbers of faithful Catholics want to see addressed honestly and openly.

The Canadian bishops developed some forty-one pages of candid and practical advice in a manner wholly consistent with what Bernard Hubert, president of the Canadian Conference of Catholic Bishops, characterized in 1985 as being the effort of the CCCB to "bring to light the questions, remarks and suggestions from the Christian communities at home" to provide "the universal Church with a rich and loyal contribution for the benefit of all."[37] They addressed some of the real issues, such as an exhausted clergy who are fewer in number, who often do not balance work, relaxation, and prayer, who sometimes cannot let go of the traditional priest who shoulders the whole load and who wants to control everything in his parish, not really trusting the laity to share the burden; issues like the need to cope with a loss of status and respect in a post-Christian world; media image and, in the minds of some, media persecution, particularly in pursuit of accusations of sexual abuse; the image some of the older priests present to prospective candidates for the priesthood: some older priests who are "perceived as uncommitted, cold, turned in on themselves, middle class, arrogant and legalistic." There is also a call to "break the closed circle" in seminary training, to integrate the laity, men and women, into seminary formation, so that laypeople have a say in the choice of candidates to the priesthood, and there is a call, too, for the active priest to image a fraternal spirit and inner joy that would encourage vocations.

The Canadian bishops' response laid bare some of the nagging issues: "It will be necessary to dare to raise questions about the ministry of married priests in the Latin Church of tomorrow. It will be necessary also for the bishops to courageously reflect together on the questions still raised by many about the ordination of women. Can the Synod refrain from giving careful attention to the problem of the link between celibacy and priestly ministry. . . ?" All of these issues were raised before by Canadian delegations—in 1987 the delegates added the question of women deacons to their list of topics that needed to be studied.

The final reflection by the Canadian bishops: "How can we inculturate the Gospel in a world that we don't know, that we fear or even that we condemn?" All in all, it was a wonderful document, one that would have made most Canadian Catholics justly proud had it been generally available.

On their return from the 1987 Episcopal Synod, the Canadian delegates to that year's Synod issued a report to the Canadian Church in which they admit that "the Synod was also a trying experience." Bishop Fred Henry made local headlines with his intervention of the psychosexual maturity of candidates for the priesthood, but for the most part the Synod was a non-event. Some 200 bishops gathered to exchange ideas with one another, all moving relentlessly to a prewritten conclusion. The usual response: "It was really helpful to have the opportunity to meet bishops from around the world"; and "When in Rome. . . ." Cardinal Aloisio Lorscheider, the archbishop of Fortaleza in Brazil, rose to address the Synod in the name of the Americas. He captured the tone one hears so often in the corridors outside the Synod hall:

> The disillusions and frustrations begin when proposals are formulated. Many bishops, who have taken part in previous Synods, have expressed their view that there seems to be a lack of reliability, claiming that the proposals are not put down as originally intended, and above all when they refer to subjects under discussion in the Church right now, or when they offend somebody's sensibilities. Many Bishops say that they do not recognize the proposals which appear, after much discussion and the preparing of it by the relator in the Hall of the Synod. [The relator is an administrative secretary who compiles, synthesizes, and relates information to the synod.] They talk of "short circuits." This is the moment when the real frustrations which the Synod can cause are born. There are also a lot of frustrations which arise from the information service of the Synod. The circulation of the news of what took place in the Synod is considered largely insufficient. Little is announced and this does not give a true image of the Synod as well as arriving too late to those whom it really interests—that is to say to the Christian people and public opinion.[38]

Because Lorscheider was so public a figure and so outspoken, the press were anxious to hear him out. So, when he gave an interview to Alberto Bobbio, a journalist with the Italian magazine *Famiglia Christiana*, his comments were widely reported, especially his observation that he had ordained two *viri probati* (married men who had been tried and found faithful) with the Pope's blessing. Reacting to the flurry of media attention, the Vatican was forced to issue a press release explaining that it was indeed possible for married men to be ordained in the Latin rite if they agreed to remain celibate as priests, if their wives and children were in agreement with the ordination, and if the priest and his wife no longer shared the same dwelling. The Vatican release went on to point out that the Church's decision to ordain a number of married Anglican priests was an exception to the rule "and should not be understood as implying any change in the Church's conviction of the value of priestly celibacy. . . ." As for the matter of the *viri probati*, John Paul II had the last word, noting in his October 27 address to the closing session of the Synod that those who looked to the *viri probati* as a means for solving the crisis in vocations were misguided. It is a suggestion, he cautioned, that is "too often evoked within the framework of systematic propaganda which is hostile to celibacy. Such propaganda finds support and complicity in the mass media."

Not everyone agreed even with the proposition that there was a crisis in the priesthood, with Pio Laghi, the pro-prefect for the Congregation for Catholic Education, arguing that "The trend is a positive one. There were 16,505 less priests in 1989 than there were in 1979 (5,761 diocesan; 10,744 religious)." Indeed, the concluding Message to the People of God reported that the number of men studying for the priesthood had increased 53 percent worldwide over the past thirteen years. (The key word is "worldwide"; there is no mention of attrition percentages.) Enthusiastic references to a "springtime of vocations" in some Third World countries were countered by concerns about creeping materialism with its negative impact on family, commitment, the place of the sacred in society, as well as about its emphasis on individualism and sensual pleasure—all of which are seen to have had a negative impact on priestly vocations. There were also stated concerns that not all vocations are properly motivated, that for some the priesthood could be a means of advancement in societies where advancement does not come easily. In Kenya, for example, delegates felt it was important that seminarians be trained to be "good and faithful stewards of church land and property, not using them for family or friends," a sure sign of the existence of a problem. Subsequent political events in Catholic countries like Poland and the concomitant decrease in vocations—vocations have decreased by a third since their 1986–1987 peak—suggest that these concerns were not misplaced.[39]

A number of delegates urged the Synod to look to local situations and to be sensitive to local cultures when shaping programs for the formation of candidates to the priesthood. Exhortations such as these not only advocated a consideration of forms of seminary life that differed from the European model, but encouraged a reconsideration of the value of celibacy within various cultures. The bishop of Port Elizabeth in South Africa, Michael Gower Coleman, pushed the thesis of inculturation in a direction that Alex Carter of Canada had counselled at the 1971 Synod on Priesthood; Coleman recommended that "In formation, far more weight needs to be given to the demands and the richness of local cultures. Their oral tradition should be respected and their antipathy towards celibacy should be seriously addressed lest we get the wrong kind of priestly leadership in our Church." Bishop Lawrence A. Burke, bishop of Nassau in the Antilles, expanded the argument, urging that "Our vision of priesthood must not be static but fitting present needs. Churches of new independent countries must not be shackled with cultural vestiges suited to Europe's experience. Specifically, we may ask whether today ordained priesthood should be limited to male celibates." And Bishop Henri Goudreault of Labrador City-Schefferville introduced a practical element into the debate, noting that in his diocese there is a large population of Anglican Inuit and that 30 percent of its clergy are married Native priests, whereas he has twenty-five parishes, 13,000 parishioners, and no Native clergy. Still, most delegates, Goudreault among them, confirmed the Pope's position, arguing in favour of retaining the discipline of celibacy for priests in the Latin rite. Some noted that problems of celibacy could be dealt with by praying to the Blessed Virgin, others insisted that it is a matter of weakness, a lack of self-control; that is, "ascesis."

So the question of celibacy was put to bed and problems of pedophilia were not aired. The Synod confirmed the papal positions that Pio Laghi recalled in his report to the Synod that John Paul II stated in unambiguous terms in an address to the Canadian bishops on November 7, 1988 in which the Pope said: "Today there are many who interpret the decrease in vocations as a sign that the priesthood should be replaced, rather than joined by new and complementary forces of the ministry. Others believe that the need for celibacy should be abolished, for priests of the Latin rite; others maintain that the traditional doctrine of the priesthood, based on the institution of this Sacrament by Christ and on Christian theology, should be abandoned, if possible, so that women can be ordained. In this way, it is said or understood, one could be assured of a large number of workers for the Lord's mass. Would it not be better to say, in following the way of the Lord and not our own, that ordained priesthood and the love and understanding of it on the part of the Church are now being put to the test, so that the essentials can be reinforced, purified and renewed in a spiritual rebirth which will make it ever more fruitful?"

Although many Synod delegates disagreed with the Pope both publicly and privately, the majority did not, and the Synod made it clear that its delegates were not simply reaffirming the Pope's position out of institutional loyalty. Archbishop Daniel Pilarczyk of Cincinnati told a news conference that the discipline of celibacy was more important in today's world than it had been in times past and questioned the efficacy of testing seminarians to control potential deviant behaviour; Cardinal Joseph Bernardin told the same news conference that the question had been settled at the Synod in 1971. So the final statement of the Synod, its Message to the People of God, celebrated the Synod's conviction that "celibacy has shone out for us in a new light and with new clarity" and the statement confirmed the traditional thesis that "priests should be free from ties of marriage and family, not attached to possessions and comfort, not demanding complete personal autonomy"; in addition, the Synod's proposals stated clearly its wish to "affirm that chastity in celibacy is a precious gift from God which perfectly fits the priest's image in the eyes of the Latin church and in the eyes of many of the Oriental churches today more than ever. In a world marked by individualism, priestly celibacy rightly lived is called to be a sign of God's gratuitous love for humanity through the total dedication of the priest as a person."[40]

Ignored in the process were not only simmering issues like the Newfoundland Mount Cashel scandal, but professional interventions such as the one provided by Father Timothy J. Costello, a Jesuit professor of theology at the Pontifical University of St. Thomas Aquinas in the United States. Entitled "The Discernment of the Priestly Vocation," Costello's intervention examined aspects of the psychological issues associated with sexual predilection, celibacy, and other personal sexual characteristics that might well have a bearing on one's ability to fulfil one's priestly obligations in a faithful manner. Drawing on the lessons of modern depth psychology and referring specifically to the work done by fellow Jesuit Luigi Rulla, Costello explained that "it is possible for a perfectly normal person *consciously* to desire and profess certain religious ideals yet also be moved, at the same time, and without being aware of it, by *unconscious* forces which may be contrary to these same ideals. Like a revolving door, it is possible for a person to say a conscious 'YES' and a hidden 'NO' at one and the same time. This leaves him in a state of dichotomy and inner tension, which is called 'vocational inconsistency'."

The resulting psychosomatic and psychosexual tension, Costello suggests, could reduce one's ability to honour one's priestly commitments. With this in mind, Costello argued for careful training of those entrusted with the formation of candidates for the priesthood, a recommendation that Bishop Fred Henry expanded by suggesting that those who would be priests should receive psychosexual counselling before entering the seminary, while attending the seminary, and after ordination. Given the framework of the Synod and the evaporation of the conciliar enthusiasm for consultation (perhaps even deliberation), no more than this ought to have been anticipated. The nagging issues may have been settled to the satisfaction of the Synod, but they would not go away.

In the spring of the following year, the Vatican released its first response to the practical issues raised at the 1990 Episcopal Synod.[41] Entitled "Redistributing Priests Worldwide," the directive was prepared collaboratively by members drawn from five different offices in the Vatican and presented as "emergency measures" to deal with the current shortfall in vocations while looking for long-term resolutions. The study provides some pretty sobering statistics: Latin America accounts for some 42.42 percent of the global Catholic population, but only 13 percent of its priests—in the northeast of Brazil, every priest is responsible for 18,000 faithful and in Cuba there is one priest for every 20,000 Catholics; at the same time, the Catholic population of Europe and North America accounts for 38.81 percent of the Catholic faithful and some 73.14 percent of the world's priests; that is, 52,452 priests in Latin America as opposed to 294,000 in Europe and North America. The logic of the distribution, the Vatican concludes, is redistribution.

The second part of the plan is to follow the Pope's suggestion at the conclusion of the Synod that "the communities of the faithful, which at the present time do not have the possibility of the celebration of Mass every Sunday, would be able to live and to strengthen themselves by listening to the word of God, going to holy communion and by fraternal union." To achieve this "second emergency solution," the Vatican notes, the Church will require the active participation of a number of "ministries": deacons, lectors, acolytes, catechists, extraordinary ministers of the Eucharist. These, it seems, would be needed only until Plan A is achieved: a revitalized means of restoring the health of the seminaries. The Vatican laments the fact that base communities are flourishing in Latin America, often without the services of a priest, while "organized apostolic activity has grown weak." In other words, the laity can be useful in the absence of an ordained priest, but alternative forms of parish life are not on the table. In addition, given the Vatican's closure of two Brazilian seminaries at Recife within months of the Synod's opening session, the message is clear with respect to cultural differences and priestly formation. In the case of the Recife Institute of Theology, one of the principal complaints seems to have been an objection to locating the seminarians in small groups throughout the city rather than providing a single facility in which the students could be housed. The European conception of seminary life would seem to be the only legitimate model that will receive the blessing of the Vatican.

The second formal response to the 1990 Episcopal Synod was issued on April 7, 1992. Entitled *Pastores dabo vobis*, the apostolic exhortation on the formation of priests begins on a positive note, borrowing the promise from Jeremiah 3:15: "I will give you shepherds after my own heart."[42] While recalling that the 1971 Synod had dealt in part with the question of priesthood, John Paul acknowledges that both social change—the rise of an "inhuman capitalism" and a concomitant commitment to a subjective morality—and the stress under which declining numbers of priests must serve their parishioners have pointed to the need to revisit the question of priestly formation. It is, moreover, a question that has become all the more important with the increasing role being assigned to the laity since "the more the laity's own sense of vocation is deepened, the more what is proper to the priest stands out."[43]

Curiously, as the Pope catalogues and discusses the ills of the present day, he points to a bias against the teaching of the conciliar Magisterium and an erroneous understanding of conciliarism as "undoubtedly . . . one of the reasons for the great number of defections" that the Church has had to endure; the 1990 Synod, he suggests, has rediscovered the depths of priestly identity.[44] The key word here is "rediscovered." Acting in imitation of Christ, the priest is the servant of the Church and related to Christ "through sacramental participation in the priestly order." Given the requirements of the time, there needs to be a new form of evangelization, new ways of preaching the Gospel. "This task demands priests who are deeply and fully immersed in the mystery of Christ and capable of embodying a new style of pastoral life, marked by a profound communion with the pope, the bishops and other priests, and a fruitful cooperation with the lay faithful, always respecting and fostering the different roles, charisms and ministries present within the ecclesial community."[45]

The process is clearly one of rediscovery. The tone and the text are wholly traditional, including the Pope's absolute assurance that it is the will of the Synod that no one should have any doubts about the firm determination of the Latin Church with respect to its discipline, which "demands perpetual and freely chosen celibacy" both for those priests already in service and those men contemplating a priestly vocation.[46] Candidates presenting for priestly studies, therefore, are expected to bring with them a degree of psychological and sexual maturity in addition to an authentic prayer life; the seminarian should place himself under the guidance of a spiritual director who will help to shape him personally, socially, and spiritually, as well as introduce him to the germinal documents with respect to priestly celibacy and sexuality in marriage. There is here, nonetheless, an effort to confront the real needs of modern society. For example, contrary to what the Pope characterizes as a contemporary tendency to downplay the importance of academic preparation, priestly formation should take seriously the need for rigorous academic study and an introduction to the principles of inculturation, all of which will be provided by teachers who demonstrate "total fidelity to the magisterium; for they teach in the name of the church, and because of this they are witnesses to the faith."[47] It is, John Paul argues, a learning process that should not end with the seminary, but be a lifelong project. At the same time, the Pope also stresses the need for the seminarian to develop a sensitivity for learned human experience, for daily contact with those living outside the seminary as a means of understanding the day-to-day demands on the lives of the laity. Finally, John Paul calls on priests to develop a "more tender devotion" to the Virgin Mary, the person who responded in perfect obedience to the call of God: *Pastores dabo vobis* concludes with a litany to the Virgin.

Much of what John Paul has to say in *Pastores dabo vobis* is theological and traditional; some of it is a practical response to the crisis in the priesthood. One needs to ask, however, whether when the dust has settled on the 1990 Synod on the Formation of Priests in the Circumstances of the Present Day the Church is better prepared to meet the social and ecclesial demands that lie ahead, or, indeed, the demands that confront us even now. One might also wonder about the practical consequences. A. Richard Sipe, author of the much celebrated *Sex, Priests, and Power*, is lamenting almost a decade after the Synod that the Church is still lacking in adequate methods for the detection and screening of potential sexual offenders from among those applying to study for the priesthood.[48] At the same time, Sipe refers to several studies that suggest that disproportionate numbers of those attracted to the priesthood may suffer from "prepsychotic personalities"; in any event, preselection assumes that there are no systemic causes of the incidents of sexual abuse by Catholic clergy, an assumption that Sipe's analysis suggests is questionable in the extreme, not the least of which is the Church's teaching on sexuality itself.

Despite the fact that the 1990 Synod did not wish to place either the pain or the problem of pedophilia on its agenda, preferring to dodge the events in Newfoundland rather than deal with them, the Mount Cashels will not go away. And despite the lofty sentiments about the virtue of celibacy and the need for ascesis, sexual misconduct by priests is nothing new, as the literature of the Middle Ages makes so abundantly clear. What is new is the social will to address the problem, even if the ecclesial will is not yet actively present beyond those national conferences that have had to react to unpleasant realities.

Donald Cozzens talks about institutional denial. It is, we think, a denial most of us have seen rationalized in one manner or another. Those of us who work with priests have heard the stories all too often. Jim McHugh, writing as a Resurrectionist priest who was counselling both the victims and the perpetrators of clerical sexual abuse, talks about his unwillingness to believe that fellow priests, some of them his friends, had been guilty of sexual molestation, yet he could no longer deny. "An Abuse of Power, A Betrayal of Trust: The Emperor Has No Clothes" is the story he tells of his experience as a marriage and family therapist as well as a counsellor of priests found guilty of pedophilia.[49] Although McHugh would not draw a causal connection between the clerical discipline of celibacy and pedophilia, he does suggest that celibacy contributes to other causes of the sexual abuse of children, causes such as loneliness, a lack of intimacy, the absence of meaningful personal relationships. The overwhelming common denominator relates to sexual immaturity, to an abuse of power, and to an abuse of trust. One ought also to note with respect to all of the above that in Canada both the Anglican and United Churches have been so racked by allegations of sexual abuse that dioceses within the Anglican Church are facing possible bankruptcy and the United Church of Canada as an institution has been placed in a perilous financial situation, yet both of these Churches provide for married clergy. As McHugh knows so well from his professional experience, traditional Christian thinking that marriage may allay the fires of concupiscence is no safeguard against abuse of power and trust or, indeed, against a penchant in some for pedophilia.

McHugh sees some real benefits in the current situation. Among them the call for the Church to accept responsibility and accountability; among them, too, is the loss of prestige once enjoyed by priests and an emerging recognition that they are "less angelic, more human"—a phenomenon that may well explain the mixed reactions to a survey conducted for the bishops of the United States as to whether the priest is a "man set apart."[50] In Canada, several bishops—the symbol of an authoritarian institution—have had the courage to apologize publicly for the abuse that the victims of clerical pedophilia have endured at the hands of our priests. Their courage, McHugh suggests, is making it possible for others in society to admit their guilt (especially fathers and mothers) and to begin the healing process within their families. Above all, he suggests, the cycle of denial has been broken: it is all right to recognize that the emperor has no clothes, to demand accountability, and to begin to right the wrongs that have for too long been tucked conveniently away, out of the accusing light of public accountability.

As if to confirm McHugh's thesis, J.A. Loftus begins his handbook for ministers, *Understanding Sexual Misconduct by Clergy*,[51] with a discussion of denial, reasoning that denial is the most prevalent response to accusations of sexual abuse by clerics. And Loftus would know. He is the past executive director of Southdown, a treatment centre for priests and nuns just north of Toronto, in which capacity he has served as administrator and counsellor; this work led quite naturally to his publication of an extensive research study of sexual misconduct by the clergy. As a result, Loftus was also a key adviser to the Canadian bishops during the Newfoundland crisis and has served for years as a special appointee to the committee dealing with accusations of sexual abuse by a Jesuit priest at Cape Croker in Ontario. Loftus's experience and that of many others does testify that denial is clearly the near universal response. When, therefore, some 300 to 400 "survivors" of clerical sexual abuse in the United States gathered at a Victims of Clergy Abuse Linkup conference in October 1992, they insisted that for them the Church's inflexible institutional denial constituted a second form of abuse, a psychological abuse that was particularly painful.[52] Sipe, too, on the basis of his own intensive research on the question of clerical sexual abuse, centres his analysis on the penchant for denial, but he carries the question to the next step: cover-up. Sipe discusses the "sexual underworld" within the realms of the Catholic clergy, an underworld in which alliances are struck and in which looking the other way becomes a systemic response both to survival and promotion.[53]

A reader cannot but experience a real sense of dissonance when moving from the biblically based and philosophically driven directives, exhortations, and encyclicals emanating from the Vatican to the social-scientific analyses of J.A. Loftus and other professionals who have contributed to the discussion of clerical sexual abuse. "Conclusion: Sexual Abuse Committed by Roman Catholic Priests: Current Status, Future Objectives," in *Bless Me Father For I Have Sinned: Perspectives on Sexual Abuse Committed by Roman Catholic Priests*,[54] for example, covers a wide range of issues relating to pedophilia and ephebophilia (sexual attraction toward and sexual activity with adolescents). Reliable data are simply not available, but the best estimates indicate that about 6 percent of the ordained Catholic priests in the United States fall into these categories, 2 percent being pedophiles (that is, about 1,200 U.S. priests may be abusing children) and 4 percent ephebophiles (that is, approximately 2,400 priests are estimated to be abusing adolescents).[55] These are best guesses; the number may be larger, and not included in the figures are consensual homosexual or heterosexual relationships with adults for which no data are available. Sipe provides a catalogue of possible statistics of instances of sexual abuse by clergy in the United States and elsewhere; even though everyone agrees that many instances go unreported, the numbers are numbing.[56] According to one study mentioned by Sipe, some 80 percent of criminals in Australian jails claim that they were sexually abused when they were children, and of this 80 percent, approximately one-half allege that the perpetrator was a Roman Catholic priest or brother.[57] Although Loftus bemoans the fact that better information is not available and suggests ways in which it could be accumulated, he makes it quite clear that no one should be surprised by the numbers since the problem is virtually as old as the Church itself.[58] Loftus also points out that when the discipline of clerical celibacy was established in 1139, the intent had nothing to do with the lofty ideals now being preached by the hierarchy of the Church, but rather as a means of dealing with medieval laws with respect to hereditary land rights: it was an effort to prevent a priest's sons from inheriting Church property.[59]

In light of the sexual abuse scandals that have surfaced internationally, and Bindoon (the Brothers' Boys' Town in western Australia) in particular, the early writings of Australian novelists Thomas Keneally and Morris West are particularly instructive since the novels of both of these authors point to the problem of sexual repression and even sexual disorder inherent in the development of clerical leadership.[60] Keneally had studied for the diocesan priesthood and West for the Christian Brothers; their novels recount stories that were apparently written on the basis of those experiences.

Thomas Keneally is anything but ambiguous in his assessment of the seminary training to which he was exposed.

I think if you live in a world where there's no danger to your faith and you're not a pilgrim, then what's the point? That's not the way we thought, of course, and therefore we have a very male-centred, sport-centred sort of philistine Catholicism in the seminary. Philistinism was safest because you didn't get any big ideas—you didn't get any ideas at all—you just believed.

As a seminarian, I was also scandalized by our living conditions. Compulsory x-rays, which obliterated TB in Australia, were yearly but they wanted to come in twice a year to examine the students because the place was so ancient and drafty. Two of my friends got TB—they were sent out of the seminary and their parents looked after their treatment, their surgery. They had to have a partial lung resection and no one from the seminary visited them except other students. I became very shocked and was angry. I think you can see the anger and a certain disorder in *Three Cheers for the Paraclete*,[61] although I think the impulses behind *Three Cheers for the Paraclete*, even though they're a bit neurotic, are still good, democratic, new-world, up-yours, bugger-the-bishop sort of attitudes. You know, "Does the bishop think it's his church?" sort of attitudes. My biggest problem with that old-fashioned, authoritarian, and extremely Jansenist, pitifully Irish brand of Catholicism is that it made for neurotics.

I'd like to say that, having been exposed to that full frontal Catholicism, if I can call it that, the full, high-tensile, Vatican, Jansenist, Irish thing, I found it very hard to adapt to the world in which you could say, "The bishops say that, but it's my church too." I've found for the rest of my life that it's hard to adapt from my earlier experience. Nonetheless, I wouldn't mind having the chance to write something like *Three Cheers for the Paraclete* again because I think it would be more measured. When you write as a young writer and you're angry, you pile on the bile. You don't let the baddies condemn themselves out of their own mouths, which you should; or you sort of let them condemn themselves out of their own mouths but you throw in the pejorative adjectives. And that's the mark of the young writer, over-signalling who the goodies are and who the baddies are. I don't do that anymore. What marks that book, I think, is the trauma of leaving, of finding out that the institution to which I'd devoted these years was a fallible institution. I'm more equable about it now.

If he is clear about his disenchantment with seminary training in Australia as well as with the authoritarian Church for which he studied,

Keneally is also clear about his perception of the heavy strain of Jansenism that garroted that Church. In *Homebush Boy*[62] Keneally recounts his experience of being drawn into the seminary as part of a social snare into which the Catholic youth of Australia were enticed. The young Thomas Keneally of *Homebush Boy* was never fully convinced of his calling, nor were his parents, nor, for the most part, were the parents of his friends and associates who found themselves drawn into lives that demanded perpetual silence or estrangement from family, or, conversely, lives that promised administrative status or games of golf. At the same time, Keneally was not wholly naive about his choice. Among the Christian Brothers who taught at Strathfield, for example, was Brother Dinny McGahan whose confused notions of sexuality triggered an intemperate tirade over some "crazed dancing" in which one of his students had engaged. Following Brother McGahan's heated admonition, an admonition the student "would probably remember all his life," Keneally observed: "Catholicism's big fear of sexuality, its morbid panic, its detestation of most sins of the flesh (including masturbation, of which I was uninformed at the time), was at play in him [Brother McGahan]. He was both the victim and promoter of that awful phobia."[63] The Christian Brothers, Keneally mused, had been infected by the scruples of Dutch theologian Cornelis Jansen whose "high stress on the essential and continual austerity which must be applied in matters of sexual morality" were visited upon the Brothers' charges. So, when the Brothers reacted to the purported episode of dirty dancing by cancelling the next year's dance, Keneally concluded that "A saner system might have imposed a different penalty altogether—a compulsory monthly dance, something to de-mystify women and prepare us to be fit lovers and husbands. But I believed at the time that we sixteen-year-old victims of Jansen were getting what we deserved."[64]

In *Three Cheers for the Paraclete* Keneally explores the implications of the pervasive Jansenism, which, he argues, has contaminated the Church in Australia. Set in an Australian seminary, *Three Cheers for the Paraclete* is populated by a liberal-thinking priest-professor, James Maitland, who bucks a system that rewards those clerics who would put law before love and who preach obedience before compassion and right reason. Among their number is a neurotic seminarian, Hurst, who tries to squirrel away the cafeteria cutlery in the backyard lest, like Origen before him, he interpret too literally the biblical mandate to become a eunuch for the kingdom—except that Hurst would have others become eunuchs too. Hurst's neurosis is explained away by the rector as "the will of God," but it is condemned by a psychiatrist experienced in dealing with priests and religious as being the result of a training that is judged to be "anti-human." And celibacy is characterized as "only a high form of sex-titillation" by the outspoken sister of a woman who had been seeking an annulment from a dysfunctional husband, but who was pursued and then abandoned by the priest who had become the *defensor vinculi* (the defender of the bond) in her case.

As *Three Cheers for the Paraclete* opens, Maitland is preaching at an outdoor Mass for a group of graduates. He develops as his theme the proposition that Christianity gave Eros, the god of sexual love, poison to drink and that the priest "lacks the self-surrender imposed by Eros to help men to enthusiasm." Maitland asks his congregation to pity the "sapless priest" and as a plea for tolerance of the priest who is more comfortable with canon law than with compassion, he quotes French poet Charles Péguy: "Because they love no one, they imagine that they love God." Keneally's novel becomes an analysis of the poison that the Christian Church has fed to Eros and of the struggle to understand the "insoluble" conflict between law and charity.

Morris West did not study for the priesthood, as Thomas Keneally had; West was a member of the Christian Brothers in Australia for some ten years before leaving the order to find his way in the world. Their attitudes toward the Church and the clerical life are, nonetheless, not dissimilar. And although Keneally's and West's experiences with seminary life go back some forty years and more, many of their criticisms of that life as well as of the contemporary Church are echoed in Donald Cozzens's recently published *Changing Face of the Priesthood*. They all decry, for example, the lack of intellectual challenge in the formation program, they express a real concern about the Church's ultrarational approach to an understanding of human sexuality, they associate the call to the clerical life as a bonding between mother and son (Cozzens describes the relationship as Oedipal), and they worry about the radical centralization that has occurred in the Church.

Morris West is arguably one of the two or three most recognizably Roman Catholic novelists of recent history, often establishing popes, cardinals, or priests as his agonized protagonists. His *Moon in My Pocket*[65] sketches in fictional form West's almost ten years as a Christian Brother—his training, his disillusionment, his laicization. The principal character of *Moon in My Pocket* is ironically named Brother Urban, ironic in that Urban's main source of anxiety is a lack of urbanization, a closeting within an artificial environment, which leaves him a sexual adolescent who is unable to cope with his emotional encounters with the opposite sex. As Brother Urban reflects on his escape from the cloister, he recalls the words of one of the women whom he has befriended: "My dear, you've so many things to learn, and I'm not sure you're in a fit state to learn them."[66] *Moon in My Pocket* is an effort to understand—ultimately, to learn. The comforting mantra he has been taught as a student is an ascetic one: "The world has little to offer but sorrow, disillusionment, pain. In following Christ in the religious life there is joy, peace, the fellowship of noble souls. . . ."[67] It is a promise, a "two-pence coloured method" of reinforcing community life, which he comes to resent.

Not only does Brother Urban find life in the monastery to be a colourless and spartan existence whose sense of self-denial and stark obedience would drain him of his individuality and stifle normal desires, but its religious discipline leaves him emotionally crippled, withdrawn "further and further from the lines of normal adolescent growth. . . . [a] sixteen-year-old postulant, shrinking from the shame of his own awakening body, his normal curiosity unsatisfied, afraid of the daily clamour of undirected affections that set him dreaming still of Beauty Unattainable, that nourished queer, unspoken, hermaphroditic attachments to his fellows in the cloister."[68] The study of philosophy became an arid exercise, pedantic, textbook answers inadequate; he yearned for the smithy of experience, but found instead an artificial separation both from the everyday world and from normal human affection. Urban recalls a high school experience, the reflex repulsion at the touch of Brother Fintan, hand on hand, as Fintan issued the formulaic warnings about sins of the flesh and the wiles of evil women. Fintan becomes for Urban the epitome of what is wrong with the system:

Brother Fintan was a product, if not typical, a least faintly characteristic of the inevitable degenerative tendency in any conventual system. Founded upon the ideal of supreme abnegation, nakedly simple pursuit of perfection, literal imitation of Christ, the religious life is justified only by the greatness of its end. When chastity becomes mere avoidance of copulation, poverty and obedience the cloaks of selfishness and avoidance of effort, when regularity degenerates into formalism, the number of by-products, mentally maimed, morally stunted, blind to the vision and the glory increases alarmingly.[69]

West's attitudes have hardly mellowed with the passing of time. A thinly veiled critique on a repentant John Paul II, for example, *Eminence* (the last novel West was to complete before his death) incorporates his concerns about the Vatican's attitudes toward sexuality, liberation theology, and, most of all, the centralization of power in the papal office. West explains his attitude toward the power of the Vatican in a way that reflects the unbending, unrelenting rule of the seminary:

It is the whole question of authority: its nature, its use, its misuse, its pushing people to liberation, or taking them into tyranny. That's a wide thing. The papacy is the greatest presumptive monarchy in the world. It is not supposed to be a monarchy, as is said in the gospel of John: "The greatest among you should be a servant." Authority as service, authority for service—that I understand. Authority for domination, regulation—no. Remember that I was in Rome during Vatican II and after, and was a great devotee of John XXIII. I could see the beginnings of Christian hope within the church and I clung to that not in desperation, but in freedom.[70]

With respect to the Church's abstract philosophical attitude toward human sexuality and its continuing inability to deal with the lived reality of human experience:

We can't quite open the questions of the importance of sexual morality or the various kinds of loving union because we don't want to put anything down in black and white. It's easier to say no or yes. Life is not like that. People are not like that. The church does not cope with very well with the fact that we have to live with one another in peace, in a community, whoever we may be.[71]

Like Keneally, West centres much of his criticism, expressly or implicitly, on the dichotomy between love and law so that his novels inevitably dwell on the love/law conflict in the life of the Church. West explains his interest in the topic:

You see, one of the effects of my reactive attitude was that I followed the road until the road stopped. I said, "Okay, what am I now expected to do? Jump off the cliff? Burst asunder in the midst?" There has to be some other alternative rather than these unjustified imperatives. My position is that I have remained an open and professing Catholic and Christian, but I do not believe a lot of the nonsense that has been handed to us down the centuries.[72]

Experience shows that the regulated law of clerical celibacy, one of those laws that have been handed down to us over the centuries, is broken by the vast majority of priests at some time in their ministerial lives. Theologians have also reacted against the dichotomy between love and law, experience and ratiocination, chastity and virginity, especially as they relate to the formation of priests and the actual pursuit of the priestly vocation. Carolyn Butler, for example, provides a quick cameo of seventeen personal histories collected in her *Faith, Hope, & Chastity: Honest Reflections From the Catholic Priesthood*.[73] In most cases, these men reflect on their struggles with the discipline of celibacy, some of them discuss preordination sexual encounters with women or other men, and almost all consider the celibate state a vocational advantage for one reason or another, though one makes it clear that he feels the Church's teaching on sexuality is both unrealistic and completely out of touch with the lives of his parishioners, while another feels that the seminary has been a stultifying experience from the perspective of one's psychosexual maturation. There are, of course, other priests who have taken principled and outspoken stances against the juggernaut of Vatican centralization. Adrian Hastings, theologian and historian at the University of Leeds, widely published author, and one-time African missionary, for example, has combined his various experiences of Church and society to argue convincingly the folly of the Vatican's insistence of clerical celibacy.

In *The Faces of God: Essays on Church and Society*,[74] Hastings argues on principle for the ordination of women and the optional right for married priests. Seminary education, he insists, needs to take into account the specific circumstances in which the priests will work; the question of celibacy can also have practical implications, like the ability of poor African dioceses to support both a priest and his family. Still, the discipline of celibacy, he insists, is not a sound one on a number of grounds: there is no biblical basis for it; there have always been exceptions to the discipline; congruity of celibacy and priests does not by extension rule out married priests; married clergy in the Eastern rite provides an example from within of the embodiment of sacramental leadership—the universalization of celibacy, on the other hand, suggests that marriage is an inferior state unworthy of the ordained priest; celibacy has lost its effectiveness as being an important and fruitful calling since the blurring of the active and contemplative ministry, the religious and secular orders of priesthood. As a result and as one component of the call for renewal, Hastings argues that the Church ought to recapture the efficacy of celibacy and assert the concomitant value of Christian marriage.[75] Hastings has, however, taken his convictions to their logical conclusion. While insisting on the worth of clerical celibacy in itself, Hastings insists that the law whose intent is to be binding on all priests in the Western Church is a bad law that he does not in conscience feel obliged to accept. *In Filial Disobedience*, therefore, stands both as his declaration and his explanation.[76] Reviewing his own progress from seminarian to missionary, Hastings traces both the development in his thinking on both practical and theoretical grounds, noting that in Britain and France there are scores of married priests—in France they even have a name: *prêtre en foyer*—many of whom are saying Mass with the full knowledge of their bishops, who would prefer to look the other way. While there are good spiritual and practical grounds for the discipline of celibacy, Hastings concludes, there are no reliable or convincing theological arguments on which one can base a general prescription for priestly celibacy. When he spoke with us, Hastings had been ordained for more than forty years and married for more than twenty. Here is what he had to say:

In Filial Disobedience has, as a first chapter, a head-on attack on celibacy as a law, which had already been published in *New Blackfriars* as an article a few months before. Then, a longish essay of autobiography just trying to say what I had been trying to do and where I was. And then several other pieces. It was my statement of policy in the late 1970s. I hadn't decided, but I was very seriously considering marriage. I think as regards to that, if I had stayed in Africa I don't think I would have wanted to marry. I couldn't cope and I had totally accepted celibacy, as one did in the 1940s or 1950s as part of a priestly package; so, I had never questioned that, just as I never questioned my priesthood. I knew absolutely that I had been called to be a priest. I knew at university—it wasn't an open option for me. Before I even went to school, I knew. My parents never even knew where it came from because it wasn't linked in any of the normal sort of ways: people who like to pretend to be saying Mass and that sort of thing. I had no ritual or liturgical attractions from that point of view at all. It was just a simple knowledge that I had been called to be a priest, and a priest as celibate, so I had never questioned it. As a student I felt annoyed or frustrated, but I accepted—I didn't seriously question the celibacy discipline. Or afterwards. And I don't think that while I was in Africa by myself I ever much questioned it, at least until just about the time I was leaving Africa in the 1970s.

I think that if I had a stable job, it might have been different. But there were obvious practical advantages to celibacy. You could live on nothing. Nobody paid me—I was a priest of an African diocese, I didn't get any money. I could be free and move around easily. I travelled around and one ate what one had, what was given, really. But, certainly coming back to England and finding myself quite outside of any Church structures, and not wanting to get into any normal Church structures— certainly not wanting to get into a religious order where one's future is somewhat bleak and one isn't much good at looking after oneself. I met someone two or three years after coming back to Britain in the early 1970s. We would have liked to have married, but I still said that it's quite impossible. I did say that I had to keep the law of celibacy and remain unmarried in order to argue the case for changing the law. I went on saying that for years and we had more or less given up on the possibility. But then when I went to Aberdeen about that time, I decided this was not my own life. Moreover, it was sort of irrational. If you say that a law is so bad, then why go on keeping it oneself? And when no one is listening to what one is saying? If I really had a position of influence in the Church, that would be different, but it was clear that I had been marginalized completely. So, I decided that I probably would marry and decided that I must explain very carefully what I am doing and why. I decided that I would write this book and publish it, and only after it has been published will I make a final decision. The book was published in the spring of 1978. And now a year later we had decided, I can't remember quite when—in the spring of 1979. I wasn't going to do anything secret. Although we did try to keep the wedding without news. We did for a couple of months and then about two months later the newspapers found out and it was on the front page of every national paper.

Others who aren't theologians have real trouble with such disclosures because they can't cope. Very few Catholics can cope with any other basic structure of ideas different from what they have learned from canon law or Roman theology. And I'm sure that this was true for Bishops Casey and Wright. So, they are forced into an awful situation of acting not in accordance with their own beliefs. They didn't have a chance to think it out. I had a very odd case. When I went to Aberdeen there was no bishop in 1976, just a very conservative vicar capitular. He was extremely unhelpful and extremely reactionary in every way. His whole view of dealing with the shortage of priests was the helicopter. Priests came down and consecrated from the elements here, and then went on and did it somewhere else. And that's all you needed. I remember his saying this. We didn't get on at all. Things got a bit easier when his successor arrived. But then a few months later this man suddenly disappeared from his parish. Of course, it was found out that he was somewhere else in Scotland with someone. It was so awful because it was entirely in contrast with his own theology. There was absolutely no congruity. I'm lucky, being a good historian and a good theologian. I just think that I have the confidence in what Christianity means or the Catholic Church means.

Although progressive-thinking Catholics supported my book, I think that I made a mistake when I published it when I got a small very

Catholic publisher to publish it. I thought it was very important to have a Catholic publisher and actually I gave it to them because there was a former priest who was their editor who had written to me asking if I had any book to publish. I had said he could have this one if he really wanted it. They accepted it, but before it was published, he was sacked and although they went on with the publication, I don't think they attempted to publicize it very well and I don't think it got around as much. And now it's certainly not available.

I was supported here, but in Africa the reaction to the thinking in my book would have been varied. Some would have agreed with me quietly, but very very few African priests would dare to speak out publicly. Just one or two. Especially more recently. What can they do? They're even more lost than Catholic priests in this country. So many priests in England—some of them come to me and say that they want to marry and they want my advice. I say to them, "Well, what are you going to do when you're married?" Again and again you find somebody who's forty-five, who has no proper qualifications, and I have to ask, "What sort of job are you going to get, realistically?" You discuss it and discuss it, and I have to say, "Well, look, it's no good thinking that because I did it you can. I had security of tenure at the university and had such qualifications and status. And of course, in England for those who do, they never get a decent job of any sort. It used to be that the younger ones could go into social work, but now even that is getting quite difficult and the status of social work has gone down and so on. A few people like Nicholas Lash went to academic life, but he'd made the transition before and he now has standing intelligence with most people. But almost none of the British clergy had any degree—some obviously had degrees and have gone on and got good jobs. I just got back from this conference in Germany where I discovered that the leading Jesuit historian in Goa, Father De Sousa, is married and has gone to Portugal where he has an academic appointment. But he'd written books and has a high status.

A Brazilian who was at the conference said that there are 3,000 priests whom the church in Brazil could have tomorrow if it changed its position on clerical celibacy, but as it is the Church is completely collapsing and Pentecostalism is taking over Brazil. The Church has no answer. It has no priests. It has nothing. The Church is dying. Here the shortage is getting particularly ridiculous because now they're trying to fill the gaps with rather conservative middle-aged Anglican clerics at the same time quite a number of Catholic priests are becoming married Anglican priests. I have literally in Leeds an ex-Anglican Catholic and an ex-Catholic Anglican both functioning not far away from one another. It's bizarre, the absurdity. But all in all it's the Catholic Church which is losing out. On the continent, in France, Germany, everywhere, it is simply dying. We are going to be a dying Church because we are a very clerical Church, we cannot really manage without a clergy, and we have blocked all the ways towards ordination. In a sense, I'm now continuing the fight for the priesthood, which seems to me to be absolutely central to the future of the Catholic Church. I was sure the change would have happened long before now.

This conservative sense of male sexual celibacy may be tied up with John Paul's Marian devotion. Clearly, in him there is this extreme devotion to Mary. I think the business of the Vatican's attack on Balasuriya is somehow tied up with some sense that he has insulted Mary. There was also this not wanting to give people communion in the hand. There are various things—there is in the Pope an old kind of sacrality which is in his own piety. There are sides which are very different, but I think that this is the side that dominates. The Latin American Church has been devastated by the attack on the base communities, and the base communities are tied to liberation theology, and he can't really cope with this. But I think that a lot of this is the fear of losing clerical control. He is very clerical, actually.

When one considers the talk in Rome about the need for sensitivity towards indigenous cultures and one thinks of the African situation, it's a network of villages badly connected by mud roads and what you need is an adapted local clergy. And even if you have a lot more people to train in hugely expensive seminaries, it's a totally inappropriate training for most of the clergy in a poor very rural continent. It's just wildly in every way an unsuitable approach. I became absolutely convinced of this in 1963 after four years in Africa. It was the first time I wrote in the *African Ecclesiastical Review* and was probably the moment when I basically came under suspicion. I was only saying that we've got to consider the ordination of married catechists. There was just no way in which the Church was not going to be on the road to disaster. It's obvious that we are on the road to disaster in this country too, just as we are almost everywhere, really. In all of western Europe—I was in a couple of churches in Munich on Sunday. Old priests, reactionary, and you can just see how tired they are. And Bavaria is one of the great heartlands of Catholicism. Large areas of France are just priestless. And here in England we were in a pretty good state and we have no future now. At home in Leeds I was talking recently to a very good parish priest and he sees that there just isn't a future. We are just sitting on top of a bomb which is just exploding because the priests are all old, or there are very very few young ones and there is no way of coping with the ordinary needs of a fairly static diocese where quite a few people actually go to church. There is a whole difference between the optimism of the Church thirty years ago and the complete depression which has now settled in with almost everyone. And you don't see a way out. And the bishops are too frightened to speak out. If only thirty of them could get together and speak out. But they haven't got the guts. Even Basil Hume is affected by the feeling that obedience is our primary duty, loyalty to the Pope, we can advise but we can't do more than that, we mustn't create a stir. . . .

There are some who are willing to create a stir. Archbishop Rembert Weakland of Milwaukee, for example, has suggested that the number of married men for whom exceptions are being made in their applications for ordination will ultimately erode the existing discipline so that in the long run the exceptions will "dictate the norm."[77] An article in *The Catholic Herald* reports that Bishop Ambrose Griffiths of Hexam and Newcastle made a similar point in a conversation during an interview prompted by the fact that the diocesan seminary at Ushaw had, for the first time in its history, registered no local candidates for the priesthood.[78] And Bishop Fritz Lobinger of Aliwal North, South Africa, makes a case for the ordination of married men in those African parishes that have been prepared to receive them. It is, Lobinger's *Like his Brothers and Sisters* suggests, the only way to reverse the shortfall of ordained ministers.[79] Similarly, at the 1971 Synod of Bishops, Canada's Maxim Hermaniuk reminded the Synod about the Orthodox and Oriental Catholic tradition of married priesthood, and Alexander Carter added that the "Canadian Bishops are nearly unanimously in favour of ordaining mature married men where there is need." Carter, who was president of the Canadian conference at the time, added a call for the reinstatement of priests who had been dispensed from their vows so they would be canonically free to leave the active ministry and marry. During their *ad limina* visit to the Vatican in the fall of 1993, the Canadian bishops raised the topic again, asking the Pope directly for his approval to provide a married clergy for Canada's Native peoples in the far north. Again, the request fell on deaf ears.[80] As Andrew Britz, Benedictine monk and editor of *The Prairie Messenger* has pointed out, the bishops have taken the route advocated by *Pastores dabo vobis*, only to discover that the cultural differences of imported priests are simply too great to allow for effective pastoral ministry, and, in any event, non-married men have no leadership credibility in the Native culture.[81] The topic of clerical celibacy has been on the table for some time, and it is obviously not likely to go away soon.[82]

GAY VOCATIONS TO THE MINISTERIAL PRIESTHOOD

Critics of John Paul II's administration and especially of its attitudes toward a married clergy, the ordination of women, and to its clumsy handling of homosexual issues have often pointed to the ironic increase in gay vocations to the priesthood and the gayification of the seminaries, which have coincided with John Paul's pontificate. Although reports concerning the numbers of gay priests and seminarians differ dramatically, there is general agreement that the Roman Catholic priesthood has attracted a percentage of gay vocations that is well in excess of percentages of gays within the general population. Vicky Cosstick, for example, speaking from her experience as a former director of pastoral theology at Allen Hall in London, suggests that although it is not possible to provide exact percentages, it certainly is possible that gays are a majority in the English seminary and it is a certainty that they form a percentage of the seminary population that is greater than that in the wider community.[83] As for the ordained ministry, various studies have concluded that in the United States the percentage of priests who are gay could range anywhere from 28 percent to 58 percent, with other estimates falling somewhere in between and others ranging much higher.[84] Andrew Greeley suggested back in 1989 that 25 percent to 35 percent of the priests in the United States were gay and that possibly half of them could be sexually active.[85] And for Greeley, the decision to admit and then ignore the presence of a growing homosexual priestly population is the direct result of an episcopal response to the shortage of priests, a response that does violence to the vow of celibacy by creating a double standard with respect to sexual activity, one for heterosexuals and one for homosexuals, since sexual liaisons with a woman would result in immediate recrimination whereas homosexual liaisons tend to be quietly overlooked. As such, Greeley reasons, the admission of growing numbers of gays to the priestly ministry undercuts the vow of celibacy and ultimately ensures its demise, does a disservice to those who have been faithful to that vow, and effectively undermines the priesthood.

Although there is no reliable information as to the relative numbers of homosexuals and heterosexuals leaving the priesthood, it is not an unreasonable supposition that many heterosexual priests decide to leave active ministry so they might marry. The result: a disproportionate number of gay priests compared to the general population. The cause: the discipline of celibacy. At the same time, while it is an open question as to whether a significant gay presence in the seminary population is in itself a deterrent to non-gay enrolment just as it is an unanswered question as to whether the increasing numbers of gays within the Roman Catholic priesthood is good, bad, or indifferent insofar as ministerial effectiveness is concerned, it is clear that a non-married clergy provides a convenient professional refuge from a society that has not yet learned to deal with the homosexual fact.

As Richard P. McBrien has pointed out, the implications of the attraction that the priesthood holds for the gay community and the impact of that attraction are both complex and essentially unknown at this time; what McBrien says is known is that there are those who are attracted to the priesthood for other than purely ministerial reasons, and the Roman Catholic priesthood may well be attractive to some men simply because its membership is unmarried. At the same time, McBrien argues, from the evidence currently available, we also know that the single greatest deterrent to the pursuit of the priestly vocation is the discipline of celibacy—a finding that makes the insistence on celibacy all the more perplexing when one considers that there is no biblical, theological, doctrinal, or any other perceivable measure by which one can argue that celibacy is essential to effective ministry. The logic of the situation would seem to suggest that the more homosexuals there are in the priesthood and the fewer heterosexuals, the less pressure there will be to dispense with the discipline of celibacy. McBrien also concludes that, should the Church decide to begin to ordain qualified women, the vow of celibacy would have a similar effect on the female population as it is having on the male: the priesthood would become particularly attractive to members of the lesbian population. For McBrien, the issue is clear. Since the discipline of celibacy is an institutional issue and not a spiritual one, the numerical problems that the discipline of celibacy has created can be remedied only by an institutional solution.[86]

Most observers of gay developments within the Catholic priesthood would agree that sexual orientation in itself is a healthy characteristic of the human person and a potentially positive component of one's priesthood as long as it is maturely integrated personally and experienced within the context of the vow of celibacy. That some priests, both heterosexual and homosexual alike, should fall victim to their sexual urges ought to be recognized as the natural result of sublunary existence; that some priests might contract AIDS, through sexual contact or some purportedly more innocent means, ought also to be recognized as the inevitable result of human social interaction. Jesuit physician and founding president of the National Catholic AIDS Network in the United States, Jon Fuller, admits that the incidence of terminal AIDS in the clerical population of the United States is higher than in the general population, but he is far from alarmist about the statistics.[87] Fuller points to the growing awareness, especially in the religious communities, of the need to deal with psychosexual issues during the formation program. By suppressing discussions of human sexuality, administrators have unwittingly contributed to unhealthy lifestyles and adolescent exploration that might well lead to instances of AIDS. By dealing more honestly with psychosexual development, more enlightened rectors have helped to foster more appropriate, healthy friendships. As a result, Fuller recounts what he sees as an increase in openness and a more compassionate understanding as well as a perceived decrease in the instance of HIV-AIDS infection. For Fuller, the question is the appropriate integration of one's sexuality into the demands of priesthood and the celibate state.

The history of the twentieth century would suggest that the Vatican remains adamant in its unwillingness to review questions of human sexuality either critically or objectively or to evaluate on their own terms the contributions that various contemporary fields of study can bring to an understanding of the institutional and human implications of our sexual natures. There are, however, increasing numbers of informed voices crying to be heard while the institutional Church grows increasingly more dysfunctional. Surely it is not merely a time to pitch in, but a time to be welcomed in.

THE KINGDOM OF PRIESTS AND THE ROYAL PRIESTHOOD

When Moses ascended Mount Sinai to pray, God spoke to him by way of a covenant, promising the people of Israel that in return for their fidelity: "You shall be to me a kingdom of priests, a holy nation" (Exodus 19:6). Simon Peter reshaped this promise as a sign of the new covenant for the troubled Christian communities of Asia Minor, encouraging them with the assurance that through the death and resurrection of Christ: "You, however, are a chosen race, a royal priesthood, a holy nation, a purchased people. . . ." (1 Peter 2:9). The kingdom of priests and the royal priesthood as envisioned in these biblical texts, however, were overtaken by historical events: the cross that led Constantine to victory in the year 312 and the canonizing of a clerical hierarchy that rose in its wake; the ascetic idealism of the desert fathers and the renouncing of earthly pleasures born of their example; the gradual centralization of spiritual and temporal power in the person of the Pope, epitomized in the reign of Innocent III; the proliferation of religious orders and the ubiquitous presence of the cleric during the high Middle Ages; the exclusion in the pre-Reformation world of the general population from the power and influence that accompany literacy and knowledge. Reacting to the entrenched clericalism of medieval society and dismayed by the centralization of power in the papacy, Protestant reformers strove to diminish clerical authority and enhance the influence of the laity (Latin *laicus*, from the Greek for "the people"). Although the Protestant concept of "the priesthood of all believers" which emerged from this reformation is a form of governance authorized by the book of Exodus and the first epistle of Peter, it was staunchly resisted by both the Council of Trent and Vatican I, only to be embraced more recently, at least in principle, by Vatican II. Despite the best intentions of the Council Fathers and of numerous local bishops, the Vatican continues, nonetheless, to cling stubbornly to its hierarchical view of the universe and the power structures that accompany that vision, turning to the laity where there is need, but assuming non-consultative authority even where consultation is appropriate.

Yves Congar's ground-breaking introduction to the role of the laity, *Lay People in the Church*,[88] first published in French in 1951, provides a seminal preconciliar comment on the nature and function of the laity. In *Lay People in the Church*, Congar stakes out rather progressive territory as he worries about the appropriateness of the neat medieval distinction between the sacerdotal and lay orders and he is enthusiastic about the possibilities for an unimaginable springtime of opportunity for the Church if only it can embrace the talent and the energy of the laity.

Indeed, Congar's approach to the question is clearly a preparatory voice for the Second Vatican Council's work on the laity, centring as Congar does on the priestly, the kingly, and the prophetic functions of Christ to which the Council returns in its *Lumen gentium*. Congar notes that not only are the two functions, the sacerdotal and the lay, as distinct as the medieval Church had portrayed them, but that in fact some of the roles traditionally performed by clerics, most notably various works of charity, have more and more been assumed by the activities of laypeople. Moreover, despite the twists and turns of history, there has always been an attack on the "hierarchology" in which the Church has become steeped. The natural reaction of the Church as institution has been to defend its turf against such attacks and, as a result, "While Protestantism was making the Church a people without a priesthood and Catholic apologists were replying by establishing the rightfulness of priesthood and institution, the Church in more than one place was finding herself reduced to the state of a priestly system without a Catholic people."[89]

There was, in other words, a developing rift between the clerical institution and the people. Yet, for Congar, there are priesthoods in addition to the hierarchical, priesthoods appropriate to the layperson: there is a moral priesthood rooted in the living of a sound Christian life, an inner priesthood rooted in the spiritual and ascetic, and a priesthood that flows from one's baptismal consecration. Even in works of the artistic imagination, insofar as they co-operate in the teaching of the sacred, the layperson participates in "a certain exertion of spiritual priesthood."[90] In fact, Congar explains, history records that laypeople have taught the Gospel, established churches, maintained the church in the absence of ordained priests, and even administered the sacraments of baptism and confession where necessity demanded—Thomas Aquinas being one of those to have made a strong case for lay administration of both of these sacraments in time of need. Laypeople, Congar reasons, can be a significant asset to the Church, being free to act as trailblazers and to take unpopular stands since they are unencumbered by tradition and authority. And although the laity have a proper and legitimate role to play in the reception and affirmation of Church teaching, and although Congar notes with some impatience: "With a very few remarkable exceptions, one finds an almost obsessive preoccupation with affirming the distinction between the teaching Church and the taught Church, and the complete subjection of the second to the first";[91] still he is very clear that "Above all, the laity must avoid setting themselves up as 'doctors of the law'; in the very act of bearing apostolic witness they still belong to the Church taught. It is for them to communicate a *lived* doctrine, but that doctrine has first been *received*."[92]

Although his writings fell under the suspicious and watchful eye of the Vatican for a time, Congar is often credited with being the most important theologian of the twentieth century and was destined to become one of the Council's most influential *periti*. Quite naturally, for example, his hand is apparent in *Apostolicam actuositatem*, the conciliar *Decree on the Apostolate of the Laity*, in which the Council Fathers take a huge stride in the development of a theology of the laity. Within its second paragraph, *Apostolicam actuositatem* makes it clear that "the laity, too, share in the priestly, prophetic, and royal office of Christ" having been consecrated "into a royal priesthood and holy people." The conciliar decree also jettisons any notion of a division of responsibilities along the old lines of the sacerdotal and the lay, the spiritual and the temporal, locating the apostolate of the laity in both spheres, each individual contributing according to one's talents and training. As a result, the Council reasoned, the layperson will not only be active in the promotion of social justice and the betterment of society, but will teach Christian doctrine, sometimes at great personal cost and even at risk of coming to personal harm.

Nonetheless, the Council Fathers have not freed themselves entirely of the clerical reflex, noting, for example, that the laity will provide "assistance in the operation of schools"[93] and "do what they can to take the place of priests"[94]—it seems not to have occurred to the Council that laypeople might actually operate the schools and not only take the place of priests, but might well do a much better job in many instances than the priest had been doing before them. One is reminded of the 1971 Episcopal Synod intervention of Maurice Roy, who was then the president of the Pontifical Commission on Justice and Peace. When Roy addressed the Synod of Bishops on October 14, 1971, he cautioned that "it is necessary also to humbly accept the fact that a lay person may at times be superior to a priest or a bishop in knowledge, prudence or holiness." Nonetheless, there is in the conciliar document on the laity, *Apostolicam actuositatem*, the same sense of hierarchical authority, oversight, and even of ability that one finds in the Council's *Decree on the Ministry and Life of Priests* (*Presbyterorum ordinis*). As a result, the response that accompanies *Apostolicam actuositatem* in Walter M. Abbott's authoritative edition of the documents of Vatican II is both frank and instructive. Dr. Cynthia Wedel, general secretary for Christian unity for the National Council of Churches, views the decree through a Protestant spectrum. Ours is a society, she reasons, in which participation is an expectation and not a concession. If the Church is really interested in lay involvement, then those exercising authority need to recognize that people who sense that their function is a secondary one or a derivative one are not likely to step forward and, from her perspective, there is in *Apostolicam actuositatem* no actual sense of shared responsibility in Church governance; in fact, Wedel finds so little real understanding of the dilemma that the Christian faces in the workaday world that she is left to wonder how many laypeople were invited to participate in the drafting of the decree on the laity. Not only that, but she notes that when it comes to the formation of the apostolate, the Protestant tradition has actually tried all of the things that the Council is suggesting—in other words, there is room for dialogue and shared insight.[95]

Vatican II provided new possibilities for a ministry patterned on shared priesthood. It was a noble beginning, though not one without its hierarchical predispositions, but a beginning nonetheless. Many of the Council's bishops returned home invigorated by the dialogue and eager to implement its directives on the local scene. Parish councils were established. Finance and building committees put in place. There was a sense of energy, enthusiasm, and hope at the local scene. Not all bishops bought into the new vision, of course, nor did all of the parish priests. To this day, one hears first-hand stories of collaborative ministries disintegrating with the change of pastors, of mass exoduses from previously collaborative parishes where the new pastor wants things done his way, and where lay involvement is not welcome. Nonetheless, the years following Vatican II were years of unbridled hope for many in the Catholic Church.

In many ways, the test of the theory would come in 1987 at the Episcopal Synod convened at the Vatican to debate The Vocation and the Mission of Lay People in the Church and in the World Twenty Years after Vatican II. Insofar as the theme of the Synod relates specifically to Vatican II, one might reasonably compare its closing document with *Apostolicam actuositatem*. It is noteworthy, in this respect, that nowhere in the Message to the People of God with which the Synod closed[96] will the reader find a reference to the royal priesthood; in addition, whereas Vatican II had specifically expanded the domain of the laity to include both the spiritual and secular, the Message is specific in relating the work of the laity to "all the spheres of life which we call 'the world.'" Though the laity are charged to permeate the workaday world with the spirit of Christ, they are also "called to announce the good news and to participate in dialogue with it." But there are other members of the faithful who have been selected to receive the sacrament of orders "which confers on them a special dignity."[97] In light of the wording of the Synod's concluding Message, the Pope's final homily to the Synod delegates is instructive for the references it does make and the way in which it makes them.[98] John Paul specifically refers to the priestly, kingly, and prophetic dignity that derives from Christ, but those characteristics are related to the Church, not to the laity; moreover, the Pope mentions the special covenant that unites the "church-communion," a communion exercised "with all the baptized," but nowhere in the midst of these hints to Exodus and the first epistle of Peter is there any indication that the laity enjoy a type of priesthood.[99] As for the mission of the laity, it resides in the "secular dimension," which is "common to all the baptized."[100] How different are the implications from the intervention by Donat Chiasson of Moncton, New Brunswick, who became the *enfant terrible* (and the darling of the press) at the 1987 Synod on the laity by insisting that the Synod had been hijacked by the hierarchy? Articulating the position of the Canadian delegation, Chiasson, like John Paul II, also talked about the "communio" that derives from one's baptism; but, unlike John Paul II, Chiasson hastened to add that the differing types of service "do not set up higher or lower classes among the people of God."

Alice Gallin's assessment of the collaborative lay-clerical arrangements at the board level in the Catholic colleges and universities in the United States provides several case studies that show what is possible when collaboration is taken seriously.[101] Gallin's theoretical starting point posits the inclusion of laypeople in governing and administrative roles within the postsecondary system as a response to the inclusivity envisioned by Vatican II, and this may well have been the case, but most of us who have been involved in these transitions would argue that they were also driven by a good bit of pragmatism. You cannot staff positions with people you do not have, nor can you create properly qualified candidates for administrative positions from a pool of people who lack either the talent or the inclination to manage effectively. Be that as it may, most of us who have been close to the scene in Canada, the United States, England, or Australia would maintain that many of our postsecondary Catholic institutions are more self-consciously and more proactively Catholic under lay direction than they were under purely religious administrations whose very presence afforded a reflex assumption of a guaranteed Catholicity.

Steve Privett, Jesuit president of the University of San Francisco, expresses a sentiment often felt by laypeople and one that indicates that he and his colleagues in religion, at least, are strides ahead of the authors of Vatican documents when it comes to "reading the signs of the times" and

working co-operatively with laypeople in the spirit of genuine co-operation that Donat Chiasson articulated so well in the Synod hall:

> The future of Catholic universities clearly does not rest with the Jesuits.
> There aren't any. There are something like thirty people in doctoral
> studies right now. That's a six-year period and there are twenty-eight
> Jesuit universities in the U.S. So I think that the future of Catholic
> universities is going to lie in our ability to enlist and engage colleagues
> in a way that they get as enthusiastic about what we're doing as we are
> and that the vision or the ideals and the values are communicable,
> they're transferable. And we ought to stop focusing on this Jesuit
> control model and start—we have started—trying to say "Okay, what
> this requires is that we figure out how one works collaboratively." And I
> think that we have to acknowledge very frankly that this didn't start out
> of conviction. It started out of necessity. We ran out of Jesuits. We are
> forced to co-operate with laypeople. And I think that now in hindsight
> we say, "Well, you know, this isn't a bad thing." I think we went into it
> saying "This is a bad thing. We've got to keep deans and vice-presi-
> dents, et cetera." We kind of defined key positions. I think most of us
> are probably over that and are saying, "Okay, we kind of got forced into
> it, but that doesn't make it not a good thing and it's about time we wake
> up and realize that."

By comparison, the tone of the Vatican's *The Religious Dimension of
Education in the Catholic School*, for example, surely does not reflect the
sense of equality in the pursuit of mission suggested by Chiasson or the
vision of an embraced collaboration discussed by Privett. In the Vatican
document, the concept of "Church" is clearly to be equated with the
ministerial hierarchy and there is both a sense of condescension and
suspicion in the Church's willingness and its reservation: "The church,
therefore, is willing to give lay people charge of the schools that it has
established, and the laity themselves establish schools. The recognition
of the school as a Catholic school is, however, always reserved to the
competent ecclesiastical authority."[102] Statements such as this ought to
bring a blush to the cheeks of those who wrote *Apostolicam actuositatem*.
Subsequent Vatican documents, however, have heightened the suspi-

cion that there is within the Holy See an anxiety about a potential loss of status and power among the clerical elite if one were to take too seriously the concept of collaboration with the laity. The November 13, 1997 Vatican Instruction with respect to collaboration between the ordained priest and the non-ordained laity, for example, was considered so important that John Paul II asked that it be drafted with the assistance of eight of his dicasteries.[103]

In the explanatory note that accompanies the Instruction on Collaboration with the Laity, the Vatican points out that the purpose of the statement is both to provide encouragement for those priests already engaged in active ministry as well as to promote vocations to the priesthood; the document is also intended to assist the laity to "understand how our fundamental equality is compatible with an essential difference." It seems that too many irregularities have crept into the practice of collaboration, practices that have had "very serious negative consequences" and that have left "the correct understanding of true ecclesial communion to be damaged."[104] Those familiar with the Vatican's anthropological definitions of maleness and femaleness will immediately detect an argument structured on complementarity, where complementarity has historically and effectively relegated women to a position of inferiority. It is instructive, therefore, to note that the authors make a point out of the need to be sensitive to vocabulary. Their intent here is to preserve from a creeping semantic corruption words such as "minister," "ministry," "pastor," "chaplain," "coordinator," "moderator" so that the role of the ordained minister is not confused with that of the non-ordained layperson—it is a confusion that the authors of the Instruction caution might well result from a misunderstanding of the "common priesthood of the faithful." (Peter Hebblethwaite had made the perceptive observation that during the Pope's visit to the United States immediately in advance of the Synod on the laity, John Paul's praise of lay involvement always referred to "mission" and never to "ministry."[105]) There is, the document explains, "a complementarity of functions which are vital for ecclesial communion."[106] It is, of course, an appropriate point. It is the dogged insistence on where the power lies, which begs the question about real co-operation. In light of the Vatican's expressed concern about the meaning of words, therefore, it is surely appropriate to wonder about the import of the wording in phrases such as "undue aspiration" in the statement "Only with constant reference to the source, the 'ministry of Christ' . . . may the term *ministry* be applied to a certain extent and without ambiguity to the lay faithful: that is, without it being perceived and lived as an undue aspiration to the ordained ministry or as a progressive erosion of its specific nature."[107]

In a similar vein, the explanation that accompanies the Instruction notes that this statement is only one small step in spelling out the differences of the roles to be filled by the ordained and the non-ordained, to which the authors add that it is their hope that this document will help the laity become "fully aware of what is specific to them and prepare them for the task that is truly theirs in the world and in the church, rather than encourage them to view as a promotion the fact that they fulfill other tasks that they exercise as substitutes." An echo of the Instruction's warning that a non-ordained person's preaching in a church or oratory "can be permitted only as a supply for sacred ministers" and that this preaching cannot "be regarded as an ordinary occurrence nor as an authentic promotion of the laity."[108] Twice the Vatican statement points out that this exercise in role definition has nothing to do with power. One wonders, therefore, what would explain the anxiety about the layperson's seeking "promotion" or harbouring of "undue aspiration." One thinks of Donat Chiasson's concern about setting up first- and second-class citizens among the people of God, or Dr. Cynthia Wedel's caution that those exercising authority need to recognize that they must share responsibility meaningfully if they are, in fact, interested in collaborative ministry. Two things are abundantly clear throughout the Instruction: first, there is here no vision of a non-hierarchical people of God; second, the document looks forward to a time when there will be a springtime of vocations and these emergency measures for lay involvement will no longer be necessary.

It would be tedious to catalogue the number of instances in which the Instruction goes out of its way to specify that lay involvement on a collaborative basis is temporary, that it must be stressed as being temporary lest there be some confusion on the layperson's part, and that the intent is to increase vocations and, therefore, return these functions to the properly ordained where they ought to reside. A sampling: ". . . the nonordained faithful do not enjoy a right to such tasks and functions. Rather, they are 'capable of being admitted by the sacred pastors . . . to those functions which, in accordance with the provisions of the law, they can discharge' or where 'ministers are not available . . . they can supply certain of their functions . . . in accordance with the provisions of law'"; "The nonordained faithful may be generically designated extraordinary ministers when deputed by a competent ecclesiastical authority to discharge, by way of supply . . ."; "if in certain circumstances it is necessary . . . , if in certain circumstances it would be useful"; "In some areas, circumstances can arise in which a shortage of sacred ministers and permanent, objectively verifiable situations . . ."; "Provisions regulating such extraordinary form of collaboration . . ."; "*Ob sacerdotum penuriam* [because of the scarcity of priests] and not for reasons of convenience or ambiguous 'advancement of the laity'"; "They are to be considered invalid, and hence null and void, any deliberations entered into (or decisions taken) by a parochial council which has not been presided over by the parish priest or which has assembled contrary to his wish"; "It must be clearly understood that such celebrations are temporary solutions . . ."; "in cases of true necessity . . ."; "So as not to create confusion, certain practices are to be avoided and eliminated where such have emerged. . . . The habitual use of extraordinary ministers of holy communion at Mass. . . ." In its conclusion the Instruction makes it clear that this is by no means an effort "to defend clerical privileges" but derives from the necessity of being "obedient to the will of Christ and to respect the constitutive form which he indelibly impressed on his church." In other words, as with the ordination of women, there is here a divinely ordained order of things that the Church could not change even if it wanted to. Except, of course, that Vatican justification for much of what the document spells out is the Church's own Code of Canon Law.

Both in the conclusion to the Instruction and in the Explanation that accompanies it, the authors go out of their way to make it clear that this is a temporary situation. They even suggest that in some areas of the world there is a "flowering of vocations"; the implication is that one day all will be well and these necessary expedients that involve collaboration with the laity will no longer be required. And steps are being taken to right the situation. The diocese of Hamilton, Canada, for example, has announced that it has decided to spend between $10,000 and $15,000 in an advertising campaign to solve its *sacerdotum penuria*.[109] According to information from the chancery office in Hamilton (which is the second largest diocese in Canada), the diocese has 143 priests, three of whom are scheduled to retire within the next ten years, yet the diocese had no ordinations in 2000, one in 1999, and none in 1998. Moreover, whereas in 1990 the diocese had thirty students in seminary formation, in 1999 there were only two; not considering early deaths or simple defections, the scene is certainly bleak, especially when one considers that nationwide there were 117 ordinations in 1969 and only fifty-seven in 1997, a period during which the Catholic population increased by several million.

Nor is the Canadian reality out of line with trends in the industrialized world. The 1,247 ordinations celebrated in the United States between 1995 and 1999 were offset by 2,654 deaths or resignations, so that the current size of the seminary classes in the United States would have to double to maintain the numerical balance.[110] In Australia, some 2,100 priests serve nearly 5 million Catholics—and the average age of Australia's priest exceeds sixty. And the seminary population of Ireland has decreased from 750 in 1970 to only ninety-one in 1999. Because of its concerns about the crisis in vocations, the Archdiocese of Dublin recently introduced a billboard campaign in an effort to attract new recruits. Is it any wonder that Belgium's Cardinal Godfried Danneels has issued warnings about the future extinction of the Church on the continent without the ability to administer the sacraments?[111] Surely the Vatican would do well to consider what real collaboration might look like in the years ahead; it might, indeed, begin to think of new forms of being Church. Certainly, it ought not to be talking down to the laity who are, after all, both the source of its mission and no doubt the resource for its future.

Yet, the Vatican continues to issue directives whose apparent purpose in part at least is to keep the laity clearly in their place—to keep the laity from intruding into the sacred space reserved for the ordained minister. The *New General Instruction of the Roman Missal* (*Institutio Generalis Missalis Romani*) is the latest of these directives.[112] Included within the new Instruction is the regulation that the priest may exchange the kiss of peace only with those in the sanctuary; by definition, therefore, the exchange is restricted to members of the clergy.

Included in the Instruction is a series of guidelines restricting the role of the extraordinary minister of the Eucharist by specifying that such a person may not be called forward if there is a capable priest in the congregation (this is an affirmation of an existing restriction); enter the sanctuary until after the priest has received communion (the word "priest" is preferred to "celebrant" throughout the Instruction as if to add a semantic dignity to the calling); break bread or pour wine into the chalice; consume any unused Eucharistic wine; purify the vessels after Mass. There would seem to be here an effort to enhance the role of the priest as if in doing so one could increase the numbers of potential vocations.

It is the same logic inherent in the Vatican instruction on collaboration with the laity where the authors suggested that the confusion of roles could actually "encourage a reduction in vocations to the (ministerial) priesthood and obscure the purpose of seminaries as places of formation for the ordained ministry."[113] As John Wijngaards observes, the document's overt stress on the sacred and the sacred place is at variance with early Christian tradition and will have a potentially deleterious effect on recent positive developments like the House Mass or Masses celebrated in the classroom, thatched huts, and the like where he has resided as celebrant.[114] Preserving and even enhancing the ordained priesthood may well be a noble objective, but one has to ask whether in its efforts to do so the Vatican has in fact put its best foot forward.

WOMEN IN THE CHURCH

Clearly, neither the 1990 Episcopal Synod nor developments that have followed that Synod have extended the promise of Vatican II. On the contrary, the penchant for centralization that has marked John Paul's pontificate, coupled with a dramatic decline in vocations to the priesthood, has set a course where traditional hierarchies have not only been honoured, they have been strengthened. Those laity who have forgotten their place within the hierarchy have been reminded. Reminded too that they are needed—needed until the blossoming of the "springtime of vocations" for which the Vatican waits so expectantly.

Yet the 1987 Synod on the Vocation and Mission of Lay People in the Church and in the World Twenty Years after Vatican II was eagerly anticipated by bishop, priest, and laity alike. Lay auditor to the Synod, Janet Somerville, left for Rome full of hope and with a forty-seven-page summary of "The Great Lay Write-In of 1987" tucked carefully in her suitcase; her counterpart, Annine Parent-Fortin, carried a similar brief from the French Sector of the Canadian Conference. The theme that ran through the Canadian preparations: On Taking Consultation Seriously.

The appointment of these two distinguished women implied a widespread recognition of the important role that women can and do play in the Church. Certainly the question of women's role in the hierarchy and the administration of the Church was often on the Synod floor. Gabriel Bullet, the auxiliary archbishop of Lausanne, Switzerland, for example, insisted that the canonical barrier to women's assuming the formal function of lector and acolyte was a source of real discrimination in the Church; Gerhard Schwenzer, bishop of Oslo, argued that the insufficient entry of women into the ecclesial environment constituted a fundamental failure on the part of the Church, and he recommended their inclusion in pastoral ministry and the diaconate; Libardo Ramirez Gomez, bishop of Garzóan, Columbia, on the other hand, urged the Synod to show an appreciation for woman's femininity, arguing in traditional tones that she should not be masculinized, but should see in the example of Mary the simple laywoman who did what her son asked of her; Rembert Weakland, archbishop of Milwaukee, took less radical and politically safer but still important ground by speaking in favour of the opening of all roles to women that do not require ordination. Other delegates, of course, supported one or another of these positions, with a surprising number favouring ordination to the diaconate as a legitimate recognition of the contribution that women make to the life of the Church.

No doubt the most radical territory staked out by any of the delegates was claimed by U.S. Jesuit priest, Joseph Fessio, who was one of the twenty theologians invited by John Paul II to participate in the Synod. Fessio's position was clear and uncompromising. He insisted that since altar boys are symbols of the ordained priest, allowing girls the privilege of dressing in priestly garments would cause an identity crisis both for the girls and for the faithful. In addition, Fessio suggested, there is a logical connection between altar boy, acolyte, lector, priest that is of such a nature that to admit women to lower positions would inevitably give them false hopes and even higher aspirations; moreover, insofar as altar boys are a major source of vocations to the priesthood, to admit women to their ranks would be detrimental to the pursuit of vocations since boys would then not want to become priests. The ultimate goal of the feminists, Fessio warned, is to eliminate all sex distinction and to create a gender-neutral society. Fessio's conclusion: "Getting approval of altar girls and women acolytes and lectors is only one aspect of the larger strategy. For now, they [the feminists] will settle for altar girls. Giving in on that point will be seen by the feminists, and rightly, a sign of weakness on the part of the pope and the Catholic Church. It will be seen as appeasement that will only increase their demands." To capitulate, Fessio argues, would create tremendous pressure on the Pope and widespread expectations for change; the media would create a situation similar to the one with which Pope Paul VI had to contend in advance of his issuing *Humanae vitae*.[115]

In light of this raft of opinion, it is instructive to note that the closing statement from the Synod, the Message to the People of God, devoted a section to "Women in the Church and in the World." In its message, the Synod affirms the equal dignity of man and woman (speaking in tones that suggest such had always been the case), noted that God's plan has been obscured by sin, and urged Mary as the perfect symbol of womanhood. It is perhaps instructive to note that during one of the press conferences conducted for the assembled media, we were assured that the women's issue is a North American preoccupation with which the rest of the Church is not particularly concerned. How peculiar, in light of all this, that the Explanation that accompanies the Vatican Instruction on collaboration of the non-ordained with the ordained priest should make the bold assertion that the document "above all builds on all that the magisterium of the church already had to say in a positive way about the role of the laity, and especially that of women, in the mission of the church and evangelization."

In the *National Catholic Reporter*'s February 5, 1988 lead article, Peter Hebblethwaite insisted that Synod organizers had boiled down propositions so that the end product no longer reflects the thrust of the Synod's thinking. In a similar vein, Archbishop Donat Chiasson of Moncton, New Brunswick, insisted that the Synod had been hijacked and that the Canadian delegation would take "Nothing" back to Canada's 11 million

Catholics except the conviction that "the Church is lived at home."[116] It is a message that both the laity and many of the ordained have learned time and time again, hence the public report issued by the Canadian delegation on November 6, 1997 upon their return home and their frank insistence that "consultation implies accountability." It is a thesis that historically has not found universal acceptance in the Vatican. Is it any wonder that the Canadian delegation concluded wistfully that "the Synod seemed to hear only faintly the cries of a world spinning into the twenty-first century"?

This unwillingness to hear the cries of the modern world is no doubt nowhere more clear than it is in the institutional Church's position with respect to the status of women in the Church. One is reminded of the well-intentioned closing message of Vatican II, its "To Women," in which the Council claims that "the Church is proud to have liberated and glorified women, and in the course of the centuries, in diversity of characters, to have brought into relief her basic equality with man."[117] On some of these difficult matters, the institutional Church seems too often to beguile itself into thinking that saying it is so actually makes it so.

Given the troublesome *sacerdotum penuria* with which the Church has been struggling for the past forty years and more, one might well wonder why, in light of the claim of the Council Fathers, women have not played a more formally significant role in the hierarchy of the Church. One reason, as we have already seen, is that the Church's anthropology has not until very recent years proclaimed in any meaningful way the innate equality of man and woman even though the authors of Vatican policy would obviously like to think otherwise.

We have previously discussed Aquinas's wholesale adaptation of Aristotle's reasoning with respect to the natural inferiority of the female and have reviewed Aquinas's conclusions concerning woman's natural incapacity for leadership; "civil subservience" is natural to woman—God designed it so, "For good order would have been wanting in the human family if some [i.e., women] were not governed by others wiser than themselves."[118] Aquinas relates these ideas explicitly to the question of women's suitability for holy orders. In the Supplement to his *Summa theologica* he explains that the male sex is properly intended for the reception of the sacrament of holy orders since "signification of the thing is required in all sacramental actions. . . . Accordingly, since it is not possible for the female sex to signify eminence of degree, for a woman is in the state of subjection, it follows that she cannot receive the sacrament of Order."[119] (In the article that follows, "Whether Boys and Those Who Lack the Use of Reason Can Receive Orders?", Aquinas explains that some boys and children who have not reached the age of reason may be validly ordained to minor orders, though ordination to higher orders does require the use of reason.) And in another context, Aquinas states that the ability to address the entire church publicly is a prerequisite for ordination to the priesthood, but since woman is subject by nature (as Genesis 3:16 stipulates) she cannot perform this function. Only men can assume this role since they are not subject by nature.[120] The Angelic Doctor adds a second impediment: a woman "teaching and preaching publicly in the church" may well cause men's minds to "be enticed to lust." And thirdly, women are barred from public teaching and preaching since "as a rule women are not perfected in wisdom." If, however, a woman should receive "the grace of wisdom or of knowledge [she] can administer it by teaching privately but not publicly." Aquinas's key argument is based on sexual inequality, a hierarchical tradition that is only recently being reviewed in official Roman Catholic thinking.

Despite apparent unhappiness within the Vatican, senior churchmen do insist on raising the issue. Jean-Guy Hamelin, for example, acting in his capacity as president of the Canadian Conference of Catholic Bishops, spoke both forcefully and eloquently in an October 9 intervention to the 1987 Synod. In his address, entitled "God's Humanity: Male and Female," Hamelin made it clear that the participation of women in the life of the Church had been strongly addressed during his delegation's preparatory consultations. Hamelin challenged the Synod to be more open to expanding women's horizons in the Church, pointing out that there is an apparent discrepancy between the roles that women play in society and in the Church, and that the discrepancy is particularly difficult to explain to young people. The women's movement in Canada, Hamelin insists, appears to be an evolution toward "justice, dignity, and partnership." But, because women are excluded from ordination, they are also excluded from the decision-making life of the Church; the Church, therefore, needs to remove whatever obstacles it can to open positions of responsibility to the laity, to men and women. As for the question of women's ordination, Hamelin adds, "we cannot avoid underlining in this assembly that the reasoning used so far to explain the reservation of sacred orders to men has not seemed convincing, especially not to young people."

Indeed, it has not. On October 11, 1971, George B. Flahiff, the cardinal-archbishop of Winnipeg, rose to address the Synod of Bishops, arguing that historical theses will not sustain the arguments for the exclusion of women from ordained ministry in the Church, that sociological arguments would support the ordination of women, and that, to the best of his knowledge, there was no compelling doctrinal reason for their exclusion. On October 14, 1980, Robert Lebel, the bishop of Valleyfield, Quebec, rose to address the Synod of Bishops, challenging the assembly to support the process of liberation, to take a prophetic stand, to envision the role of women beyond their place in the family, and to open the Church to the talents of women by making meaningful roles of responsibility available to them. And on October 3, 1983, Louis-Albert Vachon, archbishop of Quebec and primate of Canada, rose to address the Synod of Bishops, challenging them to "recognize the ravages of sexism, and our own male appropriation of Church institutions and numerous aspects of the Christian life. . . . In our society and in our Church, man has come to think of himself as the sole possessor of rationality, authority, and active initiative, relegating women to the private sector and dependent tasks. Our recognition, as Church, of our own cultural deformation will allow us to overcome the archaic concepts of womanhood which have been inculcated in us for centuries." Brave words, these, but falling mostly on deaf or defiant ears. Yet, much of it has been studied, repeated, and amplified by the 30-million strong World Union of Catholic Women's Organizations in their impressive background paper prepared as a resource for the 1987 Episcopal Synod.[121] In its broadly based and balanced presentation, WUCWO articulates a well-reasoned case for justifiable frustration. The question of women's role in the Church is a vexed one. Even conservative Catholic women like Mary Kenny see the barring of women from ordination as a form of cultural genocide rooted in ancient anxieties once apparent in such aberrant notions as suspicion of witchcraft.[122]

What are the arguments that the Church marshals to keep women in the pews and away from the altar? G. Emmett Carter's *Do This in Memory of Me* outlines the case philosophically by referring to monads and to the traditional symbolism of Christ as the bridegroom of his Church. For its part, the Sacred Congregation for the Doctrine of the Faith reviewed its objections in *Inter insigniores*, its 1977 *Declaration on the Question of the Admission of Women to the Ministerial Priesthood*. The Congregation's Declaration attempts to bring closure to the issue by explaining that as a matter of "fidelity to the example of the Lord, [the Church] does not consider herself authorized to admit women to priestly ordination."[123] In addition, *Inter insigniores* recalls that even though he was accompanied by women and appreciative of them, Jesus called only men to be his apostles; for their part, the apostles both recognized and respected Christ's intentions in this matter and did not replace Judas with a woman. The Congregation concludes that neither sociological nor biblical arguments will sustain a change in the Church's constant tradition, nor will references to the temporal world since the Church as society is wholly different from social structures in the world at large.

As much as the institutional Church had hoped that *Inter insigniores* would put an end to the discussions, it has found that the women's issue simply will not go away. John Paul's frustration with the topic became patently clear when, during a papal visit to the United States in July 1979, he chose to chide Sister M. Theresa Kane, president of the Leadership Conference of Women Religious, for publicly promoting the cause of women's ordination. Addressing the Pope at the National Shrine of the Immaculate Conception in Washington, D.C., before some 5,000 nuns, Kane asked the Pope to implement the Church's message of "dignity and reverence for all persons" by making provision for women's inclusion "in all ministries of our Church." John Paul's tactic of impatient public reprimand was every bit as effective in Washington as was his later rebuke of Ernesto Cardenal on the tarmac in Managua, Nicaragua. At the same time, John Paul has tried on a number of occasions to appear to be the defender of women's rights, just not the right to ordination. His *Mulieris dignitatem*, for example, was intended as a closing statement on the human dignity of women, a dignity that is characteristically entwined with the ideal of evangelical virginity as the perfect incarnation of Jesus Christ,[124] an ideal superior to the marriage state,[125] with the Church as the bride of Christ, and with Mary and her "fiat" as the exemplar for womanhood. Although the Pope revisits the traditional Christian anthropological definitions of male and female as they are defined in Genesis and tries to put a modern face on them, the inevitable final determination is that in the Eucharistic sacrifice, the priest is acting *in persona Christi* and Christ was a man. It is a conclusion, John Paul points out, that reiterates the findings of the declaration *Inter insigniores* previously published by Paul VI.[126]

The Vatican's determination that it "does not consider herself authorized to admit women to priestly ordination" as a matter of "fidelity to the example of the Lord" places serious obstacles to meaningful discussions before the Anglican/Roman Catholic International Commission. As a result, Pope John Paul II initiated an exchange of correspondence with Archbishop Robert Runcie of Canterbury in which the Pope regretted that from the Roman Catholic perspective, decisions taken by the Anglican community with respect to women's ordination had created "an increasingly serious obstacle" to mutual efforts at reconciliation.[127] In his response, which was directed to Cardinal Johannes Willebrands, president of the Vatican Secretariat for Promoting Christian Unity, Runcie assured the Vatican that those members of the Anglican communion who had decided to ordain women had conducted their own serious study and had concluded that one could not demonstrate from "divine law" that women were meant to be excluded from priestly ordination; on the contrary, he reasoned, since the Eucharist is by nature representative, "the priestly character lies precisely in the fact that the priest is commissioned by the church in ordination to represent the priestly nature of the whole body and also—especially in the presidency of the eucharist—to stand in a special sacramental relationship with Christ as high priest in whom complete humanity is redeemed."[128] For his part, Willebrands counters by summarizing *Inter insigniores*, and concludes with the prayerful hope that the Anglican/Roman Catholic dialogue will continue and will ultimately find a resolution that will contribute to the unity of Christ's Church.

Impatient with the continuing debate, John Paul was determined to bring closure to the discussion. On May 30, 1994, therefore, he raised the stakes by releasing the final word on the topic, *Ordinatio sacerdotalis*.

Ordinatio sacerdotalis begins by reiterating the basic conclusions at which *Inter insigniores* had arrived, noting that the Vatican's decision is consistent with the time-honoured tradition of the Church and in accord with "God's plan for the church."[129] This finding, the Pope insisted, must be seen as official Church teaching and must be held "definitively." John Paul II insists: "Wherefore, in order that all doubt may be removed regarding a matter of great importance, a matter which pertains to the church's divine constitution itself, in virtue of my ministry of confirming the brethren . . . I declare that the church has no authority whatsoever to confer priestly ordination on women and that this judgment is definitively to be held by all the church's faithful." Peter Hebblethwaite once observed of John Paul II that "Not since Pius X have we had such a *personal* pope—in the sense that the pope allows his own opinions to determine what is presented as the 'official line.' It cannot be called church 'doctrine.'"[130]

In the storm of protest that followed, hundreds of individuals signed an open letter of protest directed at the Pope as well as at the Conference of Catholic Bishops in the United States and which was published in the *National Catholic Reporter* on November 4, 1994. In the wake of that letter, Sister M. Carmel McEnroy, R.S.M., a tenured professor of systematic theology at St. Meinrad School of Theology in St. Meinrad, Indiana, was dismissed from her position for adding her name to the long list of signatories—an action that prompted an official denunciation in an additional open letter that appeared in the *National Catholic Reporter* on May 26, 1995 and which had appended to it hundreds of names, many of them of prominent academics in the United States and Canada. In England, Lavinia Byrne, prolific author, lecturer at the Cambridge Theological Federation, BBC religious personality, and sister of the Institute of the Blessed Virgin Mary, resigned from her congregation in response to pressure it was receiving from the Congregation for the Doctrine of the Faith pursuant to the publication of *Women at the Altar* in 1993—the Vatican was looking for her public acknowledgement of personal support for *Humanae vitae* and *Ordinatio sacerdotalis*.[131] She was, she said, tired of working with "one hand tied behind my back." Well after the initial shock waves over the promulgation of *Ordinatio sacerdotalis* and its aftermath had subsided, theologians, historians, and canon lawyers were still trying to determine the legal status of the Apostolic Letter. Since it had not been issued *ex cathedra*, it had not been presented as infallible. What, then, does the word "definitively" mean?[132]

Characteristically, Joseph Ratzinger upped the ante by declaring on Vatican Radio that anyone who does not accept the teaching as it is presented "obviously separates himself from the faith of the church"—a statement in which "himself" is obviously meant to be understood inclusively. (As a matter of clarification, however, Ratzinger noted that such individuals were not to be considered excommunicated.) Individual bishops in the United States quickly lined up to explain the document and their acceptance of it; in Canada where the bishops have traditionally taken a lead role in championing the cause of women's rights within the Church, the president of the Canadian Conference of Catholic Bishops issued a terse statement, which began "The Catholic bishops of Canada accept the teaching of the Pope and make it their own," and continued: "The Catholic bishops of Canada have always, and especially in these latter years, been staunch promoters of the rightful place of women in the Church. They will continue to do so, both at home in their local communities and in the universal Church, following the lead of this Apostolic letter. The bishops do not wish to see this present declaration, which reaffirms the position always held in the Church, become an obstacle to intensified efforts both on their part and on the part of all Catholics, to involve women more and more in the structures of the whole life of the communities of the faithful." This, of course, will be no small feat. Susan Ross provides one insight into the problem as well as a compelling case for a Eucharist at which the presider celebrates the giftedness of the entire community. She notes that with the changes following Vatican II, with the enhanced emphasis on the Eucharist, women often experience real pain at the male-centred celebration: women's religious communities, for example, where one imports a male into an all-female context.[133] How is it possible for any Church to provide for inclusivity within a context structured on exclusivity?

So contentious is the topic of women's participation in the life of the Church that after initiating a consultative process to study the topic, the bishops of the United States published a preliminary document in April 1988, invited further dialogue, and ultimately shelved the project unfinished.[134] The Canadian bishops, on the other hand, established a commission that reported to their plenary assembly in 1984 and, after a good bit of clandestine in-fighting, issued a Women's Green Kit in an effort at conscientization and reformation.[135] The kit was intended for use in study sessions at the parish level, but depended on the initiative of the local bishop if it was to become a vital component of the diocesan educational outreach. Very few accepted the challenge: by June 1985, 4,649 copies of the kit had been distributed in English and 2,587 in French to serve a Catholic population hovering around 11 million. So, the kit died a quiet death, but not before its potential for influencing change was quickly recognized and countered with the appearance of an anti-kit, dubbed the Blue Kit, prepared and disseminated by Women for Life, Faith, and Family and intended "to evangelize Catholic women concerning their divinely ordained roles as members of the Church." More recently, the Australian bishops have established a broadly based Commission for Australian Catholic Women to assist in the ongoing dialogue with respect to women's participation in the Australian Catholic Church. Although the bishops are clear that they are not in any way acting in opposition to official Vatican teaching with respect to women's ordination, they are looking for the means whereby women's participation can be meaningfully enhanced.[136]

THE ROLE OF THE LAITY: THE CHALLENGE FOR CHANGE

Despite official Vatican statements about the need for seminarians to be trained to work collaboratively with the laity, it is difficult to be overly optimistic about change or the potential for real collaboration when all the practical signals from the Vatican suggest retrenchment or when one is bombarded by assurances that seminaries are being populated by students whose attitudes are decidedly triumphalistic.[137] Vicky Cosstick, who is a former director of pastoral theology at Allen Hall in London (where several Neo-Catechumenate seminarians are in training), laments that too many newly ordained priests cherish a concept of a Church "that no longer exists and will never return" and who do not feel at all comfortable working collaboratively with the laity. Cosstick warns that when the Church separates seminarians from those whom they are to serve and when it espouses its current emphasis on priesthood as being "essentially different," then the Church will be forming priests who are trained to relate essentially to priests, to become part of a separate male clique. In these circumstances, Cosstick concludes, "It is little wonder if this club now attracts some unsuitable people."[138] In a context such as this, there is little prospect for empowering the laity even as a practical short-term tactic for resolving the problem of a declining number of vocations to the ordained priesthood.[139]

John Paul's call for communion in the Apostolic Letter *Novo millennio inuente* with which he marked the new millennium strikes the right chords, and its encouragement for dialogue between pastors and laypeople sounds promising, but until there is a change of heart reflected in practice, until clericalism actually makes room in a meaningful way for everyone to pitch in, fine words are hardly likely to translate into concrete action. In the meantime, national conferences plan for priestless services.[140]

In light of the squandered potential for others to pitch in, the 1989 Priestly Life and Ministry Committee's study of the morale of priests in the United States makes for sober reading indeed.[141] The Committee report is particularly hard-hitting and practical in tone and direction, worrying at the outset that, in general, priests in the United States were suffering from a "serious and substantial morale problem." It is a problem with a variety of causes: professional expectations that range from being "all things to all people" to the conviction that "I don't do windows"; expectations whose gravity is exacerbated by the paucity of priests; loneliness; sexual issues that range from a sense that the terms of the celibacy argument are simply not convincing, to matters relating to feminism or to homosexuality; tension over competing views of the Church, both among one's fellow priests and among the Catholic population at large; and the perception that not only does the priest have no control over his life but that he receives little affirmation for the long hours of selfless service. For a number of demoralized priests caught in this relentless tailspin, it is particularly distressing that perceived solutions to the shortage of ordained ministers—the ordination of married men, expanded opportunities for women in the Church, the employment of laicized priests—are simply not open to discussion.

Indeed, when the Pope declares "definitively" with respect to the question of women's ordination, he is closing one avenue for increased co-operation, and by insisting that there is no longer anything to talk about with respect to this subject, he also alienates countless others who have valued the Church as an institution where faith and reason are in dialogue one with the other and who are eager to do their part. But if, by fiat, dialogue is defined as dissent, then one has to wonder what kind of Church defines the human being as *animal rationale* and refuses its members the right to reason, or what kind of Church defines language as a property of the human person and denies its members the right to speak. Or defines human dignity as the capacity to follow one's conscience where properly informed reason leads but denies its members the right to make reasoned choices. In such a situation, demoralization or (perhaps more likely) defection, lack of interest, or disregard may well become widespread indeed.

The Vatican continues to extend its net. Noting the integral historical progression, which it insists extends from sub-deacon, to deacon, to priesthood, the Vatican has decreed that the diaconate is also an ordained ministry from which women are excluded. Given the clear direction in which John Paul's pontificate has been moving, this most recent determination can hardly be viewed as surprising. It was time to shut down the discussion. After Vatican II called for the reintroduction of the permanent diaconate, many bishops turned to the role of deacon as a means of dealing with the vocation crisis; at the same time, there have been repeated suggestions that ordaining women to the diaconate would provide a means of welcoming them into the administrative power structure within the institutional Church, suggestions that were often advanced at the 1987 Episcopal Synod on the laity. So, when in March 1998 the Vatican issued its Norms for the Formation of Permanent Deacons as well as a Directory for the Ministry and Life of Permanent Deacons, it also renewed speculation and debate with respect to the historical role of women in the Church. John Wijngaards and others have argued on the basis of historical documentation that indeed, from the fourth to the eighth century, women were ordained to the diaconate alongside men; the Vatican maintains that there were, indeed, deaconesses in the early Church, but they were not sacramental deacons. Bottom line: another potential avenue for the empowerment of women runs down a dead end road.[142]

Where does this leave the layperson who wishes to play an active role within the Catholic Church? John Paul II has frequently offered his personal and outspoken support for the various movements active within the Church, movements that are often viewed with suspicion by both the laity and the clergy alike. Nonetheless, the Pope's enthusiasm for these groups was manifest in his 1982 decision to raise Opus Dei to the rank of Personal Prelature, making of it a quasi-diocese that functions administratively outside the purview of the bishop in whose diocese its members have geographical residence. Similarly, on May 17, 1992, John Paul fast-tracked the process for the canonization of the Spanish-born founder of Opus Dei, Josémaría Escrivá, formally declaring him Blessed. It was no doubt the Pope's personal appreciation for the movements and their potential for both energizing and sanctifying the laity that accounts for the numerous supportive mentions they received during the 1987 Episcopal Synod on the laity. Still, there are those who have their doubts since their members within these organizations are often perceived as being theologically right wing, cliquish, intolerant, secretive, psychologically intimidating, and cult-like in their recruitment tactics and in their religious observance. Bishop Mervyn Alexander of the diocese of Clifton, England, for example, has concluded that the Neo-Catechumenate communities in his diocese are divisive and, as a result, he has attempted to integrate them into his parish structures.[143] In his *The Pope's Armada*, Gordon Urquart draws upon his own past experience as a leader in the Focolare movement to describe what he sees as the dangerous potential of Focolare, Communion and Liberation, and the Neo-Catechumenate; and Michael Walsh, who is an ex-Jesuit and the librarian at Heythrop College in London, England, has published several pieces that detail his concerns about Opus Dei. If Walsh's opinion of Opus Dei is more cautionary than laudatory, there are others who are quite positive about the movement; influential Italian journalist Vittorio Messori is one of these.[144]

Even though the traditionalist movements within the Church count their membership in the tens of millions, theirs is not the route most lay Catholics with an active interest in Catholicism will want to pursue. Conversely, there are more than twenty lay-organized activist groups in the United States, Canada, Australia, Britain, and Europe—groups like Catholics of Vision—which are uniting in an effort to realize the promise of Vatican II. Theirs is a platform of renewal: compassion for the poor and marginalized, ecumenical and interfaith co-operation, the development of an all-embracing atmosphere of freedom, lay consultation on appropriate issues, access to decision-making fora (including women's access to the ordained ministries), direct input in the selection of bishops. Although groups such as these can claim international support in the millions, like their traditionalist counterpoints they are not likely to serve as the vehicle for effective grassroots lay participation in the life of the Church. Grassroots Catholics have always had an enviable reputation as effective organizers: the Catholic Women's League, Knights of Columbus, Knights of the Southern Cross, Knights of Columba, Knights of the Holy Sepulcher, Knights of Malta, Teutonic Order, Catholic Action, and a host of others have taken to heart the challenge of the corporal and spiritual works of mercy. Organizations such as these, like service organizations throughout the industrialized world, sometimes struggle to maintain their membership, but they do remain popular and they do represent one more form of lay participation in the secular and the ecclesial societies.

Grant Ertel, a supreme director of the Knights of Columbus, points out that since their founding in 1881 by Father Michael McGivney at St. Mary's Church in New Haven, Connecticut, the Knights of Columbus, who are not formally a religious order of knights but use the title basically for its élan, have expanded to become the largest fraternal order within the Catholic Church. More than 1.6 million strong, the Knights admit only practising Catholics to their membership and support a long list of charitable causes with the proceeds from the more than $20 million they have raised and invested through their various activities. They are constitutionally dedicated to the service of the Holy Father, his bishops, and his priests and, as a result, provide the Pope with some $2 million annually, in addition to having constructed a modern hotel, which was recently opened in the Vatican to accommodate visiting ecclesiastical dignitaries. Ertel takes justifiable pride in the accomplishments of the Knights of Columbus:

> There is an ongoing involvement in education from grade school right through to university level. We have scholarship funds and we are particularly interested in supporting men studying to become priests. Our goal is to provide some sort of support for every seminarian.
>
> Our membership has continued to grow since the Second World War, though some councils have got into a difficult situation where

their members are dying off and they haven't recruited new members. The average age of those coming into the Knights these days is about thirty-six or thirty-seven years old, and the average age of the order is in the mid-forties. But we have gone back to our roots, and gone into our parishes, and our growth is the result of that. We want to be in the parish so we can work and support the parish. We are a lay group supporting the parish priest, but we don't see ourselves taking over any duties of the priest. We have a role of supporting the priest and keeping the parish together when he is not there. We can be a solidifying force.

Gordon Mackay, Q.C., is a member of both the Knights of the Holy Sepulcher and the Knights of Malta. He also sees groups such as these assisting the Church each in its own way at a time when the priesthood is in crisis:

I would think that all of these organizations have a very definitive role to play in the life of the Church. We are not getting the vocations that we would like and we can't leave it all to the clergy. There has to be more participation. As far as the Knights of the Holy Sepulcher are concerned, their charitable endeavours and so forth are not really locally based. What our function is and what we are told from the time we join is that our job is to support Christianity in the Holy Land. If you take the Knights of the Holy Sepulcher and all the lieutenancies throughout the world doing that, that's been a real assistance to the Latin Patriarch in keeping the faith going in the Holy Land. With the Knights of Columbus, whom I know quite well, most of their assistance has been with local charitable activities, which are all deserving. They've done a lot of good things. But the Knights of the Holy Sepulcher and the Knights of Malta are more far-afield. The Order of Malta does maintain a hospital in Jerusalem, but the Canadian association has been looking after the Safe Motherhood project in Nigeria as its principal activity, though it does support other causes as well. A few years ago when there were problems in Czechoslovakia, for example, the order raised funds from its members and asked us to support the need there.

John MacPherson, a professor emeritus from St. Francis Xavier University in Antigonish, Nova Scotia, is a high-ranking professed member of the Knights of Malta, one of eleven Knights worldwide on the council of the Knights of Malta, and a member of the papal household. Since the apostolate of the Knights of Malta centres on health care and relief work, MacPherson's association with the order blends quite naturally with his active interest in gerontology, an interest rooted in the conviction that there is a need for a Catholic and Christian conscience in the care of the elderly, lest society fall prey to the deceptive wiles of the mounting murmurs for euthanasia on demand. The Knights of Malta are a religious order of knights and dames who have virtually pioneered various health care initiatives around the world.

In Canada, for example, just outside Toronto we opened a home and training centre for mentally challenged boys which gave them an opportunity to learn a trade or skill so they could go out into the world and be self-supporting. In Quebec, we ran the first chronic care hospital for children in Canada. Then, of course, it was eventually taken over by the health care system. Before I was a member we had pioneered daycare for preschool children in this country. Shortly after the war we had set up from Quebec City out into the Canadian west a number of daycare centres for working mothers at a time when this was still a novelty in this country. So, we've been on the cutting edge of health care. There would be similar situations in other countries, but since Canada has a health care system we got the programs started and created an awareness and then they were taken over by the state. In the United States we have worked in particular with the frail and elderly, and those with limited means, setting up facilities for them. One of the things that kept us from being suppressed about the same time the Knights Templar were in the fourteenth century is the fact that we had never given up our hospitals. We had them before we were a military order and we kept them all the time that we were a military order and we still have them and as a matter of fact we are the largest single health care provider in the world.

The Knights of Malta has approximately 11,000 members throughout the world, most of them professional people, and even though it has no formal way of attracting others to its midst, it is still growing. Like the many other orders and organizations that constitute the lay Church incarnating Christian values into the lives of everyday people, the Knights of Malta represents one more face of the Church in the modern world. All of these bodies make the invisible visible; they are an expression of the wealth of talent and commitment that is today's Church.

Not everyone wants to be a knight, or a priest, or a lector, or a Eucharistic minister, but some do. And the sum total ought to be a formidable force for good. The Catholic Church is a spiritual communion with over 1 billion members, a Church large enough to make a difference in the world, a Church large enough to bring various perspectives to the question of what it means to be Catholic, and a Church that ought to be large enough to provide opportunities for those with the talent, the time, and the calling.

It would be sad, indeed, to conclude that if we have not learned from history, learned how to share power and shoulder responsibility, that we have not learned the lesson that was reiterated at Vatican II, that the Church is constantly in need of reformation. It would appear that if the Catholic Church is to survive in any meaningful way, there need to be paths of meaningful collaboration and that, it would seem, will require a *reformatio in capite et in membris*, a reformation both at its head and within its members.

5

Spiritual in Essence and Form

In his review of the 1999 retrospective of the French Symbolist Gustave Moreau at New York's Metropolitan Museum of Art, critic Peter Schjeldahl observed that "millennium or no millennium, everybody knows that we are in transition from a former world, which bores us, to a coming one, which numbs us with uncertainty."[1] One clear sign of this uncertainty and its attendant anxiety can be found in the significant rise of interest in spirituality. People are drawn in increasing numbers to explore the many complex and exciting areas of interconnection between spirituality and other areas of human endeavour and meaning. The new frontiers of knowledge so boldly pioneered by scientists and the new technology elites have opened up grand vistas of challenge and concern for the devout, the questing, and the curious.

The Genome Project is exciting, but also threatening. Science and Spirituality may be Blakean Contraries, but they are also Creative Complements. Each needs the other. Fed by the fear of the unknown—new horizons for scientific exploration and experimentation that cut to the heart of human self-definition—postmoderns are poised in large numbers to check out the "interior" world. But they need guides, a discourse, a map that will allow them entrée into a world more foreign than that of the microbe, the megabyte, and the mutual fund.

The thirst for a meaningful or living spirituality is unquenchable and there are not a few purveyors of the "spiritual arts" willing to peddle their dubious wares at a speedy rate and at cut-rate costs. Need is occasionally known to generate desperation and the snake oil salesperson is quick to rise to the entrepreneurial challenge. But spirituality is not a quick fix; it is a life project, and it has been so for centuries. Yet there are those sometimes eccentric and sometimes unnervingly modern pioneers who have chronicled their own spiritual journeys in a way that has made it possible for others to see something of the universal pattern for their own lives.

Take, for instance, Brocard Sewell. This remarkable man, who died at the age of eighty-seven in the spring of 2000, inspired generations of writers, artists, scholars, and spiritual searchers across two continents to seek the integrated life. Sewell was born in Bangkok in 1912, but was quickly spirited off to Wiltshire and Cornwall to be raised, alternately, by both his paternal and maternal grandparents. Educated variously at public schools of the calibre of Cheltenham College and Weymouth College, Sewell found himself drawn from the very beginning to the spiritual and artistic outsiders who became his lifelong company of eccentric pilgrims. For instance, not long after leaving school he sought out the Guild of Saint Joseph and Saint Dominic in the middle of Ditchling Common in the south of England. The Guild was a fellowship of Catholic artisans founded in 1920 by printer Hilary Peppler and sculptor Eric Gill. Sewell was smitten. He quickly became, through his association with the Guild, an apprentice for *G.K. Weekly's*, the official organ of the Distributist League, a body committed to establishing an economic alternative to capitalism and communism called distributism. The proponents of this noble, romantic, and doomed initiative—it lacked a hardnosed pragmatism and a serious power base—included some of the foremost Catholic luminaries of the age: Gilbert Keith Chesterton, Hilaire Belloc, and Vincent McNabb. Sewell found himself in an illustrious circle, and he was still only a teenager.

Anglican by birth and baptism, Sewell spent most of his time with Romanists of cradle and convert vintage. He would be soon numbered among the latter.

My father had told me that he was not prepared to allow me to become a Catholic until I was twenty-one. This restriction was not unreasonable, but I found it irksome. However, in 1930, when I was eighteen, he withdrew it; which was magnanimous. So I was received into the Catholic and Roman church by Dom Gilbert Higgins, at the church of Saint Peter-in-Chains, after a six months' course of instruction, from which I learned little that I did not know already.[2]

Sewell's efforts to find a spiritual home in the Roman Catholic Church resulted in several vocational experiments. He tried his hand with the Order of Preachers, the Dominicans, the Canons Regular at the Priory of Saint Mary and Saint Petroc, the Austin Canons, finally finding an hospitable environment with the Order of Carmelites of the Ancient Observance. Ordained a Carmelite friar on July 18, 1954 at Aylesford Priory, Kent, the first Catholic priest to be ordained there since the Reformation, Sewell was given liberty by his order to pursue his combined passions for art and spirituality. He founded *The Aylesford Review*, promoted young writers and artists of all religious persuasions, including those of none, and began in earnest a writing career that would see many precious memoirs, brief histories, and controversial biographies rolling off several presses, both small and big, well-established and obscure.

Sewell was drawn to those spiritual outsiders who could make life difficult for ecclesiastical authorities. He was fond of the renegades, the marginalized, the peculiar, the temerarious. He had a taste for those who challenged the accepted and the conventional, and yet he was fiercely and uncompromisingly orthodox. His personal gallery of literary subjects included Cecil Chesterton, the combative and polemical brother of the gifted G.K.; Olive Custance, the quietly noble wife of Bosie, Oscar Wilde's lover; Joseph Gard'ner, circus proprietor and founder of a religious order; John Gray and Marc-André Sebastian Raffalovich, poet-priest and literary patron respectively; Henry Williamson and Frances Horovitz, writers; and the notorious Montague Summers, specialist in the occult arts and a cleric of dubious canonical validity. Sewell wrote about them all sympathetically and judiciously.

But he also lectured and wrote about small presses; Philip Thomas Howard, the seventeenth-century Dominican cardinal; Robert Hugh Benson, the best-selling cleric-novelist of the early twentieth-century; and Frederick William Rolfe, novelist of eccentric genius and mildly sinister reputation (also known as Baron Corvo). Sewell was intellectually and theologically captivated by the spiritual questers and their individual stories cried out for the telling. He would be their voice.

But if the religious authorities looked on with relative tolerance as he published his engaging lives of these spiritual exotics, they were less inclined to do so when Sewell wrote a letter to *The Times* in 1969 deploring, in no uncertain terms, the pontifical position on artificial birth regulation as enunciated in the 1968 encyclical, *Humanae vitae*. The gauntlet was thrown down, and at the feet of the most powerful Catholic prelate in Great Britain, John Carmel Heenan, cardinal archbishop of Westminster. The cardinal suspended Sewell; the Carmelites removed him to the Black Mountains in North Wales.

Sewell then found himself whisked off to mainland Nova Scotia to assist in the founding and direction of what was to become *The Antigonish Review*. The drive to recruit Sewell had originated with the priest-professor and short story writer, R.J. MacSween. A formidable critic and wit who chaired the English Department at St. Francis Xavier University in Antigonish for many years, MacSween was on the prowl for an experienced editor, and Sewell was the ideal candidate. And, thanks to Cardinal Heenan, he was available.

In many ways it looked like a winning partnership, but it wasn't. Within a couple of years Sewell departed, MacSween secured his hold on the journal's direction, and the university lost a singular and nurturing professor.

But Sewell retained his contacts with Canada, teaching at a Carmelite junior seminary in Niagara Falls, lecturing at York University and Massey College, University of Toronto, and exploring the spiritual underground at every opportunity. He was the quintessential Victorian person. He loved to browse and ferret; he was suspicious of the specialist; he read widely and deeply; and he courted danger by advancing unpopular and controversial opinions in literary matters, political issues, and concerns of the soul. He also attended to the quiet suffering of neglected artists, supported sexual minorities, and commended spiritual pioneers when others were dismissive or indifferent.

And yet he managed to mix his heterodox side—articulated in his spiritual and literary passions—with his orthodox side—as found in his institutional membership. A deeply ecumenical person, he could still write in his autobiography:

. . . the Church on earth is made up of sinful human beings—redeemed humanity is not a sinless humanity—so she does not always appear as immediately attractive. I saw that less clearly sixty or so years ago, when I identified the "true" church with ultramontane Roman Catholicism. When, much later, I had to make a serious study of church history, I saw that this would not quite do; but I still believe that the right notion of church order is that of a visible society, with a ministry of bishops, priests, and deacons, standing in the apostolic succession, affirming the historic creeds, and administering the sacraments.[3]

Sewell's genius lay in that exquisitely tortuous skill of balancing an openness to the Spirit with a rootedness in the tradition. It was clear to Sewell that his spirituality was historical, communal, other-oriented, and transcendent. For all its idiosyncratic tones and modalities, it was in the end not a celebration of private or individual need over the spiritual communion that is the Body of Christ. Sewell's spirituality was boldly situated within the larger context of a community of believers. Theology, Church, and spirituality for Sewell, then, were not antagonistic realities but deeply interconnected components of a faith life.

Admittedly, Brocard Sewell is a bit of a theological and spiritual pastiche. In that sense, he is quite unlike many of his contemporaries. The grand orthodox thinkers of the immediate past—G.K. Chesterton, Romano Guardini, Karl Adam, and many others—were compatible company for our Carmelite friar, but they were not sufficient. He looked to others as well to nurture his modern or, better yet, postmodern soul. In that regard, Sewell was fashionable to a degree he could never have imagined. His taste for Buddhism, eccentric Catholic monks, renegade spiritual traditions, and potty outsiders on the fringe of the acceptable fit only too well with our contemporary preference for the anti-institutional and exploratory in spiritual matters. Sewell was as much a Victorian as he was a postmodern. With his compassion for the marginalized, however, Sewell was particularly drawn to a *spirituality of the wounded*, a spirituality that has exercised a compelling appeal in our time.

In 1972 the ground-breaking *The Wounded Healer* by the Dutch psychologist-priest Henri Nouwen ushered in a new attention to the "healer" and a new phrase into the lexicon of spiritual terms. Nouwen

realized that the loneliness and alienation often experienced by the healing professionals, and most especially those who are ministers of the
spirit, could be a precious gift.

A deep understanding of their own pains, however, makes it possible
for them to convert their weakness into strength and to offer their own
experience as a source of healing to those "who are often lost in the
darkness of their own misunderstood sufferings."[4]

By the time he died of a heart attack in Utrecht on September 21, 1996,
Nouwen had established an international reputation as a spiritual writer
of consequence. Author of more than forty books and a retreat-giver and
popular lecturer of promethean stamina, Nouwen stamped a generation
with his holistic approach to spirituality. Although born in the Netherlands on January 24, 1932, educated in Holland at the famed Catholic
University of Nijmegen, and ordained a priest for the Archdiocese of
Utrecht on July 21, 1957, Nouwen in fact led most of his life outside the
continent of Europe. He travelled widely and taught in numerous institutions, including stints at Notre Dame University, Yale, and Harvard. But
he also experimented with non-academic settings, including monasteries,
mission centres, and homes for the disadvantaged. Nouwen embodied in
his own life that spirit of restlessness and searching that resonated with
the youthful rebels of the 1960s, a spirit that resisted amelioration as he
aged.

Nouwen understood, both as a psychologist and as a spiritual director,
that an essentialist spirituality, a spirituality of the manuals, a spirituality
disembodied or disincarnate, could no longer speak to people. Spiritual
traditions, exercises, and formulas that failed to respond to the aching
disquiet of the individual, that discounted the deep personal experiences
of the searcher, and that did not take account of cultural shifts and adjustments failed dismally to address the needs of the time. It was the *kairos*,
the hour of the Lord, and people thirsted for a living spirituality. Nouwen
would be their oasis.

This living spirituality was profoundly Christocentric, and in a moving
passage from *Show Me the Way: Readings for Each Day of Lent*, Nouwen
recounts a Good Friday liturgy at Trosly, France, motherhouse of the

international L'Arche communities, when Père Thomas and Père Gilbert took the huge cross that hangs behind the altar and held it for the ritualistic veneration of the congregation. Nouwen was struck by the sweet juxtaposition of anguish and joy to be found in the faces of the broken and the whole as they came to kiss the dead body of Christ.

> Imagining the naked, and lacerated body of Christ stretched out over our globe, I was filled with horror. But as I opened my eyes I saw Jacques, who bears the marks of suffering in his face, kiss the body with passion and tears in his eyes. I saw Ivan carried on Michael's back. I saw Edith coming in her wheelchair. As they came—walking or limping, seeing or blind, hearing or deaf—I saw the endless procession of humanity gathering around the sacred body of Christ, covering it with their tears and their kisses, and slowly moving away from it comforted and consoled by such great love. . . . With my mind's eye I saw the huge crowds of isolated, agonizing individuals walking away from the cross together, bound by the love they had seen with their own eyes and touched with their own lips. The cross of horror became the cross of hope, the tortured body became the body that gives new life; the gaping wounds became the source of forgiveness, healing, and reconciliation.[5]

This visceral passage, teetering on the sentimental, is in many ways vintage Nouwen. It is graphic, unapologetically emotional, and classically orthodox. Nouwen engages the reader with an explicit appeal to the imagination and to the heart, grounding a theological truism in the direct experience of a people at prayer mediated through the observing, but not detached, eye of the writer.

A psychologist of the heart and the soul, Nouwen wrote not only to guide others but to discover himself. He wrote to find himself. In his spiritual enchiridion or handbook, *Making All Things New: An Invitation to the Spiritual Life*, he highlighted the spiritual confusion that afflicts our culture: "One way to express the spiritual crisis of our time is to say that most of us have an address but cannot be found there. We know where we belong, but we keep being pulled away in many directions, as if we were still homeless."[6]

Nouwen appreciated the profound displacement at the heart of contemporary humanity, a rootlessness that he shared to an often disturbing degree. He understood that everything in our culture that defines success or fulfilment is predicated precisely upon those qualities that work against our yearning for wholeness. We need to cultivate both what he calls "the discipline of solitude and the discipline of community," and we need to do this because we need to attend to the silent voice of God, to eliminate the extraneous sounds that dominate our lives.

Nouwen understood only too clearly the demands of success. His various professorships at Ivy League universities, his highly lucrative and very public writing career, and his popularity on the invitational lecture circuit combined to assure him a level of professional and personal success that was the envy of all, but the costs were great. Nouwen often found himself diminished by his achievements, and he sought protection from his own success. He frequently fled to the anonymity of monastic enclosure, requested and received spiritual direction from the abbot, and then wrote about his experience in his next book. Similarly, he would abandon the security of the academy and work in the *barrios* of Latin America. Naturally, he wrote about this experience as well. But these occasional departures from the norm of lecturing, teaching, and writing were, in the end, incapable of settling the wandering spirit.

Nouwen was desperate for that mixture of discipline and community that he passionately wrote about but which consistently eluded him. That is, until he happened upon the second largest L'Arche community in the world, Daybreak, north of Toronto. Here he would spend the last decade of his life (1985–1996), fall in love, experience a breakdown of immense proportions, be emotionally rejuvenated and, however briefly, come to terms with his homosexuality. Daybreak defined Nouwen's later years, allowed him to speak *about* the wounded *among* the wounded, and provided him with that still point that released for him a refreshing and yet unnerving spring of self-knowledge.

Nouwen's writings could be quite formulaic and predictable. He cherished patterns of three; he drew heavily on biblical stories, images, and themes; his anecdotes were autobiographical without being tantalizingly confessional, although his books written during the last half of his Daybreak years betray a taste for candid disclosure not found in the other writings; his tone was honest without being ostentatious; he maintained a syllogistic but not constrictive logic in his writing; he wrote to reveal and not conceal God's encompassing love.

More than anything, Nouwen was committed to shaping a voice for the wounded—the physically handicapped and mentally challenged, the socially marginalized and politically persecuted, the lonely and sexually oppressed/repressed. He proclaimed for all to hear a spirituality of peace-making:

> I want to speak to you about prayer in the context of our Christian voca-tion to be peace-makers; to show you a little bit about how prayer is a way of peace-making. Only then can we speak creatively about resist-ance as a form of peace-making and only then we can see how prayer and resistance can in turn build community. The three indispensable components, then, of a meaningful spirituality of peace-making are resistance, prayer, and community.[7]

Throughout his life, Nouwen sought different settings wherein to embody these three components: lecture room, monastic cell, slum, and group home. He pursued the wounded with frenetic energy and some-times exasperating zeal. Over time he came to understand his own wounds, to experience rejection as much as love, abandonment as much as affirmation. The humanizing of the celebrity proved to be liberating.

Two years before his death he wrote his finest work, *Our Greatest Gift: A Meditation on Dying and Caring.* There is an unnerving prescience about this work, a work written with the intention of befriending his death. Nouwen allows the reader to hear and share in his vulnerability, his fear, in the face of death. But more important still, he invites the reader to experience that hope that makes of death not a foe but a friend: "Our death may be the end of our success, our productivity, our fame, or our importance among people, but is not the end of our fruitfulness. In fact, the opposite is true: the fruitfulness of our lives shows itself in its fullness only after we have died."[8]

Following a funeral Mass in Utrecht, presided at by Cardinal Adrianus Simonis and with a eulogy by Jean Vanier, Nouwen's body was returned to Toronto for a three-hour Mass of the Resurrection, conducted at the

Slovak Byzantine Catholic Cathedral of the Transfiguration of Our Lord in the neighbouring town of Markham. The fruitfulness of the life of this solitary with a desperate hunger for community, of this pastor with a passion for interiority, has only begun to show itself fully.

But a *spirituality of the wounded* wasn't exclusively Nouwen territory. Although he coined the phrase "the wounded healer," he was quick to acknowledge those whose ministry with the wounded, healers or otherwise, was of long-standing and estimable quality. And none perhaps fit into this category more fully than his European eulogist, the Canadian philosopher, spiritual writer, activist, and co-founder of L'Arche, Jean Vanier.

It was Vanier who initiated a relationship with Nouwen by prompting Jan Risse, one of the North American L'Arche coordinators, to make contact with Nouwen after he first mentioned the community in his 1979 work, *Clowning in Rome: Reflections on Solitude, Celibacy, Prayer and Contemplation.* Nouwen was transfixed by Vanier. They became partners in an expanded ministry to the wounded.

Vanier is the son of Georges Vanier, a former governor-general of Canada and a man respected for his intelligence, personal nobility, heroism (he won the Military Cross for conspicuous gallantry during the First World War), and saintliness. Jean appears to have acquired something of his father's humility and commitment to serving the public, but these shared attributes and gifts would find very different expressions from those of Her Majesty's Representative. Although Jean, like his father, served in the military, he would find his life's purpose elsewhere. Upon the completion of his higher studies, Vanier taught philosophy and theology until that fateful year, 1964, when with his Dominican priest friend Thomas Philippe he bought a house in Trosly-Breuil, France, and invited two men with intellectual disabilities to come and form a community in a residence christened L'Arche, after Noah's Ark.

Now a network of more than 100 communities in more than thirty countries, the L'Arche movement is a sanctuary wherein the disabled and their caregivers can grow in mutual love, experience first-hand the dignity of the other, and build genuine life-giving community in a world only too accustomed to fear the alien and the isolated. Vanier is insistent in his public addresses and in his books that those who live in L'Arche communities:

. . . are not saviours. We are simply a tiny sign, among thousands of others, that love is possible, that the world is not condemned to a struggle between oppressors and oppressed, that class and racial warfare is not inevitable. . . . Sartre is wrong when he says that hell is other people. It is heaven that is other people. They only become hell when we are already locked into our own egoism and darkness. If they are to become heaven, we have to make the slow passage from egoism to love. It is our own hearts and eyes that have to change.[9]

To discover the heaven that is the other, to disprove Sartre's cynical judgment, Vanier has laboured to create an environment in which the broken, the shattered, and the forsaken can find healing and where healers, too, are healed. Vanier's call to community is not a romantic's fantasy. To love is messy, requires a naked openness, exposes our most acute vulnerabilities, makes no apologies in its demands. The intellectually challenged are needy, relentless, and importunate, fearing wildly, loving unconditionally. They are the principal teachers. The caregivers come to value them less as dependants and more as vessels of light. They teach us the way of the heart:

. . . a human being is more than the power or capacity to think and to perform. There is a gentle person of love hidden in the child within each adult. The heart is the place where we meet others, suffer, and rejoice with them. It is the place where we can identify and be in solidarity with them. Whenever we love, we are not alone. The heart is the place of our "oneness" with others.[10]

Throughout the years since its founding, L'Arche has drawn many to serve for a period of time as caregivers. Students, clerics, spiritual wanderers, professionals, the single, and the married, all have come to l'Arche to practise the way of the heart. James H. Clarke, lawyer, father, and writer chose with his artist wife Mary to bring his family with him to the very seat of L'Arche, Trosly-Breuil, for a nine-month period. It was not a sabbatical; it was an epiphany. Out of his time at Trosly, Clarke would write his *L'Arche Journal: A Family's Experience in Jean Vanier's Community*, a human record charged with love. Clarke does not disguise the frustrations, failures, and foibles of community living; he has no time for "cheap grace." At one point, after marvelling at Beauvais Cathedral "with its spaces of dazzling light," he pointedly observes: "Strange how dark, lifeless, and even forbidding the stained glass windows of the great cathedrals appear from the outside. But from the inside, what a contrast! Is this the experience of most people with the retarded?"[11]

Clarke quickly discovered that life with the mentally challenged was indeed different viewed from the inside: it was incandescent rather than dark, a channel of hope rather than a cavern of despair. Many years after their experience at Trosly, the Clarke family would be deeply pained by Mary's suicide, a death by drowning that prompted the now judge-poet and unforgetting lover to write "Proper Burial":

> O how we tried to give you a proper burial
>   that sunny afternoon in Easter week,
>   while your portrait gazed at us
>   from the sanctuary,
>
>   sprinkling you with holy water,
>   robing you with incense,
>   singing till we could no longer hear
>   your unquiet spirit. And still
>
>   at Eastertide I sometimes hear
>   lilies weeping in the sun, your voice
>   like Niagara, roaring in the night.[12]

Who knows if the exquisite pain of such a loss—the haunting memories, the tortured cry of love, the obsessive "why"—could not in part have been mitigated by their earlier shared experience at L'Arche. Shortly before they left Trosly, Clarke noted in his journal:

> Before going to bed Mary and I had a long discussion. Our months at L'Arche have gone by so quickly! Not only have we witnessed the unique sufferings of the mentally handicapped but we have shared their special gifts of the heart: openness, sensitivity and capacity for moral

and religious insight. . . . In a world where the massive rejection of the weak is a commonplace, we believe L'Arche is an eloquent symbol of the equality and infinite value of all.[13]

For the Clarkes, as indeed for the thousands of caregivers who have shared Vanier's vision for the wounded, the making whole of our fractured humanity is possible only when we attend to the logic of the heart. Vanier's *spirituality of the wounded* is a spirituality enmeshed in the world of broken bodies, broken minds, and broken spirits. But Vanier knows that to break open the "plague of cerebration" that poisons our culture, to expose to the open air the fallacies of reason, we must allow "the wounded" to heal our wounds, allow the maimed to touch our invisible scars of heart and mind. In short, we must be vulnerable as they are vulnerable. The "other" becomes a gift to us.

Few modern Christians understand the desperate courage involved in being as vulnerable as the most vulnerable as well as the physician and writer Sheila Cassidy. Persuaded that, in the words of her Benedictine friend Tom Cullinan, "we were given a gospel which is a wild stallion and we have domesticated it into a riding school pony," Cassidy lives her life totally for the Wild Word, shattering the conventions of professional living with the unplanned eruptions of the spirit and of grace. These eruptions have taken her to the liminal points of human experience and endurance: a torture chamber and a hospice bedside. "You can't ride a wild stallion without getting unseated from time to time and without getting a few bruises." Cassidy first rode her wild stallion in the turbulent world of post-Allende politics, on the dark landscape of Pinochet's Chile in the early 1970s:

Although I was born a Catholic and went to a convent school, it wasn't until I was in my thirties that I discovered the radical gospel. In retrospect, I think my first encounter was through Consuelo, a lapsed Catholic, an agnostic and a socialist. It was she who invaded my insular mind with the notion that all peoples had the right to enough food, decent housing, health care and education, and the uncomfortable corollary that if there weren't enough goods to go around, then they should be redistributed so that everyone had something. It was Consuelo's belief in Allende's socialist dream that took her away from a comfortable life as a plastic surgeon in England, back to a Chile that was beginning to be divided. It wasn't until after her death, however, that I began to understand that the values she stood for were truly gospel values.

My first direct meeting with the radical church was with two Holy Cross missionaries from the United States. They lived in a shanty-town on one of the outskirts of Santiago and shared the life of the Chilean poor, both in terms of material hardship and in being at odds with the security forces. I will never forget the day I went to their house and saw the way they lived. I had thought I lived simply, but they owned barely more than a change of clothes. This meeting was the beginning of a struggle to achieve a simplicity of lifestyle that somehow always eludes me. . . .

Just as my time in Chile led to an encounter with the wild word of the radical gospel of sharing and justice, so too, it acquainted me with the prophetic word. . . .

I met the Holy Cross missionaries only three months before I returned to England, but they gave me a glimpse of a church which was like none I had ever known before, and I became determined to be a part of it. Alas, when I returned to Chile, both my friends had been expelled, and I became aware only of the danger that working with the poor involved.

For several months I did nothing that would bring me into conflict with the authorities, until one day something happened that I could not ignore. I was working at the emergency hospital on the night shift. As I came down to the examination rooms, I heard a young man sobbing, "I killed a man, I killed a man." I went in and there was a young soldier lying on the couch weeping uncontrollably. In the next door cubicle was the body of a boy of seventeen, his body ripped apart by machine gun bullets. I was so furious at this wanton killing that I felt an enormous need to denounce it, though I knew I would be putting myself at risk to do so. . . .

I went next day to seek out the young man's parish priest who turned out, by a coincidence, to be a Chilean Jesuit who was already deeply involved in helping the poor. This meeting was to be crucial, for it was he who later asked me to treat the wounded revolutionary, the decision which proved instrumental in my being arrested.[14]

Her arrest, imprisonment, torture, and subsequent release are chronicled with excruciating detail and candour in her best-selling autobiographical memoir, *Audacity to Believe*. This Chilean experience proved formative for the Oxford-trained physician with a craving for God and justice and she found herself hounded by the memories of her torture and sexual humiliation and driven by the need to heal, both herself and others. In her 1991 book, *Good Friday People*, she identified in her dedicatory page those guides, philosophers, and friends who have walked with her "along the road to Jerusalem." Prominent among them was Jean Vanier.

Vanier taught her to attend closely to the "Good Friday people," those people she came to know and love in prison in Chile, those people in her hospice for the terminally ill in Plymouth. Indeed, for all the vagabonds, renegades, and nonconformists who crossed her path, she has come to understand that "the meeting with God in the desert of prison or serious illness is often a very hidden thing and we can recognize it more by the way people behave than by what they say.[15]

Cassidy, by temperament and by profession, is continuously drawn to the marginalized. Her enervating experience in Chile was merely a foretaste of the kinds of frontier spiritual encounters that would come to define a life of controversial service. A *spirituality of the wounded* is a spirituality radical and uncompromising, a spirituality that is disruptive and even cantankerous, a spirituality that allows no quarter. This is Cassidy's world, a life lived at the centre of the Wild Word.

She is not alone in her radicalness. There are others, like the late Donald Nicholl, professor, essayist, and spiritual writer. Unlike Cassidy, however, Nicholl was a husband and father who followed a rather more traditional career path. But he shared Cassidy's intense commitment to justice and espoused his own *spirituality of the wounded*, a spirituality nurtured by his wide reading and his humble origins.

Nicholl taught history and religious studies in both the United States and the United Kingdom, wrote widely and deeply about personalities and issues, and struggled throughout his life to understand what we mean by *holiness*. But to achieve holiness, one must begin somewhere and for Nicholl it begins with a call from the Holy Spirit, for

> . . . *every* call of the Holy Spirit begins with a revelation of the bank-ruptcy of one's present, habitual mode of life, its tendency towards the death of one's spirit. That moment of awakening inevitably has to be a moment of anguish, of agony, and of repentance, because it is only from the pain of awakening to the contradiction in one's life that the energy to change arises. Listen, for example, to an expression of such anguish from one of the most remarkable priests in England, Austin Smith, who has spent the last 25 years serving in the front line, in the slums of Liver-pool. Lately Fr. Austin has told us in *Vocation for Justice* how he was struck by the contrast between the way Christians protested against the celluloid *Last Temptation of Christ* of Scorsese's film yet succumb daily to the real last temptation against which Jesus had to struggle to the very end. Jesus' last temptation, in Gethsemane, was to feel that "there was still time and space to carry on [with his campaign for the kingdom] and get somewhere. And yet the message of God was, 'It is time to suffer and die.' This temptation was, if one may so express it, to keep the show going when the show has really run out of steam. Or, to put it another way, a much more radical way, it is the temptation to keep going when we are really washed up, or, if you prefer it, washed out. We keep going when the very gospel of Jesus is saying to us, 'Your day is done.' We are seduced by the thought that we still have something to offer. We will not die to our present comfortable state to rise to a new state."[16]

Our fear to rise to a new state, to undergo the dramatic process of *metanoia*, conversion, to cut oneself off from the old ways in order to answer the call to a "new, dangerous form of existence," is a fear that hobbles and diminishes us. Although each person's *metanoia* will follow a different direction, we are all called to discard the false self, "infected by death," for the true self, open to the Spirit of Life.

Throughout his own life Nicholl sought bravely to change, to resist always the blandishments of successful and homogenizing ideologies, to avoid the easy comforts of establishment living, to hear the cries of the poor and abandoned, to forge out of the sufferings and crises of both religious and artistic leaders as well as out of the anonymous multitudes a genuinely liberating *spirituality of the wounded.*

To that end, Nicholl read the Russian mystics and poets, explored the spirituality of resistance that occasionally found expression among German Catholics to the Nazis' tyranny, argued for intelligent and respectful dialogue between Catholicism and the other great religions, and campaigned vigorously in the interests of peace. Nicholl believed that humanity could find a common ground of the spirit by pursuing what he called a *scientia cordis*, or science of the heart. This *scientia cordis* is a genuine science with an appropriate authority, but it is not a positive science,

> . . . because positive science tries to formulate immutable laws about what *is*, psychology too attempts to freeze human beings in terms of laws about needs and demands that can be specified—but the aspirations of the heart always go beyond what can be specified in such laws; and it is these aspirations which keep the heart in motion and prevent it from being frozen into immobility.[17]

Because the *scientia cordis* concerns itself with human aspirations, its medium of expression is not some law or formula—characteristic of the positive sciences—but the narrative, the story, which is more proper to art in form. Nicholl, then, told stories, plenty of them, because he knew that in matters of aspiration, the chief motto and mode of disclosure is Newman's *cor ad cor loquitur* ("heart speaks to heart"), because he knew that along the path of storytelling "dancing and joy and truth can travel." But these stories arose out of Nicholl's own empathy for the suffering and alienated; they spoke of grace and heroism dearly bought; there is nothing light and frolicsome about them. Out of Nicholl's *spirituality of the wounded* comes a sweet incandescence, luminous wonders in a darkening landscape.

Kathy Shaidle, too, tells stories—her stories. Columnist, poet, and pop culture essayist, with a penchant for the *pensées* of the seventeenth-century French mathematician, mystic, and theological controversialist Blaise Pascal—aphoristic encapsulations of potent spiritual insights—Shaidle is a thirty-something *enfant terrible* with a spiritual attitude. Diagnosed at the age of twenty-seven with lupus, an incurable autoimmune disease, she confronted her chronic disability with acidic equanimity:

> I had once been a fast talker, fast walker, fast thinker—full of energy and independence, plus lots of ill-concealed impatience for anyone I deemed lazy, slow, useless. Now, my sense of humour dwindled from wit to sarcasm, then simply vanished. My fit, youthful figure shrank to a cadaverous 40 kilograms. Bedridden and in constant pain for the better part of a year, I could barely think, let alone write. But I could pray, although not, to my surprise, for relief or explanations. I'd been "experimenting" with prayer and meditation before my illness, but saw now that I'd been toying with mysticism. With my huge ego and spiritual pride fatally punctured, stripped of words and ideas, my pain now became my silent prayer. . . .
>
> In my lighter moments I consoled myself with the knowledge that being a mystical invalid is actually a viable Catholic career option.[18]

And so began in earnest Shaidle's "Catholic career option." It is not surprising, given her literary gifts and struggle with lupus, that she would find a soul sister in the southern U.S. writer Flannery O'Connor, a Catholic who died of lupus on the very day that Shaidle was born in 1964. Shaidle not only admires O'Connor's Gothic spunk, her skilful intermingling of the spiritual with the grotesque, but also her stand-alone defiance of the conventions of the literary establishment of her day. In a nicely orchestrated whine over the tendency among some Canadian feminists to elevate to literary sainthood "authors of their own misfortune" like writers Gwendolyn MacEwen, Pat Lowther, and Elizabeth Smart, Shaidle tartly notes: "but try finding a book about Flannery O'Connor, the devout Catholic novelist who lived with her mother and died a virgin. In spite of her widely acknowledged genius and influence on innumerable artists, O'Connor is evidently too boring and 'uptight' to merit a decent biography."[19] If Shaidle appears defensive about O'Connor, in large measure it can be attributed to her identification with this tragic and noble Georgia belle:

> I study the photograph again—
> peer past your crutches, your snapped-shut lips;

the still screen door: its rusty last slam
that rings through the years to my ears—

Isn't that your mother baby standing in the shadows? |

(sorry once again:
that's a song just past your time,

and so am I:
born here the year that you died down there)

Checkmate, captured queen, you stare me down.
But doctor's-ordered not to work.
Allowed 'to write a little'.[20]

The doomed and underappreciated O'Connor is Shaidle's patron saint. Shaidle invokes her memory, seeks her intercession, and celebrates her genius whenever the opportunity presents itself. O'Connor's wounded spirituality stands in judgment on the easy and individualistic self-pampering that masquerades as self-fulfilment. "Art's been reduced to Craft and Creativity; Sanctity to Sabbaticals, Seminars, and Self-Improvement—spawning more Charlie Browns than Charles Borromeos [the Counter-Reformation cardinal-archbishop of Milan and fervent reformer who was canonized in 1610]."[21]

Shaidle's dismissal of New Age wizardry isn't just a case of counterculture punchiness, a sign of the young poet's restive spirit and dislike for the fashionable, although one can make the argument that that is precisely the case. Still, there is more. In Flannery O'Connor—broken of body and whole of spirit—Shaidle finds an icon of genuine wholeness, a healing *spirituality of the wounded.*

In addition to O'Connor, she has developed a deep sympathy for and understanding of the life and work of one of O'Connor's most intelligent admirers: Thomas Merton.

It is Thomas Merton, Trappist monk, poet, and spiritual writer who, more than any other figure in the twentieth century, reclaimed and redefined monasticism, and who embodied in the boldest way the notion of the monk as archetype. As comparative religions scholar Raimundo Panikkar notes:

> . . . the monk is the expression of an archetype which is a *constitutive dimension of human life*. This archetype is a unique quality of each person, which at once needs and shuns institutionalization. . . .
>
> Monkhood represents the search for the center. Inasmuch as we try to unify our lives around the center, all of us have something of the monk in us.[22]

Merton spent a lifetime defining the centre, defining a *spirituality of the monastic cell*, but doing so in a way as to appeal to those both inside and outside the cloister. Merton resolved to bring the wisdom of the desert to the inhabitants of plaza and condominium, the sage counsels of the ancient holy ones to the struggling masses of the modern metropolis.

By the time of his death [December 10, 1968], Thomas Merton, born in France, a citizen of the United States, and a monk for twenty-seven years in the Trappist Abbey of Our Lady of Gethsemani in Kentucky, had an international following of enviable proportions, a publication record of staggering range, and an influence by no means limited to the Catholic world. Merton was, and remains, a phenomenon, an utterly engaging figure, controversial, iconic, the paradigmatic monk for our century. Since his death he has been the subject of hundreds of theses and dissertations, countless essays and reviews, and dozens of studies and biographies. His life and thought have been the subject of radio and television documentaries; songs have been composed and dances choreographed, inspired by his poetry and performed internationally; and there have been numerous learned and popular conferences and workshops on his life, work, and spirituality. In short, there is a veritable Merton industry.[23]

Merton was an intensely personal writer. With little taste for the driest of abstractions and possessed of a keen eye for the common yet unacknowledged epiphanies of the divine at the very heart of the ordinary, he examined every thought, feeling, and impression through the lens of his own experience. The monk who sought the elimination of the "I" was the very same writer who nurtured it. In sum: the paradox of the divided self, the monk-celebrity, the marriage of heaven and hell.

Merton was a literary essayist, poet, calligrapher, photographer, controversialist, social and political commentator, editor, monastic scholar, anthologist, translator, and sometime cartoonist. He was a religious thinker of Blakean propensities, a correspondent of gargantuan energy, and a belle-lettrist of startling virtuosity. But we continue to read him primarily for the same reason that we read St. Augustine, Blaise Pascal, and Simone Weil—for the personal voice, the personal revelation, the confessional tone.

It is not surprising, then, that Thomas Merton's more explicitly autobiographical writings continue to enjoy the greatest popularity in his formidable canon. Although Merton did try his hand at other genres, such as the biographies of Mother M. Berchmans and St. Lutgarde of Aywieres, published as *Exile Ends in Glory* and *What Are These Wounds?*, respectively, and although he did try his hand at a systematic exposition of the ascetical theology of St. John of the Cross known as *The Ascent to Truth*, Merton's preference was clearly for the self-exploratory possibilities of both pure and disguised autobiography.

Merton's arduous quest for the real or true self could be seriously undertaken only once he resolved to examine the myriad masks he donned in both the public and the private realm, and so we have the tantalizing striptease of the would-be anonymous monk. Merton's *strategy of disclosure*, for all its presumed candour and spontaneity, is a deftly handled process involving stringent editing and careful construction. Merton strips with modesty.

Autobiography is a mode of theological investigation; it is also Merton's *via negativa*, a way of sundering and reconstituting, a way of purgation and integration. The voluble eremite draped with the mantle of enclosure redefines silence through the power of words. He lives, as he would have it, in the "belly of a paradox," and he invites his many readers to travel with him on his *peregrinatio*, his "going forth into strange places," in order to better understand the mystery of the "I." Merton will explore the dread region of the Shadow—both external and internal—and the cadaver so minutely dissected for public show will be none other than himself.

Merton's autobiographical writings may smack on occasion of rank exhibitionism, and undoubtedly the lonely child of Montauban, France, Cambridge, England, and Columbia University in New York can be divined at the very heart of many an emotional and spiritual maelstrom, but there is, more importantly, a luminous, grace-suffused honesty about Merton's self-disclosures that continues to engage the interest of critical and mature readers.

Thomas Merton's honesty compelled him to chronicle his search for the true self in such a way that his readers could and can continue to share vicariously in both the light and the dark sides of spiritual growth. Merton simply could not stay his hand. He had to write: it was a psychological imperative. His superiors—abbots Frederic Dunne, James Fox, and Flavian Burns—were wise in their determination to channel Merton's literary gifts for the good of the Trappist order. And although he would be reined in by the censors on the matter of peace and nuclear war up until the mid-1960s, by and large he enjoyed considerable latitude and not a little abbatial indulgence. His diaries were his private reflections; they were also his public voice.

As a diarist, Merton recorded a fully catholic range of subjects. He wrote of the various hues and contours of the clouds, of the flora and fauna to be found on the vast Gethsemani grounds, of the litany of characters to be found both within and adjacent to the monastic enclosure, of the variety of sounds to be heard in the Gethsemani woods, and of the changing of the seasons in the Kentucky hillside.

Merton's enthusiasm for a new book, a just discovered author, a fascinating idea, would jostle with cynical asides and sardonic humour on the same page. His diary entries were a means of self-exploration, a mode of earnest dialogue with the anonymous reader and himself. Some of the entries are nature portraits, some are compilations of things done or books to be read, some are introspective exercises, some are mature meditations or *pensées*, and some are simply vehicles for frustration or anger. There are diary entries that serve as short essays, like the piece on Adolf Eichmann and Hannah Arendt's notion of the "banality of evil," and there are diary entries that function as short mystical expositions, like his piece on the "virgin point" or the *point vierge*.

Merton's diaries reveal the man. They are direct, personal, and most especially, they are uncompromisingly honest. But, and this is critical to remember, they were subject to careful editing and rewriting. In short, the fresh, private voice of the diarist is a fine example of disciplined spontaneity. Merton wrote to be published; he intended that his private ruminations become, in the end, public property.

Accessible to the many rather than to the elite, more inclined to use the colloquial over affected discourse, Merton could communicate with the erudite one moment and ask some of his visitors to bring a six-pack of Budweiser beer the next. Readers like the Merton of the diaries because he is without cant, exalted self-regard, or magisterial pretensions.

The diary structure gave Merton the freedom he needed to roam, to finely hone the individual *pensée*, to merely alight on a subject in order to be quickly nourished and then move on to something else, to capture in an aphoristic style the insights of a dense, systematic study. Although there is a dilettantish air about the diaries, there is also a searching and vigorous intelligence at work. His diaries convey his fierce struggles with the many contradictions that defined his life—the writer who is vowed to silence, the Columbia University bohemian who becomes a consecrated religious, the solitary figure compelled to address the public order, the "hidden one" scarred by fame.

The diaries reveal the many voices of Thomas Merton—the voice of the garden with its discipline and the voice of the field with its wildness; and—as Canadian biographer and critic George Woodcock observed in his 1978 work, *Thomas Merton, Monk and Poet: A Critical Study*, apropos a discussion of Merton's poetry—the voice of the choir and the voice of the desert. Merton's diaries are at once seductive, disturbing, amusing, and oracular. They are eclectic and alogical with a heavy dose of Swiftian irony and Zen wisdom.

The finest of the Merton diaries consist of his skilful juxtapositions of shadow with light, of the luminous with the demonic, the tranquil scene with the menacing spectre. His diary entries more often unsettle than soothe. Their homiletic power is to be found less in the grand rhetorical flourish, and more in their capacity to jar us out of moral complacency and the tyranny of William Blake's Single Vision.

The diaries remind us that the spiritual enterprise in which Merton was engaged from 1941 to 1968 was nothing less than the supreme enterprise of emptying himself:

I see more and more that my understanding of myself and of my life has always been inadequate. Now that I want more than ever to *see*, I realize how difficult it is. . . . Yet my job and that of the Church remain this: to awaken in myself and in others the sense of real possibility of truth, of obedience to Him who is holy, a refusal of pretenses and servitudes, without arrogance and pride and without any specious idealism.[24]

It is this kind of honesty that continues to draw readers worldwide to Merton, an honesty wedded to a vision and intensity captured by Merton's old friend, fellow poet and hermit, exile in the world, Bob Lax:

He lifted the level of debate on philosophical, theological and spiritual matters to a point where it had never been before except in the minds of certain individuals throughout history. The task was always there to be done for the world at large. And following his own inner light upward into infinity with heaven's constant and unfailing help, Thomas Merton did it.[25]

For his former scholastic John Eudes Bamberger, abbot of the Trappist Abbey of the Genesee in northern New York State, and a psychiatrist, Merton was

. . . not an intimate friend of mine. We were very different. He was a very gifted person who was very much of an artist, but lived very simply among us as a brother. You felt he was very approachable and he had a wonderful sense of humour. He had a great facility, I felt, for contacting people, and above all he was a very sympathetic person. If he thought that you needed help, he was wholly attentive to your need and proved always a very good listener. One difficulty in having Merton for a teacher, precisely because he was so brilliant and energetic in his response to things, was the simple difficulty in keeping up with him. However, this was not the case so much when he functioned as a spiritual director. I always found him stimulating, but there was a certain danger in that everyone likes to be somewhat like his teacher, but Merton was too gifted for others to be like him. I think that his writings,

too, can be misleading for many people precisely because he was sponta-
neously artistic, that is to say, he transmuted or transformed experience
so that he could make things sound like they fit in the real world whereas
in truth they were the artist's world. Like a landscape of Cezanne,
although it is not a photograph of the hills, it's an interpretation of how
they're put there, etc. It's not a distortion; it's an interpretation.
Merton's writings, I believe, are stamped very strongly by that tendency,
even when he was not adverting to it. I think he did advert to it at times,
but even when it was spontaneous, he thought in symbols and style
mattered to him always. No one can reproduce another's world, but as a
teacher he was always very stimulating and ever passionate.[26]

Merton, the monk-poet of unquenchable enthusiasms, could prove a
dangerous exemplar of monastic living for fellow monks, as Dom
Bamberger carefully outlines, but for the multitude of readers drawn to
him from different cultures and faith traditions, Bamberger insightfully
delineates the special gift he had as a contemplative:

In my opinion it was his long experience of contemplative prayer *joined*
with his singular ability to give effective expression to fundamental
truths concerning God and man while establishing with his readers a
climate of spiritual intimacy that distinguishes Merton's work from other
spiritual writers and theologians: "I seek to speak to you, in some way, as
your own self. Who can tell what this may mean?" Many, as they read
him, experience thoughts rising in their hearts that confront them with
the mysterious ways of the living God. They experience the issues he
treated as affecting them, as being important for their spiritual life. I
submit that this power of spiritual communication, serving as a channel
of the Holy Spirit, is one of Merton's chief contributions to spirituality.[27]

Merton made monasticism palatable for his contemporaries. But he
wasn't the only one to do so. Benedictine Dom John Main, a one-time
professor of international jurisprudence at Dublin's Trinity College,
sought in his many books and lectures to teach a form of meditation that is
accessible to those outside the cloisters:

So when you begin to meditate take a couple of moments to assume a comfortable posture. The only essential rule is to have your spine as upright as possible. And then the stillness of spirit, the way to that still-ness that we have in our monastic tradition, is to learn to say silently in the depth of your spirit a word or short phrase. And the art of medita-tion is simply learning to repeat that word over and over again. And the word I recommend you to use is the Aramaic word—Aramaic is the language that Jesus spoke—the Aramaic word "maranatha," and to say it in four equally stressed syllables.[28]

John Main's personal quest for meaningful prayer was different from Merton's, but there were ways in which their paths were strikingly simi-lar. For instance, the role of the East and its spiritual traditions and teach-ers played as critical a part in the direction Main was to follow as it did for Merton. The Kentucky Trappist had Bramachari, Suzuki, and Chakravarty. As Main biographer Neil McKenty notes, the Irish Benedic-tine had Satyananda:

One of the most significant things in Main's life happened in Malaysia: he met a Hindu swami, Satyananda, on the outskirts of the capital, Kuala Lumpur, almost at the edge of the jungle. He was enormously impressed by the Swami's charity. The Swami had a school, an orphan-age, and a meditation centre and they all bore the strong marks of authenticity characteristic of the Swami. He asked Satyananda to teach him how to pray, how to meditate, but he was reluctant. The Swami was persuaded that Christians don't pray the same way as the Hindus. Main persisted. The Swami relented, but only on the condition that Main come out to the meditation centre once a week so that they could pray together. In addition, Main was to pray twice a day in his own digs and he was to do so in the following way: he was to say to himself quietly a mantra or prayer word to be drawn from his own Christian tradition, and to do nothing else while praying other than that.[29]

Some years later while Main was being instructed by his novice master in the ways of Benedictine prayer, he was told to give up what he had learned from the Swami because, in the eyes of the novice master, it was not a Christian form of prayer. Laurence Freeman, Main's successor as prior of the short-lived Benedictine Priory of Montreal, an author, and the organizing presence behind the international network of Christian meditation centres rooted in Main's old/new spiritual insight, understood the unsettling but energizing effect the novice master's prohibition had on Main:

It was a very difficult decision for Main to accept the order of his novice master. He said that the form of simple prayer that he had learned from the Swami had brought him to the monastery and now he was being asked to give up what was the basis of his spiritual life. So he wrestled with it and couldn't really understand the dilemma, but he came to the conclusion that if he had become a monk to be *obedient* and to give up his own will, then here was the first hurdle. So he took the hurdle, and gave up the prayer he had learned from the Swami, and entered what he would later describe as a spiritual wasteland for years. In retrospect, he saw that period of the desert as a very fruitful and preparatory one because when he came to take up meditation again he took it up entirely on God's terms and not on his own, which I think explains not only the speed with which the Spirit led him after that recovery, but also the intensity of his authority in communicating it.

So some years after that, he was a monk in Washington, D.C. He was headmaster of a Benedictine school there and, as he describes it himself, it was the busiest period of his monastic life. During this time he came across the works of the seventeenth-century English monk called Augustine Baker, particularly a book named *Holy Wisdom*, one of the great classics of monasticism that few monks have read from beginning to end—like most classics. Main came across a quotation from John Cassian, one of the great monastic figures of the fourth and fifth centuries, to be found in his Tenth Conference. This quotation underscored exactly the same way of meditation that he had been taught by the Indian monk so many years earlier. And so, as he describes it, he had returned home, his cycle was completed, the way of meditation that he rediscovered in Cassian was precisely the way of the mantra his novice master had discouraged. He began to practise it again and realized that this was to be the focus of his life.

He returned to England, started a meditation centre in Ealing Abbey in London, and it was at this point that I joined the community. It became very clear to him, and to everyone associated with the centre, that this was a teaching of tremendous relevance to men and women of our own time, within the Church especially, but outside the Church as well. Father John's vision, I think, was to be found in his understanding of the contemplative renewal of the Church. Father Bede Griffiths, the great Benedictine monk living in India and celebrated author, had the highest appreciation of Main's place in the Church. In fact, he said that in his own experience he saw John Main as the most important spiritual guide in the Church today.[30]

Main's death in 1982 in Montreal did not bring to an end his work in contemplative renewal throughout the Church. Through his several writings, taped conferences, and worldwide network of meditation centres, Main's disciples have ably articulated and expanded the contemplative vision of the lawyer-monk. In his seminal lecture "Prayer and Peace," Freeman crisply defines the essence of Main's teaching and shows how it can be contrasted favourably with the passion for the superficial and narcissistic that constitutes so much of current "spirituality":

John Main reidentified as a tradition available, necessary, and integral to the life of every person an ancient tradition of meditation reclaimed from the mists of time. It is a tradition which is characterized above all by its simplicity, by coming to an inner silence deeper than words, deeper than thought. If we want to pray we must stop asking; if we want genuinely to pray we must stop thinking. The great truth of the spiritual tradition of the mantra is that the experience of prayer— entering into the stream of the Spirit—is an experience that is deeper than thought. But as we are so thought-full, so destructive with our thinking, bombarded by outside pressures and influences, it is vital that we have a practical way to travel to that place of "no-thinking" where we are deeper than thought. This is the tradition of the mantra, the formula, the single phrase or word that you repeat continually during the time of meditation in order to leave all thoughts and all words behind. This is, in essence, the work of John Main and the work that we who see great value in it continue to share with the church and society in general.

Now, it should be made clear, this understanding of meditation as a spiritual discipline is quite distinct from psychological techniques like the Human Potential Movement for instance. There is a very great difference between a spiritual discipline and a technique. We need to be very aware today, especially in the Church, of the danger of a culture of narcissism, the danger of reducing our spirituality to a series of techniques that we practice in a self-oriented and self-centred way. You have to be very careful about living what amounts to be a sort of "health club spirituality." The danger of a narcissistic spirituality is one that we can only avoid if we are committed to a process of prayer as self-transcendence. This does not mean that one of the primary goals of contemporary spirituality should not be self-knowledge, but we need to ask ourselves what it is that we mean by self-knowledge. I heard recently of a story that I believe James Joyce liked very much and immortalized. It is about a fisher living on a remote island off the Irish coast a long time ago. He lived a very primitive life. One day he came into town and was walking around when he came across something that he had never seen before: a mirror. He picked up the mirror and looked into it and said, "Oh, my God, it's my father." He was so amazed that he found a picture of his father that he took it home with him where he wanted to keep it hidden from his wife. Every so often, however, his wife saw him gazing at it and began to fear that it was a picture of a rival, another woman in his life. So, when he was out of the house one day, she found the mirror and looked at it and then exclaimed, obviously relieved: "Ha, that's no competition." Joyce, the misogynist that he was, told us that this proved the filial piety of men and the vanity of women, but what it tells us about self-knowledge is that we rarely recognize ourselves when we see ourselves. We have all sorts of techniques that hold the mirror up to us and that give us all sorts of information about ourselves, but rarely indeed do we come to know ourselves in that way. I think that we need to understand the important difference between self-knowledge and self-consciousness.

If we meditate *with* faith we will come to self-knowledge and *that* self-knowledge, the Christian tradition has always emphasized, is an essential part of the journey into the knowledge of God. This is also an essential part of John Main's anthropology and theology that we must come to know ourselves before we can come to know God, to love ourselves before we can come to love God. So self-knowledge is a valid and necessary part of the spiritual journey, but it is not an end in itself. It comes through self-transcendence. Whoever has found his/her light must lose it. I think that if we meditate *with* faith as part of the spiritual tradition then we will come to see a deepening connection between our personal and our social life and we will, accordingly, avoid the pitfalls of a narcissistic spirituality.[31]

For Freeman and Main, an authentic spirituality liberates; self-emptying is the means to spiritual plenitude; wordlessness brings us into the presence of the Word, the stilled mind into the heart of Christ. The original insight of Cassian, reclaimed by a searching twentieth-century monk desperate for true freedom, has become the common property of all who seek Christ. And essential for any truly meaningful relationship with Christ is prayer, prayer in its purest and most stripped-down form, naked prayer fed in and by silence. To discover prayer at its most raw, English writer John Skinner sought out the strict cloisters of Parkminster, the single Carthusian monastery left in England, and requested permission of the prior to live there for a short time in order to gather the information and experience necessary to better facilitate the writing of his book on the Carthusians, *Hear Our Silence*.

The Prior listened patiently to my request, patiently sifting my motives. For a while, I thought my cause lost, but eventually he agreed: I could join in the community's daily routine of work and prayer for just two weeks. The details are in the book—the stillness of the daily round, the drama of the great Night Office which begins at half-past midnight, the intensely prayerful Eucharist when the whole community comes together around Christ's table. The surprise was that they would not go away. Certainly I left them to their life-call and in due course wrote my book. End of story. No. They would keep on coming back. Of course, I could no longer visit them. Yet I knew they were still engaged in that familiar rhythm of their daily routine, so that somehow they stayed with me as part of my own experience. Most of all, they began to seep into my prayer. Whereas before I had been busy at prayer, striving as if to make it work, now a gentler, more peaceful attitude began to take shape.

When I was living at Parkminster, for the first week the Prior would come to my room every three days—"just to see how you are getting on"—as he put it. During one of these short conversations I asked him outright: "Tell me about prayer." It seemed a golden opportunity not to be missed. Here was a man whose entire life had been spent as a professional prayersmith. What he didn't know was not worth worrying about. "Prayer is a way of life," came the answer thin and short. I carried the sentence away with me to tease out like some Buddhist mantra given once for all. What I think this master meant was that if we isolate prayer into some secret exercise, cut off from the rest of life, we miss the point. Real prayer is none other than our living, loving relationship with God, a never-ending story. And if we take life itself as the ground of our prayer, then the Carthusian message is simplicity itself: first and foremost, God's love for us and flowing from this comes our reciprocal love. Such is the stuff of life.[32]

It has become quite possible, as Skinner demonstrates, to find a "professional prayersmith" as much out of the monastery as in. These exclaustrated "monks"—lay and sometimes not even Catholic—have become a remarkable spiritual phenomenon. Their most outstanding exemplar is the best-selling Benedictine Oblate, poet, and American spiritual writer Kathleen Norris. In her two uniquely crafted memoir/reflection compendia, *The Cloister Walk* (1996) and *Amazing Grace: A Vocabulary of Faith* (1998), Norris takes the reader through a liturgical cycle that draws on the rich experience of being human. She leaves out nothing. *Everything is a means of grace.* Her diaries scorn nothing. Norris uses the architecture of the Benedictine vocation—its monastic rhythms, simplicity of life, high learning, gracious hospitality—to structure her meditations. An Oblate of Assumption Abbey in North Dakota and an occasional resident at the Institute for Ecumenical and Cultural Research at St. John's Abbey in Collegeville, Minnesota, Norris, a bone fide poet and a Protestant, creatively draws from the wells of an ancient Catholic monastic order in order to partly slake the spiritual thirst of the unchurched multitudes. In both *The Cloister Walk* and *Amazing Grace*, Norris allows the poet's imagination free rein. In fact, the titles of her discrete meditations betray her ability to take a generic subject—the garden, dreaming of trees, monks and women, road trip, resistance, righteousness, hell, theology, etc.—and then indulge the poet's love for the alogical and luminous riff.

What Norris achieves in her "monastic writing" is a means of *engagement* with the world in such a way that the cloistered and the uncloistered, the practising and the disaffected, can taste the beauty of belief. She is an apologist for a revivified spirituality, a spirituality that embraces and ennobles all the senses, a spirituality that is nurtured by the poetic, by nature, by the wisdom of centuries. But it is not a romanticized spirituality—safe, nostalgic, comforting, and naively Pre-Raphaelite—as her extended reflection, "Maria Goretti: Cipher or Saint?," disconcertingly demonstrates. The murder of the young Italian peasant girl, Maria Goretti, in 1902 at nearly twelve years of age by the tenant farmer Alessandro Serenelli began a chain of events that culminated in her canonization in 1950 by Pope Pius XII. Offered to the world as a model of the virgin-martyr, Goretti has been victimized again by a misguided devotionalism and Latin sentimentalism that has robbed her heroic death of its contemporary validity by making her a figure of fun or derision in the eyes of a cynical and "liberated" world. Norris resolves to reclaim her by setting her tragic death within the context of the horrific torture and murder of a young Canadian girl, Kristen French.

Goretti was knifed to death in an attempted rape. Her virginity intact, dying, she forgave her assailant. These are the rough details, but from these the saint-makers began to weave a story that many moderns have difficulty accepting as meaningful and heroic. She was celebrated for her valour in defending her virginity, and many Church officials and teachers chose to see St. Maria Goretti's holiness in terms of her preference for death over dishonour. Her hagiographers, argues Norris, often missed the point of Goretti's true witness. She writes:

Much of our difficulty with Maria Goretti comes from the fact that her hagiography is of the nineteenth century, but she is a twentieth-century martyr, one with great significance in an age when violence against women is increasingly rejected as a norm, and properly named as criminal violence. Ironically, it is the overload of devotional material and sappy titles such as "Lily of the marshes" or "Lily of Corinaldo," designed to prove Goretti's sanctity, that make it so difficult for people to take her seriously today.[33]

Norris found one way of "tak[ing] her seriously today" and that is in the context of the brutal humiliation and murder of a teenager from a Catholic high school in southern Ontario in the 1990s. The deaths of Leslie Mahaffey and Kristen French by the depraved married couple Karla Homolka and Paul Bernardo have been permanently etched onto the Canadian consciousness. The knowledge that the rapes and mutilations were videotaped, the list of unspeakable villainies, the protracted court cases, the trials and verdicts, the sentencing, plea bargaining, defence mishaps, the books licit and otherwise, the tabloid coverage, the palpable grief of the families, etc., have imprinted themselves on the collective memory of all living Canadians. Exorcism has not worked.

Norris read in *Newsweek* the particulars concerning the death of Kristen French, the high school student from Holy Cross Secondary in St. Catharines, and found new meaning in the witness of Maria Goretti:

> Because they videotaped their victims, the defiance of one fifteen-year-old, Kristen French, is on record. "Ordered to perform a particular sex act," the article notes, "she refused, insisting, 'Some things are worth dying for.' The girl never gave in, even when her tormentors showed her the videotaped death of another of their victims. I am not suggesting that this young girl is better off "pure" and dead than raped and alive. I am stating emphatically that in this extreme situation, no doubt having realized that her death was inevitable, she had every right to act as she did. To choose a free death. . . . The mystery of holiness infuses such defiance.[34]

What Norris does most successfully is retrieve from irrelevance, or worse yet mockery, the neglected ideas, conventions, and personalities of the Christian past and then presents them anew to a reluctantly believing society. Monasticism gives her the framework, faith inspires her, and the imagination does its work. Her diary structure is reminiscent of Merton at his best, and she continues the tradition of his *pensées* or meditations with a similar poetic disposition.

Irma Zaleski, the writer and periodic anchorite or hermit, continues the Merton tradition in a different way. Like Norris, Zaleski is drawn to the spiritual oasis that is monastic enclosure, but unlike Norris she is unmarried, a member of Madonna House in Combermere, Ontario (a foundation of the Baroness Catherine de Hueck Doherty, Merton's friend and mentor from his days at Friendship House in Harlem in the 1930s), and a knowledgeable student of the spiritual traditions of the Orthodox churches. In addition, influenced by Merton's assiduous efforts to reclaim the wisdom of the fourth-century monastics for his time, Zaleski has fashioned out of history and imagination the wonderful composite: Mother Macrina. This fictive "desert mother" and "contemporary holy woman" is a fount of sane discernment and practical wisdom. Like Merton's hermits in *The Wisdom of the Desert*, Zaleski uses sayings, parables, and Zen koans to dispense insight. In sharp contrast with the spiritual Prozac offered by the New Age mavens, Zaleski reminds her readers that the path to fulfilment is *kenosis* (self-emptying):

> A friend told Mother Macrina that she had been feeling very discouraged of late. She had been trying to become a better person and to be easier to live with, but was finding it so hard she was ready to give up the struggle.
>
> "I have gone to counsellors and therapists and have joined a self-help group," she said. "I have attended healing workshops, followed special diets, tried acupuncture and shiatsu massage. I now know a whole lot more about myself than I have ever known—or even wanted to know— but this does not seem to have improved me very much at all. I am still the same miserable self and I doubt I shall ever change."
>
> "You probably won't," Mother agreed. "But then, you are not asked to *improve* your 'miserable self.' You are asked to *lose* it!"[35]

Mother Macrina's "saying" on self-improvement implodes the secular myth of limitless self-fulfilment through concentration on self. It is in death to the self that one truly lives. This is the wisdom of the desert, the simple fruit of monastic living, a radical subversion of the panacea proffered by the high priests of self-expansion and self-enrichment. Like Main, Freeman, Skinner, and Norris, Zaleski finds in the writings and life of Thomas Merton the foundation upon which a *spirituality of the monastic cell* in daily living can be secured. Merton is their common source. Still, they depart in different yet complementary directions. In this the architects of the *spirituality of the monastic cell* are similar to those engaged in accommodating to our own time the spiritual tradition of that sixteenth-century gallant-turned-mystic St. Ignatius of Loyola, the founder of the Society of Jesus.

The *spirituality of the Ignatian way* is both rigorously apostolic and contemplative. It is first and foremost grounded in the spiritual life of Ignatius himself:

> I was on my way—out of a feeling of devotion—to a church a little more than a mile from Manresa, called St. Paul the Hermit. I came upon the River Cardoner, and before venturing to cross it, I sat down on the shores of the river and continued my meditation. Suddenly, I had this extraordinary illumination, the eyes of my understanding were flooded with insight, and I perceived many things spiritual, theological, many things in a way that made them new to me. There was *no* vision. I cannot explain in detail what I understood, but I know that I received such a lucidity, such a clarity of understanding, that even now, in my sixty-second year, were I to accumulate every grace God has given me, every bit of learning that I possess, and add them all together, they would not add up to what I received by the River Cardoner.[36]

Ignatius (at this point in his life still called Inigo) spent almost a year in Manresa, from March 1522 until February 1523. It proved to be the most important year of his life. And out of this experience would come his classic contribution to the spiritual life, the *The Spiritual Exercises*. These exercises are a structured religious experience. They are designed to elicit a profound experience of God and of human freedom. They engage the whole person—the imagination, reason, will, and emotions—and they define Jesuit identity. They bear the stamp of Ignatius's personality—his introspectiveness, his preference for an orderly way of experiencing God in the world.

The *Exercises* is not a spiritual treatise nor a major theological tome. There is nothing in it of the controversies of the day, no factual or philosophical rebuttals of the learned opinions of the Reformers, and unlike Ignatius's other writings—*The Spiritual Diary*, the *Constitutions*, the letters, or the *Autobiography*—there is very little in the way of personal disclosure in its pages. It is terse, undecorative, skeletal, and compact. Compendium, program, and teaching aid, the *Exercises* is greater than the sum of its parts. And it is, primarily, to be experienced. . . . The *Spiritual Exercises* is not an arcane collection of unworldly maxims, nor a manual for the gnostic or spiritually elite. It is the product . . . of "a simple lay person with very little education who had this great experience at Manresa." . . . The spirituality of Ignatius—as crystallized in the *Exercises*—is a spirituality for everyone. It is egalitarian, accessible, and non-esoteric. It is there for the taking, or perhaps more precisely, for the doing. But the doing was really only done for Jesuits and by Jesuits for centuries. Ignatian spirituality was almost exclusively identified with Jesuit spirituality: it was their property. And then a revolution occurred.[37]

This "revolution" was the directed retreat movement as envisioned by Paul Kennedy, the legendary Tertian director at the Jesuit Retreat House in St. Beuno's in North Wales, and as defined and practised by John English, the long-serving spiritual director attached to the Guelph Centre of Spirituality in southern Ontario. English recalls the heady days of the late 1960s when the directed retreat idea—one-to-one retreats, one Jesuit and one exercitant—exploded:

From 1965 on, just after the conclusion of the Second Vatican Council, the North American Jesuit masters of novices were having their meetings. There was Dominic Marruca, Tom Walsh, Vince O'Flaherty, and Bobby Rimes. We had this group of top-flight men and when we first got together we talked about crazy things like the timetable of the novitiate, the clothing, etc. But, gradually, at around the third or fourth year of these meetings, we were getting deeply involved in the meanings of the Spiritual Exercises, the spirit of Ignatius, etc. What happened, I think, as far as Guelph is concerned, revolved around seven-week institutes for women religious. Then we started just to have thirty-day retreats as well over at the retreat house. And in some instances we would have a team of nuns directing their own sisters. This went on for two or three years. Fellow Jesuit John LeSarge and I got together and talked to the Mothers General in Ontario and told them that the demands are so great that we can't possibly fulfil them. Our plan was to run six thirty-day retreats concurrently in Toronto, Guelph, Hamilton, and London, so we did workshops with about forty sisters and twenty Jesuits. Now these were very practical workshops. Very quickly we organized them into teams, told them where they were going to be, who their chairperson was, and the nature of the process. In some instances all you would work with was Scripture and we developed a game plan built around Scripture. I think that there were some 360 sisters in the thirty-day Exercises at the same time in southern Ontario. Of course, this jamboree, as we called it, cleared away the big demand and created a whole number of spiritual directors for the sisters to use. It introduced, in a really grand way, the notion and practice that sisters could direct other sisters. From this beginning, of course, sisters went on to direct men, even priests. It was a great breakthrough. I think it was after these retreats that some of the centres in the United States started moving in the same way, giving a directed retreat, giving workshops on how to direct, etc. Wernersville, Monroe, Cambridge—all these places began in the 1970s.[38]

It would not be long before the Exercises—text and experience—would become not only the property of the Jesuits and the sisters they trained in their directed retreats, but indeed the property of all people seeking spiritual integration and peace. But knowing *why* this happened in the latter part of the twentieth century is essential according to British Jesuit and author Gerry Hughes:

To say why it happened is very difficult. One very obvious reason was that the Second Vatican Council encouraged going back to the sources of your religious community and studying them. Individual Jesuits had, in fact, been studying the sources, but I went right through my Jesuit training, which began in 1942 and finally finished in 1960, and I didn't even realize (now, I was slow on the uptake!) that the Exercises were initially given individually, one to one. I had no idea of that. It was only years later that I discovered this, and that made all the difference.

Ignatius's annotation about giving his Spiritual Exercises to people is "Let them discover for themselves." And Ignatius's presupposition is that individuals are all different. You can't mass process people in spirituality and, therefore, there is a need for individual work. So I recall the thrill I got reading about the early Jesuits and how they set about giving the Exercises and how they would spend a long, long time with individuals before they even gave them the Spiritual Exercises. Ignatius didn't even give the Spiritual Exercises to Francis Xavier, with whom he lived, for about seven years. He said he was the most difficult retreatant he ever had, or something to that effect.

Why did it come—this opening up and universalizing of the Exercises? It was partly, as I said, the Second Vatican Council encouraging people to get back to your original charisms by studying the documents, but it was part also of the whole climate at the time. People were more reflective because of the Second World War, all the devastation. Having had the war which was going to end all wars, the first one, we then had this second one, plus the Holocaust, and God knows what. People were forced to reflect more, and there was dissatisfaction with the spirituality as we were receiving it. It didn't seem to be integrated enough. And once this reflection began and people were encouraged to discover things for themselves, the approach started spreading rapidly.

I think there's a message to be learned from all that. You think of this great breakthrough of Ignatius in the sixteenth century and yet how quickly his genius was forgotten or lost sight of. The Spiritual Exercises were given en masse, you know, to masses of people because it's less labour-intensive than doing it one to one. There were all the good excuses they had for giving it to groups: it's much quicker, people encourage one another, people keep one another up to the mark. There were letters stating all this. Gradually the preached retreat came in. In Ignatius's own time Jerome Nadal, a contemporary, was asked: "For whom are these Spiritual Exercises suitable?" And Jerome Nadal said, "For Catholics, for Protestants and for pagans." I love that comment. I think it is so essential. But that was lost sight of too. So the Exercises were preached. To whom were they preached? Mostly to Roman Catholics, mostly to religious and to priests, very rarely to the laity.

In the late seventies, I had just gotten to St. Beuno's and wanted to have a retreat for laity individually given. It wasn't allowed. "We must have the traditionally preached retreat." It soon changed, but as late as the seventies. The reason I am mentioning this is because of the question as to why they forgot it so quickly in the sixteenth century. So in all these centuries of preached retreats, and with the sudden recovery of the individually directed retreat in the twentieth century, I think we have got to be aware of the history.

An awareness of this history is vital not only for the effective reinstatement of the earlier tradition of the one-to-one retreats but also for the recovery of the genuine inclusiveness of the original Ignatian vision. That inclusiveness, so forcefully expressed by Jerome Nadal and repeated by Gerry Hughes, is also realized in the work and life of Margaret Hebblethwaite. A journalist, editor, theological writer, and spiritual director, Hebblethwaite has been giving the Exercises for years to all sorts of people and in all sorts of situations. She observes of the Exercises that:

. . . one of the things I value most is its individual emphasis. It's not a program that's the same for everyone—you know, do you fit this mould? The whole point of it, I always feel and I always explain to people, is that it is based on noticing what happens in your prayer anyway, and then responding to that and building on that. The matter you're dealing with is the individual's prayer, that you listen to, and then help them to notice what's going on and respond. That makes it very suitable for laypeople, who can't always be slotted into a program or a mould. A lot of people nowadays are very keen on breathing awareness and mantras; there is a lot of interest in the Eastern traditions. But you can find that reflected in Ignatius's three methods of prayer. A lot of people value set prayers, and that is present in Ignatius as well: particular prayers that he recommends, or, as he says, you can use others. And the body as well. He talks about actually entering, physically, your place of prayer, standing before it for a moment and then physically walking into it. You may not be going into church, but you can still have a few square inches of your carpet in which you are consciously entering the presence of God.[39]

It was one thing for Hebblethwaite to speak, write, and give the Exercises while in Britain; it is quite another thing to take the Exercises so to heart and intellect that you embark on a new and risky experience. Taking an indefinite leave from her position as assistant editor of *The Tablet* in 1999, Hebblethwaite, the Oxford-educated daughter of a distinguished Catholic family, left the safety and security of England to work in a campo in Paraguay. It was the next step on her Ignatian journey.

There's a lot in the Exercises about the third degree of humility and all that—these huge ideals of abnegation which we fall very far short of. So in a way one of the things I feel is that this is an invitation to divest myself of my heritage as a Western woman from a developed country. Over there you just feel so embarrassed if you have two kids rather than one. So I feel it's an invitation to divest myself. . . . The people out there are also incredibly loving. Those communities in the areas where I am going, which is called Misiones, are very Ignatian-based. Carlos de la Cruz, a Cuban Jesuit, established them as a specific Ignatian foundation. That is what is distinctive in his work. So that is familiar to those people. They are just so loving. You go into that group and they come and they kiss you on both cheeks and they have never seen you before! It is a very terrifying thing to go into a country where—not that I don't speak the language, but where I am a child in the language. I'm at a disadvantage: I don't know the system and other people are going to have to look after me. I'm vulnerable, so to be welcomed with that unconditional love is a tremendous privilege. It's humbling, but I hope it will teach me something about loving.

The Exercises open one to true loving. Although finding Christ in the campo is different from finding him in the drawing room, the spirituality of Ignatius Loyola, as distilled in the *Spiritual Exercises* and as witnessed by directors throughout the world, is a spirituality that humanizes and liberates. Found *in* a handbook or enchiridion, it is not in the end a spirituality *of* the handbook. It is a spirituality to be lived in its fullness, a spirituality of right-knowing and of making things just. As Jesuit Joseph A. Tetlow remarks about the perduring quality of the *Spiritual Exercises*:

> It is arguably the only centuries-old handbook that can still be used. What else would there be? And as the book is understood better and better, the spiritual experiences it offers prove more and more available in every culture. Perhaps this is because the director of the *Spiritual Exercises* has first of all to be a listener. That may be the most important human activity in the new millennium.[40]

The art of listening and the art of discernment are best nurtured in an environment or, better yet, a culture that values silence, interiority, and prayer, for out of these gifts issues a tangible love of justice. A *spirituality of the Ignatian way* combines a strong acknowledgement of the needs of a spiritually parched laity—untouched by the spiritual traditions developed specifically for monastics, friars, cloistered religious, and vowed persons in canonical congregations—with the demands of the radical Gospel call to do justice.

But there are other spiritual ways that also unite a passion for justice with the cultivation of a deep prayer life, a *spirituality of poverty and protest*, with perhaps none clearer and more lasting in its focus than the Catholic Worker Movement, the brainchild of activist and journalist Dorothy Day and worker-philosopher Peter Maurin. Founded in 1933 in New York City, the genius of the Catholic Worker lies in its summons to simplicity of living, pacifism, personalism, community living, voluntary poverty, and strong attachment to Catholic values. With a loose federation of Catholic Worker houses all espousing the ideals of the charismatic Day, the movement continues to inspire scores of people drawn by its honest if old-fashioned revolutionary fervour and unapologetically Catholic idealism. This deep intermingling of piety with activism reflects the monastic roots of the Catholic Worker Movement itself.

The Catholic Worker Movement is best known for souplines and houses of hospitality for the homeless in the slums of large cities, and for an active pacifism that often puts its members in jail for acts of civil disobedience. With no recognized leadership, no definition of membership, vows or formal process of formation, no regular source of funds and operating without license or authorization from Church or state, precarity, rather than Benedictine stability, would seem to be the mark of the Catholic Worker. The intense, often messy activism of the Catholic Worker and the well-ordered contemplation of Benedictine monasticism could appear to be unrelated or even opposed traditions. Still, mysteriously, and despite the resemblance of many Catholic Workers to sarabites and gyrovagues (monks living without rule or discipline and those continually drifting from place to place—"It is better to keep silent than to speak of all these and their disgraceful way of life," St. Benedict rules in his *Rule* for monasteries), there is a connection, an affinity between monastics and Catholic Workers. There is a relationship that has nourished and inspired the Catholic Worker from its founding. At the risk of sounding ridiculous, I suggest that the Catholic Worker, at its heart, is a contemplative vocation.[41]

In addition to its monastic roots, the Catholic Worker Movement reflects the subversive instincts of Day and Maurin, but particularly of Day. Her robust identification with the poor, disenfranchised, homeless, and destitute in many ways predates her conversion to Catholicism. Prior to her reception into the Church of Rome in 1927, she had led a wild, bohemian lifestyle, was both sexually and politically promiscuous, and had already developed an empathy for the masses and a detestation for the governing elites that fed into her anarchism and eventual radical Gospel ethic. Although in many ways a conservative Catholic—ever deferential to the Magisterium on matters of faith and morals—she held no pious illusions about the trials of Catholic membership, or of the consequences for the individual Catholic pitted against an unjust exercise of Catholic authority. Like the great Swiss theologian Romano Guardini, she believed that the Church is the cross on which Christ died and that "one must live in a state of perpetual dissatisfaction with the Church."

Indeed, since her death in 1980, her followers have demonstrated again and again how deeply they understand the costs of discipleship, whether the issue is civil disobedience, pacifism, categorical opposition to free market capitalism, gender equality, or the priority of the poor for our attention and love. Her fierce and uncompromising opposition to abortion and homosexuality, however, has created some tension in the hospitality houses as Catholic Workers struggle to embrace a fully inclusive Catholic ethic and yet remain faithful to Church teachings and Day's muscular Catholicism. The struggle of the Catholic Worker House in Toronto—Zacchaeus—is instructive in this matter. Since 1990 Jim Loney, Dan Hunt, and William Payne—all formerly in formation with the Basilian Fathers, and gay—have significantly shaped the direction of the Catholic Worker presence in Toronto. In doing so they have found themselves, not surprisingly, in conflict with the local archdiocesan authorities, but they have also found themselves, and this was predictable, on a collision course with the Catholic Worker ethos as defined by Day herself. Social justice activist, Catholic leftist, and minstrel Andrew Cash neatly summarizes the quandary:

> The fact that several members of the Catholic Worker, including the three founders of Zacchaeus, were gay or lesbian meant relations with some Catholic Worker Houses in the U.S. were strained. (Dorothy was a resister of American militarism, but she was also a sexual conservative.) But perhaps more significantly, it made the community persona non grata with the local Catholic leadership. "We were selling bread at several churches on Sundays to help us raise money, and after we made it known through our newspaper that we were gay-positive, we were told that we couldn't sell bread at these churches any more," says Loney. Suzanne Scorsone, the Toronto archdiocese's engagingly blunt communications director, says that shouldn't be a big surprise to anyone. "No organization that diverges from a significant teaching of the Church is going to be given access to parishes to fundraise," she says. There have been other run-ins. A few years ago, at the archdiocese's annual big-money funder, which occurred on the heels of the [provincial] Harris government's 21-per-cent welfare cut and with the premier at the head table, William Payne, disguised in a tuxedo, went to the podium to make a plea for the poor. Amidst cries of "Shame on

you!," he was escorted from the banquet by security. Needless to say, the group receives no funding from the Church.[42]

It is easy to visualize Day nodding in approval of these tactics by Payne. With his social convictions she would have no trouble, but concerning his gay-positive views she would be, if not apoplectic, at least stonily silent. Still, what they have in common is their uncompromised commitment to the poor. In the latter part of the twentieth century, Day's love of the poor found expression and support in the Latin American notion of the *preferential option for the poor* and in the contextual theology of the South African Dominican theologian, writer, and teacher Albert Nolan. In 1990 the pontifically chartered Dominican University of Fribourg, Switzerland, was required, under Vatican directive, to withdraw its invitation to Nolan to receive an honorary doctorate. This invitation stemmed from the university's plan to celebrate the centenary of *Rerum novarum*, Pope Leo XIII's magna carta, the first of the papal social doctrine encyclicals, by honouring prominent social justice teachers and leaders. But it was not to be. Nolan had made a few enemies and they were busy delating him to Rome. Founder of the Institute for Contextual Theology, and a writer and lecturer of international prominence, Nolan drew fire from the many critics who feared his politicizing of the Gospel. For Nolan, the poor:

> . . . tend to be people of *faith* and *hope*. Because they do not have money, power and privileges the poor are more inclined to put their trust in God. Not that they sit back and wait for God to rescue them from their poverty. The poor are remarkably resourceful, determined, patient and hopeful. The spirituality of the poor is a reality, but we are not expected to believe that the poor are all saints any more than our children are all saints. The poor, like the child, are a symbol. They are a symbol of what it means to be human in a thoroughly inhuman world. They are a symbol simply because they are not rich, not part of the dominant culture, the materialist money culture and the world of consumerist madness. The poor are simply the people who have managed to remain human because they were excluded from the inhuman world of the rich where things are more important than people and where people are like objects that can be bought and sold. As soon

as a person comes to the awareness that they are being oppressed by the dominant culture, they begin to become free, to become human, to share in the spirit of the poor. . . . Anyone who thinks they can be converted to Jesus Christ without turning to the poor, does not know who Jesus is. Anyone who claims to be born again without discovering the spirit of the poor in Jesus, has not been born from above. Anyone who hasn't seen the face of Jesus in a child or in an oppressed human being, hasn't seen the face of Jesus. . . . To be poor in spirit is to opt for the spirit of the poor and to turn away from the spirit of the rich. To be poor in spirit means to side with the poor in their struggle against oppression by the rich. To be poor in spirit is to move out of the world of sin that is represented by the rich and to move into the world of those who are sinned against. To be poor in spirit is to discover Jesus amongst the victims of injustice. To be poor in spirit is to be born again, to suffer and to die with the poor Jesus and to rise again with all who are oppressed. "Blessed are the poor in spirit; theirs is the reign of God." . . .

Entering the world of the poor, at least in spirit if not in fact, and taking up the cause of those who are sinned against is only the first step in Christian spirituality. . . . I do not wish to attempt an elaboration of the steps and stages of this spiritual journey to relate them to what the classical spiritual writers of the past have said; I only want to insist that we haven't even started on the journey until we turn to the poor and the oppressed of our world today, until we commit ourselves to the *process* of becoming poor in spirit.[43]

The relationship of spirituality to the Gospel imperative to act justly has become a sometimes vexatious issue among some of the *spiritualities of resistance or restoration* that have come to feature prominently during the pontificate of John Paul II. In the excitement and charge of new feeling following the conclusion of the Second Vatican Council in 1965, the religious orders, congregations, pious associations, priestly societies, etc., found themselves responding to the challenge of the Council Decree on the Appropriate Renewal of the Religious Life (*Perfectae caritatis*) to return to the sources—*ressourcement*—of their foundation, to rediscover the original charism of their communities. Although the enthusiasm for this demanding injunction was to be found in large measure in all the religious congregations and orders called to renewal, there were those who resisted change, whether superficial or substantial, and who clung to the old ways and conventions, but they were clearly the minority voice in their religious communities. But as decade followed decade after the Council, the winds of renewal profoundly affected the religious orders in ways few could have anticipated. Quite simply, their numbers plummeted. Very few new members sought admission, large numbers of the younger ones left their communities and either abandoned or redefined their vocations, many of the brightest and most promising left to marry, the pool of future leaders all but dried up, and many of the orders and congregations that had weathered persecution, civil wars, revolutions, and suppression only to thrive were now confronted with the severe depletion of their numbers. Many congregations either sought some form of canonical merger with similar bodies facing diminishment or simply elected to die with dignity, choosing not to admit new members. It wasn't so much new life the orders were now keen on discovering, but rather the struggle to prevent the extinction of their very way of being as religious.

Some religious communities, for instance the Canadian Scarboro Foreign Mission Society (similar in structure and history to other national missionary bodies like Britain's Mill Hill Fathers and the Maryknoll Fathers and Sisters in the United States), have long seen the writing on the wall. They have responded to the precipitous decline in numbers by expanding their mandate to include a broader definition of evangelization and membership. A Roman Catholic missionary society of priests founded in 1918 by Monsignor John Mary Fraser to train and send missionaries to China—the Scarboro Fathers were often called the China Fathers in their early years—they were expelled from China following the Second World War and then began working in the Caribbean, Asia, and Latin America. Following a peak enrolment in 1966 of over ninety students in their St. Francis Xavier Seminary in Toronto, they began a gradual but steady decline in their numbers that saw them with one student in 2000—and that is an increase in recent years. Various efforts at recruitment have been unsuccessful, but at the same time the Society has undertaken to redefine itself as "a Canadian Catholic missionary community" and to respond to new challenges by going into areas not traditionally associated with the Society. Although remaining canonically a clerical society of priests, the Scarboro Fathers have creatively responded to the "signs of the times." As lay missioner Dean Riley tells it,

Since 1974, seventy-four lay missioners have served overseas with the Scarboro Foreign Mission Society. At present, one quarter of the people who serve the Church through Scarboro Missions are lay people. Lay women and men commit to Scarboro for a three-year term. Although an individual may renew for subsequent three-year terms, according to the 1983 Code of Canon Law, full and life-long membership as a lay person is not achievable. The Scarboro Lay Mission Programme has been growing steadily over the past number of years. At present, more laity are in association with Scarboro than at any other time in the past. In total we are twenty-one, with seventeen serving overseas [with seven new candidates being admitted into the Lay Mission Preparation Programme in January 2001]. Among us are women and men, single and married, young and old. We are teachers, providers of healthcare, carpenters and social workers. We are working in Latin America with three members in Ecuador and four in Guyana. We are present in Asia, with four members in China and two in Thailand; and we are in East Central Africa with four members living and serving in Malawi. We are scattered around the globe and some of us have never even met, yet we are inextricably bound together by our faith and commitment as Scarboro lay missioners. In a very real way, we are a close-knit family of strangers.[44]

Although hampered by Canon law to some degree from fully embracing laypeople as constitutive of a community of clerics, the priests of Scarboro Missions have opened themselves to a level of meaningful collaboration with lay missioners and as a consequence have avoided elimination from the religious radar screen. What they will metamorphose into is a matter of faith, risk, and courage. Other religious communities have simply chosen death.

What is true of most of the pre-Vatican Council religious communities does not apply in the same way to those new religious bodies emerging specifically in the post-Vatican Council Church. The Companions of the

Cross, a community of Catholic priests and candidates for the ministerial priesthood, was founded by Ottawa parish priest Bob Bedard in the post-conciliar Canadian Church. It is clearly in a growth mode. It has responded effectively to the need for a deep spirituality among diocesan priests, has ensured a sense of community that crosses the barriers of single-priest rectories, has appropriated some of the energy and joy to be found among evangelical and pentecostal churches, has drawn on the nostalgic yearnings of older men and the romantic idealism of younger men for a pastorally engaged clerical system, and has offered a modicum of hope for those clerics functioning in a moribund structure. The Companions of the Cross have spread out from their Ottawa base and have assigned several of their largely Rome-trained priest-professors to teach their own candidates through association with the Dominican College of Philosophy and Theology in Ottawa. They are but one example of the new communities of men and women erupting in pockets of Western Catholicism and that are characterized by their confidence, industry, fervent Catholicism, traditional piety, loyalty to the Pope, devotion to the Eucharist and the Blessed Virgin Mary, and attachment to the distinctiveness of the clerical and religious state. Such communities consist of the Community of St. Jean, the Community of Emmanuel, the Community of the Beatitudes, the Jerusalem Community, the Missionaries of Charity (Mother Teresa of Calcutta's foundation, and although established before the Council the Missionaries of Charity have flourished in number and importance during the pontificate of John Paul II), the Legionaires of Christ, the Franciscan Sisters of the Holy Eucharist, the Sisters of Mercy of Alma, and the Franciscan Friars of the Renewal, to name only a few.

In addition to these new outcroppings of the Spirit are signs of some growth in traditional bodies like the Sovereign Military Hospitaller Order of St. John of Jerusalem, of Rhodes, and Malta, more commonly referred to as the Knights of Malta. Founded before the taking of Jerusalem in 1099 by the armies of the First Crusade, it began as a monastic community dedicated to St. John the Baptist and actually administered a hospice-infirmary for pilgrims to the Holy Land. It is both a religious order of the Catholic Church and a Catholic order of knighthood. A sovereign power, with its own grand master who governs the order with the assistance of a Sovereign Council, its headquarters is in Rome at the Palazzo di Malte.

The grand master—currently Fra Andrew Bertie—is the seventy-fifth in line since founder Brother Gerard. The grand master is a fully professed Knight—vows of obedience, poverty, and chastity—and in that sense is a religious and not a layperson. For ceremonial occasions at the Vatican, he is ranked as a cardinal and enjoys the confidence of the Pope. On the international front, the grand master is recognized as a sovereign and the order authorized to send delegates to the United Nations and to maintain embassies and legations with countries throughout the world. The Knights own or manage hospitals and clinics in Germany, Britain, Italy, Israel, Benin, Haiti, Lebanon, as well as hospices, homes for the aged, and workshops for the disabled in several other countries. Membership in the order has now exceeded 11,000 and that is both an increase and a sign of growth.

John MacPherson, professor emeritus at St. Francis Xavier University in Nova Scotia, and the only non-European on the Sovereign Council, recounts the appeal of the order:

My involvement in the order has been a spiritual journey. I think that many people, not all, but many people find that working out their salvation is sometimes easier done in the companionship of other people and within the framework of some structure. The Knights of Malta gave me an opportunity to find that structure and so I moved from one category of religious involvement to another and then finally to the level where I took monastic vows and am now considered canonically a religious.

I joined the order in 1973. Friends of mine who were members recommended me and I was interested in the work that they were doing. Their apostolate is health care and relief work. I was drawn to this work at the time for various reasons. I had seen something of sickness in my own home at the time and was, as a consequence, aware of hospital health care in Canada. The Knights of Malta in Canada are a small organization, but nonetheless ran a number of rather interesting health care programs across the country. In many ways they pioneered these programs that in time became part of our national health care system. We ran a training centre and home for mentally challenged boys in Ontario, and in Quebec the first chronic care hospital in Canada, which of course was eventually taken over by the provincial system.

Before I joined the order, the Knights had pioneered daycare for preschool children. In fact, as Gerald Emmett Cardinal Carter, archbishop emeritus of Toronto and a Bailiff Grand Cross of Honour and Devotion in the order, observed: "the Knights have always been on the cutting edge of health care in this country." In short, even though many of the health and education-related activities undertaken, or even initiated by the order, have now been taken over by the state, the Knights look to explore new horizons.

The Knights of Malta provide an opportunity for professionals like John MacPherson to pursue a spiritual path that creatively combines a taste for traditional devotionalism, medieval ritual and pageantry, loyalty to the Holy See, a commitment to the corporal works of mercy, high culture, and internationalism. Admittedly, such a path as this is more likely to be for the few rather than for the many. In addition to these religious and military orders, there are the various fraternal orders, such as the Knights of St. Columba in England, the Knights of Columbanus in Ireland, the Knights of St. Virgil in Austria, and the Knights of the Southern Cross in Australia and New Zealand. And the largest of these, of course, is the Knights of Columbus, to be found in the United States, Canada, the Philippines, Puerto Rico, the Dominican Republic, Guam, and Mexico. Grant Ertel, recently one of the twenty-four supreme directors of the order and a Canadian, remarks on the order's uniquely American origin:

The order was founded in 1882 by Father Michael J. McGivney at St. Mary's Church in New Haven, Connecticut. He was thirty-two years old at the time and he was to die just eight years later. He founded the Knights because of a pressing need in his parish to find support for a young woman whose husband had just died and left his wife and children destitute. McGivney gathered up a group of some twelve men in the basement of his church and raised over a thousand dollars for the widow and her family. In this we have the beginnings of what has now become the third-largest fraternal insurance company in North America, with billions in assets. We dedicate our time and energy to various charitable projects, to renovation and renewal projects associated principally with the Vatican, as well as to some cultural interests. We put ourselves at the service of the local bishop and his priests to assist in any way they so desire.

Although they currently number well over a million and a half members, Ertel laments the difficulties that they have recruiting younger members. In this, they are in much the same situation as many of the service clubs, fraternities, and volunteer associations that dot the North American landscape. In an increasingly fractured and aggressively individualistic postmodern society, the appeal of such bodies as the Knights of Columbus has greatly diminished. What is true of secular society is also true of the Church. Like the traditional orders and congregations, the fraternal orders have great difficulty attracting new members. This is not the case with the new lay movements proliferating in the Church.

Although some of these ecclesial movements, many of which have the juridical status of secular institutes, predate the Second Vatican Council, all of them have greatly prospered in numbers, influence, and power during the reign of John Paul II. These movements—although they are largely lay in composition, many of them have clerics specifically ordained to serve their membership—include the highly influential Opus Dei (a personal prelature whose founder Josémaría Escrivá de Balaguer has been beatified by John Paul II), Communion and Liberation, the Neo-Catechumenate, the Focolare, Faith, Miles Jesu, and many others. Most of them are conservative, pietistic, scrupulously loyal to the Supreme Pontiff, well versed in the laws and traditions of the Church, intelligent, sincere, and tireless in expending their energies in the interests of institutional Catholicism. Some are more prophetic in their origins and thrust, like the San Egidio Community:

San Egidio is a lay community which began in 1968 when ten high school students, most of them baptized but non-practising Roman Catholics, started to read scripture together. In answer to their question, "What does it mean to be Christian?", they experienced a call to serve the poor in Rome. This service began very simply by helping poor children with their homework. The young people soon became friends with these children and their families and at the same time they themselves grew into a community. In 1973 the Vatican offered this growing community an old Carmelite monastery no longer inhabited by cloistered nuns, San Egidio in Trastevere, which they transformed into a centre. . . .

From ten students the San Egidio Community has grown to include many thousands of members in many countries in the world. These men and women live in their own homes and work to support themselves. Each member is committed to listening to the scriptures in common prayer and to working with the poor. Service to the victims of urban disintegration takes many forms and is done on a volunteer basis. . . .

San Egidio communities also work closely with local churches in the areas where they are present, like Santa Maria in Trastevere. . . . San Egidio reflects the servant model, reaching out to the poor in its very midst and reminding us that this commitment is at the heart of the gospel message. Discipleship includes feeding the hungry, clothing the naked, welcoming the stranger, and reconciling enemies. The community of San Egidio challenges us to look at our own cities and to ask: Where are the poor? Where are we?[45]

The question "Where are we?" cuts to the heart of any *spirituality of resistance or restoration*. How we answer the question depends on whether we are inclined to see our spirituality as a mode of prophetic defiance or creative restoration. If it is the latter, then we are likely to be engaged in a recovery of that sense of the transcendent, of the numinous, that has been tragically lost following the ravaging excesses of the Council's liturgical reforms. In addition, our spirituality is likely to be firmly situated within an established tradition of spirituality that is fully cognizant of the conventions and forms of piety that are historically conditioned yet desirous of their imaginative recovery or reinstatement. A spirituality with an emphasis on restoration will be characterized by a close affinity with spiritual luminaries of the past and with a visceral fidelity to the institutional Church and its hierarchy.

By contrast, a spirituality that places its emphasis on resistance is likely to be marked by a riskiness and temerity of imagination and intellect that places justice at its core. This is the kind of spirituality that is boldly described by British theologian Mary C. Grey:

Consider for a moment the many spiritualities that arose as a culture of protest against corruption and abuse of power. In fact, the monastic movements began as a retreat from city to desert, as a counter-cultural protest against the decadence of city life. A spirituality of resistance and struggle refuses to let injustice have the last word. Let us be clear: this is not an opting out from society, a retreat to an inner world where Christians settle down cosily with their own ideals, and give up on social critique. Far from it: prophetic critique today will work as far as possible with whatever forces or energies of society are leading in the right direction. The point about a spirituality of resistance is that *we already live from a different vision*. And this is what is so energising. . . .

Resistance is a far deeper concept than simply activism. Because, in the depth of our hearts, we have said "no" to injustice and oppression on a global level, something has been liberated deep within us and in the solidarity of the groups with whom we are in relation. *We can recover our collective soul.*[46]

A genuine spirituality of resistance, grounded in a love both for justice and for the contemplative dimension, will have little time for the easy spiritualities that are so effortlessly marketed in Western culture as the next phase in self-fulfilment. The *Chicken Soup for the Soul* school of spirituality espouses a strategy of self-enhancement techniques, a feel-good process of self-affirmation that appeals to contemporary readers hungry for spiritual fulfilment but disinclined to struggle for spiritual enlightenment. The alternative to the Chicken Soup school can be found in the writings of Kathleen Norris and Jean Vanier, as discussed earlier in this chapter, writers who "speak out of a living tradition, a communal faith, a theological history. There is no chicken soup for the soul here, no energizing spirituality seminar, no self-help strategy. They don't need a psychiatrist's note. Their integrity is intact. And damned if they aren't bestsellers to boot."[47]

A spirituality that is communal, historical, theological, with justice as part of its very definition, is a spirituality best poised to thrive in the new century, a spirituality of resistance that is not dismissive of the past, hampered by a crippling nostalgia, or self-occupied and insular. But there are other spiritualities—postinstitutional and with a touch of the antinomian—that offer a desperate challenge to a desperate Church in a new time. Classicist and Church historian Mary T. Malone nicely frames such a spirituality in the life and witness of the author of the *Mirror of Simple Souls*, the Beguine Marguerite Porete executed by the Inquisition in Paris in 1310:

> One of Marguerite's beliefs was that two Churches exist: Holy Church the Less is the Church based on reason; Holy Church the Greater is the Church based on Love, and it is the latter's mission to try to persuade the "Little Church" to move from reason to Love. It was a radical vision and did not win her many institutional friends. But is it not, in a sense, the reality of the situation? Without in any way decrying the agenda of the institutional Church . . . has it not always been the reality that it is love which will heal and renew, not "putting theory into practice?" Has it not always been the reality that it is an evangelical vision that leads to the edge of the abyss, not conciliar doctrine, however sublime? Perhaps, this is the time for Marguerite Porete, the time for standing back in wordless awe at the mystery of "unmanifest nothingness," rather than discoursing in calculated and predictable proof texts which do not feed the soul.[48]

It may not be quite divine symmetry, but it is nonetheless apposite to return to the beginning and quote once more from Peter Schjeldahl's article on Gustave Moreau in which we can see expressed something of that dangerous emptiness represented in the life of Porete and tentatively argued for in the prose of Malone: "don't we pine for spiritual enthusiasm, in our present era, which is sick with speeches."

Endnotes

CHAPTER 1 PETER'S UNSTEADY BARQUE

1 "The Papacy and the Burden of History," *The Tablet* Open Day 1998 Lecture, published in an abridged version as "The Popes: Theory and Fact," *The Tablet* (July 4, 1998), 873.

2 "The Third Millennium," *Sir Peter Ustinov's Inside the Vatican*, John McGreevy Productions, 1993.

3 J. Derek Holmes, "The 20th Century Popes," *The Tablet* (May 22, 1982), 514.

4 As quoted in Anthony Rhodes, *The Vatican in the Age of the Dictators, 1922–1945* (London: Hodder and Stoughton, 1973), 6.

5 Ronald Rolheiser, o.m.i., *The Catholic Herald* (June 30, 2000), 12.

6 Lawrence E. Schmidt, "Simone Weil's Understanding of Adolf Hitler, a Genius of the 'Physics of Human Matter'," an unpublished paper delivered to the annual colloquy of the American Weil Society, University of Chicago, April 23, 1999; pp. 6–7.

7 James M. Cameron, quoted in the Canadian Broadcasting Corporation's *Ideas* series, "Catholics," by Michael W. Higgins, originally aired in May 1984. This excerpt is from Program One: "After Me, the Flood."

8 Peter Hebblethwaite, quoted in *Ideas*, "Catholics," Program One: "After Me, the Flood."

9 Ibid.

10 Peter Hebblethwaite, *John XXIII: Pope of the Council* (London: Geoffrey Chapman, 1984), as quoted in *Ideas*, "Catholics," Program One: "After Me, the Flood."

11 Hebblethwaite, quoted in *Ideas*, "Catholics," Program One.

12 Peter Hebblethwaite, "The Mind of John Paul II," *Grail: an Ecumenical Journal*, vol. 1 (March 1985), 25.

13 John Paul II, *Crossing the Threshold of Hope*, Vittorio Messori, ed. (New York: Alfred A. Knopf, 1994), 158–159.

14 James Bentley, *God's Representatives: The Eight Twentieth-Century Popes* (London: Constable, 1997), 145.

15 Michael Walsh, "The Papacy in the Twentieth Century: 1878–The Present Day," in *The Papacy*, Michael Walsh, ed. (London: Weidenfeld & Nicolson, 1997), 206–207.

16 Michael W. Higgins and Douglas R. Letson, *My Father's Business: A Biography of His Eminence G. Emmett Cardinal Carter* (Toronto: Macmillan, 1990), 223–224.

17 John Cornwell, *A Thief in the Night: The Death of Pope John Paul I* (Harmondsworth: Penguin Books, 1990), 342.

18 Paul Johnson, "Introduction," in *The Papacy*, 6, 8.

19 J.M.R. Tillard, O.P., "The Mission of the Bishop of Rome: What Is Essential, What Is Expected?", *Ecumenical Trends*, vol. 27 (January 1998), 7, 8.

20 J.M.R. Tillard, O.P., *The Bishop of Rome* (Wilmington: Michael Glazier, 1983), 44.

21 As quoted in Michael W. Higgins, "Synod Diary," *Grail: An Ecumenical Journal*, vol. 2 (March 1986), 97.

22 Bernard Cooke, "New Light on the Papacy—Part Three," *National Catholic Reporter* (March 10, 1995), 13.

23 Patrick Granfield, *The Papacy in Transition* (Garden City: Doubleday, 1980), 194–195.

24 George Weigel, "The Chapel in the Mine," *The Tablet* (October 21, 2001), 1407.

25 John Paul II, *Crossing the Threshold of Hope*, 142.

26 Karol Wojtyla, *Easter Vigil & Other Poems*, translated by Jerzy Peterkiewicz (London: Hutchinson, 1979), 42.

27 Tad Szulc, *Pope John Paul II: The Biography* (New York: Scribner, 1995), 197.

28 André Frossard, *"Be Not Afraid:" André Frossard in Conversation with John Paul II*, translated by J.R. Foster (London: The Bodley Head, 1984), 125–127.

29 Garry Wills, *Papal Sin: Structures of Deceit* (New York: Doubleday, 2000), 215.

30 As quoted in Edward Stourton, *Absolute Truth: The Catholic Church in the World Today* (London: Viking, 1998), 79.

31 John Paul II, *Gift and Mystery: On the Fiftieth Anniversary of My Priestly Ordination* (New York: Doubleday, 1996), 33.

32 Claude Ryan, "Christians in Public Life," the inaugural John J. Wintermeyer Lecture in Christianity and Public Policy, St. Jerome's University, Waterloo, Ontario, October 18, 2000.

33 Luke Timothy Johnson, "A Disembodied 'Theology of the Body,'" *Commonweal* (January 26, 2001), 12–13.

34 Anthony Kenny, "The Pope as Philosopher," *The Tablet* (June 26, 1999), 876.

35 Dow Marmur, as quoted on "The Case of Martyr Teresa Benedicta," *Ideas*, by Myrna Kotash, originally aired in November 2000.

36 Istvan Deak, *The New York Review of Books* (March 23, 2000), 49.

37 John F. Morley, "Pacelli's Prosecutor," *Commonweal* (November 5, 1999), 28.

38 "Preliminary Report: The Vatican and the Holocaust," *Origins*, vol. 30, no. 22 (November 9, 2000), 345.

39 Ibid., 348, 351.

40 Cardinal Basil Hume, "Papal Primacy and Episcopal Authority—the Bishop in a Universal Church," *The Catholic Herald* (July 16, 1999), 5.

41 Father Richard Barrett, "Doubts *&* Queries," *The Catholic Herald* (June 16, 2000), 12.

42 Michael W. Higgins and Douglas R. Letson, eds., *Soundings: Conversations About Catholicism* (Ottawa: Novalis, 2000), 80–81.

43 Ibid., 27.

44 As quoted in Tim Ryan, S.F.M., "The Boff Case," *Grail: An Ecumenical Journal*, vol. 9 (September 1993), 31, 36.

45 Walter Principe, C.S.B., "Changing Church Teachings," *Grail: An Ecumenical Journal*, vol. 6 (September 1990), 36, 38, 39.

46 As quoted by Lawrence Barmann, letter to the editor, *Commonweal* (August 11, 2000), 2.

47 As quoted by Robert Markus in his review of Garry Wills's *Papal Sins: Structures of Deceit*, *The Tablet* (September 2, 2000), 1161–1162.

48 John Wilkins, "The Next Pope: The Papacy in the New Millennium," St. Jerome's University, Waterloo, Ontario, April 7, 2000.

CHAPTER 2 HEALTH CARE AND EDUCATION: THE PERILS OF SECULAR SOCIETY

1 For an excellent analysis of the situation, see "The Church in Quebec: The Catholic Church and the Political Evolution of Quebec, 1960–1980," written by that province's former leader of the Liberal Party, Claude Ryan. *Canadian Catholic Review*, vol. 2 (January 1984), 17–24.

2 Reginald Bibby, *Fragmented Gods: The Poverty and Potential of Religion in Canada* (Toronto: Irwin, 1987), 20.

3 Arthur Jones, "Huge Nonprofit System Feels Pressure to Cut Costs, Merge and Get Bigger," *National Catholic Reporter* (June 16, 1995), 15.

4 Richard McCormick, "The End of Catholic Hospitals?" *America*, vol. 179, no. 1 (July 4, 1998), 6.

5 Patricia Cahill, "The Environment in Which Catholic Health Care Finds Itself," *Origins*, vol. 27 (May 24, 1997), 28.

6 Dennis Brodeur's address is summarized in the marginalia of Joseph Bernardin, "Managing Managed Care," *Origins*, vol. 26, no. 2 (May 30, 1996), 22.

7 Joseph Bernardin, "The Case for Not-for-Profit Health Care," *Origins*, vol. 24, no. 32 (January 26, 1995), 541.

8 Joseph Bernardin, "The Consistent Ethic of Life and Health Care Reform," *Origins*, vol. 24, no. 4 (June 9, 1994), 63.

9 John Curley, Jr., "For-Profit Chains Seeking to Buy Catholic Hospitals," *Origins*, vol. 25, no. 5 (June 15, 1995), 79.

10 See Arthur Jones's special series of articles and graphs, which form a special section dealing with health care reform in the *National Catholic Reporter* (June 16, 1995), 11–17.

11 Jones, "Huge Nonprofit System Feels Pressure to Cut Costs, Merge and Get Bigger," 12.

12 See, for example, Bernardin, "The Consistent Ethic of Life and Health Care Reform," 60–64 and "Managing Managed Care," 21–26; Anthony Bevilacqua, "Catholic Health Care Collaborative Relationships," *Origins*, vol. 28, no. 38 (March 11, 1999), 657–660; Patricia Cahill, "Collaboration Among Catholic Health Providers," *Origins*, vol. 24, no. 12 (February 1, 1994), 212–214; Bernice Coreil, D.C., "Forging a Future for Catholic Health Care," *Origins*, vol. 22, no. 24 (November 26, 1992), 411–412.

13 Jones, "Huge Nonprofit System Feels Pressure to Cut Costs, Merge and Get Bigger," 12.

14 Cahill, "The Environment in Which Catholic Health Care Finds Itself," 27.

15 Joseph Bernardin, "Crossroads for Church's Health Care Ministry," *Origins*, vol. 22, no. 24 (November 26, 1992), 410.

16 Cahill, "Collaboration Among Catholic Health Providers," 212–214.

17 See the National Conference of Catholic Bishops' "Ethical and Religious Directives for Catholic Health Care Services," *Origins*, vol. 24, no. 27 (December 15, 1994), 449–462.

18 Justin Rigali, "Proposed Sale of Two Catholic Hospitals to For-Profit Chain," *Origins*, vol. 27, no. 21 (November 6, 1997), 362–364.

19 Bernard Law, "Statement Opposing the Sale of St. Louis University Hospital," *Origins*, vol. 27, no. 21 (November 6, 1997), 363.

20 See Lawrence Biondi, S.J., "A Context of Wrenching Changes in Health Care: The Plan to Sell St. Louis University Hospital," *Origins*, vol. 27, no. 30 (January 15, 1998), 502–505; and Justin Rigali, "St. Louis University Hospital Sold to For-Profit Corporation," *Origins*, vol. 27, no. 38 (March 12, 1998), 629–633.

21 Curley Jr., "For-Profit Chains Seeking to Buy Catholic Hospitals," 79.

22 Such, for example, was her message to the meeting of the Catholic Health Association meeting in Toronto on September 28, 2000.

23 Notes by the Honourable Elizabeth Witmer, minister of Health and Long-term Care, at the Catholic Health Association of Ontario, Toronto, September 28, 2000.

24 Michele Landsberg, "St. Mike's Religious Rules Undemocratic," *The Toronto Star* (May 30, 1998), A2.

25 Christopher J. Kaufman, *Ministry and Meaning: A Religious History of Catholic Health Care in the United States* (New York: Crossroads, 1995), 290–291.

26 Committee on Doctrine, United States Conference of Bishops, *Origins*, vol. 24, no. 27 (December 15, 1994), 453.

27 Ibid., 457, par. 45.

28 Rita Daly, "Defender of St. Mike's," *The Toronto Star* (December 14, 1997), F1.

29 Ibid., F2.

30 "The End of Catholic Hospitals?", 10.

31 Ibid., 6.

32 Catherine Thompson, "Hospital Merger Opposed," *The Record* (December 15, 1997), B1.

33 "Hospitals in Peril," *The Tablet* (March 6, 1999), 331.

34 Bernardin, "The Consistent Ethic of Life and Health Care Reform," 61.

35 Dalton Camp, "Conspiracy of Silence in Health Care," *The Toronto Star* (May 14, 2000), A13.

36 Joseph Gremillion, *The Gospel of Peace and Justice: Catholic Social Teaching Since Pope John* (New York: Orbis Books, 1976), 143–144.

37 See Douglas R. Letson, "Gerald Emmett Cardinal Carter: The Essence of Catholic Education," in *The Philosophy of Catholic Education*, Caroline DiGiovanni, ed. (Ottawa: Novalis, 1992); and Michael W. Higgins and Douglas R. Letson, *My Father's Business: A Biography of His Eminence G. Emmett Cardinal Carter* (Toronto: Macmillan, 1990).

38 See Douglas R. Letson and Michael W. Higgins, *The Jesuit Mystique* (Toronto: Macmillan, 1995).

39 D.W. Robertson, Jr., trans., *On Christian Doctrine* (New York: Bobbs-Merrill, 1958).

40 Charles C. Osgood, trans. *Boccaccio on Poetry* (New York: Bobbs-Merrill, 1956).

41 See, for example, Bernard F. Huppé, *Doctrine and Poetry* (New York: State University of New York, 1959) and *Fruyt and Chaf* (Princeton, New Jersey: Princeton University Press, 1963); and D.W. Robertson Jr., *A Preface to Chaucer: Studies in Medieval Perspectives* (Princeton University Press, 1964).

42 For a comment on the use of biography—that is, non-hagiographic story—as a teaching

device embedded in the Catholic tradition, see Michael W. Higgins, "Faith, Witness, and the Narrative: Biography as Teacher," in *Catholic Education: Transforming Our World, A Canadian Perspective* (Ottawa: Novalis, 1991), 115–128.

43 For a modern English translation, see Gussie Hecht Tanenhaus, "Bede's *De schematibus et tropis*—A Translation," *The Quarterly Journal of Speech*, vol. 48 (October 1962), 238–253.

44 See, for example, Jerome Taylor, trans., *Didascalicon of Hugo of St. Victor* (New York: Columbia University Press, 1961).

45 Herman Shapiro, trans., *Medieval Philosophy: Selected Readings from Augustine to Buridan* (New York: Modern Library, 1964), 368–383.

46 The reference is to the Jesuits' founding document, *Regimini militantis ecclesiae* as translated in John C. Olin, *The Catholic Reformation: Savonarola to Ignatius Loyola* (New York: Fordham University Press, 1992), 205.

47 Interview conducted in John Padberg's office on December 22, 1992.

48 Andrew M. Greeley and Peter H. Rossi, *The Education of Catholic Americans* (Chicago: Aldine Publishing, 1966).

49 William J. Gibbons, s.J., *7 Great Encyclicals* (New York: Paulist Press, 1963), 40.

50 Ibid., 45.

51 For comment on this and other decisions taken at the Third Plenary Council of Baltimore (1883–1884), see Stephen J. Denig, "Catholic Education in the United States," in *Commitment to Diversity: Catholics and Education in a Changing World*, Mary Eaton, Jane Longemore, and Arthur Naylor, eds. (London: Cassell, 2000), 224–225.

52 Although Canon 798 states that "Parents are to send their children to those schools which will provide for their catholic education," the 1983 revised Code of Canon Law is ambiguous in that it directs that "Catholic parents have also the duty and the right to choose those means and institutes which, *in their local circumstances*, can best promote the catholic education of their children" (Canon 793; italics added).

53 Gibbons, *7 Great Encyclicals*, 63. For an example of how this approach to objective study can be skewed by searching out a Catholic or Christian message in a manner wholly inconsistent with the text under review, see Patrick Kelly, "Frankenstein: In Defense of the Monster," *Canadian Catholic Review*, vol. 1, no. 1 (January 1983), 5–6.

54 Gerald Emmett Carter, *Psychology and the Cross* (Milwaukee: Bruce Publishing, 1959), 29.

55 For more detailed information on Carter's theory of Catholic education, see Letson, "Gerald Emmett Cardinal Carter" and Higgins and Letson, *My Father's Business*.

56 Gerald Emmett Carter, *The Catholic Public Schools of Quebec* (Toronto: W.J. Gage, 1957), 105.

57 Ibid., 111.

58 Gremillion, *The Gospel of Peace and Justice*, 339–340.

59 Walter M. Abbott, s.j., *The Documents of Vatican II* (Piscataway, New Jersey: New Century Publishers, 1966), 639–640.

60 Ibid., 642–643.

61 Sacred Congregation for Catholic Education, *The Catholic School* (Washington: Publications Office of the United States Catholic Conference, 1997), par. 1, p. 3. *The Catholic School* was issued under the authority of Cardinal Gabriel-Marie Garrone, the prefect of the Congregation for Catholic Education on March 19, 1977. The Congregation's 1988 document, "The Religious Dimension of Education in a Catholic School," begins with a similar reference to Vatican II and is in harmony with it, though this analysis is more practical and less philosophical and less inspirational in its development. See *Origins*, vol. 18, no. 14 (September 15, 1988), 213–228.

62 Ibid., par. 38, p. 218.

63 Interview with Doug McCarthy, s.j., in Toronto on July 7, 1994.

64 Abbott, *The Documents of Vatican II*, 649.

65 *Documents of the 31st and 32nd General Congregations of the Society of Jesus* (Saint Louis: The Institute of Jesuit Sources, 1977), 432.

66 Jon Sobrino, s.j., Ignacio Ellacuría, s.j., et al., *Companions of Jesus: The Jesuit Martyrs of El Salvador* (Maryknoll, New York: Orbis, 1990), 150.

67 Andrew M. Greeley, *The Catholic Myth: The Behaviour and Beliefs of American Catholics* (New York: Macmillan, 1990).

68 *Lay Catholics in Schools: Witnesses to Faith* was issued on October 15, 1982 under the name of the prefect of the Congregation, Cardinal William Baum, and its secretary, Archbishop Antonio Javierre. It appears in *Origins*, vol. 12, no. 29 (December 30, 1982), 457–469.

69 Andrew M. Greeley, William C. McCready, and Kathleen McCourt, *Catholic Schools in a Declining Church* (Kansas City: Sheed and Ward, 1976), 9.

70 Greeley, *The Catholic Myth*, 173–174.

71 Bruce S. Cooper, "National Crisis, Catholic Schools and the Common Good," in Terence McLaughlin, Joseph O'Keefe, s.j., and Bernadette O'Keeffe, eds., *The Contemporary Catholic School: Context, Identity, and Diversity* (Washington: Falmer Press, 1996), 42.

72 Ibid., 47.

73 Joseph O'Keefe, s.j., "No Margin, No Mission," in Terence McLaughlin, Joseph O'Keefe, s.j., and Bernadette O'Keeffe, eds., *The Contemporary Catholic School: Context, Identity, and Diversity* (Washington: Falmer Press, 1996), 182–188.

74 Ibid., 178–179.

75 Kathleen Kenna, "School Vouchers Colour U.S. Vote," *The Toronto Star* (September 17,

2000), B1, B4. For signs of the continuing debate in California and Michigan, see "Proposition 38: School Vouchers" and "Proposal 1: School Vouchers," *Origins*, vol. 30, no. 18 (October 12, 2000), 282–284.

76 Kenneth Westhues, "Catholic Separate Schools: An Ambiguous Legacy," *Grail: An Ecumenical Journal*, vol. 1, no. 1 (March 1985), 51–64; and "Separate Schools and Canadian Social Trends," *Grail: An Ecumenical Journal*, vol. 1, no. 2 (March/June, 1994), 168–186.

77 Kenneth Westhues, "Public vs. Sectarian Legitimation: The Separate Schools of the Catholic Church," *Canadian Review of Sociology and Anthropology*, vol. 13 (1976), 137–151.

78 See *Catholic New Times* (November 15, 1999), 1 and *The Record* (July 20, 2000), A4.

79 For a pre-referendum analysis of the situation, see Bonaventure Fagan, "The Royal Commission Report, Our Children, Our Future: A Challenge to Newfoundland's Denominational Education System," *Grail: An Ecumenical Journal*, vol. 9, no. 4 (December 1993), 62–81.

80 For a journalistic testimony to the events, see *The Catholic Register* (September 17, 1994), 3; (November 5, 1994), 3; (January 28, 1995), 3; (July 12, 1995), 1; (September 11, 1995), 1, 3; (November 13, 1995), 1, 3; *Catholic New Times* (December 15, 1996), 1, 15.

81 See *Catholic New Times* (May 4, 1997), 6, 7.

82 For an analysis of the full-funding event, see Higgins and Letson, *My Father's Business*, chapter ten, "Educator and Lobbyist" where the Donato cartoon is also reproduced.

83 Michael Swan, "Catholic Boards Win Preferential Court Case," *The Catholic Register* (November 8, 1999), 1.

84 Westhues, "Public vs. Sectarian Legitimation," 137–151.

85 Greeley et al., *Catholic Schools in a Declining Church*, 324–325.

86 See Susan Chalker Browne, "Resurrecting Catholic Education: Newfoundland Parents Find the High Cost of Religious Education Is Worth the Price," *The Catholic Register* (June 5, 2000), 9.

87 For an interesting historical analysis of the "dual system" of education in England, see Priscilla Chadwick, *Shifting Alliances: Church & State in English Education* (London: Cassell, 1997).

88 "Catholic Schools Top of the Class," *The Tablet* (December 12, 1998), 1666.

89 "A Century and a Half of Catholic Schools," *The Tablet* (October 4, 1997), 1272.

90 For a concise review of the issue, see Michael P. Hornsby-Smith, "Catholic Schooling in England and Wales," in *Commitment to Diversity: Catholics and Education in a Changing World*, Mary Eaton, Jane Longemore, and Arthur Naylor, eds. (London: Cassell, 2000), 194–195.

91 Terence McLaughlin, "Does This Vision Work?" *The Tablet* (October 9, 1999), 1357.

92 The case of St. Philip's receives detailed attention in *The Tablet* beginning in 1992, but for an

overview, see Vince Murray, "Other Faiths in Catholic Schools: General Implications of a Case Study," in McLaughlin et al., *The Contemporary Catholic School*, 239–253.

93 Michael Walsh, "The Battle of Philip's," *The Tablet* (October 10, 1992), 1261–1262; Gerard W. Hughes, s.j., "Shades of the Ghetto," *The Tablet* (November 7, 1992), 1396–1397.

94 Priscilla Chadwick, *Schools of Reconciliation: Issues in Joint Roman Catholic-Anglican Education* (London: Cassell, 1994), 25, 39, and 52.

95 McLaughlin et al., *The Contemporary Catholic School*, 13.

96 "Birmingham Plans to Scrap Ecumenical School," *The Tablet* (July 24, 1999), 1033.

97 Vincent Nichols, "My Difficult Decision," *The Tablet* (May 20, 2000), 701.

98 Priscilla Chadwick, "A Beacon Extinguished," *The Tablet* (May 20, 2000), 674–675.

99 Chadwick, *Schools of Reconciliation*, 39.

100 For a comment on a 1979 study, see ibid., 51.

101 See Robert Hughes, *The Fatal Shore* (London: Harvill Press, 1987), especially 181–195.

102 J.J. Mol, "The Effects of Denominational Schools in Australia," *The Australian and New Zealand Journal of Sociology*, vol. 4, no. 1 (April 1968), 18–35.

103 Manning Clark, *A Short History of Australia* (Toronto: Penguin, 1995), 28 and 48.

104 Edmund Campion, *Australian Catholics* (Toronto: Penguin, 1988), 71. See also the biography of Father Maurice O'Reilly, which Campion sketches in *Great Australian Catholics* (Richmond, Victoria: Aurora Books, 1997), 84.

105 Campion, *Australian Catholics*, 141.

106 Campion, *Great Australian Catholics*, 6.

107 Campion, *Australian Catholics*, 147.

108 Ibid., 62, 65.

109 Ibid., 235.

110 See, for example, McLaughlin, et al., *The Contemporary Catholic School*; Caroline Di Giovanni, ed., *The Philosophy of Catholic Education* (Ottawa: Novalis, 1992); Michael W. Higgins, Brian McGowan, Dennis Murphy, and Larry Trafford, eds., *Catholic Education: Transforming Our World, A Canadian Perspective* (Ottawa: Novalis, 1991); and *Grail: An Ecumenical Journal*, vol. 9, no. 4 (December 1993).

111 See Dennis Murphy, "Catholic Education: Towards the Third Millennium," *Grail: An Ecumenical Journal*, vol. 8, no. 2 (June 1992), 70.

112 "Formation of Priests in the Circumstances of the Present Day," Vatican Lineamenta, *Origins*, vol. 19, no. 3 (June 1, 1989), 40.

113 *Apostolic Constitution of the Supreme Pontiff John Paul II on Catholic Universities* (Vatican City: Libreria Editrice Vaticana, 1990), par. 31.999

114 Higgins and Letson, *My Father's Business*, 42.

115 "Rigorous Researchers, Faithful Disciples," *Origins*, vol. 30, no. 5 (June 15, 2000), 76.

116 For a detailed review of the case of Charles Curran, including his historical analysis of academic freedom and the evolution of Rome's current attitudes toward Canon 812, see *National Catholic Reporter*, "Is a Catholic College or University a Contradiction in Terms?" (December 2, 1988), 11, 14–15.

117 Morley Callaghan, *Such Is My Beloved* (Toronto: McClelland and Stewart, 1982), 74.

118 Richard McCormick, s.j., "Punishing Dissent: Corralling Theologians, Containing Bishops," *Commonweal* (August 14, 1998), 13.

119 Rosemary Radford Ruether, "Does 'Survival of the Fittest' Apply to Theologians?" *National Catholic Reporter* (December 2, 1988), 13.

120 *Origins*, vol. 18, no. 40 (March 16, 1989), 663.

121 Gibbons, 7 *Great Encyclicals*, 108.

122 Michael W. Higgins and Douglas R. Letson, eds. *Soundings: Conversations about Catholicism* (Ottawa: Novalis, 2000), 172–174.

123 Sobrino et al., *Companions of Jesus*, 157.

124 Henri Goudreault, o.m.i., "The Hierarchy and Roman Catholic Colleges," *Grail: An Ecumenical Journal*, vol. 6, no. 4 (December 1990), 71–72.

125 "'*Dominus Iesus*': On the Unicity and Salvific Universality of Jesus Christ and the Church," *Origins*, vol. 30, no. 14 (September 14, 2000), 217.

126 *Origins*, vol. 30, no. 14 (September 14, 2000), 220.

127 For a detailed discussion of the development of *Ex corde ecclesiae* and its political history up to its 1990 promulgation, especially as it relates to the United States, see Alice Gallin, o.s.u., *American Higher Education: Essential Documents, 1967–1990* (Notre Dame, Indiana: Notre Dame University Press, 1992).

128 "Observations of the Sacred Congregation for Catholic Education on the Project Document prepared by the Council and the Committee of the International Federation of Catholic Universities (fiuc/[ifcu]) during the meeting held at Grottaferrata-Rome" (February 3–5, 1972), May 20, 1972, par. A3.

128 *Apostolic Constitution of the Supreme Pontiff John Paul II on Catholic Universities*, par. 29.

130 John P. Langan, s.j., ed., *Catholic Universities in Church and Society: A Dialogue on "Ex Corde Ecclesiae"* (Washington, D.C.: Georgetown University Press, 1993).

131 See, for example, Leonard A. Kennedy, "The New Vatican Document on Catholic Universities," *Homiletic and Pastoral Review* (November 1989), 18–23; and Lynn Boughton, "Identity Crisis: What Constitutes a Catholic University?" *Christifidelis* (August 22, 1994), 4–8. Contrast the style and point of view with Francis J. Buckley, s.j., "Liberating the University: A Commentary on *Ex Corde Ecclesiae*," *Horizons*, vol. 19, no. 1 (1992), 99–108.

132 For Rome's response, see *Origins* (June 12, 1997), 53–55.

133 Goudreault, "The Hierarchy and Roman Catholic Colleges," 64.

134 Charles L. Currie, s.j., "Sunset or Sunrise?", *America*, vol. 182, no. 8 (May 20, 2000), 7–11.

135 See Douglas Letson, "Catholic Universities in the Modern World," *The Tablet* (February 10, 2001), 186–189.

136 See Arthur Naylor, "Teacher Education in Catholic Colleges in England," in *Commitment to Diversity: Catholics and Education in a Changing World*, Mary Eaton, Jane Longemore, and Arthur Naylor, eds. (London: Cassell, 2000), especially 12ff.

137 Dean Ashenden and Sandra Milligan, *The Good Guide to Australian Universities* (Subiaco, Western Australia: Ashenden Milligan Pty, 1966), 150.

CHAPTER 3   AND THE GREATEST OF THESE IS VIRGINITY:
SEX AND MARRIAGE

1 James Joyce, *A Portrait of the Artist as a Young Man* (Toronto: Penguin, 1966), 249.

2 Ibid., 253.

3 "Behind the Veil: Nuns," Margaret Wescott, director (Montreal: National Film Board of Canada, 1985).

4 Michael W. Higgins and Douglas R. Letson, *My Father's Business: A Biography of His Eminence G. Emmett Cardinal Carter* (Toronto: Macmillan, 1990), 47.

5 Douglas R. Letson, "Personal Reflections on the 1990 Synod of Bishops," *Grail: An Ecumenical Journal*, vol. 7, no. 1 (1991), 34. For outspoken examples of popalatry and the abuse of papal power, see Paul Collins, *Papal Power: A Proposal for Change in Catholicism's Third Millennium* (London: HarperCollins, 1997) and Garry Wills, *Papal Sin: Structures of Deceit* (Toronto: Doubleday, 2000).

6 Douglas R. Letson, ed. *Sex and Marriage in the Catholic Tradition: An Historical Overview* (Ottawa: Novalis, 2001), 27.

7 Ibid.

8 Ibid., 29.

9 Ibid.

10 Ibid., 30.

11 Arthur Jones, "Sex: Female, Religion: Catholic, Hopes: Few," *National Catholic Reporter* (September 12, 1986), 18.

12 Nathaniel Hawthorne, *The Scarlet Letter* (New York: W.W. Norton, 1961), 50.

13 John T. McNeil and Helena M. Gamer, eds., *Medieval Handbooks of Penance* (New York: Octagon Books, 1965), 197.

14 Ibid., 254.

15 Douglas R. Letson, ed. *Sex and Marriage in the Catholic Tradition*, 29.

16 Anthony Kosnik, et al., *Human Sexuality: New Directions in American Catholic Thought* (New York: Paulist Press, 1977), 42.

17 Douglas R. Letson, ed. *Sex and Marriage in the Catholic Tradition*, 91.

18 John H. Fisher, ed., *The Complete Poetry and Prose of Geoffrey Chaucer* (Toronto: Holt, Rinehart and Winston, 1977), 359.

19 Ibid., 869.

20 Douglas R. Letson, ed. *Sex and Marriage in the Catholic Tradition*, 36.

21 Ibid., 28–29.

22 Michael Novak, *Confessions of a Catholic* (New York: Harper and Row, 1983), 145.

23 Edith Hamilton and Huntington Cairns, eds., *The Collected Dialogues of Plato* (Princeton University Press, 1980), "Paedro," 81e, pp. 65–66; "Phaedrus," 250c, p. 497; "Cratylus," 400c, p. 437.

24 Walter Kaufmann, "The Inevitability of Alienation," in *Alienation*, Richard Schacht, ed. (New York: Doubleday, 1970).

25 W.S. Mackie, ed., *The Exeter Book* (Oxford University Press, 1958), 75–77.

26 Fisher, ed., *The Complete Poetry and Prose of Geoffrey Chaucer*, 312.

27 Helen Gardner, ed., *The Metaphysical Poets* (London: Penguin, 1975), 65.

28 Miriam K. Starkman, ed., *Seventeenth-Century Poetry* (New York: Alfred A. Knopf, 1967), vol. 1, 226.

29 Ibid., 219.

30 Hardin Craig, ed., *The Complete Works of Shakespeare* (Chicago: Scott Foresman and Company, 1951), III, iv, 17–19.

31 W.H. Gardner, ed., *Gerard Manley Hopkins* (London: Penguin, 1961), 31.

32 Joyce, *A Portrait of the Artist as a Young Man*, 122.

33 *Ecclesiastical History of the English Church*, I, xxvii, in Douglas R. Letson, *Sex and Marriage in the Catholic Tradition*, 90.

34 Ibid., 31.

35 Ibid., 30.

36 Fisher, ed., *The Complete Poetry and Prose of Geoffrey Chaucer*, 389.

37 Augustine, *The Good of Marriage* in *Treatises on Marriage and Other Subjects*, Charles T. Wilcox, M.M., trans., *The Fathers of the Church*, vol. 27 (Washington, D.C.: Catholic University of America Press, 1955), 9. Although Augustine had argued the absolute superiority of the virgin state, in his eyes even virginity is not as important as obedience since he also advised that "the more obedient wife is to be preferred to the less obedient virgin" (p. 46).

38 Fisher, ed., *The Complete Poetry and Prose of Geoffrey Chaucer*, 577.

39 John Milton, *Paradise Lost*, Merritt Y. Hughes, ed. (New York: Odyssey Press, 1962), 97.

40 As quoted by Donald Demarco in "Diary of an Embattled 'Sexist'," *Fidelity*, vol. 5 (April, 1986), 10.

41 Seymour L. Flaxman, *Three Plays by Ibsen* (New York: Bell Publishing, 1959), 197.

42 Benjamin Thorpe, *The Homilies of the Anglo-Saxon Church*, vol. 1 (New York: Ælfric Society, 1844), 148–149.

43 Fisher, ed., *The Complete Poetry and Prose of Geoffrey Chaucer*, 386.

44 Augustine, *Treatises on Marriage and Other Subjects*, *The Fathers of the Church*, vol. 27.

45 John Paul II, *The Role of the Christian Family in the Modern World: "Familiaris consortio"* (Boston: Daughters of St. Paul, 1981), 29–30.

46 F.A. Wright, *Select Letters of St. Jerome* (Cambridge, Mass.: Harvard University Press, 1930), 57.

47 Ibid., 253.

48 Ibid., 241.

49 Fisher, ed., *The Complete Poetry and Prose of Geoffrey Chaucer*, p. 116, l. 614.

50 Douglas R. Letson, ed. *Sex and Marriage in the Catholic Tradition*, 90.

51 *City of God*, XIV, xxiv–xxvi.

52 Douglas R. Letson, ed. *Sex and Marriage in the Catholic Tradition*, 37.

53 For an encapsulated examination of Augustine's attitudes on sex and marriage as well as of the thinking of the early Church Fathers, including the inclusion of primary Augustinian texts, see Elizabeth Clark, *St. Augustine on Marriage and Sexuality* (Washington, D.C.: Catholic University of America Press, 1996). The quotation is taken from Augustine's *Confessions* and is on p. 14.

54 Fisher, ed., *The Complete Poetry and Prose of Geoffrey Chaucer*, 388.

55 Malcolm Godden, ed., *Ælfric's Catholic Homilies* (Toronto: Oxford University Press, 1979), p. 343, ll. 263–264.

56 In his *The Good of Marriage*, Augustine argues that among married couples intercourse for the purpose of procreation is no sin, but intercourse simply for pleasure is a venial sin. Complete abstinence, he reasons, is the better plan. *Treatises on Marriage and Other Subjects*, 17.

57 Josef Raith, ed., *Die Altenglische Version des Haltgar'schen Bussbuches* (Darmstadt: Wissenschaftliche Buchgesellschaft, 1964), p. 28 par. 21.

58 McNeil and Gamer, eds., *Medieval Handbooks of Penance*, 197, 208.

59 Claudia Carlen, I.H.M., ed., *The Papal Encyclicals, 1878–1903* (McGrath Publishing, 1981), par. 28.

60 Augustine, *The Good of Marriage* in *Treatises on Marriage and Other Subjects*, 12.

61 William J. Gibbons, ed., *7 Great Encyclicals* (New York: Paulist Press, 1963), 5.

62 Ibid., 20.

63 Ibid., 79.

64 "Women Enhance a Man's Outlook, Especially Biblically," *The Record* (November 4, 2000), H8.

65 Bernard Häring, "Consulting the Faithful," *The Tablet* (July 24, 1993), 941.

66 As quoted by Peter Stanford, *Cardinal Hume and the Changing Face of English Catholicism* (London: Geoffrey Chapman, 1993), 172.

67 For an excellent summary of the mounting pressure in Europe, see Robert Blair Kaiser, *The Encyclical That Never Was* (London: Sheed and Ward, 1987).

68 For a complete list of the participants, see ibid., 297–300.

69 Report from Rome in *The Tablet* (October 31, 1987), 1189.

70 David Knowles, "Authentic Teaching," *The Tablet* (July 24, 1993), 939.

71 Paul VI, *Of Human Life: Humanae vitae* (Boston: St. Paul Books & Media, 1968).

72 Häring, "Consulting the Faithful," 941.

73 John Marshall, "Inside the Commission," *The Tablet* (July 24, 1993), 938.

74 Joyce, *A Portrait of the Artist as a Young Man*, 214.

75 Julian Morris [Morris West], *Moon in My Pocket* (Sydney: Australian Publishing Company, 1945), 176.

76 Ibid., 163.

77 Kaiser, *The Encyclical That Never Was*, 240–263.

78 Andrew Greeley, *The Catholic Myth* (Toronto: Maxwell Macmillan, 1990), 10–11.

79 Paul Collins, *Papal Power: A Proposal for Change in Catholicism's Third Millennium* (Toronto: HarperCollins, 1997), 88.

80 Donald Cozzens, "Telling the Truth," *The Tablet* (August 5, 2000), 1044.

81 Higgins and Letson, *My Father's Business*, 103.

82 Derived from an undated document sent to Rome after its approval by the Canadian Catholic Conference apparently in April 1964 and entitled "Report Concerning Birth Control in the Light of the Questionnaire Sent Out from the Holy See."

83 John Marshall, "True Meaning of Marriage," *The Tablet* (September 4, 1993), 1122.

84 Ibid., 1122–1123.

85 Andrew Greeley, *The American Catholic* (New York: Basic Books, 1977), 149.

86 Greeley, *The Catholic Myth*, 91.

87 The final report of the commission is reprinted from *The Tablet* (April 22, 1967) in Kaiser, *The Encyclical That Never Was*. Reference here is to pp. 6–7.

88 Kaiser, *The Encyclical That Never Was*, 10.

89 Ibid., 11.

90 *The Winnipeg Statement*, like several subsequent Canadian statements on *Humanae vitae*, are reprinted in E.F. Sheridan, s.j., ed., *Love Kindness! The Social Teaching of the Canadian Catholic Bishops* (Toronto: Jesuit Centre for Social Faith and Justice, 1991). Reference is to p. 144.

91 Ibid., 147.

92 Ibid., 127–134.

93 Ibid., 155.

94 Ibid., 165.

95 Cardinal Gerald Emmett Carter, *A Shepherd Speaks* (Toronto: Mission Press, undated), 72.

96 Ibid., (September 27, 1980), 82.

97 Ibid., (October 11, 1980), 87–88.

98 Ibid., (September 27, 1980), 81.

99 Ibid., 96.

100 Ibid., 99–100.

101 Michael McAteer, "Canadian Bishops Angry, Bitter Over Synod," *Toronto Star* (October 30, 1987), A1–A23.

102 For an analytical summary of Canadian participation in Episcopal Synods, see Michael W. Higgins and Douglas R. Letson, "Canadian Participation in Episcopal Synods, 1967–1985," *Historical Studies of the Canadian Catholic Historical Association*, vol. 54 (1987), 145–157.

103 Clifford Longley, "Hume's Mission Impossible," *The Tablet* (November 20, 1999), 1572.

104 Francis X. Murphy, C.Ss.R., "Of Sex and the Catholic Church," *The Atlantic Monthly* (February 1981), 44–57.

105 For a copy of the final message, see *The Tablet* (November 1, 1980), 1087–1089.

106 Kaiser, *The Encyclical That Never Was*, 279.

107 See, for example, Letson, "Personal Reflections on the 1990 Synod of Bishops," 34.

108 Kenneth Baker, "The 1980 Synod on the Family," *Homiletic and Pastoral Review*, vol. 81, no. 6 (February 1981), 18.

109 Pope John Paul II, *The Role of the Christian Family in the Modern World: "Familiaris Consortio"* (Boston: Daughters of St. Paul, 1981).

110 Annabel Miller, "How Natural Is NFP?", *The Tablet* (December 2, 2000), 1633.

111 Jack Dominian, "Sexuality—From Law and Biology to Love and Person," *Grail: An Ecumenical Journal*, vol. 4, no. 3 (September 1988), 41.

112 Jack Dominian, "The Use of Sex: Christian Marriage in a Changing World," *The Tablet* (February 11, 1984), 127.

113 Jack Dominian, *Proposals for a New Sexual Ethic* (London: Darton, Longman and Todd, 1977), 70.

114   Ibid., 81, 83.

115   Jack Dominian, "Person to Person: Christian Marriage in a Changing World," *The Tablet* (February 4, 1984), 101.

116   Ibid., 102.

117   Dominian, "Sexuality—From Law and Biology to Love and Person," 38–39.

118   Kate Saunders and Peter Stanford, *Catholics and Sex: From Purity to Perdition* (London: Heinemann, 1992).

119   Stanford, *Cardinal Hume and the Changing Face of English Catholicism*, 168.

120   Ibid., 170.

121   Joseph Ratzinger, "Vatican Says Father Curran Can't Teach Theology," *Origins*, vol. 16, no. 11 (August 28, 1986), 201.

122   Ibid., 203.

123   André Guindon, *The Sexual Creators: An Ethical Proposal for Concerned Christians* (Boston: University Press of America, 1986), 175.

124   Art Babych, "Coalition Explores Idea of 'Dysfunctional Church'," *Catholic New Times* (May 16, 1993), 13.

125   Art Babych, "Father André Guindon Dies Suddenly," *Catholic New Times* (November 7, 1983), 1.

126   André Guindon, *The Sexual Language: An Essay in Moral Theology* (Ottawa: University of Ottawa Press, 1976).

127   André Guindon, *Moral Development, Ethics and Faith* (Ottawa: Novalis, 1992).

128   Guindon, *The Sexual Language: An Essay in Moral Theology*, 2.

129   Ibid., 25ff.

130   Guindon, *The Sexual Creators*, 68.

131   Ibid., 32.

132   Ibid., 51.

133   Guindon, *The Sexual Language*, 199.

134   Joseph Gremillion, *The Gospel of Peace and Justice* (Maryknoll, New York: Orbis, 1976), *Gaudium et spes*, section 52, p. 289.

135   Ibid., section 62, p. 298.

136   Ibid., section 62, p. 299.

137   Douglas R. Letson, ed. *Sex and Marriage in the Catholic Tradition*, Ia Q. 92, art. 1 reply 1, p. 29.

138   "The Good of Marriage," in Douglas R. Letson, ed. *Sex and Marriage in the Catholic Tradition*, p. 83. See also p. 69 and p. 75.

139   Guindon, *The Sexual Language*, 63.

140 Ibid., 367.

141 Ibid., 368.

142 Congregation for the Doctrine of the Faith, "The Pastoral Care of Homosexual Persons," *Origins*, vol. 16, no. 22 (November 13, 1986), 380.

143 Ibid., 380.

144 "Bishop Speaks of Church's Sins Against Homosexuals," *The Tablet* (January 6, 2001), 28.

145 Jeannine Gramick and Robert Nugent, *Building Bridges: Gay and Lesbian Reality and the Catholic Church* (Mystic, Conn.: Twenty-Third Publications, 1992).

146 Jeannine Gramick and Robert Nugent, eds., *Voices of Hope* (New York: Centre for Homophobia Education, 1995).

147 An interview with Dr. Mary Sheridan, in ibid., 25.

148 Gramick and Nugent, *Voices of Hope*, 92.

149 Ibid., 107.

150 Ibid., 132.

151 Ibid., 188.

152 Joseph Ratzinger, "Notification Regarding Sister Gramick and Father Nugent," *Origins*, vol. 29, no. 9 (July 29, 1999), 133–136.

153 See, for example, Simon Caldwell, "Gay Group Challenges Vatican Ban," *The Catholic Herald* (July 30, 1999), 1–2; "Vatican Was Jury, Judge and Prosecutor, Gramick Says," *The Tablet* (July 31, 1999), 1059–1060 as well as the letters to the editor in the same edition, pp. 1050–1051 as well as in subsequent issues, especially November 13 and November 20; Sidney Callahan, "Sexuality and Homosexuality: The Church's Gordian Knot," *Commonweal* (September 10, 1999), 7–8; Lisa Sowle Cahill, "Silencing of Nugent, Gramick Sets a Novel Standard of Orthodoxy," *America* (August 14, 1999), 6–11; Gerald Coleman, "Ministry to Homosexuals Must Use Authentic Church Teaching," *America* (August 14, 1999), 12–14; "A Response: Two Persons Whose Ministry to Gays and Lesbians Has Come Under Scrutiny from a Critic," *America* (October 9, 1999), 16–17; Bishop Joseph Fiorenza, "Statement Regarding Vatican Notification on Sister Gramick and Father Nugent," *Origins*, vol. 29, no. 26 (December 9, 1999), 417–420; "Sister Gramick and Father Nugent Called to Rome," a series of related statements by the School Sisters of Notre Dame, Jeannine Gramick, the Salvatorian Province, and Robert Nugent, *Origins*, vol. 30, no. 4 (June 8, 2000), 62–64.

154 "Bishop Meets Homosexual Challengers," *The Tablet* (June 20, 1998), 824. A report based on an article by Chris McGillion, reporter for the *Sydney Morning Herald*.

155 Eileen P. Flynn, "Responding to the 'Gay Agenda'," *America* (September 30, 2000), 16.

156 Shawn Zeller, "Dignity's Challenge: Can Homosexuals Feel at Home in Catholicism?"

Commonweal (July 14, 2000), 17–19. For a balanced and anecdotal analysis of Courage and other such initiatives within a Canadian context, see Anne Bacani, "Gay Catholics Look to Their Faith," *The Catholic Register* (June 19, 2000), 9.

157   Laureen McMahon, "Same-Sex Decision Disappoints Bishop," *The Catholic Register* (June 12, 2000), 16.

158   Zeller, "Dignity's Challenge," 18. See also Cardinal Roger Mahony, "Statement on Proposition 22, Same-Sex Marriage Initiative," *Origins*, vol. 29, no. 29 (January 6, 2000), 465–467. The sidebar in the *Origins* article provides a quick history of the question of same-sex marriages in the United States.

159   Andrew M. Brown, "Marriage Rate Lowest Since 1926, as Divorce Rate Rises," *The Catholic Herald* (February 6, 1998), 3.

160   James Griffin, "Marriage: Foundation of Social Life," *Origins*, vol. 29, no. 34 (February 10, 2000), 557.

161   National Catholic Conference of Bishops, "Marriage Preparation and Cohabiting Couples: Information Report," *Origins*, vol. 29, no. 14 (September 16, 1999), 213–224.

162   Michael Sheehan, "Cohabitation and Marriage in the Church," *Origins*, vol. 29, no. 14 (September 16, 1999), 224–225.

163   Report by President Jack Costello, "From the President's Desk," *The Regis News* (Fall 1997), 2.

164   See, for example, Susan A. Ross, "Extravagant Affections: Women's Sexuality and Theological Anthropology," in *In the Embrace of God: Feminist Approaches to Theological Anthropology*, Ann O'Hara Graff, ed. (Maryknoll, New York: Orbis, 1995), 105–121; Lisa Sowle Cahill, "Feminism and Christian Ethics," in *Freeing Theology: The Essentials of Theology in Feminist Perspective*, Catherine Mowry LaCugna, ed. (San Francisco: HarperSanFrancisco, 1993), 211–234; and Lisa Sowle Cahill, *Women and Sexuality* (New York: Paulist Press, 1992).

165   Walter M. Abbott, s.j., ed., *The Documents of Vatican II* (Piscataway, N.J.: New Century Publishers, 1966), 733.

166   Social Affairs Committee of the Assembly of Quebec Bishops, *A Heritage of Violence? A Pastoral Reflection on Conjugal Violence*, Antoinette Kinlough, trans. (Montreal: L'Assemblée des évêques du Québec, 1989), 34–40.

167   William Langland, *Piers the Ploughman*, J.F. Goodridge, trans. (Toronto: Penguin, 1971), 215.

168   John Paul II, "The Ratified and Consummated Sacramental Marriage," *Origins*, vol. 29, no. 34 (February 10, 2000), 555.

169   Timothy J. Buckley, C.Ss.R., *What Binds Marriage?: Roman Catholic Theology in Practice* (London: Geoffrey Chapman, 1997).

170   Ibid., 7.

171 Eamon Duffy, *Saints and Sinners: A History of the Popes* (London: Yale University Press, 1997).

172 Richard P. McBrien, *Lives of the Popes: The Pontiffs from St. Peter to John Paul II* (Toronto: HarperCollins, 1997).

173 Edmund Campion, *Australian Catholics* (Toronto: Penguin, 1987), 108.

174 A. Richard Sipe, "The Problem of Prevention in Clergy Sexual Abuse," in *Bless Me Father For I Have Sinned: Perspectives on Sexual Abuse Committed by Roman Catholic Priests*, Thomas J. Plante, ed. (Westport, Connecticut: Praeger, 1999), 121–122.

175 Thomas C. Fox, "Sex and Power Issues Expand Clergy-Lay Rift," *National Catholic Reporter* (November 13, 1992), 18.

176 "Survey of U.S. Priests Ordained Five to Nine Years," *Origins*, vol. 20, no. 42 (March 28, 1991), 690.

177 Rembert Weakland, "Reflections for Rome," *America*, vol. 178, no. 13 (April 18, 1988), 12.

CHAPTER 4   THE CURSE OF CLERICALISM

1 "Sex, Power and Priesthood," *The Tablet* (March 24, 2001), 432–433; "Abused Nuns: The Evidence," *The Tablet* (March 31, 2001), 467–468.

2 John Paul II, *The Role of the Christian Family in the Modern World: "Familiaris Consortio"* (Boston: Daughters of St. Paul, 1981), art. 60, p. 89.

3 Walter M. Abbott, s.J., ed., *The Documents of Vatican II* (Piscataway, New Jersey: New Century Publishers, 1966), *Lumen gentium*, art. 10, p. 27.

4 Ibid., art. 11, p. 29.

5 Ibid., art. 21, p. 41.

6 Ibid., art. 28, p. 53.

7 Ibid., art. 31, p. 57.

8 Ibid., art. 9, pp. 553–554.

9 Ibid., art. 13, p. 562.

10 Ibid., art. 8, p. 24.

11 Michael W. Higgins and Douglas R. Letson, *My Father's Business: A Biography of His Eminence G. Emmett Cardinal Carter* (Toronto: Macmillan, 1990), 47.

12 "Right so as bees out swarmen from the hyve, / Out of the develes ers ther gonne dryve / Twenty thousand freres in a route. . . ." Geoffrey Chaucer, *The Complete Poetry and Prose of Geoffrey Chaucer*, John H. Fisher, ed. (Toronto: Holt, Rinehart and Winston, 1977), "The Summoner's Prologue," p. 134, ll. 1693–1695.

13 Chaucer's "Retraction," in ibid., p. 397, l. 1083.

14 Ibid., p. 307, l. 3443.

15 See Dante's letter to Lord Can Grande della Scala in P. Toynbee, ed., *Dantis Alagherii Epistolae* (Oxford: Clarendon, 1966), 198 where Dante discusses the polysemous nature of *The Divine Comedy* and relates the allegorical structure to biblical exegesis.

16 See Charles G. Osgood, trans., *Boccaccio on Poetry* (New York: Bobbs-Merrill, 1956), 58–69.

17 Augustine, *On Christian Doctrine*, D.W. Robertson, Jr., trans. (New York: Bobbs-Merrill, 1958), 135.

18 Thomas Wright, ed., *The Political Songs of England from John to Edward II* (London: John Bowyer, 1839), 32–33.

19 Ibid., 45.

20 Ibid., 137–148.

21 Ibid., 155–159.

22 J.A.W. Bennett and G.V. Smithers, eds., *Early Middle English Verse and Prose* (Oxford: Clarendon Press, 1966), 136–144.

23 William Langland, *Piers the Ploughman*, J.F. Goodridge, trans. (Toronto: Penguin, 1971), 27.

24 John Gower, *Confessio Amantis*, Terence Tiller, ed. (Toronto: Penguin, 1963).

25 Abbott, ed., *The Documents of Vatican II*, art. 12, pp. 558–559.

26 Fisher, ed., *The Complete Poetry and Prose of Geoffrey Chaucer*, p. 109, ll. 115–117.

27 Abbott, ed., *The Documents of Vatican II*, art. 16, p. 567.

28 Ibid., art. 13, pp. 561–562.

29 Ibid., art. 6, p. 545.

30 Donald Cozzens, *The Changing Face of the Priesthood* (Collegeville, Minnesota: Liturgical Press, 2000), 120. Cozzens is referring here specifically to the crisis of clerical abuse with respect to child sexual abuse, but his book is much more far-reaching and the sentiment is hardly restricted to this one issue.

31 "Study of U.S. Diocesan Priesthood Statistics: 1966–2005," *Origins*, vol. 20, no. 13 (September 6, 1990), 206–208.

32 Canadian Conference of Catholic Bishops, "The Ministry of Priests," *Origins*, vol. 19, no. 41 (March 15, 1990), 661–664.

33 "The Winter Report on Sexual Abuse: Conclusions," *Catholic New Times* (September 9, 1990), 9–12.

34 For an overview of the Canadian scene in the late 1980s and early 1990s, see Michael W. Higgins, "Catholics in Shock," *The Tablet* (September 22, 1990), 1187–1188; and "Focus on Sexual Abuse," *The Tablet* (February 13, 1993), 194–196. See also the Canadian Conference

of Catholic Bishops, "Fifty Recommendations: The Church and Child Sexual Abuse," *Origins*, vol. 22, no. 7 (June 25, 1992), 97–107.

35 See, for example, Michael W. Higgins and Douglas R. Letson, "Canadian Participation in Episcopal Synods, 1967–1985." *Historical Studies of the Canadian Catholic Historical Association*, vol. 54 (1987), 145–157.

36 Thomas P. Rausch, "Forming Priests for Tomorrow's Church: The Coming Synod," *America*, vol. 162, no. 7 (February 24, 1990), 168–172.

37 "Canadian Participation in the 1985 Extraordinary Synod," CCCB bulletin number 1178. For an extended discussion on the Synod process as well as of the 1990 Episcopal Synod, see Douglas R. Letson, "Personal Reflections on the 1990 Synod of Bishops," *Grail: An Ecumenical Journal*, vol. 7, no. 1 (1991), 24–48.

38 Taken from an unpublished copy of his remarks, which he made available for the use of the media attending the Synod.

39 Jonathan Luxmoore, "Act VII: Enter Pope John Paul," *The Tablet* (May 31, 1997), 698.

40 Both the text of the Message to the People of God and a sampling of the forty-one proposals can be found in *Origins*, vol. 20, no. 22 (November 8, 1990), 351–353, 353–355.

41 "Redistributing Priests Worldwide," an intercongregational Vatican document published by *Origins*, vol. 20, no. 42 (March 28, 1991), 681–685.

42 John Paul II, *Pastores dabo vobis*, *Origins*, vol. 21, no. 45 (April 16, 1992), 719–758.

43 Ibid., 720.

44 Ibid., 724.

45 Ibid., 726.

46 Ibid., 731.

47 Ibid., 749.

48 A. Richard Sipe, "The Problem of Prevention in Clergy Sexual Abuse," in *Bless Me Father For I Have Sinned: Perspectives on Sexual Abuse Committed by Roman Catholic Priests*, Thomas J. Plante, ed. (Westport, Connecticut: Praeger, 1999), 111–134.

49 Jim McHugh, "An Abuse of Power, A Betrayal of Trust: The Emperor Has No Clothes," *Grail: An Ecumenical Journal*, vol. 7, no. 2 (June 1991), 18–39.

50 A summary of the findings appears in *Origins*, vol. 20, no. 42 (March 28, 1991), 688–690. Another finding of note is that U.S. priests ordained between five and nine years (the target group for the survey) said that they are "least comfortable with the governance of the church and with its moral teachings."

51 John Allan Loftus, S.J., *Understanding Sexual Misconduct by Clergy: A Handbook for Ministers* (Washington, D.C.: Pastoral Press, 1994), 4–5.

52   Thomas C. Fox, "Sex and Power Issues Expand Clergy-Lay Rift," *National Catholic Reporter* (November 13, 1992), 17.

53   Sipe, "The Problem of Prevention in Clergy Sexual Abuse," 123–125.

54   Thomas J. Plante, ed., *Bless Me Father For I Have Sinned: Perspectives on Sexual Abuse Committed by Roman Catholic Priests* (Westport, Connecticut: Praeger, 1999).

55   Thomas J. Plante, "Conclusion: Sexual Abuse Committed by Roman Catholic Priests: Current Status, Future Objectives," in ibid., 172.

56   Sipe, "The Problem of Prevention in Clergy Sexual Abuse," 114–115.

57   Ibid., 127.

58   John Allan Loftus, "Sexuality in Priesthood: *Noli me tangere*," in *Bless Me Father For I Have Sinned: Perspectives on Sexual Abuse Committed by Roman Catholic Priests*, Thomas J. Plante, ed. (Westport, Connecticut: Praeger, 1999), 7–20.

59   Ibid., 10.

60   Much has been written about the problems encountered by the Christian Brothers in Australia. For a brief overview, see Alan Gill, "Children for Export," *The Tablet* (August 8, 1998), 1029–1030; and "Christian Brothers in the Dock," *The Tablet* (August 8, 1998), 1046.

61   Thomas Keneally, *Three Cheers for the Paraclete* (Toronto: Penguin, 1968).

62   Thomas Keneally, *Homebush Boy* (London: Hodder & Stoughton, 1995).

63   Ibid., 81–82.

64   Ibid., 86–87.

65   Julian Morris (Morris West), *Moon in My Pocket* (Sydney: Australian Publishing Company, 1945).

66   Ibid., 5.

67   Ibid., 18.

68   Ibid., 29.

69   Ibid., 12.

70   Michael W. Higgins and Douglas R. Letson, eds., *Soundings: Conversations About Catholicism* (Ottawa: Novalis, 2002), 192.

71   Ibid., 193.

72   Ibid., 192.

73   Carolyn Butler, ed., *Faith, Hope, & Chastity: Honest Reflections from the Catholic Priesthood* (London: HarperCollins, 1999).

74   Adrian Hastings, *The Faces of God: Essays on Church and Society* (London: Geoffrey Chapman, 1975).

75   Ibid., 148–150.

76   Adrian Hastings, *In Filial Disobedience* (Great Wakering, Essex: Mayhew McCrimmon, 1978).

77 *The Catholic Register* (November 11, 1996), 2. The reference is to an essay in the editorial section of the October 27 issue of the *Milwaukee Journal-Sentinel*. See also his previous determination to raise the issue, *The Tablet* (February 2, 1991), 143, "Archbishop Weakland Ready to Propose Married Priests."

78 Luke Coppen, "Days of Priestly Celibacy Could Be Numbered, Says Bishop," *The Catholic Herald* (October 16, 1998), 3.

79 "Ordain Mature Married Men, Bishop Urges," *The Tablet* (July 8, 2000), 935.

80 John Thavis, "Canadian Bishops Ask Vatican for Married Priests in the North," *Catholic New Times* (October 10, 1993), 1.

81 Andrew Britz, o.s.b., "Married Priests: Enculturating the Gospel Among Native Peoples," *Catholic New Times* (October 24, 1993), 5.

82 Bishop Francis T. Hurley of Anchorage, Alaska, admits that the discussion is not about to cease, but he argues in favour of maintaining the discipline in "The Return to Ministry of Inactive Married Priests," *America*, vol. 178, no. 6 (February 28, 1998), 13–16.

83 Letter to the editors of *The Tablet* (May 29, 1999), 747.

84 Cozzens, *The Changing Face of the Priesthood*, 98–99, provides a quick survey of recent studies.

85 Andrew Greeley, "Bishops Paralyzed Over Heavily Gay Priesthood," *National Catholic Reporter* (November 10, 1989), 13.

86 Richard P. McBrien, "Homosexuality and the Priesthood: Questions We Can't Keep in the Closet," *Commonweal* (June 19, 1987), 380–383.

87 Jon Fuller, "Priests with aids," *America*, vol. 182, no. 9 (March 18, 2000), 7–9.

88 Yves Congar, *Lay People in the Church* (London: Geoffrey Chapman, 1985).

89 Ibid., 47.

90 Ibid., 304.

91 Ibid., 271.

92 Ibid., 323.

93 Abbott, ed., *The Documents of Vatican II*, art. 11, p. 503.

94 Ibid., art. 17, p. 507.

95 Walter M. Abbott, s.j., ed., *The Documents of Vatican II*, "A Response to Apostolicam actuositatem," 522–525.

96 The Message is reprinted in *Origins*, vol. 17, no. 22 (November 12, 1987), 385–389.

97 Ibid., item 3, p. 387.

98 The Pope's homily is reprinted in *Origins*, vol. 17, no. 22 (November 12, 1987), 390–392.

99 Ibid., items 5 and 6, p. 391.

100 Ibid., item 7, p. 391.

101 Alice Gallin, o.s.u., *Independence and a New Partnership in Catholic Higher Education* (Notre Dame, Indiana: University of Notre Dame Press, 1996).

102 Sacred Congregation for Catholic Education, "The Religious Dimension of Education in a Catholic School," *Origins*, vol. 18, no. 14 (September 15, 1988), 38, 218.

103 "Some Questions Regarding Collaboration of Nonordained Faithful in Priests' Sacred Ministry," *Origins*, vol. 27, no. 24 (November 27, 1997), 397–409; the document is followed by the Vatican's explanation as to the significance of the document: "The Instruction: An Explanatory Note," 409–410.

104 "Some Questions Regarding Collaboration of Nonordained Faithful in Priests' Sacred Ministry," 400.

105 Peter Hebblethwaite, "Visiting Pope Listed, Rejected Lay 'Ministry'," *National Catholic Reporter* (October 2, 1987), 5.

106 "Some Questions Regarding Collaboration of Nonordained Faithful in Priests' Sacred Ministry," 402.

107 Ibid., 403.

108 Ibid., 404.

109 "Call to Priesthood Falling on Deaf Ears," *The Record* (February 24, 2001), H7.

110 Donald Cozzens, "Facing the Crisis in the Priesthood," *America*, vol. 183, no. 14 (November 4, 2000), 17. See also Robert G. Kennedy, "Will We Ever Have Enough Priests?" *America*, vol. 177, no. 6 (September 13, 1997), 18–22.

111 Chris McGillion, "Rome, Take Note: Father's Days Are Numbered," *The Sydney Morning Herald* (August 8, 2000), 13; Joe Jenkins and Andrew M. Brown, "Dublin Acts to Counter Vocations Crisis," *The Catholic Herald* (October 24, 1997), 1.

112 Vatican Congregation for Divine Worship and the Sacraments, "Summary of the New General Instruction of the Roman Missal," *Origins*, vol. 30, no. 10 (August 3, 2000), 153–160.

113 "Some Questions Regarding Collaboration of Nonordained Faithful in Priests' Sacred Ministry," 401.

114 John Wijngaards, "Don't Cage the Sacred," *The Tablet* (September 23, 2000), 1256–1257.

115 Joseph Fessio's intervention has been reprinted in *Origins*, vol. 17, no. 22 (November 12), 397–399.

116 Michael McAteer, "Canadian Bishops Angry, Bitter Over Synod," *The Toronto Star* (October 30, 1987), A1, A23.

117 Walter M. Abbott, s.j., ed., *The Documents of Vatican II* (Piscataway, New Jersey: New Century Publishers, 1966), "*To Women*," 733.

118 Ia, Q. xcii, ad. 2. Ecclesiastical History Society, *Women and the Church: A Sourcebook*, p. 15.

119   St. Thomas Aquinas, *Summa Theologica*, vol. 3, translated by the Fathers of the English Dominican Province (New York: Benzinger Brothers, 1947, 1948). Supplement, Q. 39, art. 1: "Whether the Female Sex Is an Impediment to Receiving Orders," p. 2698.

120   Ibid., IIa, IIae, Q. 177, art. 2.

121   See "Women and Church," *Origins*, vol. 14, no. 46 (May 2, 1985), 750–756.

122   The Synod interventions and Mary Kenny's January 26, 1985 *Tablet* article "Could the Feminists Destroy Christianity?" have been reprinted in *Women and the Church: A Sourcebook*.

123   Michael W. Higgins and Douglas R. Letson, eds. *Women and the Church: A Sourcebook* (Toronto: Griffin House, 1986), 127. *Inter insigniores* can also be found in *Origins*, vol. 6, no. 33 (February 3, 1977).

124   John Paul II, *Mulieris dignitatem*, "On the Dignity and Vocation of Women," *Origins*, vol. 18, no. 17 (October 6, 1988), 275.

125   Ibid., 276.

126   Ibid., 279.

127   The exchange of correspondence between John Paul II, Robert Runcie, and Joannes Willebrands is published in *Origins*, vol. 16, no. 8 (July 17, 1986), 153–160.

128   *Origins*, vol. 16, no. 8 (July 17, 1986), 157.

129   John Paul II, *Ordinatio sacerdotalis*, "Apostolic Letter on Ordination and Women," *Origins*, vol. 24, no. 4 (June 9, 1994), 49.

130   Peter Hebblethwaite, "From JPII Superstar to a Super Surprise?", *National Catholic Reporter* (September 11, 1992), 5.

131   Patsy McGarry, "Nun Decides to Quit Rather Than Recant," *Catholic New Times* (February 6, 2000), 14.

132   See, for example, Charles Donahue, Jr., "Theology, Law & Women's Ordination: *Ordinatio sacerdotalis* One Year Later," *Commonweal* (June 2, 1995), 11–16.

133   Susan A. Ross, "Like a Fish Without a Bicycle? Virtually No Women's Religious Community Deals the Eucharist Without Some Pain," *America* (November 27, 1999), 10–13.

134   The initial draft was published in *Origins*, vol. 17, no. 45 (April 21, 1988), 757–788.

135   See Jean Forest, "Women in the Canadian Context," *Grail: An Ecumenical Journal*, vol. 1, no. 4 (December 1984), 13–23; Elisabeth Lacelle, "From Today to Tomorrow: Women in the Canadian Catholic Church, *Grail: An Ecumenical Journal*, vol. 1, no. 2 (June 1984), 25–32; "Jean Forest," in Michael W. Higgins and Douglas R. Letson, *Portraits of Canadian Catholicism* (Toronto: Griffin House, 1986); CCCB Information release OPI-355, by Bonnie Brennan on October 25, 1985, "Role of Women in the Church." *The Globe and Mail* editorial for October 29, 1984, entitled "In Reasonable Tones," recounts some of the divisions

that surfaced at the plenary session and denounces the Toronto bishops for their opposition to the women's presentation; a subsequent article by Denys Hogan, "RC Debate on Women's Issues: Power Remains Solely for Men," *The Globe and Mail*, 16, details some of the contrary positions taken by various of the bishops.

136 Australian Bishops, "Response to Research: Women's Participation in the Church," *Origins*, vol. 30, no. 18 (October 12, 2000), 276–280.

137 See, for example, a comment on the situation in the United States by Albert DeIanni, "A View of Religious Vocations," *America*, vol. 178, no. 6 (February 28, 1998), 8–12; see, too, Paul Wilkes, "The Hands That Would Shape Our Souls," *The Atlantic Monthly* (December 1990), 59–88, in which Wilkes notes not only the conservatism of the modern seminarian but the fact that Catholic seminaries, for the most part, no longer attract top-quality students academically; indeed, Wilkes argues that the academic quality would be only mediocre on average if it were not for the presence of bright women who are also registered in seminary programs. For a Canadian comment, see Art Babych, "Few Diocese Tap into Order's Priestly Resources," *The Catholic Register* (October 18, 1999), 1, 3, and Eugene McCarthy, "Latin Attachment," *The Saturday Record* (April 8, 2000), 8.1. And for an English perspective, see "The New Traditionalists," *The Catholic Herald* (March 20, 1998), 7.

138 Vicky Cosstick, "Let Down the Drawbridge," *The Tablet* (July 29, 2000), 1012.

139 Kennedy, "Will We Ever Have Enough Priests?", 21–22, argues that one way to solve the problem of numerical shortfall is to empower the laity, an option he says will never be realized unless the pastors have a dramatic change of heart with respect to clerical–lay collaboration.

140 See, for example, Joe Jenkins and Deborah Jones, "Bishops Plan Guide to No-Priest Services," *The Catholic Herald* (June 6, 1977), 1.

141 Priestly Life and Ministry Committee of NCCB, "Reflections on the Morale of Priests," *Origins*, vol. 18, no. 31 (January 12, 1989), 497–505.

142 John Wijngaards, "When Women Were Deacons," *The Tablet* (May 8, 1999), 623–624; see also, the supporting response by Kyriaki Karidoyanes FitzGerald, *The Tablet* (May 29, 1999), 746. For the original documentation, see "The Permanent Diaconate," *Origins*, vol. 28, no. 11 (August 27, 1998), 179–181; "Basic Norms for the Formation of Permanent Deacons," *Origins*, vol. 28, no. 11 (August 27, 1998), 181–191; "Directory for the Ministry and Life of Permanent Deacons," *Origins*, vol. 28, no. 11 (August 27, 1998), 191–204.

143 Elena Curti, "Who Are the Neo-Cats?", *The Tablet* (January 6, 2001), 10–11.

144 Michael Walsh, *Opus Dei: An Investigation into the Secret Society Struggling for Power within the Roman Catholic Church* (Toronto: HarperCollins, 1991); Vittorio Messori, *Opus*

Dei: Leadership and Vision in Today's Catholic Church (Washington, D.C.: Regnery Publishing, 1997).

CHAPTER 5   SPIRITUAL IN ESSENCE AND FORM

1 Peter Schjeldahl, "High Folderol," *The New Yorker* (July 19, 1999), 89.

2 Brocard Sewell, O.Carm., *The Habit of a Lifetime: An Autobiography* (Padstow: Tabb House, 1992), 46.

3 Ibid., 163.

4 Michael Ford, *Wounded Prophet: A Portrait of Henri J.M. Nouwen* (New York: Doubleday, 1999), 46.

5 Henri J.M. Nouwen, *Show Me the Way: Readings for Each Day of Lent* (New York: Crossroad, 1995), 134.

6 Henri J.M. Nouwen, *Making All Things New: An Invitation to the Spiritual Life* (San Francisco: HarperSan Francisco, 1981), 36.

7 Henri J.M. Nouwen, "A Spirituality of Peace-Making," inaugural Devlin Lecture delivered at St. Jerome's University, Waterloo, Ontario, September 12, 1982.

8 Henri J.M. Nouwen, *Our Greatest Gift: A Meditation on Dying and Caring* (San Francisco: HarperSanFrancisco, 1994), 38.

9 Jean Vanier, *Community & Growth: Our Pilgrimage Together* (Toronto: Griffin House, 1979), 199.

10 Jean Vanier, *Becoming Human* (Toronto: Anansi/CBC, 1988), 86.

11 James H. Clarke, *L'Arche Journal: A Family's Experience in Jean Vanier's Community* (Toronto: Griffin House, 1973), 35.

12 James H. Clarke, *The Raggedy Parade* (Toronto: Exile Editions, 1998).

13 Clarke, *L'Arche Journal*, 137–138.

14 Sheila Cassidy, "The Word Is Wild," *Grail: An Ecumenical Journal*, vol. 3 (March 1987), 57, 61–62.

15 Sheila Cassidy, *Good Friday People* (New York: Orbis, 1991), 79.

16 Donald Nicholl, "Holiness—A Call to Radical Living," *Grail: An Ecumenical Journal*, vol. 5 (December 1989), 68–69.

17 Donald Nicholl, *"Scientia Cordis," The Beatitude of Truth: Reflections of a Lifetime* (London: Darton, Longman and Todd, 1977), 161.

18 Kathy Shaidle, "Illness a Harsh But Welcome Teacher," *The Toronto Star* (December 13, 1998), F4.

19 Kathy Shaidle, "Women, Poetry and the Cult of the Victim," *The Toronto Star* (February 6, 2000), B2.

20 Kathy Shaidle, "That Photograph of Flannery O'Connor," *Lobotomy Magnificat* (Ottawa: Oberon, 1997), 24.

21 Kathy Shaidle, *God Rides a Yamaha: Musings on Pain, Poetry, and Pop Culture* (Vancouver: Northstone, 1998), 118.

22 Raimundo Panikkar, *Blessed Simplicity: The Monk as Universal Archetype* (New York: The Seabury Press, 1982), 11, 15.

23 Michael W. Higgins, *Heretic Blood: The Spiritual Geography of Thomas Merton* (Toronto: Stoddart, 1998), 2–3.

24 Thomas Merton, *A Vow of Conversation: Journals 1964–1965* (New York: Farrar, Straus, Giroux, 1988), 200–201.

25 Michael W. Higgins and Bernie Lucht, *Heretic Blood: An Audiobiography of Thomas Merton*, Canadian Broadcasting Corporation, 1998.

26 John Eudes Bamberger, OCSO, quoted in the Canadian Broadcasting Corporation's *Ideas* series, "Monasticism as Rebellion," by Michael W. Higgins, originally aired in December 1986. This excerpt is from Program Three: "At the Heart of Emptiness."

27 John Eudes Bamberger, OCSO, "Thomas Merton and Henri Nouwen: Living with God in Modern America," *The Merton Seasonal: A Quarterly Review* (Summer 2000), 30–31.

28 Dom John Main, O.S.B., quoted in *Ideas*, "Monasticism as Rebellion," Program Three: "At the Heart of Emptiness."

29 Neil McKenty, quoted in *Ideas*, "Monasticism as Rebellion," Program Three: "At the Heart of Emptiness."

30 Laurence Freeman, O.S.B., quoted in *Ideas*, "Monasticism as Rebellion," Program Three: "At the Heart of Emptiness."

31 Laurence Freeman, O.S.B., "Prayer and Peace," a public lecture delivered at the St. Jerome's Centre for Catholic Experience, St. Jerome's University, Waterloo, Ontario, January 29, 1988.

32 John Skinner, "Prayer Is a Way of Life—It's All Very Simple," *The Catholic Herald* (November 5, 1999), 5.

33 Kathleen Norris, *The Cloister Walk* (New York: Riverhead Books, 1996), 232.

34 Ibid., 234–235.

35 Irma Zaleski, *Mother Macrina* (Ottawa: Novalis, 2000), 57.

36 As quoted in the Canadian Broadcasting Corporation's *Ideas* series, "The Jesuit Mystique," by Michael W. Higgins, originally aired in November and December 1995. This excerpt is from Program One.

37   Michael W. Higgins and Douglas R. Letson, *The Jesuit Mystique* (Toronto: Macmillan, 1995), 80, 82, 83.

38   "The Directed Retreat: John English, s.J., in conversation with Tom Clancy, s.J., October 7, 1977," Symposium on Ignatian Spirituality: The Formation of Christian Leadership for the New Millennium—Implications of the Contribution of John English, s.J., to the Ministry of the Spiritual Exercises, held at Loyola House, Guelph Centre of Spirituality, Guelph, Ontario, July 18–21, 1999.

39   CBC's *Ideas*, "The Jesuit Mystique," Program One.

40   Joseph A. Tetlow, s.J., "The Spiritual Exercises in the Twentieth Century," *Jesuits: Yearbook of the Society of Jesus 2000* (Rome: General Curia of the Society of Jesus, 1999), 36.

41   Brian Terrell, "Monastic Roots of the Catholic Worker Movement," *The Mustard Seed* (Easter 2000), 7.

42   Andrew Cash, "Tough Love," *Now* (July 6–12, 2000), 17, 30.

43   Albert Nolan, o.P., "Poor in Spirit," *Grail: An Ecumenical Journal*, vol. 7 (March 1991), 20, 22, 23.

44   Dean Riley, "Sharing a Common Vision," *Scarboro Missions* (October 2000), 3.

45   Ellen Leonard, "Emerging Communities of Dialogue and Mission," *Grail: An Ecumenical Journal*, vol. 8 (September 1992), 12–13, 23.

46   Mary C. Grey, *The Outrageous Pursuit of Hope: Prophetic Dreams for the Twenty-First Century* (London: Darton, Longman and Todd, 2000), 32, 33.

47   Michael W. Higgins, *The Muted Voice: Religion and the Media* (Ottawa: Novalis, 2000), 9.

48   Mary T. Malone, "Living Without a Why," *Doctrine & Life*, vol. 49 (September 1999), 403–404.

Bibliography

INTERVIEWS

Antonello, Bruce. Chair of the Catholic Health Association of Ontario and President of St. Mary's
 General Hospital. Kitchener, Ontario. February 3, 2000.

Baumann, Paul. Associate Editor, *Commonweal*. New York, New York. December 18, 1996.

Baum, Greg. Theologian, McGill University. Montreal, Quebec. December 11, 1996.

Bélanger, Martin, P.S.S., Rector, Pontifical Canadian College. Rome, Italy. May 4, 1999.

Carpenter, Peter. Dean of Arts and Science, ACU, Mount St. Mary Campus. Strathfield, Australia.
 April 20, 1998.

Carter, Gerald Emmett. Cardinal. Toronto, Ontario. December 4, 1996.

Casanova, José. Chair, Department of Sociology, New York School for Social Research.
 Waterloo, Ontario. September 22, 2000.

Coughlan, Michael. Principal and CEO, Trinity and All Saints College. Horsforth, Leeds,
 England. December 10, 1999.

Daly, Gabriel, O.S.A. Theologian. Dublin, Ireland. February 19, 1997.

Davenport, Tony. Director, Programmes, Newman College. Bartley Green, Birmingham,
 England. December 13, 1999.

Dempsey, Luke, O.P. Theologian, Basilica of San Clemente. Rome, Italy. April 26, 1999.

Drake, Peter. Founding President, Australian Catholic University. Clareville, Australia. April 21,
 1998.

Eaton, Mary. Vice-Principal, St. Mary's College. Strawberry Hill, Twickenham, England.
 December 7, 1999.

Ertel, Grant. Member, Supreme Council of the Knights of Columbus. Waterloo, Ontario. February 25, 2000.

Falez, Stefan. Ambassador, Knights of Malta to the Vatican. Rome, Italy. May 3, 1999.

Gascoigne, Robert. Chair of Theology, ACU, Mount St. Mary Campus. Strathfield, Australia. April 20, 1998.

Griffith, Michael. Department of Literature and Languages, ACU, Mount St. Mary Campus. Strathfield, Australia. April 20, 1998.

Gumbleton, Thomas. Bishop of Detroit. Waterloo, Ontario. February 10, 1998.

Hansen, Ron. Novelist. Santa Clara, California. April 18, 2000.

Hass, Richard. Business Manager, *Commonweal*. New York, New York. December 18, 1996.

Hastings, Adrian. Theologian. Oxford, England. February 18, 1997.

Hayes, Michael. Chaplain, Digby Stuart College, Roehampton Institute. London, England. December 7, 1999.

Hebblethwaite, Margaret. Assistant Editor, *The Tablet*. London, England. December 9, 1999.

Hellwig, Monika. Executive Director and Theologian, ACCU. Washington, D.C. February 3, 1998.

Hope, Harriet. Director, Santa Sabina Retreat Centre. St. Rafael, California. April 17, 2000.

Hoyt, Robert G. Senior Writer, *Commonweal*. New York, New York. December 18, 1996.

Hughes, Gerry, S.J. Spiritual Director and author. Birmingham, England. December 11, 1999.

Jordan, Patrick. Managing Editor, *Commonweal*. New York, New York. December 18, 1996.

Kelly, Jim. Sociologist, Fordham University. New York, New York. December 17, 1996.

Keneally, Thomas. Novelist. Bilgola Beach, Australia. April 21, 1998.

Kenny, Mary. Journalist. London, England. December 8, 1999.

Lucie-Smith, Alexander. Parish priest and novelist. London, England. February 17, 1997.

MacDonald, Sutherland, C.R. Superior General of the Congregation of the Resurrection. Rome, Italy. May 1, 1999.

Mackay, Gordon, Q.C. Knight of Holy Sepulchre, Knight of Malta, Knight of Columbus. Waterloo, Ontario. April 14, 1999.

MacPherson, John. North American representative to the Sovereign Council for the Knights of Malta. Halifax, Nova Scotia. February 10, 1999.

Malarkey, Susannah, O.P. Coordinator, Santa Sabina Retreat Centre. St. Rafael, California. April 17, 2000.

Maloney, Frank. Theologian, ACU, Christ Campus. Melbourne, Australia. April 22, 1998.

McCormack, Alan. Canon Lawyer. Casa del' Clero, Italy. April 26, 1999.

McDonagh, Enda. Theologian, St. Paul's University. Ottawa, Ontario. October 16, 1997.

McKittrick, Tony. Director, International Education, ACU, MacKillop Campus. North Sydney, Australia. April 20, 1998.

McLoughlin, David. Chaplain and Professor of Theology, Newman College. Bartley Green, Birmingham, England. December 13, 1999.

Porter, Bernadette. Rector and CEO, Roehampton Institute. London, England. December 7, 1999.

Prendergast, Terrence, S.J. Archbishop of Halifax. Halifax, Nova Scotia. February 11, 1999.

Prince, Bernard. Msgr. Official, Congregation for the Evangelization of Peoples. Rome, Italy. April 30, 1999.

Privett, Steve, S.J. President-Elect, San Francisco University. Santa Clara, California. April 18, 2000.

Prusak, Bernard G. Intern journalist, *Commonweal*. New York, New York. December 18, 1996.

Ray, Brian. Principal and CEO, Newman College. Bartley Green, Birmingham, England. December 13, 1999.

Rigelhof, T.F. Novelist and journalist. Montreal, Quebec. December 11, 1996.

Sheehan, Peter. President, Catholic University of Australia, MacKillop Campus. North Sydney, Australia. April 20, 1998.

Skillin, Edward S. Publisher, *Commonweal*. New York, New York. December 18, 1996.

Spackman, Frances. Acting Principal, Digby Stuart College, Roehampton Institute. London, England. December 7, 1999.

Stanford, Peter. Journalist and author. London, England. December 8, 1999.

Steinfels, Margaret O'Brien. Editor, *Commonweal*. New York, New York. December 18, 1996.

Tanguay, H. E. Ambassador Fernand. Canadian Ambassador to the Vatican. Rome, Italy. April 30, 1999.

Taylor, Arthur. Principal and CEO, St. Mary's College. Strawberry Hill, Twickenham, England. December 7, 1999.

Taylor, Pamela. Vice-Principal, Newman College. Bartley Green, Birmingham, England. December 13, 1999.

Taylor, Ruth E. Advertising Manager, *Commonweal*. New York, New York. December 18, 1996.

Wahl, Jim, C.R. Professor of History and member of the Marriage Tribunal, St. Jerome's University. Waterloo, Ontario. February 17, 2000.

West, Morris. Novelist. Avalon, Australia. April 21, 1998.

SOURCES

Abbott, Walter M., S.J. *The Documents of Vatican II*. Piscataway, New Jersey: New Century Publishers, 1966.

Allen, John L., Jr. "Exclusive Claim," *National Catholic Reporter*, September 15, 2000.

Apostolic Constitution of the Supreme Pontiff John Paul II on Catholic Universities. Vatican City: Libreria Editrice Vaticana, 1990.

Ashenden, Dean, and Sandra Milligan. *The Good Guide to Australian Universities*. Subiaco, Western Australia: Ashenden Milligan Pty, 1966.

Augustine, Saint. "The Good of Marriage." In *Treatises on Marriage and Other Subjects*, translated by Charles T. Wilcox, M.M. The Fathers of the Church, vol. 27. Washington: Catholic University of America Press, 1955.

———. *On Christian Doctrine*. Translated by D.W. Robertson, Jr. New York: Bobbs-Merrill, 1958.

Babych, Art. "Father André Guindon Dies Suddenly," *Catholic New Times*, November 7, 1983.

———. "Coalition Explores Idea of 'Dysfunctional Church'," *Catholic New Times*, May 16, 1993.

———. "Few Diocese Tap into Order's Priestly Resources," *The Catholic Register*, October 18, 1999.

Bacani, Anne. "Gay Catholics Look to Their Faith," *The Catholic Register*, June 19, 2000.

Baker, Kenneth. "The 1980 Synod on the Family," *Homiletic and Pastoral Review* 81:6, February 1981.

Bamberger, John Eudes, O C S O. Quoted in the Canadian Broadcasting Corporation's *Ideas* series, "Monasticism as Rebellion," by Michael W. Higgins, originally aired December 1986. Excerpt from Program Three: "At the Heart of Emptiness."

———. "Thomas Merton and Henri Nouwen: Living with God in Modern America," *The Merton Seasonal: A Quarterly Review*, Summer 2000.

Barrett, Richard. "Doubts & Queries," *The Catholic Herald*, 16 June 2000.

Bennett, J.A.W. and G.V. Smithers, eds. *Early Middle English Verse and Prose*. Oxford: Clarendon Press, 1966.

Bentley, James. *God's Representatives: The Eight Twentieth-Century Popes*. London: Constable, 1997.

Bernardin, Joseph. "Crossroads for Church's Health Care Ministry," *Origins* 22:24, November 26, 1992.

———. "The Consistent Ethic of Life and Health Care Reform." *Origins* 24:4, June 9, 1994.

———. "The Case for Not-For-Profit Health Care," *Origins* 24:32, January 26, 1995.

———. "Managing Managed Care," *Origins* 26:2, May 30, 1996.

Bevilacqua, Anthony. "Catholic Health Care Collaborative Relationships," *Origins* 28:38, March 11, 1999.

Bibby, Reginald. *Fragmented Gods: The Poverty and Potential of Religion in Canada*. Toronto: Irwin, 1987.

Biondi, Lawrence, S.J. "A Context of Wrenching Changes in Health Care: The Plan to Sell St. Louis University Hospital," *Origins* 27:30, January 15, 1998.

Britz, Andrew, o.s.b. "Married Priests: Enculturating the Gospel Among Native Peoples," *Catholic New Times*, October 24, 1993.

Brown, Andrew M. "Marriage Rate Lowest Since 1926, as Divorce Rate Rises," *The Catholic Herald*, February 6, 1998.

Buckley, Timothy J., C.Ss.R., *What Binds Marriage? Roman Catholic Theology in Practice*. London: Geoffrey Chapman, 1997.

Butler, Carolyn, ed. *Faith, Hope, & Chastity: Honest Reflections from the Catholic Priesthood*. London: HarperCollins, 1999.

Burtchaell, James Tunstead. *The Dying of the Light: The Disengagement of Colleges and Universities from Their Christian Churches*. Grand Rapids, Michigan: William B. Eerdmans, 1998.

Cahill, Patricia. "Collaboration Among Catholic Health Providers," *Origins* 24:12, February 1, 1994.

———. "The Environment in Which Catholic Health Care Finds Itself," *Origins* 27:2, May 24, 1997.

Cahill, Lisa Sowle. *Women and Sexuality*. New York: Paulist Press, 1992.

———. "Feminism and Christian Ethics." In Catherine Mowry LaCugna, ed., *Freeing Theology: The Essentials of Theology in Feminist Perspective*. San Francisco: HarperSanFrancisco, 1993.

———. "Silencing of Nugent, Gramick Sets a Novel Standard of Orthodoxy," *America* 181, August 14, 1999.

Caldwell, Simon. "Gay Group Challenges Vatican Ban," *The Catholic Herald*, July 30, 1999.

Callaghan, Morley. *Such Is My Beloved*. Toronto: McClelland and Stewart, 1982.

Callahan, Sidney. "Sexuality and Homosexuality: The Church's Gordian Knot." *Commonweal*, September 10, 1999.

Cameron, James M. Quoted in the Canadian Broadcasting Corporation's *Ideas* series, "Catholics," by Michael W. Higgins, originally aired in May 1984. Excerpt from Program One: "After Me, the Flood."

Camp, Dalton. "Conspiracy of Silence in Health Care," *The Toronto Star*, May 14, 2000.

Campion, Edmund. *Australian Catholics*. Toronto: Penguin, 1987.

———. *Great Australian Catholics*. Richmond, Victoria: Aurora, 1997.

Carter, Gerald Emmett. *The Catholic Public Schools of Quebec*. Toronto: W. J. Gage, 1957.

———. *Psychology and the Cross*. Milwaukee: Bruce Publishing, 1959.

———. *The Modern Challenge to Religious Education*. New York: William Sadler, 1961.

———. *A Shepherd Speaks*. Toronto: Mission Press, undated.

Cash, Andrew. "Tough Love," *Now*, July 6–12, 2000.

Cassidy, Sheila. "The Word is Wild," *Grail: An Ecumenical Journal* 3, March 1987.

Cassidy, Sheila *Good Friday People*. New York: Orbis, 1991.

"Catholic schools are vital for handing on the faith." *The Tablet*, July 31, 1999.

"Catholic University in the Modern World." Paper presented to the Congress of the Catholic Universities of the World, Rome, November 20–29, 1972.

Chadwick, Priscilla. *Schools of Reconciliation: Issues in Joint Roman Catholic-Anglican Education*. London: Cassell, 1994.

———. *Shifting Alliances: Church and States in English Education*. London: Cassell, 1997.

———. "A Beacon Extinguished," *The Tablet*, May 20, 2000.

Chalker Browne, Susan. "Resurrecting Catholic Education: Newfoundland Parents Find the High Cost of Religious Education is Worth the Price," *The Catholic Register*, June 5, 2000.

Clark, Elizabeth. *St. Augustine on Marriage and Sexuality*. Washington: Catholic University of America Press, 1996.

Clark, Manning. *A Short History of Australia*. Toronto: Penguin, 1995.

Clarke, James H. *L'Arche Journal: A Family's Experience in Jean Vanier's Community*. Toronto: Griffin House, 1973.

———. *The Raggedy Parade*. Toronto: Exile Editions, 1998.

Code of Canon Law. Ottawa: Canadian Conference of Catholic Bishops/Collins, 1983.

Coleman, Gerald. "Ministry to Homosexuals Must Use Authentic Church Teaching," *America* 181, August 14, 1999.

Collins, Paul. *Papal Power: A Proposal for Change in Catholicism's Third Millennium*. London: HarperCollins, 1997.

Congar, Yves. *Lay People in the Church*. London: Geoffrey Chapman, 1985.

Congregation for Catholic Education. *The Catholic School*. Washington: Publications Office of the United States Catholic Conference, 1997.

———. "Lay Catholics in Schools: Witnesses to Faith," *Origins* 12:29, December 30, 1982.

———. "The Religious Dimension of Education in a Catholic School," *Origins* 18:14, September 15, 1988.

Congregation for the Doctrine of the Faith. "The Pastoral Care of Homosexual Persons," *Origins* 16:22, November 13, 1986.

———. "Vatican Says Father Curran Can't Teach Theology," *Origins* 16:11, August 28, 1986.

———. "Notification Regarding Sister Gramick and Father Nugent," *Origins* 29:9, July 29, 1999.

———. "Dominus Iesus: On the Unicity and Salvific Universality of Jesus Christ and the Church," *Origins* 30:14, September 14, 2000.

Cooke, Bernard. "New Light on the Papacy—Part Three," *National Catholic Reporter*, March 10, 1995.

Cooper, Bruce S. "National Crisis: Catholic Schools and the Common Good." In Terence McLaughlin, Joseph O'Keefe, s.j., and Bernadette O'Keeffe, eds., *The Contemporary Catholic School: Context, Identity, and Diversity*. Washington: Falmer Press, 1996.

Coppen, Luke. "Days of Priestly Celibacy Could Be Numbered," *The Catholic Herald*, October 16, 1998.

Coreil, Bernice, D.C. "Forging a Future For Catholic Health Care," *Origins* 22:24, November 26, 1992.

Cornwell, John. *A Thief in the Night: The Death of Pope John Paul I*. Harmondsworth: Penguin Books, 1990.

Cosstick, Vicky. "Let Down the Drawbridge," *The Tablet*, July 29, 2000.

Cozzens, Donald. *The Changing Face of the Priesthood*. Collegeville, Minnesota: Liturgical Press, 2000.

———. "Telling the Truth," *The Tablet*, August 5, 2000.

———. "Facing the Crisis in the Priesthood," *America* 183:14, November 4, 2000.

Craig, Hardin, ed. *The Complete Works of Shakespeare*. Chicago: Scott Forseman and Company, 1951.

Curley, John Jr. "For-profit Chains Seeking to Buy Catholic Hospitals," *Origins* 25:5, June 15, 1995.

Curran, Charles E. *Catholic Higher Education, Theology, and Academic Freedom*. Notre Dame, Indiana: Notre Dame University Press, 1990.

Currie, Charles L., s.j. "Sunset or Sunrise?" *America* 182:18, May 20, 2000.

Curti, Elena. "Who are the Neo-Cats?" *The Tablet*, January 6, 2001.

Daly, Rita. "Defender of St. Mike's," *The Toronto Star*, December 14, 1997.

Deak, Istvan. *The New York Review of Books*, March 23, 2000.

DeIanni, Albert. "A View of Religious Vocations," *America* 178:6, February 28, 1998.

Demarco, Donald. *Fidelity* 5, April 1986.

Desiato, Tonia. "End Funding Inequity, Keep Preferential Hiring, Education Report Says," *The Catholic Register*, January 11, 1995.

Di Giovanni, Caroline, ed. *The Philosophy of Catholic Education*. Ottawa: Novalis, 1992.

Documents of the 31st and 32nd General Congregations of the Society of Jesus. St. Louis: The Institute of Jesuit Sources, 1977.

Dolphin, Frank. "Catholic Hospitals Feel Threatened by Coming Reforms to Canadian Health Care System," *The Catholic Register*, April 8, 1995.

———. "Loss of Separate Schools Feared: Catholic Educators Prepare Battle Against Alberta Legislation," *The Catholic Register*, July 15, 1995.

Dominian, Jack. *Proposals for a New Sexual Ethic*. London: Darton, Longman and Todd, 1977.

———. "Person to Person: Christian Marriage in a Changing World," *The Tablet*, February 4, 1984.

———. "The Use of Sex: Christian Marriage in a Changing World," *The Tablet*, February 11, 1984.

———. "Sexuality—From Law and Biology to Love and Person," *Grail: An Ecumenical Journal* 4:3, September 1988.

Donohue, Charles Jr. "Theology, Law & Women's Ordination: *Ordinatio sacerdotalis* One Year Later," *Commonweal*, June 2, 1995.

Duffy, Eamon. *Saints and Sinners: A History of the Popes*. London: Yale University Press, 1997.

Edwards, David. *A Concise History of English Christianity: From Roman Britain to the Present Day*. London: HarperCollins, 1998.

English, John, S.J. "The Directed Retreat: John English, S.J., in Conversation With Tom Clancy, S.J., October 7, 1977." In *Symposium on Ignatian Spirituality: The Formation of Christian Leadership for the New Millennium—Implications of the Contribution of John English, S.J. to the Ministry of the Spiritual Exercises*, July 18–21, 1999. Held at Loyola House, Guelph Centre of Spirituality, Guelph, Ontario.

Fagan, Bonaventure. "The Royal Commission Report, *Our Children, Our Future*: A Challenge to Newfoundland's Denominational Education System," *Grail: An Ecumenical Journal* 9:4, December 1993.

Fiorenza, Joseph. "Statement Regarding Vatican notification on Sister Gramick and Father Nugent," *Origins* 29:26, December 9, 1999.

Fisher, John H., ed. *The Complete Poetry and Prose of Geoffrey Chaucer*. Toronto: Holt, Rinehart and Winston, 1977.

Flaxman, Seymour L. *Three Plays by Ibsen*. New York: Bell Publishing, 1959.

Flynn, Eileen P. "Responding to the 'Gay Agenda'," *America* 180, September 30, 2000.

Ford, Michael. *Wounded Prophet: A Portrait of Henri J. M. Nouwen*. New York: Doubleday, 1999.

Fox, Thomas C. "Sex and Power Issues Expand Clergy-Lay Rift," *National Catholic Reporter*, November 13, 1992.

———. *Sexuality and Catholicism*. New York: George Braziller, 1995.

Freeman, Laurence, O.S.B. Quoted in the Canadian Broadcasting Corporation's *Ideas* series, "Monasticism as Rebellion," by Michael W. Higgins, originally aired December 1986. Excerpt from Program Three: "At the Heart of Emptiness."

———. "Prayer and Peace," a public lecture delivered at the St. Jerome's Centre for Catholic Experience, St. Jerome's University, Waterloo, Ontario, January 29, 1988

Frossard, André. *"Be Not Afraid": André Frossard in Conversation with John Paul II*, translated by J.R. Foster. London: The Bodley Head, 1984.

Fuller, Jon. "Priests with AIDS." *America* 182:9, March 18, 2000.

Gallin, Alice, o.s.u. *American Higher Education: Essential Documents, 1967–1990*. Notre Dame, Indiana: University of Notre Dame Press, 1992.

———. *Independence and a New Partnership in Catholic Higher Education*. Notre Dame, Indiana: University of Notre Dame Press, 1996.

Gardner, Helen, ed. *The Metaphysical Poets*. London: Penguin, 1975.

Gardner, W.H., ed. *Gerard Manley Hopkins*. London: Penguin, 1961.

Gibbons, William J., s.j. *7 Great Encyclicals*. New York: Paulist Press, 1963.

Gill, Alan. "Children for Export," *The Tablet*, August 8, 1998.

Godden, Malcolm, ed., *Ælfric's Catholic Homilies*. Toronto: Oxford University Press, 1979.

Goudreault, Henri, o.m.i. "The Hierarchy and Roman Catholic Colleges," *Grail: An Ecumenical Journal* 6:4, December 1990.

Gramick, Jeannine, and Robert Nugent. *Building Bridges: Gay and Lesbian Reality and the Catholic Church*. Mystic, Connecticut: Twenty-Third Publications, 1992.

Gramick, Jeannine, and Robert Nugent, eds. *Voices of Hope*. New York: Centre for Homophobia Education, 1995.

Gramick, Jeannine, and Robert Nugent. "A Response: Two Persons Whose Ministry to Gays and Lesbians Has Come Under Scrutiny Respond to a Critic," *America* 181, October 9, 1999.

Granfield, Patrick. *The Papacy in Transition*. Garden City: Doubleday, 1980.

Greeley, Andrew M., and Peter H. Rossi. *The Education of Catholic Americans*. Chicago: Aldine Publishing, 1966.

Greeley, Andrew M., William C. McCready, and Kathleen McCourt. *Catholic Schools in a Declining Church*. Kansas City: Sheed and Ward, 1976.

Greeley, Andrew M. *The American Catholic: A Social Portrait*. New York: Basic Books, 1977.

———. "Bishops Paralyzed Over Heavily Gay Priesthood," *National Catholic Reporter*, November 10, 1989.

———. *The Catholic Myth: The Behavior and Beliefs of American Catholics*. New York: Macmillan, 1990.

Grey, Mary C. *The Outrageous Pursuit of Hope: Prophetic Dreams for the Twenty-First Century*. London: Darton, Longman and Todd, 2000.

Gremillion, Joseph. *The Gospel of Peace and Justice: Catholic Social Teaching Since Pope John*. New York: Orbis Books, 1976.

Griffin, James. "Marriage: Foundation of Social Life." *Origins* 29:34, February 10, 2000.

Guindon, André. *The Sexual Language: An Essay in Moral Theology*. Ottawa: University of Ottawa Press, 1976.

———. *The Sexual Creators: An Ethical Proposal for Concerned Christians*. Boston: University Press of America, 1986.

———. *Moral Development, Ethics and Faith*. Ottawa: Novalis, 1992.

Hamilton, Edith, and Huntington Cairns, eds. *The Collected Dialogues of Plato*. Princeton University Press, 1980.

Häring, Bernard. "Consulting the Faithful," *The Tablet*, July 24, 1993.

Hastings, Adrian. *The Faces of God: Essays on Church and Society*. London: Geoffrey Chapman, 1975.

———. *In Filial Disobedience*. Great Wakering, Essex: Mayhew McCrimmon, 1978.

Hawthorne, Nathaniel. *The Scarlet Letter*. New York: W.W. Norton, 1961.

Hebblethwaite, Peter. "Visiting Pope Listed, Rejected Lay 'Ministry'," *National Catholic Reporter*, October 2, 1987.

———. Quoted in the Canadian Broadcasting Corporation's *Ideas* series, "Catholics," by Michael W. Higgins, originally aired in May 1984. Excerpt from Program One: "After Me, the Flood."

———. *John XXIII: Pope of the Council*. London: Geoffrey Chapman, 1984.

———. "The Mind of John Paul II," *Grail: An Ecumenical Journal* 1, March 1985.

———. "From J P II: Superstar to a Super Surprise?" *National Catholic Reporter*, September 11, 1992.

Higgins, Michael W., and Douglas R. Letson. "Canadian Participation in Episcopal Synods, 1967–1985." *Historical Studies of the Canadian Catholic Historical Association* 54, 1987.

———. *Women and the Church: A Sourcebook*. Toronto: Griffin House, 1986.

Higgins, Michael W. "Synod Diary," *Grail: An Ecumenical Journal* 2, March 1986.

Higgins, Michael W., and Douglas R. Letson. *My Father's Business: A Biography of His Eminence G. Emmett Cardinal Carter*. Toronto: Macmillan, 1990.

Higgins, Michael W. "Catholics in shock," *The Tablet*, September 22, 1990.

Higgins, Michael W., Brian McGowan, Dennis Murphy, *et al*, eds. *Catholic Education: Transforming Our World, A Canadian Perspective*. Ottawa: Novalis, 1991.

Higgins, Michael W. "Focus on Sexual Abuse," *The Tablet*, February 13, 1993.

———. Quoted in the Canadian Broadcasting Corporation's *Ideas* scries, "The Jesuit Mystique," orginally aired in November and December 1995. Excerpt from Program One.

———. *Heretic Blood: The Spiritual Geography of Thomas Merton*. Toronto: Stoddart, 1998.

Higgins Michael W., and Bernie Lucht. *Heretic Blood: An Audiobiography of Thomas Merton*. Toronto: Canadian Broadcasting Corporation, 1998.

Higgins, Michael W. *The Muted Voice: Religion and the Media*. Ottawa: Novalis, 2000.

Holmes, J. Derek. "The 20th Century Popes," *The Tablet*, May 22, 1982.

"Hospitals in Peril," *The Tablet*, March 6, 1999.

"Hospital Loses its Catholic Identity, Critics Fear Abortion May Be on Way," *The Catholic Register*, February 4, 1995.

Hughes, Gerard W., s.j. "Shades of the Ghetto," *The Tablet*, November 7, 1992.

Hughes, Richard T., and William B. Adrian, eds. *Models for Christian Higher Education: Strategies for Success in the Twenty-First Century*. Grand Rapids, Michigan: William B. Eerdmans, 1997.

Hughes, Robert. *The Fatal Shore*. London: Harvill Press, 1987.

Hume, Basil, o.s.b. "Papal Primacy and Episcopal Authority: The Bishop in a Universal Church," *The Catholic Herald*, July 16, 1999.

Hurley, Francis T. "The Return to Ministry of Inactive Married Priests," *America* 178:6, February 28, 1998.

Hutchison, Mark. "Religion and University Education in Australia: Debates Over the Introduction of Chaplaincies to Macquarie University," *The Journal of Religious History* 17:3, June 1993.

Jenkins, Joe, and Andrew M. Brown. "Dublin Acts to Counter Vocation Crisis," *The Catholic Herald*, October 24, 1997.

John Paul II. *The Role of the Christian Family in the Modern World: 'Familiaris consortio'*. Boston: Daughters of St. Paul, 1981.

——. "*Dignitatem mulieris*: On the Dignity and Vocation of Women." *Origins* 18:17, October 6, 1988.

——. "*Ordinatio sacerdotalis*: Apostolic Letter on Ordination and Women," *Origins* 24:4, June 9, 1994.

——. *Crossing the Threshold of Hope*, edited by Vittorio Messori. New York: Alfred A. Knopf, 1994.

——. *Gift and Mystery: On the Fiftieth Anniversary of My Priestly Ordination*. New York: Doubleday, 1996.

——. "The Ratified and Consummated Sacramental Marriage," *Origins* 29:34, February 10, 2000.

Johnson, Luke Timothy. "A Disembodied 'Theology of the Body'," *Commonweal*, January 26, 2001.

Jones, Arthur. "Huge Nonprofit System Feels Pressure to Cut Costs, Merge and Get Bigger." *National Catholic Reporter*, June 16, 1995.

——. "Sex: Female, Religion: Catholic, Hopes: Few," *National Catholic Reporter*, September 12, 1986.

——. "Can Things Get Too Big?" *National Catholic Reporter*, June 16, 1995.

——. "How Profitable?" *National Catholic Reporter*, June 16, 1995.

——. "Stories of Hardship and Endurance," *National Catholic Reporter*, June 16, 1995.

——. "Contradictions Erupt Over the Union Issue," *National Catholic Reporter*, June 16, 1995.

Jones, Deborah. "Bishops Plan Guide to No-Priest Services," *The Catholic Herald*, June 6, 1977.

Joyce, James. *A Portrait of the Artist as a Young Man*. Toronto: Penguin, 1966.

Kaiser, Robert Blair. *The Encyclical That Never Was*. London: Sheed and Ward, 1987.

Kaufman, Christopher J. *Ministry and Meaning: A Religious History of Catholic Health Care in the United States*. New York: Crossroads, 1995.

Kaufmann, Walter. "The Inevitability of Alienation." In Richard Schacht, ed. *Alienation*. New York: Doubleday, 1970.

Kenna, Kathleen. "School Vouchers Colour U.S. Vote," *The Toronto Star*, September 17, 2000.

Kennedy, Robert G. "Will We Ever Have Enough Priests?" *America* 177:6, September 13, 1997.

Knowles, David. "Authentic Teaching," *The Tablet*, July 24, 1993.

Kosnik, Anthony, *et al. Human Sexuality: New Directions in American Catholic Thought*. New York: Paulist Press, 1977.

Kotash, Myrna. "The Case of Martyr Teresa Benedicta." Quoted in the Canadian Broadcasting Corporation's *Ideas* series, originally aired in November 2000.

Landsberg, Michele. "St. Mike's Religious Rules Undemocratic," *The Toronto Star*. May 30, 1998.

Langan, John P., ed. *Catholic Universities in Church and Society: A Dialogue on "Ex Corde Ecclesiae"*. Washington: Georgetown University Press, 1993.

Langland, William. *Piers the Ploughman*. Translated by J.F. Goodridge. Toronto: Penguin, 1971.

Law, Bernard. "Statement Opposing the Sale of St. Louis University Hospital," *Origins* 27:21, November 6, 1997.

Leo XIII. *"Arcanum."* In Claudia Carlen, I.H.M., ed., *The Papal Encyclicals, 1878–1903*. College Park, Maryland: McGrath Publishing, 1981.

Letson, Douglas R. "Gerald Emmett, Cardinal Carter: The Essence of Catholic Education." In Caroline DiGiovanni, ed., *The Philosophy of Catholic Education*. Ottawa: Novalis, 1992.

———. "Personal Reflections on the 1990 Synod of Bishops," *Grail: An Ecumenical Journal* 7:1, 1991.

———. "Catholic Universities in the Modern World," *The Tablet*, February 10, 2001.

Letson, Douglas R., and Michael W. Higgins. *The Jesuit Mystique*. Toronto: Macmillan, 1995.

Leonard, Ellen. "Emerging Communities of Dialogue and Mission," *Grail: An Ecumenical Journal* 8, September 1992.

Loftus, J.A., S.J. *Understanding Sexual Misconduct by Clergy: A Handbook for Ministers*. Washington: Pastoral Press, 1994.

———. "Sexuality in Priesthood: *Noli me tangere*." In Thomas G. Plante, ed., *Bless Me Father for I Have Sinned: Perspectives on Sexual Abuse Committed by Roman Catholic Priests*. Westport, Connecticut: Praeger, 1999.

Longley, Clifford. "Hume's Mission Impossible," *The Tablet*, November 20, 1999.

Luxmoore, Jonathan. "Act VII: Enter Pope John Paul," *The Tablet*, May 31, 1997.

Mackie, W.S., ed. *The Exeter Book*. London: Oxford University Press, 1958.

Malone, Mary T. "Living Without a Why," *Doctrine & Life* 49, September 1999.

Marshall, John. "Inside the Commission," *The Tablet*, July 24, 1993.

———. "True Meaning of Marriage," *The Tablet*, September 4, 1993.

Mahony, Roger. "Statement on Proposition 22, Same-Sex Marriage Initiative," *Origins* 29:29, January 6, 2000.

McAteer, Michael. "Canadian Bishops Angry, Bitter Over Synod," *The Toronto Star*, October 30, 1987.

McBrien, Richard P. "Homosexuality & the Priesthood: Questions We Can't Keep in the Closet," *Commonweal* 114:12, June 19, 1987.

———. *Lives of the Popes: The Pontiffs from St. Peter to John Paul II*. San Francisco: HarperSanFrancisco, 1997.

McCormick, Richard. "Technology, the Consistent Ethic and Physician-Assisted Suicide," *Origins* 25:27, December 21, 1995.

———. "The End of Catholic Hospitals?" *America* 179:1, July 4, 1998.

McGarry, Patsy. "Nun Decides to Quit Rather Than Recant," *Catholic New Times*, February 6, 2000.

McGillion, Chris. "Rome, Take Note: Father's Days Are Numbered," *The Sydney Morning Herald*, August 8, 2000.

McHugh, Jim. "An Abuse of Power, a Betrayal of Trust: The Emperor Has No Clothes," *Grail: An Ecumenical Journal* 7:2, June 1991.

McLaughlin, Terence, Joseph O'Keefe, s.j., and Bernadette O'Keeffe, eds. *The Contemporary Catholic School: Context, Identity, and Diversity*. Washington: Falmer Press, 1996.

———. "Does This Vision Work?" *The Tablet*, October 9, 1999.

McMahon, Laureen. "Same-Sex Decision Disappoints Bishop," *The Catholic Register*, June 12, 2000.

McNeil John T., and Helena M. Gamer, eds. *Medieval Handbooks of Penance*. New York: Octagon Books, 1965.

Merton, Thomas. *A Vow of Conversation: Journals 1964–1965*. New York: Farrar, Straus, Giroux, 1988.

Messori, Vittorio. *Opus Dei: Leadership and Vision in Today's Catholic Church*. Washington: Regnery Publishing, 1997.

Miller, Annabel. "How Natural is n f p?" *The Tablet*, December 2, 2000.

Mol, J.J. "The Effects of Denominational Schools in Australia," *The Australian and New Zealand Journal of Sociology* 4:1, April 1968.

Morley, John F. "Pacelli's Prosecutor," *Commonweal*, November 5, 1999.

Morris, Julian [Morris West]. *Moon in My Pocket*. Sydney: Australian Publishing Company, 1945.

Murphy, Dennis. "Catholic Education: Towards the Third Millennium," *Grail: An Ecumenical Journal* 8, June 1992.

Murphy, Francis X., C.Ss.R., "Of Sex and the Catholic Church," *The Atlantic Monthly*, February 1981.

Murray, Vince. "Other Faiths in Catholic Schools: General Implications of a Case Study." In Terence McLaughlin, Joseph O'Keefe, s.j., and Bernadette O'Keeffe, eds. *The Contemporary Catholic School: Context, Identity, and Diversity*. Washington: Falmer Press, 1996.

National Conference of Catholic Bishops: Committee on Priestly Life and Ministry. "Reflections on the Morale of Priests," *Origins* 18:31, January 12, 1989.

National Conference of Catholic Bishops. "Ethical and Religious Directives for Catholic Health Care Services," *Origins* 24:27, December 15, 1994.

———. "Marriage Preparation and Cohabiting Couples: Information Report," *Origins* 29:14, September 16, 1999.

New Jersey Bishops. "The Rationale of Catholic Health Care," *Origins* 25:27, December 21, 1995.

Nicholl, Donald. "Holiness: A Call to Radical Living," *Grail: An Ecumenical Journal* 5, December 1989.

———. *"Scientia Cordis," The Beatitude of Truth: Reflections of a Lifetime*. London: Darton, Longman and Todd, 1977.

Nichols, Vincent. "My Difficult Decision," *The Tablet*, May 20, 2000.

Nolan, Albert, o.p. "Poor in Spirit," *Grail: An Ecumenical Journal* 7, March 1991.

Norris, Kathleen. *The Cloister Walk*. New York: Riverhead Books, 1996.

Nouwen, Henri J.M. *Making All Things New: An Invitation to the Spiritual Life*. San Francisco: HarperSan Francisco, 1981.

———. "A Spirituality of Peace-Making." Inaugural Devlin Lecture delivered at St. Jerome's University, Waterloo, Ontario, September 12, 1982.

———. *Our Greatest Gift: A Meditation on Dying and Caring*. San Francisco: HarperSanFrancisco, 1994.

———. *Show Me the Way: Readings for Each Day of Lent*. New York: Crossroad, 1995.

Novak, Michael. *Confession of a Catholic*. New York: Harper and Row, 1983.

"Observations of the Sacred Congregation for Catholic Education on the Project Document prepared by the Council and the Committee of the International Federation of Catholic Universities (f.i.u.c. / [ifcu]) during the meetings held at Grottaferrata-Rome, February 3–5, 1972. Published May 20, 1972.

O'Connor, John. "The Temptation To Become Just Another Industry: Health Care," *Origins* 25:27, December 21, 1995.

O'Keefe, Joseph, s.j. "No Margin, No Mission." In Terence McLaughlin, Joseph O'Keefe, s.j., and Bernadette O'Keeffe, eds. *The Contemporary Catholic School: Context, Identity, and Diversity*. Washington: Falmer Press, 1996.

Olin, John C. *The Catholic Reformation: Savonarola to Ignatius Loyola*. New York: Fordham University Press, 1992.

Osgood, Charles G., trans. *Boccaccio on Poetry*. New York: Bobbs-Merrill, 1956.

Panikkar, Raimundo. *Blessed Simplicity: The Monk as Universal Archetype*. New York: Seabury Press, 1982.

Paul vi. *Of Human Life: Humanae vitae*. Boston: St. Paul Books & Media, 1968.

Philips, Walter. "A Review of Edmund Campion, *Australian Catholics*," *The Journal of Religious History* 16:1, June 1990.

Place, Michael. "Planned Sale of St. Louis University Hospital To For-Profit Chain," *Origins* 27:30, January 15, 1998.

Plante, Thomas G. "Conclusion: Sexual Abuse Committed By Roman Catholic Priests: Current Status, Future Objectives." In Thomas G. Plante, ed., *Bless Me Father for I Have Sinned: Perspectives on Sexual Abuse Committed by Roman Catholic Priests*. Westport, Connecticut: Praeger, 1999.

"Preliminary Report: The Vatican and the Holocaust," *Origins,* November 9, 2000.

Priestly Life and Ministry Committee of n c c b, "Reflections on the Morale of Priests," *Origins* 18:31, January 12, 1989.

Principe, Walter, c.s.b. "Changing Church Teachings," *Grail: An Ecumenical Journal* 6, September 1990.

Rausch, Thomas P. "Forming Priests for Tomorrow's Church: The Coming Synod," *America* 162:7, February 24, 1990.

Raith, Josef, ed. *Die Altenglische Version des Halitgar'schen Bussbuches*. Darmstadt: Wissenschaftliche Buchgesellschaft, 1964.

Rhodes, Anthony. *The Vatican in the Age of the Dictators, 1922–1945*. London: Hodder and Stoughton, 1973.

Riley, Dean. "Sharing a Common Vision," *Scarboro Missions*, October 2000.

Rigali, Justin. "Proposed Sale of Two Catholic Hospitals To For-Profit Chain," *Origins* 27:21, November 6, 1997.

——. "St. Louis University Hospital Sold To For-Profit Corporation," *Origins* 27:38, March 12, 1998.

Rolheiser, Ronald, o.m.i. *The Catholic Herald*, June 30, 2000.

Ross, Susan A. "Extravagant Affections: Women's Sexuality and Theological Anthropology." In
    Ann O'Hara Graff, ed., *In the Embrace of God: Feminist Approaches to Theological Anthropol-
    ogy*. Maryknoll, New York: Orbis, 1995.

———. "Like a Fish Without a Bicycle? Virtually No Women's Religious Community Deals With
    the Eucharist Without Some Pain," *America*, November 27, 1999.

Ruether, Rosemary Radford. "Does 'Survival of the Fittest' Apply to Theologians?" *National
    Catholic Reporter*, December 2, 1988.

Rutty, Christopher. *A Circle of Care: 75 Years of Caring, St. Mary's General Hospital*. Waterloo,
    Ontario: Waterloo Printing Company, 1999.

Ryan, Claude. "The Church in Quebec: The Catholic Church and the Political Evolution of
    Quebec 1960–1980," *Canadian Catholic Review* 2, January 1984.

———. "Christians in Public life." Inaugural John J. Wintermeyer Lecture in Christianity and
    Public Policy, St. Jerome's University, Waterloo, Ontario, October 18, 2000.

Ryan, Tim, S.F.M. "The Boff Case," *Grail: An Ecumenical Journal* 9, September 1993.

Saunders, Kate, and Peter Stanford. *Catholics and Sex: From Purity to Perdition*. London: Heine-
    mann, 1992.

Schjeldahl, Peter. "High Folderol," *The New Yorker*, July 19, 1999.

Schmidt, Lawrence E. "Simone Weil's Understanding of Adolf Hitler, a Genius of the 'Physics of
    Human Matter'." Presented to the annual colloquy of the American Weil Society, University of
    Chicago, April 23, 1999.

"Seven big players in a fluctuating field," *National Catholic Reporter,* June 16, 1995.

Sewell, Brocard, O.Carm. *The Habit of a Lifetime: An Autobiography*. Padstow: Tabb House,
    1992.

Shaidle, Kathy. "Illness a Harsh but Welcome Teacher," *The Toronto Star*, December 13, 1998.

———. "Women, Poetry and the Cult of the Victim," *The Toronto Star*, February 6, 2000.

———. "That Photograph of Flannery O'Connor," *Lobotomy Magnificat*. Ottawa: Oberon, 1997.

———. *God Rides a Yamaha: Musings on Pain, Poetry, and Pop Culture*. Vancouver: Northstone,
    1998.

Shapiro, Herman, trans. *Medieval Philosophy: Selected Readings from Augustine to Buridan*. New
    York: Modern Library, 1964.

Sheehan, Michael. "Cohabitation and Marriage in the Church," *Origins* 29:14, September 16, 1999.

Sheridan, E.F., ed. *Love Kindness! The Social Teaching of the Canadian Catholic Bishops*.
    Toronto: Jesuit Centre for Social Faith and Justice, 1991.

Sipe, A. Richard. "The Problem of Prevention in Clergy sexual Abuse." In Thomas J. Plante, ed.,
    *Bless Me Father for I Have Sinned: Perspectives on Sexual Abuse Committed by Roman Catholic
    Priests*. Westport, Connecticut: Praeger, 1999.

Skinner, John. "Prayer is a Way of Life: It's All Very Simple," *The Catholic Herald*, November 5, 1999.

Sobrino, Jon, s.j., Ignacio Ellacuría, s.j., *et al. Companions of Jesus: The Jesuit Martyrs of El Salvador*. Maryknoll, New York: Orbis, 1990.

Social Affairs Committee of the Assembly of Quebec Bishops. *A Heritage of Violence? A Pastoral Reflection on Conjugal Violence*. Antoinette Kinlough, trans. Montreal: L'Assemblée des évêques du Québec, 1989.

"Some Questions Regarding Collaboration of Non-Ordained Faithful in Priests' Sacred Ministry," *Origins* 27:24, November 27, 1997.

Starkman, Miriam K., ed. *Seventeenth-Century Poetry*. New York: Alfred A. Knopf, 1967.

Stanford, Peter. *Cardinal Hume and the Changing Face of English Catholicism*. London: Geoffrey Chapman, 1993.

Stourton, Edward. *Absolute Truth: The Catholic Church in the World Today*. London: Viking, 1998.

"Synod Propositions," *The Tablet*, January 31, 1981; February 7, 1981; February 14, 1981.

Swan, Michael. "Catholic Boards Win Preferential Court Case," *The Catholic Register*, November 8, 1999.

Szulc, Tad. *Pope John Paul II: The Biography*. New York: Scribner, 1995.

Tanenhaus, Gussie Hecht. "Bede's *De schematibus et tropis* — A Translation," *The Quarterly Journal of Speech* 48, October 1962.

Thavis, John. "Canadian Bishops Ask Vatican For Married Priests in the North," *Catholic New Times*, October 10, 1993.

Thompson, Catherine. "Hospital Merger Opposed," *The Record*, December 15, 1997.

Thorpe, Benjamin. *The Homilies of the Anglo-Saxon Church*, vol. 1. New York: Ælfric Society, 1844.

Tillard, J.M.R., o.p. "The Mission of the Bishop of Rome: What is Essential, What is Expected?"*Ecumenical Trends* 27, January 1998.

Toynbee, P., ed. *Dantis Alagherii Epistolae*. Oxford: Clarendon, 1966.

Vanier, Jean. *Community & Growth: Our Pilgrimage Together*. Toronto: Griffin House, 1979.

Vanier, Jean. *Becoming Human*. Toronto: Anansi/cbc, 1988.

Vatican Congregation for Divine Worship and the Sacraments, "Summary of the New General Instruction of the Roman Missal," *Origins* 30:10, August 3, 2000.

Walsh, Michael. "The Battle of St. Philip's," *The Tablet*, October 10, 1992.

———. *Opus Dei: An Investigation into the Secret Society Struggling for Power Within the Roman Catholic Church*. Toronto: HarperCollins, 1991.

———. "The Papacy in the Twentieth Century: 1878 – the present day." In Michael Walsh, ed., *The Papacy*. London: Weidenfeld & Nicolson, 1997.

Weakland, Rembert, o.s.b. "Reflections for Rome," *America* 178:13, April 18, 1988.

Weigel, George. "The Chapel in the Mine," *The Tablet*, 21 October 2001.

Wescott, Margaret, director "Behind the Veil: Nuns." Montreal: National Film Board of Canada, 1985.

Westhues, Kenneth. "Public vs. Sectarian Legitimate: The Separate Schools of the Catholic Church," *Canadian Review of Sociology and Anthropology* 13, 1976.

———. "Catholic Separate Schools: An Ambiguous Legacy," *Grail: An Ecumenical Journal* 1:1, March 1985.

———. "Separate Schools and Canadian Social Trends," *Grail: An Ecumenical Journal* 1-2, March/June 1994.

Wilcox, Charles T., trans. *Treatises on Marriage and Other Subjects*, The Fathers of the Church, vol. 27. Washington: Catholic University of America Press, 1955.

Wilkes, Paul. "The Hands That Would Shape Our Souls," *The Atlantic Monthly*, December 1990.

Wilkins, John. "The Next Pope: The Papacy in the New Millennium." Devlin Lecture, St. Jerome's University, Waterloo, Ontario, April 7, 2000.

Wills, Gary. *Papal Sin: Structures of Deceit.* Toronto: Doubleday, 2000.

Wijngaards, John. "When Women Were Deacons," *The Tablet*, May 8, 1999.

———. "Don't Cage the Sacred," *The Tablet*, September 23, 2000.

Wojtyla, Karol. *The Place Within.* Translated by Jerzy Peterkiewicz. London: Hutchinson, 1979.

Wright, F.A. *Select Letters of St. Jerome.* Cambridge, Massachusetts: Harvard University Press, 1930.

Wright, Thomas. *The Political Songs of England.* London: John Bowyer Nichols, 1839.

Zaleski, Irma. *Mother Macrina.* Ottawa: Novalis, 2000.

Zeller, Shawn. "Dignity's Challenge: Can Homosexuals Feel at Home in Catholicism?" *Commonweal*, July 14, 2000.

Permissions

Index

abortion, 50, 52–54, 101, 213, 232, 371

Adam, Karl, 22, 333

Adrian, William, 166

Ælfric (the Grammarian), 198, 200, 202

Agagianian, Cardinal Gregory Peter (iv), 19–20

Agca, Mehmet Ali, 42

Albert the Great, 236

Alexander, Bishop Mervyn, 324

Amato, Angelo, 151

Andreotti, Giulio, 27

Antonello, Bruce, 106–13

Apostolic Constitution on Catholic Universities, 146

Apostolic Constitution on Ecclesiastical Universities and Faculties (encyclical). See *Sapientia christiana*

Apostolicam actuositatem (decree), 6, 302–4, 306

Aquaviva, Claudio, 117

Aquinas. *See* Saint Thomas Aquinas

Arcanum (encyclical), 203–4, 208

Arendt, Hannah, 350

Arinze, Cardinal Francis, 81

Aristotle, 187–89, 314

the arts, 3

As the Third Millennium Draws Near (letter). See *Tertio millennio adveniente*

At the Beginning of the New Millennium (letter). See *Novo millennio ineunte*

Athenagoras II, 26

Augustine of Canterbury, 190, 201

Augustine of Hippo, 6, 114, 123

Australian Catholic University, 178–81

Baggio, Cardinal Sebastiano, 29

Baker, Augustine, 355

Baker, Kenneth, 223–24

Balaguer, Josémaría Escrivá de, 324, 379

Balasuriya, Tissa, 73, 84, 148, 295

Bamberger, John Eudes, 352–53

Banco Ambrosiano, 28, 30

Barrett, Richard, 75

Baum, Gregory, 90

Bedard, Bob, 376

Bede, the Venerable, 190, 195, 201

Bedoyere, Quentin de la, 48

Belloc, Hilaire, 330

Benson, Robert Hugh, 331

Beran, Cardinal Josef, 12

Berchmans, Mother M., 349

Berger, Philip, 103

Bernardin, Cardinal Joseph, 6, 80, 96–97, 104, 113, 141, 145–46, 259, 277

Bertie, Fra Andrew, 377

Biondi, Lawrence, 98

birth control. *See also* contraception, 101

Bissel, Kevin, 189

Black Madonna, 41

Blair, Tony and Cherie, 136

Blessed Virgin. *See* Saint Mary

Bobbio, Alberto, 274

Boccaccio, Giovanni, 263, 265

body (human), relationship to soul, 192–94, 208

Boethius, Anicius M. S., 191

Boff, Leonardo, 73, 83–84, 148

Bon Secours Sisters, 113

Bonaventure, 123

Bonhoeffer, Dietrich, 271

Boswell, James, 249

Bouchard, Premier Lucien, (Quebec) 131

Bourke, Richard, 142

Bramachari, 354

Brodeur, Dennis, 96

Buber, Martin, 63

Buckley, Timothy J., 249

Bullet, Archbishop Gabriel, 312

Burke, Bishop Lawrence A., 276

Burns, Flavian, 350

Burtchaell, James, 166

Butler, Carolyn, 290

Byrne, Lavinia, 79–80, 148, 319

Cahill, Patricia, 95, 97–98

Callaghan, Morley, 2, 5, 148, 266

Calvi, Roberto, 28, 30

Cameron, James M., 16–17

Camp, Dalton, 113

Campion, Edmund, 117, 142–44

Capitalism, 10–11, 330

Capovilla, Archbishop Loris, 20

Cardenal, Ernesto, 36, 82, 317

Carmelites (Order of), 39–40, 60, 331

Carpenter, Peter, 179

Carter, Bishop Alexander, 255, 259, 276, 297

Carter, Cardinal Gerald Emmett, 6, 214, 226, 317, 378
    on clerical power, 185–86
    on the 1980 Synod re the family, 220–21
    on teaching, 114, 120–21, 123, 145, 147
    Vatican finances and, 30

Vatican II and, 258–62
on women in the church, 317
the Carthusians, 358
Casaroli, Cardinal Agostino, 11–12
Casey, Bishop Eamon, 293
Cash, Andrew, 371
Cassian, John, 355, 358
Cassidy, Cardinal Edward Idris, 64
Cassidy, Sheila, 341–43
Casti connubii (encyclical), 204–5,
    208–9, 212, 225, 227
Catholic Church. *See also* Catholics;
    celibacy; infallibility; laity;
    pilgrim status; women
anti-intellectual phases of, 123
collegiality and, 34–36
confession of sins of, 71
contraception and, 221–25
denial of sexual abuse in, 5, 49,
    74–76, 88–90, 232–34, 252,
    283, 323
divorce and, 248–51
doctrinal changes of, 87–89
educational guidelines of, 118–26
the elderly and, 327
erosion of respect for, 133
the Eucharist and, 268–69
family rights and, 225
fundamental nature of the, 22–23
hierarchical development in,
    300–301
hierarchical legacy of, 187–89
historical humanism of, 23
homophobia and, 231
homosexuality and, 241–46
homosexual pastoral care, 237–41
infallibility and, 262
Jansenism in, 285–87
Jewish relations and, 23, 62–68
marriage and, 245–51
Marxism and, 82–83
mass media and the, 74
need for a better understanding of,
    4–6
past errors of, 235
plummeting numbers of new
    priests, 95, 269–72, 295, 298,
    310
potential division of, 249, 251
power and, 252
pretence of consultations by,
    229–30
reaction to the Reformation by,
    254
religious liberty and the, 23
request for pardon by, 70
resistance to change of, 205–6
rigidified by Aristotelian theory,
    189–90
role of prayer in, 23

sexuality and, 51, 200–3, 228, 230,
    252–53
signs of commitment to, 5
synods and the, 33–35
women and, 77–81, 247–49, 312–17
Catholic education ministries
change in, 93–95
decline in religious personnel for,
    94
historic raison d'être, 113–18
Catholic health care ministries
AIDS and, 102–3
in Canada, 100–104
change in, 93–95
decline in religious personnel for,
    94, 109
ethical guides for, 99, 102–3
historic raison d'être, 94–97, 104,
    107, 113
hospital boards and, 100
poor prognosis for, 99
Catholics. *See also* Catholic Church
obligations of, 4, 6
The Catholic School (statement),
    122–24
Catholic Schools
in Australia, 141–45
in Canada, 129–33
closures of, 127–28
current challenges of, 145–46
lay contributions to, 305–6
non-Catholics in, 128, 139, 144–45
success of, 126–27
in the U.K., 134–41
Catholic universities
bishops' role regarding, 153–54
degrees of freedom in, 147–53
financial state of, 168
importance of, 146–47
lay contributions to, 306
non-doctrinal challenges to,
    165–83
resolving tensions concerning,
    152–53
Vatican policy concerning, 155–65
Catholic universities (Jesuit), future
    of, 167–69
Catholic Worker Movement, 369–72
Catholics of Vision (movement), 324
Cavour, Camillo Benso di, 9
celibacy. See also *Sacerdotalis
    coelibatus*
clerical arguments against, 291–92,
    299
loneliness and, 267, 282
origin of policy respecting, 284
renewed call for, 268, 276–77
risks due to, 277–78
the will to power and, 185–86
censorship, 3

Centisimus annus (encyclical), 47
Chadwick, Priscilla, 138–40, 146
Chair of Peter. *See* papacy
Chakravarty, Amiya, 354
charity, clerics and, 301
Chaucer, Geoffrey, 2, 115, 191,
    193–97, 199, 202, 247–48, 254,
    262–63, 265
Chenu, Marie-Dominique, 17
Chesterton, Cecil, 331
Chesterton, Gilbert Keith, 330, 333
Chiasson, Archbishop Donat, 313–14,
    222, 305–6, 308
Chicherin, Georgi, 10
Chmielowski, Adam, 46
Chrétien, Prime Minister Jean, 130
Christ, Jesus, 75, 153
His attitude about power, 260
celibate life of, 199, 204, 267–68
in each person, 125
the mind of, 220
as mother and teacher, 113, 123
mystical body of, 4
obedience to and by, 196
perceived demands of, 223
His priestly function, 257, 301
revelation from, 259
role of His Apostles, 211
on self-transcendence, 51
His will, 309
the unshakable Truth of, 58
women and, 78, 317
Christian Family Movement, 213
Clarizio, Archbishop Emmanuele, 214
Clark, Manning, 142
Clarke, James H., 339–40
Clarke, Mary, 339–41
clericalism
defined, 255
sexual, 255–56, 270–71, 276, 282
clerical life, medieval call to, 254
clerical pedophilia, estimated rates of,
    283–84
clerical "sexual underworld", 283
clerics, early images of, 254
Code of Canon Law, 122
Cody, Cardinal John, 28–29, 217
Coleman, Michael Gower, 276
Collins, Paul, 148, 214
Communion and Liberation
    (movement), 72, 379
communism, Marxist, 10–12
Community of Emmanuel, 376
Community of St. Jean, 376
Community of the Beatitudes, 376
community vs. individuality, 126
The Companions of the Cross, 375–76
Congar, Yves, 17, 22, 86, 301–2
Congregation for Catholic Education,
    99

Congregation for Institutes of
    Consecrated Life and for Societies
    of Apostolic Life, 79, 99
Congregation for the Doctrine of the
    Faith, 73–74, 79, 83–87, 150, 232,
    237, 241–43, 245, 271, 319
Congregation of the Resurrection, 1
Conrad, Theodor, 59
conscience, 48–49
    contraception and, 218
    "dynamic Christian", 220
    the media and, 225
    primacy of, 239, 242
*Constitution on the Church in the
    Modern World.* See *Gaudium et spes*
contraception, 50, 74, 79, 88, 102, 108
    Catholic debate over, 209–19,
    221–25, 232–33
    evil nature of, 206
"contraceptive intent", 216–17
"contraceptive mentality", 225
Cooke, Bernard, 35
Cools, Anne, 131
Cornwell, John, 31, 65–67
Cosstick, Vicky, 297, 321
Costello, Timothy J., 277–78
Coughlan, Michael, 163, 171–73
The Council of Constance, 261
The Council of Trent, 18–19, 205,
    254, 259, 261, 301
Cozzens, Donald, 3, 214, 269, 272,
    281, 287
Crowley, Pat and Patty, 213
Cullinan, Tom, 341
Curley, John Jr., 96, 99
Curran, Charles, 73, 148, 232
Currie, Charles L., 167
Custance, Olive, 331

Danneels, Cardinal Godfried, 310
Dante Alighieri, 263, 265
Daughters of Charity, 97
Davis, Charles, 230–31
Davis, Premier William (Ontario), 132
Dawkins, John, 178
Day, Dorothy, 369–72
De doctrina christiana (teaching
    document), 114
De Fontibus revelationis (Council
    document), 24
Deak, Istvan, 65
death, fruitfulness of, 337
death penalty, 50
Declaration of Independence (U.S.), 113
Declaration on Christian Education
    (document). See *Gravissimum
    educationis*
Declaration on Religious Freedom
    (document). See *Dignitatis
    humanae*

*Declaration on the Question of the
    Admission of Women.* See *Inter
    insigniores*
Decree on the Apostolate of the Laity.
    See *Apostolicam actuositatem*
*Decree on the Ministry and Life of
    Priests.* See *Presbyterorum ordinis*
Dempsey, Luke, 152
Dignitatis humanae (document), 3, 121
Dionysius, 207
DiPede, Tony, 103
distributism (philosophy), 330
Dives in misericordia (encyclical), 47
Divini illius magistri (encyclical), 118
Divini redemptoris (encyclical), 10
Dogmatic Constitution on the Church.
    See *Lumen gentium*
Dominian, Jack, 226–28
Dominus Iesus (statement), 151–52
Donum veritatis, 74
Drake, Peter, 178
Drinan, Robert, 36
Duffy, Eamon, 7–8, 71, 251
Dulles, Cardinal Avery, 4
Dunne, Frederic, 350
Dupuis, Jacques, 73, 148

Ecclesia semper reformanda (motto),
    150
eclecticism, 57
education. *See also* Catholic
    educational ministries
    parents and, 225
    for profit, 94
    seminary, 146–47
Eichmann, Adolf, 350
Ellacuría, Ignacio, 126
Elliott, Elizabeth, 197–98
emptiness in contemplation.
    See prayer, selfless
English, John, 364
Ertel, Grant, 325–26, 378–79
Eucharist. *See also* Catholic Church,
    Eucharist and
    male province of the, 318, 320
euthanasia, 50, 54, 232
Evangelium vitae (encyclical), 50
Ex corde ecclesiae (document), 146,
    157–58, 161, 163–65, 171

Faith (movement), 379
Faith and Reason (encyclical). See
    Fides et ratio
faith vs. reason, 147, 154
Familiaris consortio (statement), 199,
    224–25
Fascism, 10–11
Fessio, Joseph, 80–81, 312–13
Fiand, Barbara, 148
Fides et ratio, 56–58

Fielding, Henry, 264
Fitzgerald, Penelope, 3
Flahiff, Cardinal George B., 316
Fleischner, Eva, 67
"flesh," concept of, 190
Flynn, Eileen, 244
Focolare, 379
Fogarty, Gerald, 67
Fox, James, 350
Fox, Matthew, 148
Franciscan Friars of the Renewal, 376
Franciscan Sisters of the Holy
    Eucharist, 376
Franco, Francisco, 10
Fraser, John Mary, 374
freedom, nature of, 51
Freeman, Laurence, 355–58
French, Kristen, 360–61
Fuller, John, 299–300

Gahl, Robert Jr., 243
Gallin, Alice, 159, 305
Gard'ner, Joseph, 331
Garibaldi, Giuseppe, 9
Gascoigne, Robert, 180–81
Gasparri, Cardinal Pietro, 9
Gasquet, Cardinal Aidan, 15
Gaudium et spes (Pastoral Constitu-
    tion), 3, 6, 208–9, 211–14, 234–35,
    249
Gebara, Ivone, 148
The Gift of Truth (instruction). See
    Donum veritatis
Gelli, Licio, 28, 30
Gill, Eric, 330
Gilroy, Cardinal Sir Norman, 20
Gipps, George, 142
globalization, medical services and,
    111
God
    intentions of, 238
    mirrored in society, 196
    His plan, 206
    the provider, 205
    responsibilities of Popes to, 33
    revelation and, 24
    Word of, 7
Gomez, Bishop Libardo Ramirez, 312
Goretti, Maria. *See* Saint Maria Goretti
The Gospel of Life (encyclical). See
    Evangelium vitae
Goudreault, Bishop Henri, 151, 162, 276
Gower, John, 266
Graham, David, 106–13
Gramick, Jeannine, 148, 241, 243
Granfield, Patrick, 37
Gravissimum educationis (document),
    3, 121–22, 126
Gray, John, 331
Great Benedictine Reform, 261

Greeley, Andrew, 118, 126–27, 133, 214, 217, 298
Greene, Graham, 266
Gregorian Reform, 261
Gregory of Nyssa, 201
Gregory the Great. *See* papacy, of Gregory (the Great)
Grey, Mary C., 380–81
Griffiths, Bede, 356
Griffiths, Bishop Ambrose, 296
Guardini, Romano, 333, 370
Guindon, André, 148, 232–33, 236–37
Gumbleton, Bishop Thomas, 238–39, 243
Gutiérrez, Gustavo, 148

Haight, Roger, 73, 148
Hamelin, Jean-Guy, 315
Hansen, John-Erik Stig, 51
Häring, Bernard, 84, 148, 149, 212, 249
Harris, Premier Michael (Ontario), 101, 132, 371
Hastings, Adrian, 290–96
Hawkes, Brent, 245
Hawthorne, Nathaniel, 189
Hayes, Michael, 182
healing, ministries of, 333–35
health care. *See also* Catholic health care ministries
technology and, 100
Health Services Restructuring Commission (Ontario), 101, 106–7
Hebblethwaite, Margaret, 367–68
Hebblethwaite, Peter, 18, 22, 307, 313, 319
Heenan, Cardinal John Carmel, 210, 231, 235–36, 332
Henry, Bishop Fred, 278
Hesburgh, Theodore, 153, 159
Hickey, James, 270
historicism, 57
Hitler, Adolf, 10, 13–14
Hochhuth, Rolf, 66
Holy Office of the Roman Inquisition, 85
Holy Spirit, 35, 88, 344
homosexuality, 101, 232–33, 236–46, 371
Christian love and, 240
homosexuals, attraction to the priesthood of, 298
Hopkins, Gerard Manley, 194
Horovitz, Frances, 331
hospital care, for profit, 94–105
Howard, Philip Thomas, 331
Hubert, Bishop Bernard, 273
Hugel, Baron Friedrich von, 88
Hughes, Gerry, 138, 365–67
Hughes, Richard, 166

Hugh of St. Victor, 123
Humanae vitae (encyclical), 26, 55–56, 197, 211–14, 216, 223–24, 233–35, 249–51, 313, 319, 332
Hume, Cardinal Basil, 27, 75, 80, 136, 223, 228, 230–31, 296
humour
on lacking a sense of, 197
as a spur to reformation, 264–65
Hunt, Dan, 371
Hunthausen, Archbishop Raymond, 241
Husserl, Edmund, 59

Ibsen, Henrik, 2, 197–98
Ignatius of Loyola. *See* Saint Ignatius of Loyola
Illich, Ivan, 84
Incarnationis mysterium (Bull), 70
index, puzzling self-reference to, 436
Index Librorum (prohibited books), 85, 148–49
indulgences. *See* simony
infallibility doctrine. *See* papacy, infallibility and; Vatican Council (First)
Inopportunists, 15
Inquisition. *See* Holy Office of the Roman Inquisition
Instruction on Collaboration with the Laity, 307–9
Insulis, Alanus de, 123
Inter insigniores (1997 Declaration), 317–19
International Commission of Theologians, 86
IOR. *See* Vatican Bank
Isabella (Catholic Queen of Spain), 66

Jerusalem Community, 376
Jewish outrage over canonization, 61–62, 66
Jews, Catholicism and, 23
John Paul II. *See also* Catholic Church; papacy
approach to Anglicans, 318
perceived authoritarianism of, 289
assassination attempt on, 42–43
concern for social justice, 225
creation of saints by, 45–47
debut in the *aula*, 24–25
despotic regimes and, 12–14
devotion to centralization of, 311
dissent and, 73–74
early influences upon, 37–43
ecumenical dialogue and, 36–37
Edith Stein and, 60–63
election of, 32
faith and reason discussed by, 147
his frustration over women's issues, 317–19

importance of forgiveness to, 69–70
importance of martyrs to, 58–59
interfaith matters and, 74
Jewish relations and, 62–66
the laity and, 323–24
liberationist theology and, 82–83
Marian devotion of, 295, 317–18
"Marian thread" in his life, 40–45
marriage and, 199, 238
Marxism and, 74
philosophical writings of, 47–52
policies on politics and virtue, 54–55
political interests of, 36
priesthood crisis and, 279–81
preferences for philosophical abstraction of, 55–59
reactions to, 229
reserves priestly roles to clergy, 304–5
resistance to change of, 205, 222–25
suspicion of academics under, 148–52, 155
his talks on bodily love, 55
Vatican Council (Second) and, 26, 32–33
Vatican finances and, 30
women's ordination and, 77–79
Johnson, Luke Timothy, 55
Johnson, Paul, 31–32
Johnson, Samuel, 249
Jones, Arthur, 97
Jovinian, 199
Joyce, James, 2, 184, 194, 357
Jubilee years, 69–72

Kaiser, Robert Blair, 214, 223
Kalwaria Zebrzydowska (sanctuary), 41
Kane, M. Theresa, 317
Kasper, Cardinal Walter, 45
Kaufmann, Walter, 192
Kelly, Jim, 161–62
Keneally, Thomas, 266, 284–87
Kennedy, Paul, 364
Kenny, Anthony, 58
Kenny, Mary, 207, 316
Kluger, Jerzy, 63–64
Knights of Columbanus, 378
Knights of Columbus, 325–26, 378–79
Knights of Malta, 325–28, 376–78
Knights of St. Columba, 378
Knights of St. Virgil, 378
Knights of the Holy Sepulchre, 325–26
Knights of the Southern Cross, 378
Knowles, David, 211
Knox, Ronald, 3
Kolbe, Maximillian Mary, 63

Kosnik, Anthony, 190
Kowalska, Maria Faustina. *See* Saint Maria Faustina
Krol, Cardinal John, 30
Küng, Hans, 73, 148

Laborem exercens (encyclical), 47
Lagan College, 138
Laghi, Cardinal Pio, 99, 158, 163, 275–76
laity
    as participants in the priesthood, 257, 259
    isolation of seminarians from, 321–22
    limits to any power of, 307–9
    obedience of the, 258
    pilgrim nature of, 258
    priesthood of, 300–303
    religious collaboration with, 6, 15, 305–11
Landsberg, Michele, 102
Langland, William, 248, 265
L'Arche (healing community), 336, 339–41
    founding of, 338
Lash, Nicholas, 294
Lateran Treaties, 9
Law, Bernard, 98
Lax, Robert, 352
Lay Catholics in Schools (document), 126
leadership, as a giving of oneself, 260–61
Lebel, Bishop Robert, 316
Ledesma, Diego, 117, 121, 123
Lefebvre, Archbishop Marcel, 26
Légaré, Henri, 222
Léger, Cardinal Paul-Emile, 23
Legionaires of Christ (organization), 376
Leibrecht, Bishop John, 159
Lercaro, Cardinal Giacomo, 23
LeSarge, John, 365
Levinas, Emmanuel, 63
life, meaning of, 57
Lobinger, Bishop Fritz, 296
Locatelli, Paul, 169
Lodge, David, 217, 266
Loftus, J. A., 282
loneliness. *See* celibacy, loneliness and; priesthood, loneliness and
Loney, Jim, 371
Lorscheider, Cardinal Aloisio, 34, 274
love. *See also* married love
    Christian, 214, 339
    human, 55–56
    of justice, 381
    messy nature of, 339
    self-transcendence and, 358

of the state, 14
    vs. church law, 290
    vulnerability and, 368
Lowther, Pat, 346
Lubac, Henri de, 17
Luciani, Albino. *See* papacy, of John Paul I
Lumen gentium (Dogmatic Constitution), 3, 6, 23, 257–58, 266, 272, 301
Luther, Martin, 116, 266

MacEwen, Gwendolyn, 346
Mackay, Gordon, 326
MacPherson, John, 327, 377–78
MacSween, R. J., 332
Madonna. *See* Our Lady; Saint Mary
Magee, Bishop John, 29
the Magisterium. *See also* Catholic Education, 48–49, 74, 119, 149, 212, 214, 219, 225, 227, 232, 234, 236, 313, 370
Mahaffey, Leslie, 361
Mahoney, Jack, 231
Main, John, 353–58
Malone, Bishop James, 34
Malone, Mary T., 382
Maloney, Frank, 179–80
mandatum (teaching), 160
Manning, Cardinal Henry Edward, 75, 134
Manning, Joanna, 78
Mannix, Archbishop Daniel, 144
Marcinkus, Archbishop Paul, 28–29
Marian religious thought and devotion, 40–47
Marinelli, Luigi, 148
Markus, Robert, 89
Marmur, Rabbi Dow, 61–63
marriage
    core basis of, 226–27
    nature of, 209, 220–25
    purposes for, 202–6, 208–10, 221
    spiritual status of, 199–202
married love
    life-giving values of, 218
    selfless, 214, 247
Marruca, Dominic, 364
Marrus, Michael, 67
Marshall, John, 212, 216–17, 226
Martinus, Hedwig, 59
martyrdom, 58–59, 61–63, 72–73, 360–61
martyrs, modern, 255
Marvell, Andrew, 193
masturbation, 232–33
matter, perceived place of, 187
Maurin, Peter, 369–70
Mazzini, Giuseppe, 9
McBrien, Richard P., 251, 298
McCarthy, Doug, 124

McCormick, Richard, 51, 95, 102–6, 149
McDonagh, Enda, 85–87, 150, 239–41
McEnroy, M. Carmel, 148, 319
McGahan, Dinny, 286
McGivney, Michael J., 325, 378
McHugh, Jim, 281–82
McKenty, Neil, 354
McKittrick, Tony, 179
McLaughlin, Terence H., 137, 139
McLaurin, David, 266
McLoughlin, David, 137, 164–65, 175–77
McNabb, Vincent, 330
McNeill, John J., 73
media (mass), 275
    effects on clerical morale by the, 273
meditation. *See* prayer, selfless
Mello, Anthony de, 148
Memory and Reconciliation, 70–71
Menzies, R. G., 144
Merton, Thomas, 347–53, 362–63
Messori, Vittorio, 324
Miles Jesu (movement), 379
Milosz, Czeslaw, 45
Milton, John, 190
Mindszenty, Cardinal József, 12
Missionaries of Charity, 376
Mohler, Johann Adam, 22
Mol, J. J., 141–42
the monastic, as archetype, 348
Montfort, Pere St. Louis-Marie Grignion, 39–40
Montini, Cardinal Giovanni Battista, 23
Monty Python. *See* Python, Monty
Moore, Brian, 266
moral relativism, 13
Moran, Cardinal Patrick Francis, 142, 144
Moreau, Gustave, 382
Morgan, Frank, 207
Morley, John F., 67
Moro, Aldo, 27
Morrisey, Frank, 162
Mount Cashel School (Newfoundland), 133
Muggeridge, Anne Roche, 220
Murphy, Francis X., 222
Murray, Les, 266
Mussolini, Benito, 9–10
The Mystery of the Incarnation (papal Bull). *See* *Incarnationis mysterium*

Nadal, Jerome, 366–67
Naylor, Arthur, 174, 177
Neo-Catechumenate, 379
New General Instruction of the Roman Missal, 310

Newman, Bishop William, 241
Newman, Cardinal John Henry, 15–17, 88, 220, 258
Nicholl, Donald, 343–45
Nichols, Archbishop Vincent, 140
nihilism, 58
Nolan, Albert, 372–73
Non abbiamo bisogno (encyclical), 9
Norris, Kathleen, 359–62, 381
Notre Dame University, 168
Nouwen, Henri, 333–38
Novak, Michael, 192, 194
Novo millennio inuente (letter), 72, 90, 322
Nugent, Robert, 148, 241, 243–44
nuns, clerical sexual abuse of, 256

O'Brien, Archbishop Keith, 91
Ocáriz, Fernando, 151
O'Connor, Cardinal John, 30
O'Connor, Flannery, 346–47
Of Chaste Wedlock (encyclical). See *Casti connubii*
Of Human Life (encyclical). See *Humanae vitae*
O'Flaherty, Vince, 364
Of New Things (encyclical). See *Rerum novarum*
O'Hagan, H. B., 143
O'Keeffe, Bernadette, 139
O'Keefe, Joseph, 139
On Consulting the Faithful in Matters of Doctrine, 15, 17
On the Christian Education of Youth (encyclical). See *Divini illius magistri*
On Human Work (encyclical). See *Laborem exercens*
On the Hundredth Anniversary of Rerum Novarum (encyclical). See *Centisimus annus*
On Reconstruction of the Social Order. See *Quadragesimo anno*
On Social Concern (encyclical). See *Sollicitudo rei socialis*
Ontario Secondary School Teachers Assn., 132
Opus Dei (movement), 72, 151, 324, 379
Ordinatio sacerdotalis, 77, 318–19
Ostpolitik, 11
Ottaviani, Cardinal Alfredo, 24, 212
Our Greatest Gift: A Meditation on Dying and Caring (book), 337
Our Lady of Fatima, 42–43
Our Lady of Guadalupe, 41
Our Lady of La Salette, 41
Our Lady of Lourdes, 41
Our Lady of the Rosary. See Our Lady of Fatima
Pacelli, Eugenio, 17

Padberg, John, 116–18
Panikkar, Raimundo, 348
papacy
    of Boniface VIII, 69
    despotic regimes and, 10–12, 14–15
    of Eugene III, 36
    executive powers of the, 12
    of Gregory (the Great), 89, 190, 195, 201
    infallibility and the, 15, 21, 31, 319–20
    of Innocent III, 261, 300
    of John XXIII, 18–26, 113–14, 121–22, 144, 208, 210
    of John Paul I, 12, 27–32
    of John Paul II. See John Paul II
    of Leo XIII, 114, 120–21, 203–4, 206, 234, 372
    nature of, 7–15, 31–35, 37–38
    of Paul VI, 11–12, 25–27, 30, 32, 78, 85, 149, 209–10, 215
    of Pelagius II, 89
    of Pius IX, 9, 14–15, 16, 43, 150
    of Pius X, 148
    of Pius XI, 9, 68, 118–21, 123, 205–7, 234, 255
    of Pius XII, 17–20, 31, 43, 65–67, 155, 213, 216
    realpolitik and, 10
    reforms of, 35
Papal City States, 9
papal indulgences. See simony
Parent-Fortin, Annine, 312
Pascal, Blaise, 345, 349
Pastoral Constitution on the Church. See *Gaudium et spes*
Pavelich, Ante, 10
Payne, William, 371
pedophilia. See clerical pedophilia
Pell, Archbishop George, 244
penitential of Pseudo-Ecgbert (handbook), 202
penitential of Theodore (handbook), 189–90
Penney, Archbishop Alphonsus, 270
Peppler, Hilary, 330
Philippe, Thomas, 338
philosophy, errors of, 57–58
philosophy, sapiential dimension to, 57
Physicians for Global Peace, 112
Pilarczyk, Archbishop Daniel, 277
Pilgrim People of God, 4
pilgrim status. See also laity, pilgrim nature of
    church and, 6, 222
    in life, 284
    societies and, 2
poetry, education and, 114–15
Pohier, Jacques, 73

Poland
    communism in, 38
    religious culture of, 37–38
politics
    compromise and, 53
    faith and, 52–55
pontifical commission on contraception, 210–14, 216–20
pontificate. See papacy
"popalatry", 186
Pope(s). See papacy
Populorum progressio (encyclical), 26
Porete, Marguerite, 382
Porter, Bernie, 165, 173
A Portrait of the Artist as a Young Man (book), 2, 184
Postman, Neil, 113
Power, Bishop Pat, 244
power (personal/positional)
    clergy and, 185–86
    clericalism and, 255–57
    ecclesiastical, 225–26
    resistance to dissent and, 186
    responsibility & accountability devolving from, 255–57
    sexual relations and, 256
pragmatism, 57
prayer
    as peacemaking, 337
    selfless, 39, 354–59, 362–69
premarital cohabitation, 246
premarital intercourse, 232–33
Presbyterorum ordinis (decree), 266–68
priesthood. See also Catholic Church, plummeting numbers of new priests
    inner, 302
    lay. See laity, priesthood of
    loneliness and, 267, 334
    moral, 302
Priestly Celibacy. See *Sacerdotalis coelibatus*
Priestly Ordination (letter). See *Ordinatio sacerdotalis*
priests
    female, 272
    heroism of, 269
    homosexual, 297–300
    low morale of, 322–23
    married, 272, 274–75, 294, 297
    redistribution of, 278
Principe, Walter, 87
private schools, funding of, 130–33
Privett, Steve, 105–6, 152, 160–61, 167–70, 305–6
Progress of Peoples (encyclical). See *Populorum progressio*
Prus, Jozef, 39
Python, Monty, 197, 201, 217

Quadragesimo anno (enclyclical), 255
Quinn, Archbishop John, 36, 223–24

Raffalovich, Marc-André Sebastian, 331
Rahner, Karl, 86
Ramsey, Archbishop Michael (of Canterbury), 26
Ratzinger, Cardinal Joseph, 45, 70, 73, 77, 80, 83, 148, 151, 222–23, 232–33, 237, 243–44, 269, 320
Rausch, Thomas P., 272
Ray, Brian, 164, 173–74
Read, Piers Paul, 266
realpolitik, 2, 103
reason. *See also* faith vs. reason, 56–58
Redemptor hominis, 74
Reinach, Adolf, 59
relationships, "disposable", 227
The Religious Dimension of Education in a Catholic School (Document), 124, 126, 306
religious orders, drop in numbers of, 374
Rerum novarum (encyclical), 114, 204, 372
Rich in Mercy (encyclical). See *Dives in misericordia*
Richards, Hubert, 230–31
Ricouer, Paul, 233
Rigali, Archbishop Justin, 98–99
Rigelhof, T. F., 266
Riley, Dean, 375
Rimes, Bobby, 364
Risse, Jan, 338
Rolfe, Frederick William, 331
Rolheiser, Ronald, 13
Roman Curia, 90
Roncalli, Angelo. *See* papacy, of John XXIII
Ross, Susan, 320
Rossi, Peter H., 118
Roy, Cardinal Maurice, 303
Royackers, Martin, 255
Ruether, Rosemary Radford, 149
Rulla, Luigi, 278
Runcie, Archbishop Robert (of Canterbury), 318
Ryan, Bill, 221
Ryan, Claude, 52–54

Sacerdotalis coelibatus (encyclical), 26
Sacred Congregation for Catholic Education, 122–23, 126, 153–57, 159, 162
Sacred Congregation for the Doctrine of the Faith, 148, 151, 317
Saint Alphonsus Liguori, 207
Saint Augustine, 53, 199, 201–2, 234–35, 251, 263, 349

Saint Bernard of Clairvaux, 36
Saint Catherine of Siena, 78
Saint Charles Borromeo, 18, 347
Saint Edith Stein, 59–63, 68
Saint Edmund, 200
Saint Francis of Assisi, 84
Saint Francis Xavier, 366
Saint Ignatius of Loyola, 116, 363–69
Saint Jerome, 198, 200
Saint John of the Cross, 38–39, 60, 349
Saint Lutgarde of Aywieres, 349
Saint Maria Faustina, 46
Saint Maria Goretti, 360–61
Saint Mary. *See also* Marian religious thought; Our Lady, 40–41, 56, 77, 184
    changing status of, 44–45
    helper with celibacy, 276
    as model for all women, 312–13
    perfect obedience of, 281
    virginal life of, 198–99
Saint Paul, 89, 188–89, 196, 249
Saint Teresa of Avila, 60, 78
Saint Thomas Aquinas, 47, 53, 58, 119–20, 186–90, 192, 195–96, 199, 201–2, 231, 234, 236, 302, 314–15
San Egidio Community, 379–80
Sapieha, Prince-Cardinal Adam, 39
Sapientia christiana (encyclical), 155
Sartre, Jean-Paul, 339
Satyananda, 354
Saunders, Kate, 228
Scarboro Fathers, 1, 374–75
Scheler, Max, 47, 59
Schillebeeckx, Edward, 73, 148
Schjeldahl, Peter, 329, 382
schools. *See* Catholic Church, education; Catholic schools; private schools; *and see below under* St.
Schools of Reconciliation (book), 138–39
Schwenzer, Gerhard, 312
scientia cordis (teaching), 345
scientism, 57
Scorsone, Suzanne, 371
Second Vatican Council. *See* Vatican Council (Second)
self-transcendence, 51
    and prayer, 357–58
seminaries
    original purpose of, 254
    origins of, 182
    restricted experience in, 321–22
Serenelli, Alessandro, 360
Sewell, Brocard, 330–33
sexuality
    Aristotle's theory of, 188
    complex nature of, 233
    facilitating love, 226–27

as gift, 206
    opposition to spirituality of, 187
    perceived as sinful, 201–3
Shaidle, Kathy, 345–47
Shakespeare, William, 193–94
Sharpe, Justice Robert, 132
Shaw, George Bernard, 147, 182
Sheehan, Michael, 246
Sheehan, Peter, 163
Shoah, 61, 64, 70
Simonis, Cardinal Adrianus, 337
simony, 265–66
sin, death and, 50
Sindona, Michele, 28, 30
Singha, Bishop Georges, 35
Sipe, A. Richard, 252, 281, 283–84
Sisters of Mercy of Alma, 376
Skinner, John, 358–59
Slipyi, Cardinal Josyf, 12
Smart, Elizabeth, 346
Smith, Austin, 344
Sobrino, Jon, 150–51
social sciences, 3
Societies of Apostolic Life, 79
Society of Jesus, 116–18
    General Congregation (#32), 124–26
Sodano, Cardinal Angelo, 42
Sollicitudo rei socialis (encyclical), 47
Somalo, Cardinal Eduardo Martinez, 99
Somerville, Janet, 312
spiritual crisis, current, 335–36
spiritual discipline vs. technique, 357
The Spiritual Exercises (of Ignatius), 363–69
spirituality
    biases against, 13
    essentialist, 334
    human needs for, 329–33
    narcissistic ("health club"), 357
spirituality of resistance/restoration, 373, 380–82
spirituality of the wounded, 333–47
spiritual values, 8
The Splendour of Truth (encyclical). See *Veritatis splendor*
SSM Healthcare, 98
St. Augustine of Canterbury (school), 139–40
St. Bede's (joint school), 138
St. Francis Xavier University, 170
St. Joseph's Health Care System (Ontario), 107, 109–12
St. Philip's (joint school), 137–39
Stanford, Peter, 228–32
Stepinac, Cardinal Alojzije, 62–63
sterilization, 54, 213
Stock, Mark, 139
Stoppard, Tom, 5

storytelling, path of, 345
Suchecky, Bernard, 67
Suenens, Cardinal Leo Josef, 23, 210
Summers, Montague, 331
Suzuki Roshi, 354
Synod(s). *See also* Catholic Church,
    synods and the; 1, 91
    fate of, 34
    governance of, 34
    1971 (on priesthood), 276, 316
    1980 (on The Role of the Family),
        220–24
    1985 (retrospective on Vatican II),
        34
    1987 (The Vocation and Mission
        of Lay People), 221–22, 304–5,
        311–16, 316, 323–24
    1990 (Formation of Priests), 147,
        271–77, 278, 281, 311

Talbot, George, 15
Taylor, Pamela, 175–76
technology, dangers of, 57
Tenet Healthcare Corp., 98–99
Tertio millennio adveniente (letter),
    69
Tetlow, Joseph A., 369
Tetzel, Johann, 266
That They May Be One (encyclical).
    See *Ut unum sint*
Theology of the Body (compilation), 55
Tillard, J. M. R., 33
time limited ministries, 272
Tobin, Brian, 130
truth, change and, 88–89
Tyranowski, Jan, 38

Ullathorne, Bishop W. B., 16
*Understanding Sexual Misconduct by
    Clergy* (handbook), 283
Unity Health System, 98
Urquart, Gordon, 324
Ustinov, Sir Peter, 8–9
Ut unum sint (encyclical), 36

Vachon, Archbishop Louis-Albert,
    316
Vallauri, Luigi Lombardi, 148
Vanier, George, 338
Vanier, Jean, 337–38, 343, 381
Vatican
    organizational difficulties of,
        90–92
    perceived isolation of, 186
    response to clerical sexual abuse,
        256
    secrecy of, 68, 210
Vatican Bank "affair", 28–30
Vatican City, 9
Vatican Council (First). *See also*
    papacy, infallibility and; 14–15, 21,
        259, 261, 301
Vatican Council (Second: 1962–65), 3,
        14, 16–27, 32, 36, 64, 93, 112,
        118–19, 121–24, 126, 144,
        148–50, 208, 210, 218, 227,
        247, 255, 257–58, 261–62, 301,
        304–5, 311, 324
    documents of the, 21–22
    Holy Spirit and, 25
Vatican finances, 30–31
Vaughn, John, 83
Veritatis splendor (encyclical), 47–50
Villot, Cardinal Jean, 28–29
virginity, 360–61
    spiritual status of, 198–200
Virgin Mary. *See* Saint Mary
viri probati. *See* priests, married
vocational clergy. *See* priesthood
"vocational inconsistency" (psychic
    tension), 278
Voices of Hope (book), 241–42, 245

Wahl, James A., 250
Wahl, John, 149
Waldman, Arieh, 129
Walsh, Michael, 138, 324
Walsh, Tom, 364
Ward, Wilfrid, 88

Weakland, Archbishop Rembert G.,
    80, 253, 296, 312
Weber, Max, 92
Wedel, Dr. Cynthia, 303–4, 308
Weigel, George, 37, 55
Weil, Simone, 13–14, 349
West, Morris, 213, 266, 284, 287–88
Westhues, Ken, 129, 132–133, 135
widowhood, death-like nature of, 200
Wijngaards, John, 311, 323
Wilkins, John, 91
Willebrands, Cardinal Johannes, 318
Williamson, Henry, 331
Wills, Garry, 43–44, 214
The Winnipeg Statement, 218–19
Wistrich, Robert, 67
Witmer, Elizabeth, 101
Wojtyla, Karol. *See* John Paul II
women. *See also* Catholic Church,
    women and; *Inter insigniores*;
    priests, female
    ordination of, 77–81, 316–20, 323
    perceived place of, 187
    rights of, 248
    seen as "flesh", 190–92
    seen as sinfully sensual, 195
    St. Mary as model for, 312–13
    their subservience to men, 206
Women for Life, Faith, and Family
    (organization), 321
Woodcock, George, 351
World Union of Catholic Women's
    Organizations, 316
Worlok, Archbishop Derek, 231
Wright, Cardinal John, 293
Wright, Lloyd, 106

Yallop, David, 28–31

Zaleski, Irma, 362–63
Zoungrana, Cardinal Paul, 186